MEUBLES

DE LA ROYNE DESCOSSE

DOUAIRIERE DE FRANCE.

Inventaires De La Royne Descosse Douairiere De France: Catalogues Of The Jewels, Dresses, Furniture, Books, And Paintings Of Mary Queen Of Scots : 1556-1569

Bannatyne Club (Edinburgh, Scotland)

Inuentaires

de la Royne Descosse Douairiere de France.

CATALOGUES OF THE JEWELS, DRESSES,

FURNITURE, BOOKS, AND PAINTINGS

OF

MARY QUEEN OF SCOTS.

1556–1569.

EDINBURGH: MDCCCLXIII.

THE CONTRIBUTION

OF

THE MARQUESS OF DALHOUSIE

TO

THE BANNATYNE CLUB.

THE BANNATYNE CLUB.

SEPTEMBER MDCCCLXIII.

THE EARL OF ABERDEEN, K.G. AND K.T.—(Deceased.)

WILLIAM PATRICK ADAM, Esq.

THE EARL OF ASHBURNHAM.

THE LORD BELHAVEN AND HAMILTON, K.T.

WILLIAM BLAIR, Esq.

BERIAH BOTFIELD, Esq., M.P.—(Deceased.)

THE MARQUESS OF BREADALBANE, K.T.—(Deceased.)

SIR THOMAS MAKDOUGALL BRISBANE, Bart.—(Deceased.)

GEORGE BRODIE, Esq.

10 CHARLES DASHWOOD PRESTON BRUCE, Esq.

THE DUKE OF BUCCLEUCH AND QUEENSBERRY, K.G.

VERY REV. DEAN RICHARD BUTLER.—(Deceased.)

SIR HUGH HUME CAMPBELL, Bart.

JAMES CAMPBELL, Esq.—(Deceased.)

THOMAS CARNEGY, Esq.—(Deceased.)

THE EARL CAWDOR.—(Deceased.)

PATRICK CHALMERS, Esq.—(Deceased.)

RIGHT HON. SIR GEORGE CLERK, Bart.

DAVID CONSTABLE, Esq.

20 THOMAS CONSTABLE, Esq.

ANDREW COVENTRY, Esq.

DAVID COWAN, Esq.

JAMES THOMSON GIBSON CRAIG, Esq.—(*TREASURER.*)

SIR WILLIAM GIBSON CRAIG, Bart.

THE MARQUESS OF DALHOUSIE, K.T.—(Deceased.)

THE EARL OF DALHOUSIE, K.T.

GEORGE HOME DRUMMOND, Esq.

HENRY DRUMMOND, Esq., M.P.—(Deceased.)

RIGHT HON. SIR DAVID DUNDAS.

30 GEORGE DUNDAS, Esq.

WILLIAM PITT DUNDAS, Esq.

THE EARL OF ELLESMERE, K.G.—(Deceased.)

JOSEPH WALTER KING EYTON, Esq.

LIEUT.-COL. ROBERT FERGUSON.

THE COUNT DE FLAHAULT.

THE EARL OF GOSFORD, K.P.

WILLIAM GOTT, Esq.

ROBERT GRAHAM, Esq.—(Deceased.)

THE EARL OF HADDINGTON, K.T.—(Deceased.)

40 THE DUKE OF HAMILTON AND BRANDON.—(Deceased.)

SIR THOMAS BUCHAN HEPBURN, Bart.

JAMES MAITLAND HOG, Esq.—(Deceased.)

PROFESSOR COSMO INNES.

DAVID IRVING, LL.D.—(Deceased.)

JAMES IVORY, Esq.

DAVID LAING, Esq.—(*SECRETARY.*)

JOHN BAILEY LANGHORNE, Esq.

THE EARL OF LAUDERDALE—(Deceased.)

VERY REV. PRINCIPAL JOHN LEE, D.D.—(Deceased.)

50 THE LORD LINDSAY.

JAMES LOCH, Esq.—(Deceased.)

THE MARQUESS OF LOTHIAN.

THE LORD LOVAT.

JAMES MACKENZIE, Esq.

JOHN WHITEFOORD MACKENZIE, Esq.

KEITH STEWART MACKENZIE, Esq.

WILLIAM FORBES MACKENZIE, Esq.—(Deceased.)

JAMES MAIDMENT, Esq.

SIR WILLIAM MAXWELL, Bart.

60 THE HON. WILLIAM LESLIE MELVILLE.—(Deceased.)

THE EARL OF MINTO, G.C.B.—(Deceased.)

JAMES MONCREIFF, Esq., M.P.

JAMES PATRICK MUIRHEAD, Esq.

HON. SIR JOHN A. MURRAY, LORD MURRAY.—(Deceased)

ROBERT NASMYTH, Esq.

HON. CHARLES NEAVES, LORD NEAVES.

THE EARL OF NORTHESK.

ALEXANDER PRINGLE, Esq.—(Deceased.)

JOHN RICHARDSON, Esq.

70 THE DUKE OF ROXBURGHE, K.T.

REV. HEW SCOTT, A.M.

JAMES ROBERT HOPE SCOTT, Esq.

THE EARL OF SELKIRK.

PROFESSOR JAMES YOUNG SIMPSON, M.D.

ALEXANDER SINCLAIR, Esq.

JAMES SKENE, Esq.

WILLIAM SMYTHE, Esq.

JOHN SPOTTISWOODE, Esq.

EDWARD STANLEY, Esq.

---

80 PROFESSOR WILLIAM STEVENSON, D.D.

THE HON. CHARLES FRANCIS STUART.—(DECEASED.)

THE DUKE OF SUTHERLAND, K.G.—(DECEASED.)

ARCHIBALD CAMPBELL SWINTON, ESQ.

ALEXANDER THOMSON, ESQ.

SIR WALTER CALVERLEY TREVELYAN, BART.

WILLIAM B. D. D. TURNBULL, ESQ.—(DECEASED.)

ADAM URQUHART, ESQ.—(DECEASED.)

88 ALEXANDER MACONOCHIE WELWOOD, ESQ.—(DECEASED.)

LIBRARIES.

THE BRITISH MUSEUM.

THE SOCIETY OF LINCOLN'S INN, LONDON.

THE FACULTY OF ADVOCATES, EDINBURGH.

THE SOCIETY OF ANTIQUARIES OF SCOTLAND.

THE SOCIETY OF WRITERS TO H. M. SIGNET, EDINBURGH.

THE UNIVERSITY OF CAMBRIDGE.

THE UNIVERSITY OF EDINBURGH.

THE UNIVERSITY OF GLASGOW.

TRINITY COLLEGE, DUBLIN.

10 THE ROYAL LIBRARY, BERLIN.

THE SMITHSONIAN INSTITUTION, WASHINGTON, UNITED STATES.

THE CONTENTS.

THE CONTENTS.

THE EDITOR'S PREFACE.

THE crowds which hurried to the shore of the Forth, on the morning of the nineteenth of August 1561, to welcome the return of their young Queen, heard with wonder of the multitude and splendour of the dresses, the diamonds, the plate, the furniture, and the tapestry which she was bringing with her. Fairer or costlier gems, it was told, were nowhere to be seen in Europe;[1] and such, it was whispered among the followers of the Reformed faith, was the sumptuous- ness of her apparel and household stuff, that her kinsman, the dreaded Cardinal of Lorraine, would fain have hindered their leaving the banks of the Seine.[2] It was easy to dazzle a people, the sight of whose poverty brought tears to the eyes of their sovereign;[3] but the appointments of the rich Dowager of

---

[1] 'Attour the Quenes Hienes fornitour, hingingis, and appareill, quhilk wes schippit at Newheavin and careit in Scotland, was also, in hir awin cumpanye, transportit with hir Majestie in Scotland, mony cost- lye jewells and goldin wark, precious stanis, orient pearle, maist excellent of any that was in Europe, and mony coistly abilyeamentis for hir body, with meikill silver wark of coistlye cupbordis, cowpis, plaite.'—(Bishop Lesley's History of Scotland, p. 299.)

'Shee brought with her als faire jewells, pretious stones and pearles as wer to be found in Europe.'— (Knox's History of the Reformation in Scotland, vol. ii. p. 267, note 4. Mr. David Laing's edit. Calder- wood's History of the Kirk of Scotland, vol. ii. p. 142. Wodrow Society's edit.)

[2] 'Interea Carolus [Gusius] Cardinalis [Lotharin- gus], inter tot publicas curas sui non oblitus, con- sulebat Reginae, ut supellectilem, mundumque muliebrem, magni precii, Regina velut in alium orbem transitura, apud se deponeret, donec de sui itineris eventu certius cognosceret. Illa facile intel- lecta fraude, ut quae hominis ingenium probe nosset, respondit, Cum se periculo committeret, non videre, cur mundo magis quam sibi caveret.'—(G. Buchanani Rerum Scoticarum Historia, lib. xvii. cap. 7; Opera, vol. i. p. 328, edit. 1715.)

[3] 'La Reyne y alla à cheval, et ses dames et seign- eurs sur des hacquenées guilledines du pays, telles quelles, et harnachées de mesme : donc, sur tel appareil, la Reyne se mist à pleurer et dire que ce n'estoit pas les pompes, les apprestz, les magnifi- cences, ni les superbes montures de la France, dont

France[1] seem to have been admired by men who were familiar with the grandest court of the age.[2]

Lists of the Queen's ornaments and attire were drawn up for different purposes at different periods of her reign; and it is the object of this volume to bring together such of these Inventories as are now known to exist.[3]

Inventory of Jewels etc. sent to Queen Mary in France, in June 1556.

The first, in order of time, is of the summer of 1556, when Mary Stewart was a girl of fourteen at the court of France.

The jewels and plate left by the King her father had come, in 1542, into

elle avoit joüy si long-temps; mais puisqu'il lui falloit changer son paradis en un enfer, qu'il falloit prendre patience.'—(Brantôme, Vies des Dames Illustres, disc. iii. Marie Stuart; Oeuvres, t. v. p. 95. edit. Paris, 1823.)

Mary had not been a month in Scotland before the quick eye of the English envoy discovered that 'the povertie of her subjectes greatlye advanceth whatsomever she intendethe.' — (Letter from Randolph to Cecil, 12. Sept. 1561, in Selections illustrating the Reign of Mary Queen of Scotland, p. 96. Maitland Club.)

Queen Mary's French dowry.

[1] Her dowry, as settled by her marriage-contract in April 1558, and by an ordinance of King Charles IX. in December 1560, was 60,000 livres a year.—(Acts of the Parliaments of Scotland, vol. ii. p. 512. M. Teulet, Papiers d'Etat relatifs à l'Histoire de l'Ecosse, t. i. pp. 734-739.)

It appears from a letter of Sir Francis Knollys to Sir William Cecil (13. June 1568), that Queen Mary's French jointure was reckoned in sterling money at L. 12,000 a year.—(Anderson's Collections relating to Mary Queen of Scotland, vol. iv. part i. p. 79.)

This was probably twice as much as the Crown revenue of Scotland in that day. But, poor in one respect as her kingdom was, Queen Mary brought no mean portion to her French husband, as he was reminded in the fine verses which the great Latin poet of Errope wrote upon the match :—

'Ampla si dote movaris
Accipe dotales Mavortia pectora Scotos.

Hanc tibi dat conjux dotem, tot secula fidam
Conjunctamque tuis sociali foedere gentem,' etc.

—(G. Buchanani Silvae, iv. 'Francisci Valesii et Mariae Stuartae, Regum Franciae et Scotiae, Epithalamium.')

[2] 'Estant habillée à la sauvage (comme je l'ay veüe) et à la barbaresque mode des sauvages de son pays, elle paroissoit, en un corps mortel et habit barbare et grossier, une vraye déesse. . . . Que pouvoit elle donc parestre se representant en ses belles et riches parures, fust à la Françoise ou à l'Espaignolle, ou avec le bonnet à l'Italienne, ou en ses autres habits de son grand deuil blanc.'—(Brantôme, t. v. p. 85.)

[3] There are traces of several Inventories which appear now to be lost.

A list of all the dresses which she had had since she left Scotland in August 1548, was sent by the Queen in France to' her mother in Scotland, in December 1555 : 'Je vous envoye l'inventoire de tous mes habits depuis que je suis en France.'—(Letter of Queen Mary, printed by Prince Labanoff in his Lettres de Marie Stuart, t. i. pp. 29-32.)

A marginal note on one of the Inventories of 1561, refers to a list of the Queen's linen, drawn up by the keeper of the house of Fecamp, when she left France (p. 47). Mary visited Fecamp in July or August 1561, to pay her last duty to the remains of her mother, which then lay in state there, on their way from Scotland, where she died, to their last resting-place in her sister's abbey of St. Pierre at Rheims.

After the Queen was sent to Lochleven, on the 17th of June 1567, the Confederated Lords 'went doun to the Palace of Halyrud hous, and tooke up an inventar of the plait, jewells, and other movables.'—(Calderwood's History of the Kirk of Scotland, vol. ii. p. 366.)

the custody of the Earl of Arran, who, as next heir to the throne, was appointed Governor of Scotland, and Tutor to the infant Queen. He gave up these high offices in 1554, when he had royal and parliamentary discharges,[1] in the amplest terms, of all the property of the crown which had been in his keeping. But some jewels, tapestry, and cloths of state, were still left in his hands; and these, in the summer of 1556, he sent to France, by Sir James Hamilton, a gentleman of his household, who received an acquittance from the Queen, which takes the first place in the following sheets.[2] Among the articles which it enumerates, is a richly jewelled dagger, the gift, as we learn elsewhere, of King Francis the First of France to his son-in-law, King James the Fifth of Scotland.[3] It was brought back to Holyrood in 1561, and

Jewelled dagger given by Francis I. to James V.

The Inventories made during the eighteen years of Mary's captivity do not fall within the scope of this volume. Prince Labanoff has printed the most interesting of them—the 'Inventaire de la Garde-Robe,' made at Chartley in June 1586; the 'Inventaire de différentes Broderies et Ouvrages,' made at Chartley in July 1586; the 'Inventaire des Bijoux, de l'Argenterie et d'autres menus objets,' made at Chartley in August 1586; and the 'Inventarye of the Jewells Plate Money and other goods found in the custody of the severall servantes of the late Quene of Scottes,' made at Fotheringhay, in February 1587.—(Lettres de Marie Stuart, t. vii. pp. 229-274.)

[1] They acquit him of 'all poisis sowmes of money plait weschell of silvir or gold with all vthir gold and silvir baith cunyeit and vacunyeit jowellis ringis targattis precius stanis baith sett in ringis targattis and abilyementis or vthirwayis or yit vnsett in ony thing arraymentis clething with all kynd of abilyementis hornis buttonis of gold or silvir and all vthir accowtrementis thairof all tappessaries hingaris ornamentis of housis and chalmeris bedding with all maner of plennissing and insycht of palacijs hallis chalmeris and houssis quhatsumeuir,' and 'all bannatis coueringis of beddis claithis of estait veschellis caparisonis harnissingis sadillis and vtheris accoutrimentis for horss with all garnissingis thairof veluote and all vther kynd of silkis schaipin or vnschaipin with all vthir guidis geir Jowellis and thingis quhatsumeuer.'—(Acts of the Parliaments of Scotland, vol. ii. pp. 600-604. Miscellany of the Maitland Club, vol. iv. pp. 112-115.)

The terms of this enumeration have obvious reference to the contents of the 'Inventaris of the Silver Werk Jowellis and Abilyementis' of King James v. in 1542, printed in the late Mr. Thomas Thomson's Collection of Inventories of the Royal Wardrobe and Jewelhouse, pp. 55-106. Edinb. 1815.

[2] Pp. 3-6.

It is apparently to these jewels that the Queen refers in a letter to her mother, conjectured by Prince Labanoff to be of the year 1552, but more probably of the year 1555 or 1556: 'J'é entendu par les gens de mon cousin le Conte de Chatelleraut [Arran], que son père me vouloit envoier un gentillome qui m'aporterait quelques bagues à ses paques, toutesfois je n'en suis pas sertaine.' — (Lettres de Marie Stuart, t. i. p. 6.)

The acquittance in the text is included in Mr. Thomson's Collection of Inventories, pp. 116-120.

The original is in the charter-room of the Duke of Hamilton, to whom it has descended with the titles and estates of his ancestor, the first Duke of Chatelherault, or, as he wrote himself during his Regency, 'James, by the grace of God, Earl of Arran and Lord Hamilton, Governor and Prince of Scotland.'—(Epistolae Regum Scotorum, vol. ii. pp. 154, 155, 159, 162, 164, 165, 176, 177.)

[3] P. 6. It is described in the Inventory of King James v. in 1542, as 'ane quhinyear with ane scheith of gold quhilk the King of France gaif to the Kingis Grace set with ane gryt sapheir on the heid with xix rubeis and thrie dyamonttis upoun the heft and upoun the scheith twantie sevin rubeis gryt and small sex

is last heard of, five years afterwards, in the hands of that Lord Ruthven who rose from his deathbed to play such a memorable part in the murder of Riccio.[1]

It does not appear how far the scanty list of 1556 is to be received as an account of all that then remained in the Jewel-House and Wardrobe of Scotland. We are told only that most part of the not inconsiderable treasures which they contained at the death of the Queen's father, had been sold to support the war with England during the first years of the Regency.[2] More than one object of note would seem thus to have been lost, such as the coat worn by King James the Fifth when, receiving honours never before paid to any foreign prince, he rode through the streets of Paris to seek the hand of the eldest Daughter of France;[3] the little cups of gold, basin of agate, ewer of jasper,

amerantis greit and small sex dyamontis tablit with ane gryt knop of gold and fass of gold wyre and silver set with small rubeis and perle upoun the end of the fass.'—(Mr. Thomson's Collection of Inventories, p. 70.)

[1] P. 13 : 'Ledit poygnar a estez enuoye a Millor Roven en Engleterre.'
Lord Ruthven fled to England immediately after Riccio's murder, 'his conscience bearing him record,' as he wrote to Cecil, that all that he had done was 'for the good of religion.' He died there on the 13th of May 1566. Morton, his companion in exile, described his end as 'so godly that all men that saw it did rejoice.'—(Calendar of State Papers relating to Scotland, vol. i. pp. 231-233, 838. Registrum Secreti Sigilli, vol. xxxvi. fol. 30. MS. Register House.)
Lord Ruthven and his second wife, Janet Stewart, were in such favour with the Queen, that, in order to have them beside her, she gave them one of the conventual buildings within the precinct of Holyrood.—(Registrum Magni Sigilli, 1. Decemb. 1564, lib. xxxii. no. 335. MS. Register House.)
Lord Ruthven's remarkable narrative of the assassination of Rizzio, reports a conversation between him and the Queen, while she was yet ignorant of the fate of the Italian : 'Remember ye not, said she, what the Earl of Murray would have had me done to you for giving me the ring ? The said Lord Ruthven answered that he would bear no quarrel for that cause, but would forgive him and all others for God's sake ; and as to that ring, it had no more virtue than another, and was one little ring with a pointed diamond in

it. Remember ye not, said her Majesty, that ye said it had a virtue to keep me from poisoning ? Yea, madam, said he ; I said so much that the ring had that virtue, only to take that evil opinion out of your head of poisoning, which you conceived that the Protestants would have done.'—(Lord Ruthven's Relation of the Death of David Rizzi, in Scotia Rediviva, pp. 347, 348.)—Among Queen Mary's jewels at Fotheringhay were two stones, one 'medicinable against poyson,' the other 'medicinable for the collicke.'—(Prince Labanoff, Lettres de Marie Stuart, t. vii. p. 255.)

[2] 'The noble and mychtie prince James duke of Chattellarawlt erle of Arrane lord Hammiltoun . . . having fund . . . this . . . realme . . . vndir cruell weris regnand betuix the samyn . . . and the realme of Ingland . . . hes . . . expendit . . . all kynd of jowellis ringis preciouss stanis abulyeamentis garnist and vngarnist with stanis and vthirwayis hingaris tapesreis . . . and all vthir thingis quhatsumeuer quhilkis pertenit to vmquhile Oure Souerane Ladijs fader . . . the tyme of his deceiss.'—(Acts of the Parliament of Scotland, vol. ii. p. 603.)
It is said that when the Regent Murray, after his victory at Langside, seized Hamilton Palace, he found in it some of the household stuff of King James v.—(G. Buchanani Rerum Scoticarum Historia, lib. xix. c. 12.)—But we must not give too much trust to one who, born a Lennox man, was the hereditary enemy of the house of Hamilton.

[3] 'Ane cott of sad cramasy velvott quhilk was the Kingis Graces enterie coitt in Pareis reschit all our

and flagon of rock-crystal, made for his fond bride when she was a child ;[1] the church-plate and vestments, and the dresses which she brought with her to the country where she was so soon to find a grave ;[2] a mystical cap or diadem blessed at Rome by the successor of St. Peter, on Christmas eve,—either the cap which Pope Julius the Second sent to King James the Fourth, along with what is now shown as the Sword of State of the Scottish Regalia,[3] or, more probably, the cap which Pope Paul the Third sent to King James the Fifth, along with a sword which he was vainly exhorted to draw against the King, his near kinsman and neighbour, who had been too long allowed to bear that title of Defender of the Faith which was now offered to the King of the Scots.[4] A loss still more to be regretted is that of the cup from which Bruce was used to drink.[5] It was the last memorial of the great King which remained in the Treasury. His four mazers[6] had disappeared in the previous reign,

Relics of King Robert Bruce.

with gold cuttit out on plane clayth of gold freinyeit with gold and all cuttit out knit with hornis and lynit with reid taffate.'—(Mr. Thomson's Collection of Inventories, pp. 80, 81. M. Teulet, Papiers d'Etat relatifs à l'Histoire de l'Ecosse, t. i. pp. 122-125. Bishop Lesley's History of Scotland, p. 151.)

[1] ' Twa lytill small culppis of gold maid to Quene Magdalene quhane scho was ane bairne. Item ane bassing and laver siclyk maid for hir in hir barneheid the tane of aget the uther of jespe sett in gold with ane lytill flacone of cristalline of the samyne sort.'—(Mr. Thomson's Collection of Inventories, p. 63.)

[2] ' The Alter grayth quhilk wes Quene Magdalenis . . . The Claythis quhilk pertenit to umquhill Quene Magdalene quhome God assoilyie.'—(Mr. Thomson's Collection of Inventories, pp. 58, 100, 101.)

[3] ' The Hatt that cam fra the Paipe of gray velvett with the Haly Gaist sett all with orient perle.' —(Mr. Thomson's Collection of Inventories, pp. 49, 76.)

' Julius the Secound, Paip for the tyme, send ane ambassadour to the King, declaring him to be Protectour and Defendour of Christen faythe, and in signe thairof, send unto him ane purpour diadame wrocht with flouris of gold, with ane sword, having the hiltis and skabert of gold, sett with precious stains.'— (Bishop Lesley's History of Scotland, p. 75. Leslaei

De Rebus Gestis Scotorum, lib. viii. p. 345, edit. 1578. Papers relative to the Regalia of Scotland, pp. 23, 44. Sir W. Scott's Miscellaneous Prose Works, vol. vii. pp. 307, 308, edit. 1834.)

In saying that the title of Defender of the Faith was given to King James IV., Bishop Lesley has apparently confused the Papal Embassy of 1507, with the Papal Embassy of 1536. The letter of thanks sent by King James IV. to Pope Julius II. acknowledges the cap and sword—'ensem et pileum, sacratissima Nativitatis Domini nocte, tua felici manu benedictum' —but is silent as to any gift of style or title.—(Epistolae Regum Scotorum, vol. i. p. 82.)

[4] ' History of Scotland, by William Drummond of Hawthornden, pp. 304-306, edit. 1681 ; Works, pp. 101, 102, Edinb. 1711. Mr. Tytler's History of Scotland, vol. iv. p. 223, edit. 1845.

[5] 'Ane culp quhilk was King Robert Bruicis gilt.'—(Inventar of the Silver Wark in the Register Hous within the Castell [29. November 1542], in Mr. Thomson's Collection of Inventories, pp. 73, 111.)

Bruce's cup.

[6] ' Foure Masaris callit King Robert the Brocis with a cover . . . Item the hede of silver of ane of the coveris of masar.'—(Jowellis fund in the Castell [17. June 1488], in Mr. Thomson's Collection of Inventories, p. 8.)

Bruce's mazers

The mazer was a bowl or drinking vessel of wood,

together with his shirt,[1] which had long hung in the Castle, and his sword,[2] which had been recovered from the battlefield on which King James the Third lost his life. The spoil of cloth of gold and silk won by that sword at Bannockburn still clothed the priests, and glittered on the altars of many an abbey and cathedral church;[3] but these trophies also were soon to perish in the tumult of the Reformation, or the more fatal neglect which followed, suffering even the sepulchre of Bruce himself to be swept away.

Inventories of the Crown Jewels of France delivered by Queen Mary to Catharine of Medicis, in February 1561.

The two Inventories next in date belong to the first days of the Scottish Queen's first widowhood.

generally the knotty-grained maple, often richly mounted with silver or gold.—(Note by Mr. Albert Way, in the Promptorium Parvulorum, vol. ii. p. 328.) Two or three mazers are mentioned among the spoil taken by King Edward I. from the Castle of Edinburgh in 1296.—(Archæological Journal, vol. xiii. p. 247. Lond. 1856.) 'The mazer of St. Erkenwald' appears in an Inventory of the Dean and Chapter of St. Paul's at London, in 1295. 'The mazer of St. Thomas of Canterbury' was among the treasures of King Charles VI. of France, in 1399. 'The mazer of St. Louis' was shown at St. Denis in 1470.—(M. le Comte de Laborde, Notice des Emaux, Bijoux et Objets Divers, exposés dans les galeries du Musée de Louvre, par. ii., 'Glossaire,' pp. 371-377, edit. 1853.)

Bruce's shirt. [1] 'Item ressavit in the cloissat of Davidis Tour . . . King Robert Brucis serk.'—(Jowellis fund in the Castell [17. June 1488], in Mr. Thomson's Collection of Inventories, p. 8.)

Shirt of St. Lewis. In the same way the shirt of King Lewis IX.—'la chemise Saint Loys, dont il fault une manche'—was preserved among the treasures of France.—(Inventory of King Charles VI. in 1420, quoted by M. le Comte de Laborde, Notice des Emaux, par. ii., 'Glossaire,' p. 481.)

St. Margaret's shirt. The shirt of our own St. Margaret—'camisia Beate Margarete Regine;' 'Sanct Margaretis sark'—was kept beside her shrine in Dunfermline; and the Queens of Scotland still continued, in the fifteenth and sixteenth centuries, to clothe themselves in it in their hour of travail.—(Rotuli Scaccarii Regum

Scotorum, no. 211, A.D. 1450-1451. MS. Register House. Compotum Thesaurarii Regis Scotorum, 10. Martii 1511-1512. MS. Register House.)

St. Duthac's shirt. In the fourteenth century, the Earls of Ross went to battle in the shirt of St. Duthac, which hung in one of the churches within his sanctuary at Tain.—(J. Major De Gestis Scotorum, lib. v. cap. xii.)

St. Columba's shirt. So early as the close of the seventh century the shirt in which St. Columba died—'tunica qua etiam hora exitus ejus de carne indutus erat'—was believed to be endowed with preternatural powers, and was used by the monks of Iona, as a charm to bring down rain upon their corn-fields.—(Adamnan's Life of St. Columba, pp. 175, 321-323. Dr. Reeves's edit.)

Bruce's sword. [2] 'Waltero Simsoun pro . . . recuperacione . . . cuiusdam gladii quondam Regis Roberti Bruce in bello prope Striueling in die Sancti Barnabe apostoli et Domino Regi deliberati.'—(Compotum Camerarii de Menteth, 1488-1489, Rotuli Scaccarii Regum Scotorum, no. 295. MS. Register House.)

It was, perhaps, a sword of Bruce which was shown in the armoury of the French King in 1499, as 'the sword of the Hardy King of Scots:' 'Une espée, la poignée de fouet blanc, au pommeau une Nostre Dame d'un costé et Saint Michel de l'autre, nomme *l'Espee du Roy d'Escosse, qui fust fort Hardy,* laquelle fust donnée au feu Roy Loys quant il espousa Madame la Dauphine.'—(Inventaire du Château d'Amboise, quoted by M. le Comte de Laborde in his Notice des Emaux, par. ii., 'Glossaire,' p. 482.)

Spoils of Bannockburn. [3] 'Tapetes autem quos multos ex regio ceperat tentorio ex bysso pretiosissima auro intextos coenobiis

Her sickly husband, King Francis the Second, died in December 1560; and Mary, hastening to quit a court which was now under the sway of one whom, in her brief day of power, she had taunted with being a merchant's daughter,[1] followed the Duke of Guise to Joinville in March 1561. On the eve of her departure, she made over to Catharine of Medicis, the Queen Mother, the crown jewels of France, as described in two lists, which set forth the price at which each jewel was valued by a goldsmith of the French King, and by two goldsmiths of the King of Navarre.[2] A diamond cross, it will be seen, is reckoned at 50,000 crowns; a large diamond, which had been bought by King Francis the First, at 65,000 crowns; a big ruby, known as the Egg of Naples, at 70,000 crowns. In all, the forty-two pieces enumerated are estimated to be worth 490,914 crowns.

It was stipulated in Queen Mary's marriage-contract, that if she survived her husband, she might either abide in France, or return to Scotland, at her

Inventory of Queen Mary's Jewels at her leaving France, in August 1561.

Praedicatorum per regnum diuisit, vt inde ad sacrorum vsum ornamenta fierent: quae hac nostra adhuc extant memoria.'—(H. Boethii Scotorum Historiae, lib. xiv. fol. 303. edit. 1575.)

'The goldin and silkin claithis, of quhilkis King Edwardis palyonis war maid, war distribut amang the abbayis of Scotland, to be vestamentis and frontallis to thair altaris; of quhilkis mony yit remanis to our days.'—(Archdean Bellenden's Translation of H. Boece's History of Scotland, book xiv. chap. xi.)

'King Edwardis tent, all of ane clayth of gold, . . .
Wes consecrat to Halie Kirk, to be
Maid vestiment, quhilk yit is for to se
In sindrie places now of the Black Freiris,
And yit wilbe lang efter mony yeiris.'
—(Stewart's Buik of the Chroniclis of Scotland, vol. iii. pp. 237, 238.)

'Vna capella vetus ex auro textili dicta cherbulink ex spolio conflictus de Bannokburne continens vnam cappam vnam casulam vnam tunicellam et dalmaticam cum quindecim paramentis duobus antependijs ante et retro pro summo altari longitudinis eiusdem.'—(Inuentarium Ornamentorum Summi Altaris Ecclesie

Cathedralis Aberdonensis A.D. 1549, in the Registrum Episcopatus Aberdonensis, vol. ii. pp. 189, 190.)

Perhaps we should recognise tokens of Bruce's great victory in the chasuble, tunicles, and copes described in one of the Inventories of 1569 as embroidered with the arms of 'King Edward' (p. 184).

[1] 'La Regina di Scotia un giorno gli disse che non sarrebe mai altro che *figlia di un mercante.'*—(Letter of the Pope's Nuncio in France, quoted by M. Chernel in his Marie Stuart et Catherine de Médicis, p. 17. Paris, 1858.)

'Our Queen, then Douagiere of France, retired hir self be litle and litle farther and farther fra the Court of France, that it suld not seam that sche was in any sort compellit thereunto, as of a treuth sche was, be the Queen Mothers rygorous and vengeable dealing; wha allegit that sche was dispysed be hir gud dochter, during the schort regne of King Francis the Second hir husband, be the instigation of the house of Guise.'—(Memoirs of his Own Life, by Sir James Melville of Halhill, p. 88, edit. 1827.)

[2] Appendix I. and II. pp. 191-205.

They are now printed for the first time from tran-

pleasure, taking with her such plate, rings, gems, apparel, and the like, as the Queens of France had been accustomed to have, after the demise of the Kings their consorts.[1] The next Inventory[2] appears to be of the jewels which fell to her in this way, mixed up with others sent to her from Scotland,[3] or acquired in France by gift, inheritance, or purchase.[4] The list is without date, but it must have been written after the fifth of December 1560, when King Francis the Second died, for it speaks of the Queen as the Dowager of France;[5] and before the fifteenth of August 1561,[6] when she set sail from the French shore, for it describes, as still in her possession, a string of pearls which, as we are told by a note on the margin, was afterwards taken for caps to her cousins of Lorraine,[7] and a necklace of rubies, emeralds, and diamonds, which, as another note informs us, was given to her aunt the Duchess of Guise, at Calais[8]—the port where Mary took ship for Scotland, and received the last farewells of the brilliant escort of her French kinsfolks.[9]

scripts from the originals in the Bibliothèque Impériale at Paris (MS. François, no. 10370), for which the Editor is indebted to the courtesy of M. Teulet, whose learned and accurate researches in the French archives have done so much for the history of Scotland in its relations with France.

[1] 'Et si emportera ses derniers vaisselle bagues joyaulx habillemens meubles pretieux biens et aultres choses que les Roynes de France doiuent et ont accoustume davoir apres le trespas des Roys de France leurs marys.'—(Acts of the Parliaments of Scotland, vol. ii. p. 512.)

[2] Pp. 7-17.
It is now printed, for the first time, from the original in the Register House.

[3] Compare p. 13 and p. 6; p. 15 and p. 5.

[4] 'La Royne vostre fille, a desjà assez d'aultres semblables bagues [émerauldes]; et advenant qu'elle se veuille parer, la cognoissant honneste comme je faictz, je ne refuseray à luy prester des vostres; et puis s'il vous plaist luy aulmosner de celles que vous avez, ainsy qu'il vous a pleu nous promettre, nous aurons moyen de la faire bien jolye quant il en sera besoing.'—(Letter from the Cardinal of Lorraine to his sister the Queen Dowager and Regent of Scotland,

25. February 1552-53, printed by Prince Labanoff, in his Lettres de Marie Stuart, t. i. p. 12.)

Queen Mary of Guise had a dowry in France of 10,000 livres a year, as Duchess Dowager of Longueville.—(MS. Register House.)

[5] P. 7.

[6] The Inventory may have been drawn up in March 1561, when the Queen passed a day or two in Paris to 'look upon such robes and jewels as she had there.' —(Letter from Throckmorton to Queen Elizabeth, 31. March 1561, quoted by Miss Strickland, in her Lives of the Queens of Scotland, vol. iii. p. 167.)

[7] P. 11.

[8] P. 10.

[9] 'Estant acheminée par terre à Calais, accompagnée de Messieurs tous ses oncles, M. de Nemours, et de la pluspart des grands et honnestes de la Court, ensemble des dames, comme de Madame de Guyse et autres, tous regrettans et pleurans à chaudes larmes l'absence d'une telle Reyne.'—(Brantôme, t. v. p. 92. Bishop Lesley's History of Scotland, p. 297.)

Mary was accompanied to Scotland by three of her uncles (the Duke of Aumale, the Grand Prior of France, and the Marquis of Elbeuf), by M. Danville, son of the Duke of Montmorency, and by more than

The Inventory enumerates one hundred and fifty-nine articles, of which forty-three were in the Queen's cabinet,[1] a piece of furniture which was then only coming into use. Among its contents will be seen a large diamond set in gold, with a gold chain, and a large ruby attached, which, under the name of the Great Harry, came afterwards to be regarded as one of the chief jewels of the Scottish crown. It appears to have been a gift to the Queen from her boy husband's father, King Henry the Second of France, whose cypher it bore.[2] A miniature of King James the Fifth, in a gold case shaped like an apple,[3] would be doubly interesting if we could be assured that it was the work of Scottish hands. Another article in the list, is one of the roses of gold yearly blessed by the Pope, on the fourth Sunday in Lent, and sent by him to such Christian prince or potentate as he wishes specially to honour.[4] It seems to have been presented by the dissolute Borgia to the noblest of the Stewarts,[5]—by Pope Alexander the Sixth, to King James the Fourth.[6] The marginal note which records the gift of certain pearls to ' Merna' or ' Marnac,'[7] brings before us a humble name, which yet has found a place in one of the sternest pages of religious his-

The Great Harry, a jewel given by Henry II. to Queen Mary.

Miniature of King James v.

Golden Rose sent by Pope Alexander VI. to James IV.

---

a hundred gentlemen, among whom were the ever lively, self-satisfied Brantôme, and the kinsman of the chivalrous Bayard, the hapless Chastellard.—(Brantôme, t. ii. p. 368 ; t. v. pp. 92, 122.)

[1] P. 15.

[2] Pp. 7, 75, 90, 93. Mr. Thomson's Collection of Inventories, pp. 196, 197, 200, 265, 291, 307, 318, 329.

[3] P. 16.

[4] Du Cange, Glossarium Mediae Latinitatis, tom. v. col. 1497, voce ' Rosa Aurea,' edit. 1733-6.

The usage, it would seem, still continues. It is but the other day that the newspapers told us that the Golden Rose had been sent by Pope Pius IX. to the Queen of Naples.

Towards the close of the twelfth century, it would appear that the Rose was a mark of tribute due to the newly-restored Praefect of Rome, whose prerogative had not yet been shorn by Pope Innocent III. The Archbishop of Lyons writes to the Bishop of Glasgow, between the years 1199 and 1202 : ' In Dominica, qua cantatur *Laetare Jerusalem*, expleta solemni processione, in qua Rosam Auream idem summus Pontifex circumportat, ipsum [Praefectum urbis Romae] quasi pro debiti exequutione eadem Rosa remunerat.'—(Mabillonii Vetera Analecta, pp. 478-9, edit. 1723.)

[5] A fortunate digression of Erasmus, on the ambition of princes, shows how high a place King James IV. of Scotland held in the opinion of contemporary Europe : ' Erat ea corporis specie, ut vel procul Regem posses agnoscere. Ingenii vis mira, incredibilis rerum omnium cognitio, invicta animi magnitudo, vere regia pectoris sublimitas, summa comitas, effusissima liberalitas. Denique nulla virtus erat quae magnum deceret principem, in qua ille non sic excelleret, ut inimicorum quoque suffragio laudaretur.'—(Adagia, voce ' Spartam nactus es, hanc orna,' col. 1634, edit. Aurel. Allobrog. 1606.)

[6] A. D. 1494. ' The Paip Alexander the Sixt send ane protonotar callit Forman in Scotland, with ane roise and septour of gold to the King.'—(Bishop Lesley's History of Scotland, p. 63.)

[7] Pp. 11, 82.

tory,—the French valet, who, as Knox writes, not without exultation, could scarcely find handkerchiefs to dry the flood of tears to which the Queen gave way under the vehemence of the Reformer's rebuke.[1]   We see no trace of the

Diamond heart sent by Queen Mary to Queen Elizabeth.

diamond heart, which was sent by Mary, soon after her arrival in Scotland, to Queen Elizabeth,[2] along with some French verses, written, it has been said, by the Scottish Queen herself, and turned into Latin in the courts of both countries,—by Buchanan at Holyrood, and by Sir Thomas Chaloner at White-hall.[3]   It was, doubtless, bought or fashioned for the occasion.

Inventory of her mother's move-ables, delivered to the Queen in September 1561.

Hitherto we have had to speak of Inventories made in France.   The first Inventory taken in Scotland[4] is of moveables left by Mary's mother, the Queen Regent, and delivered, in September 1561, to Servais de Conde, a trusted valet of the Queen's chamber, afterwards appointed keeper of her Palace of Holyrood.[5]   Ninety-six articles are enumerated.   There are five

---

[1] 'And with these wordis, skarslie could Marnock, hir secreat-chalmer boy, gett neapkynes to hold hyr eyes drye for the tearis; and the owling, besydes womanlie weaping, stayed hir speiche.'—(Knox's History of the Reformation, vol. ii. p. 387.)

[2] Calendar of State Papers relating to Scotland, vol. i. p. 185.   Jebb, De Vita Mariae Reginae Scotorum, t. ii. pp. 23, 24, 196.

[3] 'Adamas in cordis effigiem sculptus, annuloque insertus, quem Maria Scotorum Regina ad Elizabetham Anglorum Reginam misit.'—(G. Buchanani Hendecasyllabon, xi.)—'Translatio quorundam carminum quae Gallico primum sermone conscripta, a serenissima Scotiae Regina in mutuae amicitiae pignus, una cum excellentis operis annulo, in quo insignis adamas prominebat, ad serenissinam Angliae Reginam Elizabetham missa fuerant.'—(Sir Thomas Chaloner, De Republica Anglorum Instauranda, p. 353. Lond. 1579.)

The original French seems to be lost.

Buchanan wrote other two sets of Latin verses on the same diamond.   'De adamante misso a Regina Scotiae ad Reginam Angliae.'   'Loquitur adamas in cordis effigiem sculptus quem Maria Elizabethae Angliae

misit.'—(G. Buchanani Epigrammatum, lib. i. no. 59, lib. iii. no. 8.)

[4] Pp. 18-27.

It is printed from the original in the Register House.

Although it gives account of things received in September 1561, it would seem to have been written (probably from an older Inventory) after the Earl of Murray had assumed the Regency in August 1567. It is authenticated by the signature of his secretary, Mr. John Wood of Tilliedavy, one of the Lords of Session; and may have been prepared, at the same time with another Inventory likewise authenticated by his signature, in November 1569 (pp. 179-187).

It is included in Mr. Thomson's Collection of Inventories, pp. 123-132.

In judging of the appointments of Holyrood from this Inventory, it is to be remembered that the Palace had been in the hands of the Reformers in July 1569.—(Leslaei De Rebus Gestis Scotorum, p. 551. Knox's History of the Reformation, vol. i. pp. 364, 377, 378.)

[5] 'Ane lettre maid to Seruais de Condez warlett of hir Hienes chalmer gevand to him the keiping of hir Hienes Place of Haliruidhouss in oure absence indur-

palls or cloths of state, nine beds, two Turkey carpets, twelve suits of tapestry. Six maps, and a pair of globes are mentioned. Five of the maps—one of the world, and one of each of its four quarters—appear to have been in the *Maps and globes.* Queen's possession till within a few months of her death;[1] the globes were found in her chamber after her execution at Fotheringhay.[2] There are ten paintings, all it would seem on panel, one of the Muses, another of 'Gro-*Paintings.* tesque or Conceits,' and eight of the German Doctors, or, as they seem elsewhere to be called, the New Doctors.[3] Like most of the other lists, this has a great many notes explaining how certain articles had been disposed of. These notes in the original are written on the margin, for the most part in another hand; they are here printed in smaller type under the articles to which they refer.

We have next an Inventory of furniture in Holyrood in November *Inventory of the Queen's moveables in Holyrood in November* 1561.[4] It contains a hundred and eighty-six entries, or about twice as many *ables in Holyrood in November 1561.*

---

ing oure will And the said Seruais to answer for all thingis that is within the said Palice that be deliuerit to him in keiping be Seigneur Frances superintendent of oure biggingis And gife ony thing inlaikis that be deliuerit to the said Serwais it salbe rebaittit in his feall Thairfore it is hir Hienes will that all the keyis of the Lordis chalmeris and Gentillwemen chalmeris with office houssis and vthiris and yettis within oure said Palice be deliuerit to the said Serwais at hir Hienes delugeing thairfra quhill hir hamecuming And for vsing and keiping of the said Palice oure Souerane Ladie gevis . . . to the said Serwais in yeirlie feall . . . ane hundreth merkis money . . . At Haliruidhous the twentie daye of Januare the yeir of God j^m v^c lxiiij yeiris Per signaturam.'—(Registrum Secreti Sigilli, vol. xxxii. foll. 72, 73. MS. Register House.)

[1] P. 25, nn. 68, 69.
[2] Inventaire des Bijoux, de l'Argenterie et d'autres menus objets appartenant a Marie Stuart, made at Chartley, in August 1586, printed by Prince Labanoff, in his Lettres de Marie Stuart, t. vii. p. 249.

There seems to have been a map of Scotland at Holyrood in 1565. The English envoy relates that when Lord Darnley was shown 'in the Scotch mappe' the vast territories of which the Earl of Murray had already possessed himself, he exclaimed, 'It is too much.'—(Letter from Randolph to Cecil, 20. March 1564-5, in Mr. T. Wright's Queen Elizabeth and her Times, vol. i. p. 195.)

Inventarye of the Jewells Plate money and other goods of the Quene of Scottes, made at Fotheringhay, 20. February 1587, printed by Prince Labanoff, in his Lettres de Marie Stuart, t. vii. p. 271.

[3] P. 25, nn. 70, 71 ; p. 186.
[4] Pp. 28-48.

It is printed from the original in the Register House.

Although it gives account of things received in November 1561, it would seem to have been written (probably from an older Inventory) after the Earl of Murray had assumed the Regency in August 1567. It is authenticated by the signature of his secretary, Mr. John Wood, and may have been prepared at the

as the Inventory of the moveables of Queen Mary of Guise, made two months before.   There are ten cloths of state, forty-five beds, thirty-six Turkey carpets, twenty-three suits of tapestry.   One of the embroidered cloths of state, bearing the arms of Scotland and Lorraine,[1] seems to have followed the Queen to the last but one of her many places of captivity.[2]   Twelve of the beds are described as embroidered, three as pasmented with gold or silver, five as plain, thirteen as old, and twelve as wooden, that is, simple frames without hangings. One of the suits of tapestry is spoken of as still in the embroiderers' hands.[3] Another, representing the Labours of Hercules, would seem to have lined the walls of Holyrood since the marriage of the Princess Margaret of England with King James the Fourth, in 1503.[4]   A third figured the famous victory gained by the French under the youthful Gaston of Foix, at Ravenna, in 1512.[5]   This appears to have been a favourite with the Queen; she had rooms at Chartley and at Fotheringhay[6] hung with it.   Five canopies are mentioned, one of them in terms which show that it was used by the Queen as a parasol.[7]   We find but

same time with another Inventory likewise authenticated by his signature, in November 1569 (pp. 179-187).

It is included in Mr. Thomson's Collection of Inventories, pp. 133-152.

[1] Pp. 28, 29, no. 4.

[2] 'Un autre daiz de velloux viollet, faict en broderie des armes d'Escosse et de Lorraine.'—(Inventaire de la Garde-Robe de Marie Stuart, made at Chartley, 13. June 1586, printed by Prince Labanoff, in his Lettres de Marie Stuart, t. vii. p. 236.)

At Tutbury, in April 1585, Sir Amias Poulet removed the Scottish Queen's cloth of state from her great chamber, contending that there should be only one cloth of state in England.   But a small cloth of state was suffered to remain in the room where the Queen dined and supped : 'It represented by letters the names of the Queen's father and mother, with the arms of Scotland in the middle quartered with the arms of Lorraine.'—(G. Chalmers's Life of Mary Queen of Scots, vol. ii. p. 144, edit. 1822. Calendar of State Papers relating to Scotland, vol. ii. p. 969.)

At Fotheringhay, after sentence of death had been given against her, Poulet ordered her cloth of state to

be torn down ; and some of the last letters which she wrote complain of the act as a cruel indignity.—(Jebb, De Vita Mariae Scotorum Reginae, t. ii. pp. 41, 91, 293, 294. Prince Labanoff, Lettres de Marie Stuart, t. vi. pp. 464, 469, 470, 478, 479.)

[3] P. 38, no. 74.

[4] P. 39, no. 88.   Mr. Thomson's Collection of Inventories, pp. 51, 103. Relation of John Younge, Somerset Herald, in Leland's Collectanea, vol. iv. pp. 295, 296, edit. 1774. Prince Labanoff, Lettres de Marie Stuart, tom. vii. p. 236.

[5] P. 38, no. 78.   Mr. Thomson's Collections of Inventories, p. 212.

[6] Prince Labanoff, Lettres de Marie Stuart, t. vii. pp. 236, 273.

[7] P. 33, no. 33 ; p. 156. Mr. Thomson's Collection of Inventories, p. 208.

Recent research has discovered the parasol in the paintings and sculptures of Egypt and Assyria. Du Cange quotes Aristophanes and Claudian for its use among the Greeks and the Romans. He finds the word umbrella in the twelfth century, used apparently to signify the modern parasol.—(Glossarium Mediae Latinitatis, tom. vi., coll. 1669-70, voce ' Umbellum.')

one table and one chair. The table is described as painted and gilt;[1] the chair as high, covered with velvet and cloth of gold embroidered. It was obviously a seat of state.[2] There are no more than two folding stools and three low stools, all of them covered with velvet.[3] As many as eighty-one cushions are enumerated; eleven covered with velvet, thirty-three with cloth of gold, fifteen with cloth of silver, thirteen with satin embroidered or brocaded, six with needlework of silk, three with needlework of worsted.[4] Of four table-covers, three are of velvet, one being embroidered with the lilies of France in thread of gold.[5] There are twenty-four linen table-cloths, two of them together measuring fourteen yards, other two, with a cloth for the cupboard (or, as we should now call it, the sideboard), being of damask.[6] There is mention of a litter,[7] covered with velvet fringed with gold and silk; and we learn elsewhere that the Queen had a coach,[8] although she seldom used it, choosing rather, in those early days, to ride on horseback, with a steel bonnet on her head, and a pistol at her saddle-bow, in time of war, regretting only, as she said, that she was not a man to know what life it was to lie all night

The Queen's Litter.

The Queen's Coach.

—Mr. T. Wright thinks that the umbrella, in our sense of the word, was known to the Anglo-Saxons.— (History of Domestic Manners in England, p. 75.)

[1] P. 42, no. 115.
[2] P. 34, no. 36.
[3] P. 34, nn. 37, 38.
[4] Pp. 36, 43-45.
[5] Pp. 35, 36.
[6] Pp. 46-48.
[7] P. 41.
[8] 'To the smythis in Sanctandrois for thair labouris in mending of the Quenis Graces coiche at the Maister Stabillaris command xx schillingis.' — (Computum Thesaurarii Reginae Scotorum, March 1561-2. MS. Register House.)

'Vpoun the ferd day of Maij [1562], my Lord Arrane . . . come fra Sanctandrois . . . to Edinburgh . . . in the Quenis Graces cosche, becaus of the frenasie.'—(Diurnal of Occurrents, p. 72.)

In 1550, there are said to have been but three coaches in Paris, of which Catharine of Medicis had one, Diana of France, another, and the unwieldy lord of Bois-Dauphin, the third. They increased so rapidly, that in 1563 the parliament of Paris petitioned the King to forbid their use within the capital.—(M. D. Ramée, Histoire des Chars, Carosses et Voitures, pp. 68, 76. Paris 1856.) A coach of the reign of Henry II. (1547-1559), figured in this work, looks exactly like a four-post bed on wheels.

There is mention more than once of the chariot of Mary's mother, Queen Mary of Guise. In July 1538, there was a payment of 13s. from the Treasury 'to Alexander Naper for mending of the Quenis sadill and hir cheriot in Sanctandrois;' and in January 1540-1, a payment of L.7, 16s. 'to Patrik Sklater iij elnis blak veluet to mend the Quenis cheriot with, price of the eln lij schillingis.'—(Computa Thesaurariorum Regis Scotorum. MS. Register House.)

When the daughter of King Henry VII. came to Scotland in 1503 to marry King James IV., she travelled for the most part on horseback, making her entry into the towns in a litter borne by two horses. — (Relation of John Younge, Somerset Herald, in Leland's Collectanea, vol. iv. p. 267.)

in the fields, or to walk upon the causeway with a jack and a knapscull, a Glasgow buckler, and a broadsword.[1]

Inventory of the Earl of Huntly's moveables brought to Holyrood, in December 1562.

The Inventory[2] next in order is of the household stuff of a great Scottish Earl, who had ruled half the kingdom as Lieutenant of the North, and held the office of Chancellor of the realm. Whatever may have been the object of the Queen's journey to Inverness in the autumn of 1562, it issued in the utter overthrow of the Gordons. She had scarcely returned to her capital, when two ships from Aberdeen, laden with fruits of her victory, dropped anchor at Leith. One brought the dead body of the Earl of Huntly, rudely embalmed, so that it might be placed at the bar of the Parliament, and arraigned for treason, according to the custom which Scotland had borrowed from the law of Rome.[3] The other brought the Queen's share of the pillage of the Earl's

[1] Letters from Randolph to Cecil, 18. September 1562, and 13. October 1565, quoted in G. Chalmers's Life of Queen Mary, vol. i. pp. 133, 240, and Mr. Tytler's History of Scotland, vol. v. pp. 223, 322. Cf. M. Teulet, Lettres de Marie Stuart, pp. 118, 125.

[2] Pp. 49-56.

It is printed from the original in the Register House.

Although it gives account of things received in December 1562, it would seem to have been written (probably from an older Inventory) after the Earl of Murray had assumed the Regency in August 1567. It is authenticated by the signature of his secretary, Mr. John Wood, and may have been prepared at the same time with another Inventory, likewise authenticated by his signature, in November 1569 (pp. 179-187).

It is included in Mr. Thomson's Collection of Inventories, pp. 153-158.

Trial of the dead for treason.

[3] The Earl was slain at Corrichie on the 28th October 1562. His body, which was very corpulent, was disembowelled at Aberdeen and filled with spices, by a physician, who received a fee of L. 21. 10s. On its arrival at Edinburgh, a sum of L. 28. 3s. 4d. was paid to a surgeon ' for expensis maid be him vpoun spicis vinagre aquauitie pulderis odouris and hardis

with sindrie vthiris necessaris and for his laubouris in the handeling of the said Erle of Huntleis bodie that it suld nocht putrefie.'—(Compotum Thesaurarii Reginae Scotorum, Oct.—Dec. 1562. MS. Register House.

On the 28th of May 1563, the Earl's body was brought to the bar of Parliament, and sentence of forfeiture passed against it. It lay unburied in Edinburgh till April 1566, when it was carried north to the tomb of the Gordons in the cathedral at Elgin.—(Acts of the Parliaments of Scotland, vol. ii. pp. 572-576. Diurnal of Occurrents, pp. 76, 98, 99. Knox's History of the Reformation, pp. 359, 380, 381.)

The right of the crown, in certain cases, to move for doom of treason against a dead man, was unanimously affirmed by the Scottish Parliament in 1540, and seems to have been the law of Scotland till the Union.—(Acts of the Parliaments of Scotland, vol. ii. p. 356. Sir George Mackenzie's Observations on the Statutes, in his Works, vol. i. pp. 247, 248 ; and his Laws of Scotland in Matters Criminal, part i. tit. vi. sect. xxii., in his Works, vol. ii. pp. 73, 74.)

I have seen an unpublished letter from Queen Elizabeth to the Regent Morton, pleading for the exemption of the corpse of Secretary Maitland from the last indignity of the Scottish law : ' For the bodie of

castle of Strathbogie, which, as already forfeited to the crown, was delivered
to the valet of the chamber in charge of the Palace of Holyrood.[1]

The list recounts seventy-three articles. There are nine beds,[2] quite as
costly to appearance as the beds, no more in number, left by Queen Mary
of Guise. The tapestry is not reckoned by suits, but there are fifty-six
pieces,[3] and we are told that six of them sufficed to hang the chamber in
which the King was murdered at the Kirk of the Field.[4] Eleven pieces were
of leather, stamped and gilt.[5] There is a cloth of state of satin figured
with gold, which afterwards served the Queen in her prison at Lochleven.[6]
Forty-eight table-cloths are mentioned, two of figured velvet, one of green
velvet, four of green cloth, twenty of linen. There are twenty-two cloths for
the cupboard or sideboard. There is no mention of plate, either the Earl's
own, or that which we know had been intrusted to his keeping ; both, doubtless, had been carried off by friendly hands before the castle gates were flung
open to the plunderer. A velvet cushion for a book,[7] shows that letters were
not wholly neglected at Strathbogie. We have still less doubtful tokens of taste

Book-cushion,
gilded and
coloured glass,
enamels, sculp-
ture, etc.

Liddington, who died before he was convict in judgement, and before any answer by him made to the
crymes obiectid to him, it is not our maner in this
contrey to shew crueltie vpon the dead bodies so
vnconvicted, but to suffer them streight to be buried,
and put in the earth. And so suerly we think it mete
to be done in this case, for (as we take it) it was God's
pleasure he should by death be taken away from
thexecucion of iudgment, so we think consequently
that it was his divine pleasure that the bodie now
dead should not be laceratid, nor pullid in peeces, but
be buried like to one who died in his bed, and by
sicknes, as he did.' This was written at Croydon,
on the 19th of July 1573. Maitland died at Leith on
the 9th of June, in the same year, ' some supponyng
he tok a drink,' says Sir James Melville, ' and died
as the auld Romanes wer wont to do.'—(Memoirs,
p. 256.)

Queen Elizabeth was moved to intercede with Morton by a touching letter to Lord Burleigh from Lethington's widow, who had been one of the Four Marys,
written from Edinburgh on the 21st of June 1573. It

is printed in G. Chalmers's Life of Mary Queen of
Scots, vol. iii. p. 615. Efforts had been made in
other quarters to obtain leave to lay the Secretary's
corpse in the grave.—(Calendar of State Papers relating to Scotland, vol. i. p. 378.)

[1] In November 1562, a payment of L.30. 7s. was
made, by the Queen's command, ' to Maister Johnne
Balfour for expensis maid be him for inbringing of
George Erle of Huntleis geir this instant moneth of
Nouember to the toun of Abirdene putting the samyn
in pypis cariage and fraucht of Abirdene to the port
of Leith.'—(Compotum Thesaurarii Reginae Scotorum, Nov. 1562. MS. Register House.)

[2] Pp. 49-51.

[3] P. 51.

[4] P. 51, no. 18 ; p. 177.

[5] P. 51, no. 11.

[6] P. 50, no. 6.

Another pall, wrongly described as a cloth of
estate (p. 53, no. 34), was a canopy or tabernacle for
the procession on Corpus Christi day (p. 184).

[7] P. 52, no. 20.

and refinement in the list of ewers, basins, stoups, flagons, and cups of gilded or coloured glass; enamelled plates, cups, glasses, dishes, saucers, basins, and ewers; gilded chandeliers; figures of animals, and images of a monk, a nun, and the Earl's patron St. George; a white vase; a bust of a man, sculptured in marble; and the Woman of Samaria drawing water from the Well of Jacob, carved in wood.[1]

All this was but a part, although no doubt a large one, of the spoil of Strathbogie. The Queen divided the prey with her brother, by whose wisdom and courage it had been won. She gave him possession, in the hall of Darnaway, of the long-coveted Earldom of Murray; and he seems to have found furniture for the forsaken chambers of Randolph's forest castle, in a share of the Earl of Huntly's moveables. There is, unfortunately, no list of what thus fell to his lot. We know only that, some years afterwards, when the star of the Gordons was once more rising in the north, Murray was careful to guard himself against all claim for restitution of the jewels, furniture, and chattels of the Earl, whose lifeless body he had led away with him from the glen of Corrichie.[2]

It must not be supposed that Scotland could show many castles like Strathbogie. The pile had been newly enlarged and adorned in such a way, it is said, as to move the envy of the Queen Regent and her French retinue, whom it

---

[1] Pp. 54-56.

Some of these articles are found in the King's Jewel-house in 1578: 'Ane gilt basine of glas; tua blew flaconis garnist with tyn; ane uther blew flacon; foure gilt chandilleris; ane Samaritane Woman and hir Well maid of trie; fyve pleittis of quheit anamaling; ane pleitt hollit as gif it wer wandis; thre uther pleittis of divers cullouris; thre pleittis cullourit plane; aucht blew salceris ane brokin; tua litle barrellis and ane litle thre futtit pott; ane blew lawer with ane gilt coupe; ane litle lawer blew gilt; ane quhite vais; ane coup of jasp with the cover; thre heich gobblettis tua coverit and ane without a cover; aucht couppis of sindrie fassionis; sax litle culing fannis of litle wandis.'—(Mr. Thomson's Collection of Inventories, p. 241.)

[2] By a deed, dated at Holyrood, on the 18th of April 1567, George Earl of Huntly, binds himself, his mother, his brothers, and his sisters, ' to warrand releve and keip skaithles James Earl of Murray and Maister Johnne Wod Johnne Stewart and vtheris his serwandis of quhatsumeuir gudis geir jowellis and vthir grayth quhatsumeuer intromettit with be thame pertening to our [the Earl of Huntly's] vmquhile fader the tyme of his deceis or that wes than in his possessioun. . . and neuer to move pley call nor persew the said Erle of Murray nor his saidis serwandis thairfoir,' confessing ' that thair intromissioun with the saidis gudis procedit be our Soueranis commandement.'—(Register of Deeds, vol. vii. foll. 406-408. MS. Register House. Compare Malcolm Laing's Dissertation on the Murder of Darnley, in his History of Scotland, vol. ii. p. 98, edit. 1804.)

received as guests in 1556.[1] More recently, the English envoy to the court of Holyrood, who spent two nights within its walls, described it as a fair house, the best furnished that he had seen since he passed the Tweed, and of marvellous great cheer.[2] Buchanan speaks of the Earl as by far the wealthiest noble in the land.[3] Knox tells how he was reputed the wisest, the richest, and the most powerful man in Scotland ; and adds that, in the world's estimation, the realm had not, for three hundred years, produced such another, under the degree of a prince.[4]

We might be surprised that even this great chief, the head of the Roman Catholic power in Scotland, should have so much and so sumptuous church furniture. But a little consideration enables us to discover that the articles of this sort enumerated in the Inventory are but a portion of the ornaments and vestments of the neighbouring Cathedral of Aberdeen, which the bishop, with his dean and chapter, hastened to commit to the safe keeping of the Earl, in the summer of 1559,[5] on hearing that the Reformers had sacked the monasteries of the

Ornaments and vestments of the Cathedral of Aberdeen.

Power of the Gordons.

[1] 'Inuernessam urbem proficiscenti erat in itinere Strathbogia arx, comitatus caput, amoeno situ ad confluentes Bogii et Duuerni fluminum posita, quam Huntlaeus, adjectis veteri arci novis structuris, omnia, nulli sumptui parcens, magnifice extruxerat. Hic illa [Regina Gubernatrix] liberaliter cum magno comitatu, Gallorum praesertim, excepta est. Post aliquot dies transactos, ne pregravaret hospitem, digredi parat : Huntlaeus, ad omnia illi semper obsequentissimus, et partibus firmus, demississime rogat longiorem moram ; nihil defuturum ad eam laute excipiendam, vult inspici cellas penusque copiose instructas, tanta autem volatilium et ferinae copia ejusque recentis ut mirum videri posset. Quaerentibus Gallis, unde tanta et tam recentis abundantia, refert ille habere se in aviis, in montibus, locisque sylvestribus magno numero venatores aucupesque, unde ad se referatur quotidiana praeda, quamvis locis longe distantibus. Henricus Clutinius Oisellius, e nobilitate Gallica, qui Gubernatricis consilia moderabatur, apud eam exclamat, Hunc hominem in tam angusto regno non ferendum ; illum sic aequales excedere, ut potuit Regi Scoto formidini esse ; revocandum in memoriam Duglassiorum nefandam audaciam, quae quas turbas dederit, quamque regibus formidolosas superiori saeculo, non-

dum animis hominum excidisse ; demetendas Huntlaeo alas, ne nimium superbiat.'—(Origo et Progressus familiae illustrissimae Gordoniorum in Scotia, Roberto Gordonio a Straloch auctore [circa A. D. 1650]. MS. Advocates' Library, Edinburgh. C. A. Gordon's History of the House of Gordon, pp. 85-88. Aberd. 1754. Cf. Leslaei De Rebus Gestis Scotorum, p. 528.)

Little or nothing of the Strathbogie of Queen Mary's time now remains. It was demolished by her son in 1594, at the instance chiefly of Mr. Andrew Melville, who was present at the work of destruction, clad in a cuirass, as his nephew exultingly tells us, adding, that on another occasion, he marched, for great part of a day, with a spear in his hand.—(Mr. James Melville's Diary, p. 210. edit. 1829.)

[2] Letter from Randolph to Cecil, written from Spynie on the 18th of September 1562, quoted in G. Chalmers's Life of Mary Queen of Scots, vol. i. p. 129.

[3] G. Buchanani Rerum Scoticarum Historia, lib. xvii. c. 27.

[4] Knox's History of the Reformation, vol. ii. p. 358.

[5] Registrum Episcopatus Aberdonensis, vol. i. appendix to the preface, no. II. pp. lxxxvi.-xc.

The Cathedral plate put in the Earl's keeping

d

Friars in Edinburgh and other towns, had laid the beautiful priory of the Carthusians at Perth in ruins, and given the ancient abbey of Scone to the flames. The Bishop's great mitre,[1] since it was worn by the munificent and saintly Elphinstone, had fallen into evil hands, from which it was not rescued until it had been stripped of several of its gems.[2] The Cathedral could show robes and hangings made from the cloth of gold taken in the English tents at Bannockburn, or woven in the looms of Bruges and Arras, of Venice and Florence.[3] The meagre descriptions in the Inventories do not allow us in every case to follow the history of the vestments which were sent from Aberdeen to Strathbogie, and from Strathbogie to Holyrood. But there is at least nothing to forbid the suspicion that the copes, chasubles, and tunicles of cloth of gold which the Queen profaned to secular uses in March 1567, were relics of the proudest triumph ever gained by Scottish arms;[4] and that the spoils which Bruce had set apart, in the service of religion, to nerve the hearts of his people in their struggle for national life, were given by her who inherited his throne and held his faith, to make a showy doublet for the needy, vainglorious, profligate Bothwell.[5]

weighed 843 ounces. No part of it is known to be preserved. But an image of the Blessed Virgin, committed to the care of Queen Mary's devoted servant, Bishop Lesley of Ross, is still to be seen in Brussels. It is the subject of a recent religious tract (bearing to be taken from F. A. Wichmans' Brabantia Mariana): 'Histoire de la Statue Miraculeuse de la Tres-Sainte Vierge Marie, honorée dans l'eglise de Notre-Dame de Finisterrae, a Bruxelles, sous le titre de Notre-Dame de Bon Succès. Bruxelles, 1854.'

[1] P. 54, no. 50.

[2] Registrum Episcopatus Aberdonensis, vol. ii. pp. 162-166, 179, 180, 186, 187, 195, 196; vol. i. app. to pref. p. lxxxix.

[3] Registrum Episcopatus Aberdonensis, vol. ii. pp. 189, 190, 191, 194.

Barbour, the father of our Scottish poetry, was a canon of the Cathedral of Aberdeen, and so may have served at the altar in the vestments made from the trophies of the victory which he has sung in his 'Bruce.'

Silver cross of Irish work. An inventory of the Cathedral plate in January 1549-50 describes a cross of silver gilt as of Irish work, 'opere Ibernicorum,' meaning, probably, the knotted or interlacing pattern so common in Irish art.—(Registrum Episcopatus Aberdonensis, vol. ii. p. 182.)

[4] See above, pp. xiv., xv., note 3.

[5] P. 53, no. 32. Registrum Episcopatus Aberdonensis, vol. i. app. to pref. p. lxxxix.; vol. ii. pp. 189, 190.

Bothwell's foppery: Bothwell would seem to have been noted for his love of finery. One who must have known him well, compares him to an ape in purple, 'tanquam simius in purpura.'—(G. Buchanani Actio contra Mariam Scotorum Reginam.) The same great scholar speaks elsewhere of the gorgeousness of the apparel in which Bothwell figured at the Prince's baptism at Stirling: 'Regina, non modo pecunia, sed opera etiam et industria, contendit ut Bothuelius, inter cives et hospites, singulari cultus magnificentia conspiceretur.'—(Rerum Scoticarum Historia, lib. xviii. c. 5;

The Inventory of what came into the Queen's possession on the forfei- *Inventories of articles brought from France, in June 1563; of the vestments of the Chapel Royal of Stirling, in January 1562, etc.* ture of the Earl of Huntly, is followed by lists[1] of a few things which seem to have belonged to Mary of Guise, brought from France, by Maitland of Lethington,[2] the Queen's secretary, in the summer of 1563; of three cloths of state and a table-cover of cloth of gold, portions of a gift made to the Queen in the summer of 1564, by the wife of the Lord Ruthven who bore the chief part in the murder of Riccio; and of the rich vestments of the Chapel Royal of Stirling, delivered to the valet in charge of the Queen's wardrobe in 1562.[3] Among the articles brought from France by Lethington, was a portrait of *Portrait of Queen Mary of Guise.*

Opera, p. 349). Again, in another work, but still referring to the same occasion: ' Ut Bothuelius inter proceres conspicuus esset, ipsa [Regina] partim ei ad vestimenta coemenda pecuniam erogabat, partim de mercatoribus emebat; omnibusque conficiundis tanta diligentia praeerat, quam si, non dico uxor, sed ne ancilla quidem foret.'—(G. Buchanani Detectio Mariae Reginae Scotorum.)

His ungainly person; The *simius in purpura* would appear to imply that Bothwell's person was such that his gay garments hung awkwardly upon him. Buchanan has other expressions to the same effect; and they are more than justified by the unmistakeable language of Brantôme: ' Ce Bothwell estoit le plus laid homme, et d'aussi mauvaise grace qu'il se peut voir.' Lord Hailes tried to get rid of Brantôme's evidence, by pleading that ' he never saw Bothwell,' and ' got his information from one de Cros, an officer of Queen Mary's household.' —(Remarks on the History of Scotland, chap. xi., in Annals of Scotland, vol. iii. pp. 80, 81, edit. 1819.) But a reference to Brantôme (t. v. pp. 98, 99) will show that Lord Hailes has misapprehended his meaning, and that all that he had from de Cros was an account of Mary's brief campaign between her escape from Lochleven and her flight into England, at a time when Bothwell was a prisoner in Denmark. Brantôme tells us that his own visit to Scotland was made in the train of Mary's uncle, the Grand Prior of France (t. v. p. 122). He must thus have spent nearly two months at Holyrood (from the 19th of August to the 9th of October 1561); and it is scarcely reasonable to suppose that, during all that time, he had no opportunity of seeing one already so conspicuous at Mary's court as the Earl Bothwell.

His coarse speech. But if not good-looking, neither does Bothwell seem to have had the gift of a winning tongue. 'Qui audi-

erint,' says Buchanan, ' hominis infantiam et hebetudinem non ignorent;' or, as it is rendered in the contemporary translation of the 'Actio contra Mariam:' ' thay that haue hard him ar not ignorant of his rude utterance and blockishness.'—(Anderson's Collections relating to Queen Mary, vol. ii. p. 53.) When he was the Queen's husband, we have the evidence of Sir James Melville that his ' speaking sic filthy language' drove that gentleman from the supper table at Holyrood.—(Memoirs, p. 178.)

[1] Pp. 57-59.
They are printed from the originals in the Register House. They are without date, but are written in the same hand, and apparently at the same time, with the Inventory of the Moveables of the Earl of Huntly, to which they seem to have been attached. They may be referred, therefore, to some period between August 1567 and January 1570.
They are included in Mr. Thomson's Collection of Inventories, pp. 159-161.

[2] Lethington's mission to the French court is referred to by the Queen of Scots in a letter to Catharine of Medicis, of the 18th of May 1563.—(Prince Labanoff, Lettres de Marie Stuart, t. vii. pp. 3-5.) He returned to Scotland about the end of June 1563. —(Knox's History of the Reformation, vol. ii. p. 390.)

[3] Another and somewhat fuller list of the vestments of the Chapel Royal of Stirling delivered by the Sacristan to Servais de Conde, on the 11th of January 1561-2, will be found in the Appendix to the Preface, No. I. It is reprinted, with a few corrections, from Robertson's Topographical Description of Ayrshire, p. 431. Irvine, 1820. The original is in the Crawfurdland charter chest.

Mary's mother, which appears to have accompanied her, from prison to prison, to the fatal hall at Fotheringhay.[1]

The next Inventory is of the Queen's dresses.[2] It was made at Holyrood in February 1562, and has a hundred and thirty-one entries. There are sixty gowns, for the most part of cloth of gold, cloth of silver, velvet, satin, and silk. Of fourteen cloaks, five are described as of the Spanish fashion, and two as royal mantles, one being of purple velvet, the other furred with ermine. There are thirty-four vasquines or basquines, and sixteen devants, chiefly of cloth of gold, cloth of silver, and satin. There is mention of the fardingale, and we learn elsewhere that it was expanded by girdles of whalebone,[3] into something like the vast circumference of the hoops of our great grandmothers,[4] or the ample volume of the crinoline of our own day.

[1] P. 57, no. 1. Prince Labanoff, Lettres de Marie Stuart, t. vii. pp. 248, 254.

The Inventory made at Fotheringhay, in February 1587, mentions only 'certen pictures of the late Quene's auncestors.' But we have a list of them in the Inventory made at Chartley, in August 1586. There are five Kings and one Queen of Scots, namely, James II., James III., James IV., James V., Mary, and James VI. (of whom there are two portraits). The others are the Queen's mother, Mary of Guise; two of the Queen's uncles, Charles, Cardinal of Lorraine, and Francis, Duke of Guise (old *le Balafré*); her cousin, Henry, Duke of Guise (the younger *le Balafré*); King Charles IX. of France; King Henry III. of France; and Jeanne d'Albret, Queen of Navarre.

An Inventory of Jewels, etc., in the Castle of Edinburgh in 1578, adds to this list, King Francis II. of France; Anne, Duke of Montmorency, Constable of France; and a little old picture of King James V. of Scotland.—(Mr. Thomson's Collection of Inventories, p. 238.)

All these seem to have been oil-paintings on panel or on canvas. The inventories made at Chartley and Fotheringhay enumerate miniatures of the Queen herself, her second husband King Henry, and their son King James; of her first husband, King Francis II. of France, and his mother Catharine of Medicis; of the Queen's mother, Mary of Guise; of the Queen's mother-in-law, the Countess of Lennox; of Margaret of France, wife of Emmanuel Philibert, Duke of Savoy (*Tête-de-Fer*); of King Henry III. of France, and his Queen, Louise of Lorraine; of Queen Mary of England; of Queen Elizabeth of England, and of two ladies not named.—(Prince Labanoff, Lettres de Marie Stuart, t. vii. pp. 243-245, 247, 255, 257.)

The inventories in this volume mention miniatures of the Queen herself; of Queen Elizabeth of England; of King Henry II. of France; and of King James V. of Scotland.—(Pp. 11, 16, 85, 112, 119, 123.)

I am tempted to think that the portrait of Louise of   La Reyne Lorraine is sometimes mistaken for the portrait of   Blanche. Mary Stewart. Their features were much alike, and the dress and name of *la Reyne Blanche* were common to both.—(Brantôme, t. v. p. 334.)

[2] Pp. 60-74.

It is printed, for the first time, from the original in the Register House.

[3] 'Item xij bowtis of quhaill horne to be girdis to the vardingallis the bowt v schillingis summa iij pundis ... Ane verdingale iij pundis x schillingis Item v balling of quhaill xxxv schillingis.'—(Compotum Thesaurarii Reginae Scotorum, Oct.—Dec. 1562. MS. Register House.)

[4] The Cameronian Martyrologist writing between

The Inventory of the Queen's jewels which follows is without date, but *Inventory of the Queen's Jewels, in February 1562.* would appear to have been made at the same time with the Inventory of the Wardrobe at Holyrood, which immediately precedes it.[1] It has a hundred and eighty entries, or twenty-one more than the Inventory of the Queen's jewels made at her departure from France. Among the articles thus *Jewelled cross pawned for £1000 Scots.* added, we may recognise a cross of gold set with diamonds and rubies, which Mary had lately redeemed from the hands in which it was pledged by her mother for a thousand pounds.[2] Another acquisition is of pearls, which, as they were bought from an Edinburgh goldsmith, we may perhaps presume to be Scottish.[3]

...in 27 feet in cumference. 1725 and 1728, instances 'hoops or farthingales, nine yards about, some of them in three stories,' as one of seven proofs 'that Scots blood has gone out of our veins, honesty out of our hearts, zeal off our spirits, and the English abominations drunk in as sweet wine with pleasure.'—(Patrick Walker's Life and Death of Mr. Alexander Peden, in the Biographia Presbyteriana, vol. i. p. 138.)

If England set the fashion of hoops to Scotland in the beginning of the eighteenth century, Scotland seems to have set the fashion of fardingales to England in the beginning of the seventeenth century. The 'Scottish farthingale' is commemorated among the luxuries of London ladies, in Eastward Hoe, printed in 1605, and in Westward Hoe, printed in 1607.—(Dodsley's Old Plays, vol. iv. pp. 194, 196. edit. 1825.)

[1] Pp. 75-92.
It is printed, for the first time, from the original in the Register House.
As it makes reference to the Queen's visit to St. Johnstown (Perth), it must have been drawn up after the 17th of September 1561, when Mary made her first entry into the Fair City.—(Diurnal of Occurrents, p. 69.)

[2] P. 76.
'Item the ferd day of Februare [1561-2] be the Quenis Grace speciale command to Johne Hwme of Blacader for ane croce of gold sett with dyamondis and rubeis as his acquitance schewin vpoun compt beris quhilk lay in plege to him be the Quenis Grace Regent of 1000 pundis jm pundis.' — (Compotum Thesaurarii Reginae Scotorum, Feb. 1561-2. MS. Register House.)

[3] P. 89.
Scottish topazes and pearls appear among Queen *Scottish topazes.* Mary's jewels at Chartley in 1586.—(Prince Labanoff, Lettres de Marie Stuart, tom. vii. p. 246.)

Scottish pearls are often named in inventories of *Scottish pearls.* jewels in the Middle Ages.—(M. le Comte de Laborde, Notice des Emaux du Louvre, par ii. 'Glossaire,' pp. 310, 349, 350, 437, 480. Comptes de l'Argenterie des Rois de France au xiv⁰ Siècle, pp. 26, 395.)

We have mention of them early in the twelfth century. About the year 1120, an English churchman begs the Bishop of St. Andrews to get him as many pearls as possible, especially large ones, even if the Bishop should have to ask them from the King of the Scots, who has more than any man living.—(Wharton's Anglia Sacra, vol. ii. p. 236.)

Aeneas Sylvius, afterwards Pope Pius II., who visited Scotland in 1435, speaks of Scottish pearls as one of the four commodities which the country exported: 'ex Scotia in Flandriam corium, lanam, pisces salsos, margaritasque ferri.'— (Pii Secundi Pontificis Commentarii Rerum Memorabilium quae temporibus suis contigerunt, p. 5.) In 1498, we find a Scottish merchant at Middleburg remitting a small sum 'to by perll in Scotland.'—(Account Book of Andrew Halyburton, Conservator of the Privileges of the Scottish Nation in the Low Countries, fol. 159. MS. Register House.)

The pearls of Scotland seem to have shared with those of Bohemia the reputation of being the best found in Europe. But both were regarded as very far inferior to the pearls of the East.—(Anselmi Boetii de Boodt Gemmarum et Lapidum Historia, pp. 85,

The jewels which were in the Queen's cabinet in 1561 are not included in the list of 1562. But added to it, in a different hand, is a note of certain jewels which were then with the crown, the surcoat, and the coiff.[1]

Testamentary Inventory of the Queen's Jewels, Books, &c., in May or June 1566.

On the nineteenth of June 1566, Mary gave birth in the Castle[2] to the prince who was to unite, under one sceptre, kingdoms which had been too long divided. She seems to have had uneasy forebodings of her hour of travail. Before ' taking her chamber,'[3] she gathered her nobles round her, made her will, and otherwise provided for the government of her realm. Her will was written in three copies ; one she kept in her own hands, another she left under

---

90. Du Cange, Glossarium Mediae Latinitatis, t. v. col. 393, *voce* ' Perlae.')

Some notices of Scottish pearls are given in the Descrittione del Regno di Scotia di Petruccio Ubaldini, pp. 44-51, and in Collections for a History of the Shires of Aberdeen and Banff, pp. 80, 81. One or two Scottish streams are still fished for pearls ; and the newspapers tell us that the fishing of 1861 was singularly successful, especially in the Teith. In the seventeenth century the Ythan was in most repute ; and I am informed that during the last ten years its pearl fishery has again become a source of profit.

[1] Pp. 90-92.

[2] On the 5th of April 1566, there was a meeting of Privy Council at Edinburgh, attended by the Earls of Huntly, Bothwell, Atholl, Marischal, Crawford, Caithness, and Mar ; the Bishop of Galloway (Alexander Gordon), the Commendator of Lindores (John Lesley, afterwards Bishop of Ross), Sir John Maxwell of Terregles, knight, and Sir James Balfour of Pittendreich, knight, Clerk of the Register. The following Act was passed : ' The Lordis of Secreit Counsall thinkis it maist commodious for the commoun weill of this cuntre gif it may stand with the Quenis Maiesteis plesour and with the helth of hir body that hir Maiestie remane in the Castell of Edinburgh till hir Grace be deliuerit of hir birth. And in cais hir Maiestie pas to ony vther part to remane the Counsall to remane still in Edinburgh and sum forceis with thame dureing the said space and sum nobill men to remane with the Quenis Maiestie quhair hir Grace remanis.' —(Registrum Secreti Concilii : Acta 1563-1567, p. 191. MS. Register House.)

Having discovered that there was no wine in the Queen's cellars, the Privy Council sent to Leith for eleven tuns and a half, at the price of £50 Scots a tun. —(Id. p. 201).

[3] This was a solemn ceremony in that age, as we *Ceremonial of a Queen taking her chamber.* may learn from the contemporary account of what passed when Elizabeth of York, the wife of King Henry VII. of England, was about to give birth to Queen Mary's grandmother : ' Upon Allhalow even [31st October 1489] the Quene tooke her chamber at Westmynster, gretely accompagned with ladyes and gentilwomen . . . and . . . havyng befor hir the greate parte of the nobles of thys royalme being present at this Parlement. And she was ledde by therle of Oxenforde and therle of Derby ; and the reverent fader in God, the Bishop of Excestre, songe the masse, *in pontificalibus*, and after the *Agnus Dei* ; and whan the Bishop had done, the Quene was lede as bifore. And therles of Shrewsbury and of Kente hylde the towelles whan the Quene toke her rightes [that is, received the Eucharist], and the torches ware holden by knightes. And after mass, accompayned as before, and when she was comen into hir great chambre, she stode undre hir cloth of estate. Then their was ordeyned a voide of espices and swet wyne. That doone, my lorde the Quenes Chamberlain, in very good wordes, desired, in the Quenes name, the pepul there present to pray God to sende hir the goode oure. And so she departed to her inner chambre, which was hanged and sceyled with riche clothe of arras of blew, with flour. de lisis of gold, without any other clothe of arras of ymagerye, whiche is not convenient about wymen in such case. And in that chambre was a

seal to those who were to have the chief trust in Scotland, the third she sent to her kinsfolks in France.[1] No one of these copies would seem to have been preserved, nor is it certainly known what their terms were. All that can now be learned of the Queen's feelings and wishes is to be gathered from the Testamentary Inventory of her jewels, printed in the text.[2]

It appears to have been drawn up in the end of May or in the beginning of June 1566, by Mary Livingston,[3] the lady of honour in charge of the Queen's jewels, and by Margaret Carwod, the bedchamber woman in charge of the

riche bedde and palliet, the which palliet had a marviellous riche canope of clothe of gold . . . also ther was a riche auter well furnyshed with reliques, and a riche cupborde well and richely garnyshed. And then she recomanded hir to the goode praiers of the lordes, and then my lord her Chamberleyn drew the travers. And frome thens forthe, no maner of officers came within the chambre, but ladies and gentelwomen after the old coustume.'—(Strutt's Horda Angel-Cynnan, vol. iii. pp. 157, 158.)

A relic of this formal seclusion still lives in one of the senses in which we use the word 'confinement.' The ceremony with which it began has long been forgotten, but the rite which marked its end survives in 'the Churching of Women.'

[1] Letter from Randolph to Cecil, 7th June 1566, quoted in G. Chalmers' Life of Queen Mary, vol. i. p. 269, vol. iii. pp. 30, 31 ; Mr. Tytler's History of Scotland, vol. v. p. 354 ; Miss Strickland's Lives of the Queens of Scotland, vol. iv. pp. 338, 339; Calendar of State Papers relating to Scotland, vol. i. p. 235.

[2] It is here printed, for the first time, from the original in the Register House, where it was discovered in August 1854, among some unassorted law papers.

It is in two parts or gatherings, which have been tied together by a ribbon, secured by a seal, of which the mark is still to be seen.

The first gathering (pp. 93-115 of the text) contains ten leaves, numbered consecutively in a hand of the time. The first leaf, which is not counted in the numbering, is inscribed, *Inuentayre des Brodures de la Royne.* The first page of the tenth leaf is subscribed by the Queen and Mary Livingston (as at p. 115 of the text). On the second page of the tenth leaf, being the last page of the gathering, is written in the Queen's hand (as at p. 115 of the text),

Ientands que cestuissi soyt execute au cas que lanfant ne me suruiue mays si il vit ie le foys heritier de tout MARIE R

The second gathering (pp. 116-124 of the text) contains six leaves, of which the first four are numbered consecutively in a hand of the time. The second page of the second leaf is subscribed by the Queen and Mary Livingston (as at p. 121 of the text), and the second page of the third leaf, by the Queen and Margaret Carwod (as at p. 123 of the text). The facsimile shows that the latter was but a poor pen-woman ; it would seem, indeed, that it was only on great occasions that she attempted to write at all. A writ by her, in the Register House, dated in April 1566, is subscribed in set phrase, *Margaret Carwod with my hand at the pen led be the notar vnderwrittin at my command.* The postscript in the Queen's hand (printed at p. 124 of the text) begins at the foot of the second page of the third leaf, and fills the first page of the fourth leaf. On the second page of the fourth leaf, the Queen had begun what would seem to have been some conditional instructions, but broke off abruptly after writing the two words, *Si mon.* The fifth leaf and the first page of the sixth leaf are blank. On the second page of the sixth leaf, being the last page of the gathering, is written in the Queen's hand (as at p. 124 of the text), *Iantands que cestuissi sorte acffect* MARIE R

Both gatherings are stained with water, and worn at the edges, especially towards the foot of the page. The accompanying facsimile is of the first and second pages of the third leaf, of the first page of the fourth leaf, and of the second page of the sixth leaf of the second gathering. The curved line towards the head and foot of each page represents the slit through which a ribbon was passed so as to fasten the two gatherings together under a seal.

[3] Pp. 115, 121.

Queen's cabinet.[1]　On the margin, opposite to each of the two hundred and fifty-three articles enumerated, the Queen has written, with her own hand, the name of the person to whom she bequeaths it, adding at the end a note that the bequests are to take effect only in the event of her infant dying with herself; for if he lives she makes him the heir of all.　Both the Inventory itself, and the Queen's bequests, are in the language of the country where her happier days were passed ; indeed it was not until seven years after she left France, when she had crossed the Solway in her flight from her last battlefield, that she ventured on the attempt to write in English.[2]　It will be seen from the accompanying facsimile, that it was not altogether without reason that her letters about this time contain apologies for her handwriting,[3] which, at the best, was perhaps a little too masculine.

Bequests to the Crown of Scotland.

Her first bequest is for the honour of the Crown which she inherited. She leaves to it the Great Harry, another jewel of the same fashion, a grand dia-

---

The Queen's first letters in English.

[1] Pp. 119, 123, 124.

[2] What Queen Mary describes as her first letter in English, was written to Sir Francis Knollys, from Bolton, on the 1st of September 1568 : 'Mester Knollis, y heuu har sum neus from Scotland ; y send zou the double off them y vreit to the Quin my gud sister, and pres zou to du the lyk, conforme to that y spak zesternicht vnto zou, and sut hesti ansur y refer all to zour discretion, and wil lipne beter in zour gud delin for mi, nor y kan persuad zou, nemli in this langasg ; excus my iuel vreitin for y neuuer vsed it afor, and am hestet . . . Excus my iuel vreitin thes furst tym.'—(Sir H. Ellis' Original Letters illustrative of English History, first series, vol. ii. pp. 252-4, edit. 1825.)

When Mary called this her first English letter, she forgot that she had written in English to the Commendator of St. Colm's Inch six weeks before (on the 23d of July 1568).—(Miss Strickland's Lives of the Queens of Scotland, vol. vi. p. 390.)

There are a few letters of still earlier date, written in the Queen's name, which have an English sentence or two added to them in her own hand.　The first of these postscripts which I have observed, is in a letter to the Earl of Argyll, of the 31st of March 1566 : 'Wat euer bis sayed bi sur off my gud mynd and that ye sal persayue command my to our bruder　Zour richt gud sister MARIE R.'—(Letters to the Argyll Family, pp. 5, 6, Maitland Club, 1839).　Other examples will be found in the same volume, pp. 10-12 ; and in the Miscellany of the Spalding Club, vol. iii. p. 212.

[3] On the 15th of March 1566, Mary, after her escape to Dunbar from the short captivity in which she was held by the murderers of Rizzio, writes to Queen Elizabeth : 'We thoct to haue writtin to zow this letter with oure awin hand . . . bot of trewth we ar so tyrit and ewill at ease, quhat throw rydding of twenty millis in fiue houris of the nycht, as with the frequent seiknesses and ewill dispositioun be the occasioun of our chyld, that we could nocht at this time.' On the 4th of April 1566, still writing to the English Queen, she says : 'Excusés moy si j'escris si mal; car je suis si grosse, estant en mon septiesme moys.' Again, in May 1566, she writes to her aunt, the Duchess of Guise : 'Je bayse aussi les mayns à la Mignone, et la prie m'excuser ; car, tant que je seray si empeschée de ce fardeau, je ne lui escriray point, qui ne sera plus que six semaines.'—(Prince Labanoff, Lettres de Marie Stuart, t. i. pp. 337, 355, t. vii. p. 302. Calendar of State Papers relating to Scotland, vol. i. p. 233.)

The Queen's apologies for her handwriting.

he two hundred and
h her own hand, the
: end a note that the
dying with herself;
ntory itself, and the
re her happier days
ft France, when she
, that she ventured
the accompanying
letters about this
st, was perhaps a

ch she inherited.
hion, a grand dia-

7 to our bruder Zou:
~(Letters to the Argyll
sh, 1839). Other ex-
ne volume, pp. 10-13;
ipalding Club, vol. iii

566, Mary, after her
captivity in which she
rzio, writes to Queen
: writtin to zow this
bot of trewth we ar
it throw rydding of
nycht, as with the
:oaitioun be the oc-
t nocht at this time
riting to the Eng-
oy si 7 eseris si mal;
a septiesme moys.
to her aunt, the
si les mayns à la
, tant que je seray
lui escriray point,
(Prince Labanoff,
17, 355, t. vii. p.
ung to Scotland.

tanas que est trussi sirte agtter
Phillippe

Immetanzes
Forvellus

mond cross, a chain enriched with rubies and diamonds, a necklace of diamonds, rubies, and pearls, and a large diamond set in an enamelled finger-ring. These seem to have been among her choicest gems; and she desires that an act may be passed annexing them to the Crown of Scotland in remembrance of herself, and of the Scottish alliance with the house of Lorraine.[1] Seven jewels containing what appear to have been her largest diamonds, she bequeaths for *Bequests to the Queens of Scotland;* ornaments to the Queens of Scotland, under injunctions neither to change the setting, nor to give the pieces away, but to keep them with the Crown for evermore.[2]

There are as many as twenty-six bequests to her husband the King.[3] *to the King.* Among them are a watch studded with diamonds and rubies; a little dial[4] set with diamonds, rubies, pearls, and turquoises; a St. Michael, containing fourteen diamonds; a chain of gold enamelled in white, containing two hundred links, with two diamonds in each link; and, of more interest than all, a *The Queen's marriage-ring.* diamond ring, enamelled in red, against which the Queen writes, 'It was with this that I was married; I leave it to the King who gave it me.'[5]

Nor are the King's kindred forgotten. Mary leaves a large diamond *Bequests to the Earl and Countess of Lennox;* ring, enamelled in black, to his father the Earl of Lennox,[6] and two diamond rings, one of them enamelled in black, to his mother, her own aunt, the Countess of Lennox.[7]

The Queen's kinsfolks in France have more affectionate or more costly *to the house of Guise.*

Jewelled dial, etc., given by the Earl of Lennox to the Queen.

[1] Pp. 93, 94, 97, 98, 112.

[2] Pp. 94, 95.

[3] Pp. 109, 110, 112, 114, 115, 122, 123.

[4] P. 123. It does not appear in the Inventories of 1561 and 1562, and may therefore, perhaps, be identified with the 'dial curiously wrought and set with stones,' which was given by the Earl of Lennox to the Queen in the autumn of 1564, along with 'a marvellous fair and rich jewel, whereof there is made no small account; a clock; and a looking-glass, very richly set with stones, in the four metals.'—(Letter from Randolph to Cecil, 24th October 1564, in Mr. Tytler's History of Scotland, vol. v. p. 256.)

[5] P. 112.

The English envoy at Edinburgh, in his contemporary account of the Queen's marriage, writes: 'The words were spoken; the rings, which were three, the middle a riche diamonde, were put upon her finger, theie kneel together, and manie prayers saide over them.'—(Letter from Randolph to Leicester, 31st July 1565, printed in Mr. T. Wright's Queen Elizabeth and her Times, vol. i. p. 202; and in Principal Robertson's History of Scotland, appendix, no. xi., Works, vol. ii. p. 333, edit. Oxf. 1825.)

[6] P. 112: 'A mon beau pere.'

[7] P. 112: 'A ma belle mere.'

e

remembrances. The house of Guise has a legacy of great rubies and great pearls, to be handed down from generation to generation as the inheritance of its first-born.[1] A large ruby is left to its chief,[2] the Queen's cousin, the Duke afterwards known as the second *le Balafré*, then only in his sixteenth year, but already distinguished in arms against the Turks. There are bequests to his mother,[3] then on the eve of her second marriage; to his sister,[4] conspicuous in after years for her devotion to the League; and to his brothers Charles,[5] afterwards Duke of Mayenne, the conqueror of many a Huguenot town before he was vanquished at Ivry; Lewis,[6] afterwards Cardinal of Guise; and Francis,[7] who died before he had risen above the rank of a Canon of King of Reims. He was the godson of the Queen's first husband; and it will be observed that she remembers him before his elder brothers, Charles and Lewis, and gives him a richer jewel than either.

<small>of King II.</small>

---

[1] Pp. 96, 97, 101, 102.

[2] P. 94: 'Ie le laysse a mon cousin de Guise.'

Henry of Lorraine, third Duke of Guise, born in 1550, was the eldest son of the Queen's uncle (her mother's eldest brother), Francis of Lorraine, second Duke of Guise, the first *le Balafré*, assassinated by the Huguenot Poltrot de Méré, at the siege of Orleans, in 1563. He himself was assassinated, by order of King Henry III., on the threshold of the king's cabinet at Blois, in 1588.—(L'Art de Vérifier les Dates, t. ii. pp. 606, 607, edit. 1784.)

[3] P. 93: 'Ie la laysse a ma tante Madame de Guise.'

Anne, daughter of Hercules of Este, Duke of Ferrara, was born in 1531. She married, in 1549, Francis second Duke of Guise, and, after his murder, in 1566, James of Savoy, Duke of Nemours. She died in 1607.

[4] Pp. 94, 95: 'Ie le laysse a ma cousine de Guise.'

Catharine of Lorraine, the only daughter of Francis second Duke of Guise, was born in 1552, and in 1570 became the second wife of Lewis of Bourbon, Duke of Montpensier. She died in 1596, and was buried in the choir of the conventual church of St. Peter at Reims, beside her aunt, the Queen Dowager of Scotland. 'Elle fut Ligueuse outrée,' says Father Anselme.—(Histoire Généalogique de France, t. iii. p. 486, edit. 1728.)

[5] P. 114: 'A Charles.'

Charles of Lorraine, second son of Francis second Duke of Guise, was born in 1554. The young Queen of Scots was present at his baptism, along with King Henry II. and Catharine of Medicis.—(Prince Labanoff, Lettres de Marie Stuart, t. i. pp. 19-22.) He was created Duke of Mayenne in 1573. A successful campaign in Dauphiny gained him the title of *le Preneur de Villes*. He became the chief of the League on the assassination of his elder brother, the second *le Balafré*, in 1588. He died in 1611.

[6] P. 114: 'A Loys.'

Lewis of Lorraine, third son of Francis second Duke of Guise, was born in 1556. He became Archbishop of Reims and Cardinal of Guise, being the second of his house who had the latter title. He was put to death at Blois in 1588, on the day after the murder of his brother, the younger *le Balafré*.

[7] P. 114: 'Au filleul du feu Roy.'

Francis of Lorraine, fifth son of Francis second Duke of Guise, was born in 1559. He became a Canon of Reims, where he died in 1573, before his uncle the Cardinal of Lorraine could fulfil the intention of making him Archbishop-Coadjutor of Reims.

The house of Aumale,[1] and the house of Elbeuf (or, as Mary calls it, *Bequests to the houses of Aumale and Elbeuf.* 'the house of the Marquis'),[2] have each a legacy of pearls to be kept, it would seem, as family heirlooms, like the rubies and pearls left to the parent house of Guise. There is a bequest to the eldest daughter of the Duke of Aumale,[3] Catharine, the Queen's cousin, afterwards Duchess of Mercoeur, then in her sixteenth year. There is a still larger bequest to the eldest daughter of the *The Queen's goddaughter.* Marquis of Elbeuf,[4] Mary, afterwards Duchess of Aumale, the Queen's cousin and goddaughter.

To her mother's sister, the Abbess of St. Peter's at Reims,[5] Mary be- *Bequest to the Queen's aunt, the Abbess of Reims.*

---

[1] P. 102 : 'A celle Daumalle ;' p. 98 : 'Le reste de cest acoustremant aux esnez Daumalle.'

[2] Pp. 102, 103 : 'A celle du Marquis ;' pp. 100, 101 : 'A laisne fils le la mayson du Marquis.'

[3] P. 93 : 'Ie la laysse a ma cousine Daumalle lesne ; p. 96 : 'A ma cousine Daumalle.'

Catharine of Lorraine, the eldest daughter of Claude second Duke of Aumale, by his marriage in 1548 with Louise, daughter of Louis of Brezé, grand steward of Normandy, was born in 1550, and in 1569 became the third wife of Nicholas of Lorraine, Count of Vaudemont, created Duke of Mercoeur in 1576. She died in 1606.

Her father, the Queen's uncle, was the third son of Claude of Lorraine, first Duke of Guise. He was born in 1526, and became Duke of Aumale in 1547. It was at his marriage, as we learn from a letter of King Henry II., that Queen Mary, after her arrival in France in 1548, first danced with the Dauphin. The Duke of Aumale accompanied the Queen to Scotland in 1561. He was killed at the siege of Rochelle in 1573.—(L'Art de Vérifier les Dates, t. ii. pp. 794, 795. Miscellany of the Maitland Club, vol. i. pp. 210, 219.)

[4] P. 93 : 'Ie le laysse a ma filleule fille du Marquis ;' p. 94 : 'A la fille du Marquis ma filleule,' 'A ma filleule ;' p. 97 : 'A ma cousine la fille du Marquis ma filleule.'

Mary of Lorraine, the only daughter of Rene, Marquis of Elbeuf, by his marriage in 1554, with Louise of Rieux, Countess of Harcourt, married in 1576 her cousin Charles third Duke of Aumale. She died about the year 1616.—(L'Art de Vérifier les Dates, t. ii. p. 796. Brantôme, t. v. p. 68.)

Her father, the Queen's uncle, was the eighth son of Claude of Lorraine, first Duke of Guise. He was born in 1536. In December 1559, he had a commission from Francis and Mary, King and Queen of France and Scotland, appointing him their Lieutenant-General in Scotland during the absence of the Queen Dowager. But it never took effect. In August 1561, he accompanied Queen Mary to Scotland, where he remained till the end of February 1561-2, giving such scandal to the Reformed in Edinburgh, that it drew from them a formal remonstrance to the Queen. He had an allowance from her of fifty shillings sterling a day for his table ; the payments made to him in all amounting to L.1500 Scots. He died in 1566.—(Liber Responsionum in Scaccario 1546-61, MS. Register House. Bishop Keith's History of Scotland, vol. ii. p. 101, edit. 1845. Compotum Thesaurarii Reginae Scotorum, Oct. 1561—Jan. 1562, MS. Register House. Diurnal of Occurrents, pp. 66, 67, 71. Booke of the Universall Kirk of Scotland, vol. i. pp. 11, 12. Knox's History of the Reformation, vol. ii. pp. 4, 268, 315-321. Anselme, Histoire Généalogique de France, t. iii. pp. 492, 493. Calendar of State Papers relating to Scotland, vol. i. pp. 122, 127, 131, 132, 139, 140, 142, 178, 179 ; vol. ii. p. 823. Prince Labanoff, Lettres de Marie Stuart, t. vii. pp. 282-287.)

[5] Pp. 112, 124 : 'A ma tante de St. Pierre.'

Renee of Lorraine, the third daughter of Claude first Duke of Guise, was born in 1522, and became Abbess of St. Peter's at Reims in 1546. She died in 1602, and was buried in the choir of her own abbey church, beside the stately tomb which showed her sister, the Queen Dowager of Scotland, figured in bronze, clothed in her royal vestments, holding the sceptre and the sword of justice.—(Anselme, Histoire Généalogique de France, t. iii. pp. 485, 486.) A

queaths, with other things of less note, a great mirror in a frame of white and black enamel, containing a miniature of the Queen of England.

Bequest to the Queen's uncle, the Cardinal of Lorraine.

She leaves an emerald ring to her mother's brother, the Cardinal of Lorraine,[1] that able but unscrupulous minister, 'the Tiger of France,' as so many regarded him, but the man, of all her kinsfolks and friends, whom Mary loved best and trusted most.[2]

Cancelled bequest to Madame Damville.

The Queen had bequeathed an emerald ring to one who had been her companion at the court of King Henry the Second, the wife of that flower of French chivalry, the Seigneur de Damville, afterwards Duke of Montmorency

---

prayer-book which Mary Stewart is said to have bequeathed to the abbey of St. Peter's at Reims, is still shown in the public library of that city.—(M. Francisque-Michel, Les Ecossais en France, t. ii. p. 27.)

[1] P. 114: 'A mon oncle le Cardinal.'

Mary had two uncles Cardinals, both brothers of her mother.

Her bequest is to the elder and more famous, Charles, second son of Claude first Duke of Guise. He was born in 1525, became Archbishop of Reims in 1540, Cardinal of Lorraine in 1555, and died in 1574. He was the chief minister of France during the reign of King Francis II.

His younger brother Lewis, fourth son of Claude first Duke of Guise, was born in 1527, and was made Bishop of Troyes in 1545, and Cardinal of Guise in 1553. He appears in our Scottish records, in March 1560, as Commendator of the Abbey of Kelso.—(Register of Deeds, vol. iv. fol. 93, MS. Register House.) He died in 1578, with the character of a good, easy man, who seldom troubled himself with any more serious affairs than those of the table.

The Queen and the Cardinal of Lorraine.

[2] 'Eh bien!' said Mary, when she heard of his death, 'je suis prisonnière, et Dieu prend l'une des créatures que j'aimoys le mieux.'—(Prince Labanoff, Lettres de Marie Stuart, t. iv. p. 267.)

Other eyes, such as, in her better days, had brightened as they looked upon her, saw in him only the shadow of her evil genius :

' Ni mihi tam foedus, tam dirus avunculus esset,
        Secli hujus Marie foemina prima forem.
   Sed vitiis, quibus evertit regna omnia, famam
        Polluit ille suam, polluit ille meam.'

—(G. Buchanani Epigrammatum, lib. ii. epp. 20, 21 : 'Maria Regina Scotiae puella ;' ' Eadem adulta.')

The King and the Cardinal of Lorraine.

The influence of the Cardinal of Lorraine on Mary's career was no doubt malign upon the whole ; but his counsels, if listened to, would have saved her from at least one mistake which drew others in its train. His searching eye had early seen through Darnley, and he warned his niece against marrying a great girlish nincompoop wholly unworthy of her hand : 'que ce n'estoit pas party pour elle . . . que c'estoit ung gentil hutaudeau,' that is, as M. Teulet glosses it, ' un étourneau, un jeune homme léger et inconsidéré.' —(Papiers d'Etat relatifs à l'Histoire de l'Ecosse, t. ii. p. 42.) Old Cotgrave interprets ' hutaudeau' to signify a ' cockerell, or great cocke chicke, also a caponet, a big well-grown pullet.' The word, like not a few other household terms, found its way from France to Scotland, where, with some slight change of its primary meaning, it long survived (if, indeed, it be yet extinct) in the shape of ' howtowdy.'

The King and Catharine of Medicis.

Catharine of Medicis had formed an equally contemptuous estimate of Darnley's character : 'Ce jeune fou n'a pas été longtemps Roi,' she wrote, when she heard of his murder ; 's'il eût été plus sage, je crois qu'il seroit encore en vie.'—(M. Chéruel, Marie Stuart et Catherine de Médicis, p. 51.)

The King and Buchanan.

I have already spoken (p. xii., note 2) of Buchanan's devotion to the house of Lennox, the chiefs of his race, the lords of his paternal strath. It carried him so far as to hail the worthless Darnley as 'the best of kings :'

' Optime Rex, opto, sit tibi certa salus.'

He seems, on reflection, to have seen that the bestowal of such an epithet on such a man, was beyond even a poet's license ; and the line was afterwards silently changed into

' Unum opto id, Princeps, sit tibi certa salus.'

and Constable of France.[1] But, upon second thoughts, the bequest was cancelled, and the ring is left to Riccio's brother, to be delivered to one whose
name the Queen had imparted to him in secret. The only French legacies
beyond the circle of her family, are to Mary of Beaucaire, who, as we learn from
Brantôme, had been the Scottish Queen's great favourite at the court of
France.[2] She was now the wife of the Viscount of Martigues,[3] a gallant
soldier, who had commanded the French forces sent to Scotland to sustain the
falling power of the Queen Regent, and, when he heard in Paris that Mary

Bequests to Madame de Martigues, etc.

—(G. Buchanani Epigrammatum, lib. iii. ep. 1, edit.
T. Ruddimanni.)

Bothwell and Knox.

The same feudal feeling which attracted Buchanan
to Darnley, manifested itself still more remarkably in
drawing the great Reformer of Scotland to the most
dissolute and flagitious of her nobles. ' Wold to
God,' said Knox to Bothwell in 1562, ' that in me war
counsall or judgement that mycht conforte and releave
you. For albeit that to this hour it hath nott chaunsed
me to speik with your Lordship face to face, yit have
I borne a good mynd to your house ; and have bene
sorry at my heart of the trubles that I have heard
you to be involved in. For, my Lord, my grandfather, goodsher, and father, have served your Lord-
shipis predecessoris, and some of thame have died
under thair standartis ; and this is a part of the obli-
gatioun of our Scotish kyndnes.'—(Knox's History
of the Reformation, vol. ii. pp. 323, 324.) Knox
throughout speaks of Bothwell with obvious tender-
ness.

[1] P. 113 : ' A Madame Danuille.'
Antoinette, eldest daughter of Robert de la Marck,
Duke of Bouillon, by his marriage with Frances of
Breze, Countess of Maulevrier, was born in 1542, and
married the Seigneur de Damville in 1559. She died
in 1591.—(Anselme, Histoire Généalogique de France,
t. iii. p. 605. Brantôme, t. v. p. 68.)

M. Damville.

Her husband, Henry of Montmorency, the second
son of Anne, Duke of Montmorency, Constable
of France, was born in 1534, and was known
during the lifetime of his father and elder brother
as the Seigneur de Damville. In 1561, having the
unfortunate Chatellard in his train, he accompanied
Queen Mary to Scotland, and, with the rest of her
French escort, was entertained at a banquet by the
city of Edinburgh, on Sunday the 31st of August, in
the house which had been Cardinal Beaton's in the

Blackfriars' Wynd. He took his departure with the
Queen's uncle, the Grand Prior of France (who had
Brantôme in his train) on the 9th of October ; three
of their retainers being presented by the Queen with
gold chains, one of 150 crowns, and two of 50 crowns
each. The Seigneur de Damville was made a Marshal of France in 1567, succeeded his brother Francis
as Duke of Montmorency in 1579, and became Constable of France in 1597. He died in 1614.—(L'Art
de Vérifier les Dates, t. ii. p. 656. Diurnal of Occurrents, pp. 66, 67, 69. Brantôme, t. v. pp. 92, 121-
125. Compotum Thesaurarii Reginae Scotorum, Oct.
1561—Jan. 1562, MS. Register House. M. Teulet,
Papiers d'Etat relatifs à l'Histoire de l'Ecosse, t. iii.
pp. 3, 4. Prince Labanoff, Lettres de Marie Stuart,
t. i. pp. 111, 112, 118.)

[2] Pp. 93, 98, 99, 108.

' Madame de Martigues, dite avant Madamoiselle de
Villemontays, grande favorite de la Reyne d'Escosse.'
—(Brantôme, t. v. p. 68.)

She was the daughter of John of Beaucaire, Seigneur de Puy-Gillon, and Seneschal of Poitou.—
(Anselme, Histoire Généalogique de France, t. iii.
p. 738.)

[3] Sebastian of Luxembourg, second son of Francis
second Viscount of Martigues, succeeded his brother
as fourth Viscount of Martigues, in 1553. He was
sent to Scotland in command of the French forces in
1559. He was made Duke of Penthievre in 1569,
and was killed at the siege of St. Jean-d'Angeli in the
same year.—(L'Art de Vérifier les Dates, t. ii. pp.
921, 922. Diurnal of Occurrents, pp. 55, 57, 272,
274. Bishop Lesley's History of Scotland, 280, 282.
Knox's History of the Reformation in Scotland, vol.
ii. pp. 8, 12, 57. G. Buchanani Rerum Scoticarum
Historia, lib. xvi., Opera, pp. 322, 325. Brantôme,
t. iv. pp. 397-413.)

was a prisoner in Lochleven, undertook, if the French king would grant him but three thousand harquebussiers for three months, either to deliver her in spite of all opposers, or never to set foot in France again.[1] The Queen, it will be seen, makes two bequests to his infant daughter,[2] afterwards Duchess of Penthievre in her own right, and Duchess of Mercoeur by marriage.

Bequests to the Countess of Argyll;

The first Scottish legacies, after those to the Crown, are to the Queen's kinsfolks, the offspring of her father by various concubines,—Lady Jane Stewart, Countess of Argyll,[3] a wayward and unloving wife, who had forsaken her husband's home for the court of Holyrood, and was sitting at supper with the Queen when the murderers of Riccio burst into her cabinet; Lord Robert

to the Commendator of Holyrood.

Stewart, Commendator of Holyrood,[4] afterwards Earl of Orkney, the only

---

[1] Letter from Sir Henry Norris, the English Ambassador at Paris, to Queen Elizabeth, 23d July 1567, in Selections illustrating the Reign of Mary Queen of Scotland, pp. 242, 243.—(Maitland Club.)

[2] Pp. 100, 103.
Mary of Luxembourg, born in 1562, succeeded to her father's Duchy of Penthievre in 1569, and married in 1576 Philip-Emmanuel of Lorraine, Duke of Mercoeur. She died in 1623.—(Anselme, Histoire Généalogique de France, t. iii. pp. 738, 795. Brantôme, t. iv. pp. 91-95, t. v. p. 70.)

[3] Pp. 99, 100: 'A Madame Darguilles;' p. 103: 'A ma sœur;' pp. 103, 104: 'A ma sœur Darguilles;' pp. 106-108: 'Aus dames d'Arguilles,' etc. ; p. 108: 'A Madame d'Arguilles;' p. 113: 'A ma sœur.'
Lady Jane (or Janet) Stewart, daughter of King James v. by Elizabeth Betoun (daughter of the Laird of Creich, afterwards wife of John fourth Lord Innermeath), married in 1554 Archibald fifth Earl of Argyll. As proxy for Queen Elizabeth, she stood godmother to the Prince at his christening at Stirling in December 1566. This was regarded by the General Assembly as a falling away from the Reformed faith, and the Countess was sentenced to make public repentance in the Chapel Royal at Stirling. She had left her husband in 1564, and persisting in her refusal to return, was divorced from him in 1573. There seems to have been considerable hesitation in pronouncing the sentence, which was the first sentence of divorce given on such a ground in Scotland ; and its validity, which

was challenged by the Countess, would appear not to have been beyond question. The Earl, who immediately married again, died in the same year. The Countess (for she kept the title to the last) survived till January 1587, when, dying in the Canongate, she was buried in the royal vault at Holyrood.—(Registrum Magni Sigilli, lib. xxxv. no. 275. MS. Register House. Calendar of State Papers relating to Scotland, vol. i. pp. 239, 241. Booke of the Universal Kirk of Scotland, vol. i. pp. 114, 117, 148, 149, 262, 263. Letters to the Argyll Family, pp. 59, 71, 78. Mr. Riddell's Peerage and Consistorial Law of Scotland, vol. i. pp. 547-552. Knox's History of the Reformation, vol. i. pp. 375, 376.)

[4] P. 122: 'A mon frere de St. Croyx.'
Lord Robert Stewart, bastard son of King James v. by Eupheme, second daughter of Alexander first Lord Elphinstone, was born in 1532, and made Commendator of Holyrood in 1539, and Commendator of Charlieu (in France) before 1557. He joined the Reformers in 1559, and married, in 1561, Janet Kennedy, daughter of Gilbert third Earl of Cassilis. He had a grant from the Queen, in 1565, of the crown lands of Orkney and Shetland, and in 1568, exchanged his Commendatorship of Holyrood for the lands of the Bishopric of Orkney. In 1575, he was imprisoned on the charge of procuring a charter from the King of Denmark as sovereign of the Orkneys, and was not released until 1579. He was made Earl of Orkney about 1581, and died before the close of the year 1592.

other guest at the Queen's table on that memorable night; and Lord James Bequests to the Earl of Murray, etc.;
Stewart, Earl of Murray,[1] afterwards Regent of Scotland, his wife,[2] and their
eldest daughter.[3]   There are bequests to Master John Stewart,[4] to James
Stewart,[5] and to Jane Stewart,[6] all apparently illegitimate inheritors of
the royal blood, although, perhaps, it might not be easy now to identify
them.

There is no difficulty in recognising the nephew Francis,[7] on whom to Francis Stewart, afterwards Earl Bothwell.

In her incompleted will, made at Sheffield in February 1577, Queen Mary declared his title to the Orkneys to be null and void: 'Je déclare que mon frère bastard, Robert abbé de Sainte-Croix, n'a eu que par circonvention, Orknnay, et que se ne fut jamais mon intention, comme il apert par la révocation que j'en ay fayte depuys, et a été aussi fayte d'avant l'asge de xxv ans, ce que j'aurois délibérez, si il ne m'eussent prévenu par prison, de défayré aux Estats. Je veulx donc que Orkennay soit réuni à la couronne.'—(Prince Labanoff, Lettres de Marie Stuart, t. i. p. 44, t. iv. p. 36L. Registrum Magni Sigilli, lib. xxv. no. 334. MS. Register House. Liber Cartarum Sancte Crucis, pp. xxxv. xxxvi. Mr. Balfour's Oppressions in Orkney and Zetland, pp. xlvi.-lvi. 3-11. Historie of King James the Sixth, pp. 157, 182.)

[1] P. 112: 'A mon frere de Mora;' p. 122: 'A mon frere.'
Lord James Stewart, as every one knows, was the bastard son of King James v. by Margaret, daughter of John, fourth Lord Erskine, afterwards wife of Sir Robert Douglas of Lochleven. He was born about 1531, made Commendator of the Priory of St. Andrews in 1538, Commendator of the Priory of Pittenweem, and Commendator of the Priory of Mâcon (in France), in 1555, joined the Reformers in 1556, was made Earl of Mar in February 1561-2, and Earl of Murray in September 1562. He became Regent of Scotland in August 1567, and was assassinated at Linlithgow in January 1569-70.
Mary, it will be observed, spells most Scottish names as they were pronounced in her court, and as they have continued to be pronounced by the commonalty almost to our own day. 'Mora,' 'Boduel,' and 'Hontelay,' are pronunciations of 'Murray,' 'Bothwell,' and 'Huntly,' not yet, perhaps, altogether obsolete in every part of Scotland. The fidelity with which the ancient form of a name has been preserved among the people is sometimes

very remarkable. 'Cathcart,' for example, has long been an historical name in that shape; but the Clydesdale peasant still calls the place 'Carkert,' the very form in which it was written in the twelfth century.—(Acts of the Parliaments of Scotland, vol. i. pref. p. 82; Registrum Episcopatus Glasguensis, vol. i. p. 47.)

[2] Pp. 104, 105, 108: 'A Madame de Mora.'
Agnes, Annas, or Anna Keith, daughter of William fourth Earl Marischal, married the Earl of Murray in February 1561-2. After his death, she married Colin sixth Earl of Argyll, who died in 1584. She survived till 1588.—(Letters to the Argyll Family, pp. 61-70, 79-88.)

[3] P. 100: 'A la fille de mon frere de Mora.'
The Earl of Murray had two daughters, but only one of them, Elizabeth, was born at the date of Queen Mary's bequest, in May or June 1566. In 1580, she married James Stewart (the eldest son of Sir James Stewart, Commendator of St. Colm's Inch), who, in her right, became Earl of Murray. In her incompleted will, made at Sheffield in February 1577, Queen Mary declared that the daughters of the Earl of Murray had no right of succession in his earldom: 'Les filles de Mora ne peuvent aussi hériter, ains revient la conté à la couronne.'—(Prince Labanoff, Lettres de Marie Stuart, t. iv. pp. 361, 362.)

[4] P. 118: 'A Maystre Ien Stuart.'
[5] P. 120: 'A Iame Stuart.'
[6] Pp. 105, 124: 'A Iene Stuart;' p. 109: 'A Ien Stuart.'
She was perhaps the daughter of the Commendator of Holyrood, who afterwards married Patrick Leslie, Commendator of Lindores, and, on his death, Robert Lord Melville of Raith.

[7] Pp. 110, 111: 'A Francoys mon nepueu;' pp. 111, 112: 'A mon nepueu;' p. 114: 'A mon nepuueu;' p. 123: 'A mon nepuieu.'

Mary heaps so many tokens of her regard. He was the only son of Bothwell's sister[1] by her marriage with the Queen's bastard brother, Lord John Stewart, Lord Darnley, better known as Commendator of Coldingham.[2] Mary witnessed the sports and pastimes of their wedding at Crichton,[3] and stood godmother to their child, giving him, it would seem, the name of her first husband. The infant was still at his mother's breast when his father died, bequeathing him to the Queen's protection. Mary was no careless guardian. Before the boy had completed his fourth year, she made him Commendator of Coldingham. When he was stripped of his father's lordship of Darnley, by the restoration of the Earl of Lennox, she made him Lord of Badenoch; and when he lost that lordship by the restoration of the Earl of Huntly, she made him Commendator of Culross, and gave him a large grant from the Earl of Morton's forfeited rents of Aberdour and Dalkeith.[4] Her dethrone-

Bothwell's sister.

[1] Lady Jane Hepburn, only daughter of Patrick, third Earl Bothwell. She was thrice married, first (in January 1561-2) to Lord John Stewart, Commendator of Coldingham; next (before May 1567) to John Sinclair, Master of Caithness, eldest son of George, fourth Earl of Caithness; lastly (before February 1581) to Archibald Douglas, a kinsman of the Regent Morton. She is the 'Madame de Cotiquant,' to whom the Queen gives a mourning robe in November 1563, and the 'Maistresse Catenay,' or 'Cadenay,' to whom the Queen gives a mantle and a vasquine in May 1567 (pp. 68, 71, 73), when she seems to have been the reigning female favourite at Holyrood. —(Letter from Drury to Cecil, 15th April 1567, in Mr. Tytler's History of Scotland, vol. v. p. 520. M. Teulet, Papiers d'Etat relatifs à l'Histoire de l'Ecosse, t. ii. p. 433.)

Lord John Stewart, Lord Darnley.

[2] Lord John Stewart, natural son of King James v. (it is said by Elizabeth, daughter of Sir John Carmichael, the Captain of Crawford), was made Commendator of the Priory of Coldingham in 1541, when he seems to have been in his eighth or ninth year. In February 1550-1, he had letters of legitimation under the great seal. He renounced the old faith and joined the Reformers in 1560. He married Bothwell's sister in January 1561-2, and soon afterwards had a grant of part of the forfeited domains of the Earl of Lennox, together with the title of Lord Darn-

ley. Under that style (which has been overlooked by the peerage writers, although it appears in the public records) he had grants, in June 1563, of the lordship of the Enzie, the Forest of Boyne, with the tower of Bogygeich (now called Gordon Castle), and other lands forfeited by the Earl of Huntly in the previous year. He died at Inverness, probably in October or November 1563, certainly before the close of January 1563-4.—(Registrum Magni Sigilli, lib. xxx. no. 688; lib. xxxii. no. 367. MS. Register House. Registrum Secreti Sigilli, vol. xxxi. foll. 102, 103, 105, 106, 130, 131; vol. xxxii. foll. 26, 71-73, 121. MS. Register House. Knox's History of the Reformation, vol. ii. pp. 88, 271, 293, 315, 320, 389, 391, 392. Epistolae Regum Scotorum, vol ii. pp. 115-120.)

[3] 'On Sunday the 11th of January 1561-2, the Lord John, a bastard brother of the Queen, the Commendator of Coldingham, married Jane, the sister of Bothwell, at Crichton Castle, the Queen being present; and much good sport and many pastimes there were, said Randolph to Cecil.'—(G. Chalmers's Life of Queen Mary, vol. iii. pp. 16, 17. Calendar of State Papers relating to Scotland, vol. i. p. 177.)

[4] In March 1563-4, 'Francis Lord Darnley, only lawful son of the deceased John Lord Darnley, the Queen's brother, and of Dame Janet Hepburn his wife,' has charters of the lands of the lordship of the Enzie, the Forest of Boyne, Cruickstoun, Inchinnan,

ment left her helpless to serve him further; but her affection still survived, and in her will, made at Sheffield, in the tenth year of her captivity, she entreated her son to befriend her nephew, godson, and ward.[1] King James had almost anticipated her request that the stripling might have his uncle's inheritance. If the new Earl Bothwell proved strangely ungrateful to the King, he was at least not unmindful of Mary's kindness. He told James to his face that if he gave his consent to her trial by Queen Elizabeth, he deserved to be hanged;[2] and when tidings reached Scotland that she had been put to death, Bothwell exclaimed that a steel coat was the only mourning weed which he should wear, and raised the Middle Marches in arms for the invasion of England.[3]

Neilstoun, and others. In December 1564, the Queen makes a grant to him in liferent, and to his mother in fee, of the lordship of Badenoch, in recompense of the lordships and baronies of Darnley, Inchinnan, Neilstoun, and others restored to Matthew Earl of Lennox, on the recall of his forfeiture. In January 1564-5, Francis Stewart, son of the deceased John Lord Darnley, has a grant of the lordship of Lochaber. In March 1564-5, the Queen makes a grant to Francis Lord Badenoch, her nephew, of the escheat of a lease. On the 25th of March 1565, Francis Lord Badenoch, with consent of Mary Queen of Scots, his tutrix, makes a grant of the lands of Rothmakenzie and others to Alexander Innes of Cromby. The charter (which is in the Innes charter-chest at Floors) is subscribed by the Queen; her nephew's seal shows the arms of Scotland, with a bend, and the legend SIGILLVM · FRANCISCI · DNI · DE · BADZENACH · ET · LYNGZES. In July 1565, the Queen makes a grant to her nephew, Francis Stewart, of the Commendatorship of the Priory of Coldingham. In October 1565, the King and Queen order the grant of the lordship of Lochaber, made in January 1564-5, to Francis Stewart, son of the deceased John Lord Darnley, to be deleted from the register. In April 1566, the King and Queen grant to Francis Stewart, son of the deceased John, Commendator of Coldingham, 28 chalders of victual, and £240 of money, from the rents of the baronies of Aberdour and Dalkeith, in recompense of the rents of the barony of the Enzie restored to the Earl of Huntly. In May 1566, the King and Queen appoint James Earl Bothwell to be tutor dative to Francis Stewart, son of the deceased John, Commendator of Coldingham. In February 1566-7, the Queen grants the Commendatorship of Culross and the Commendatorship of Kelso to her nephew, Francis Stewart, in lieu of the Commendatorship of the Priory of Coldingham, which he had resigned at her request.—(Registrum Secreti Sigilli, vol xxxii. foll. 71-73, 121, 130; vol. xxxiii. fol. 3; vol. xxxiv. fol. 54; vol. xxxv. foll. 76, 115, 116; vol. xxxvi. foll. 21, 101. MS. Register House. Compotum Thesaurarii Reginae Scotorum. Jan. 1564—Jun. 1566. MS. Register House. Books of Sederunt of the Lords of Council and Session, vol. ii. foll. 139, 140. MS. Register House.)

[1] 'Je recommande mon nepveu François Stuart à mon filz, et luy commande le tenir près de luy et s'en servir, et lui laisser le bien du Comte de Boduel son oncle, en respect qu'il est de mon sang, mon filleul, et m'a esté laissé en tutèle par son père.'—(Prince Labanoff, Lettres de Marie Stuart, vol. iv. p. 361.)

[2] On the 4th of October 1586, 'the Earle Bothwell, beinge asked his advise by the Kinge what he should doe, the Queene of England requiringe his consente to proceed against his mother, said, yf he did suffer it, hee were worthie to be hanged the nexte daye after; wherat the Kinge laughed, and said he would provid for that.'—(Despatches of M. Courcelles, French Ambassador in Scotland, 1586-1587, pp. 8, 22, 23, 43. Edinb. 1828: Bannatyne Club.)

[3] Mr. Tytler's History of Scotland, vol. vii. p. 127. M. Teulet, Papiers d'Etat relatifs à l'Histoire de l'Ecosse, t. iii. p. 568.

A few years afterwards, Bothwell plunged into that strange career of secret conspiracy and open tumult

f

There are legacies, of more or less value, to the Countess of Mar,[1] denounced by Knox as a Jezebel fit for the maw of Satan, but chosen with the general approval of the nation to be the governess of two generations of its princes; to her daughter, afterwards Countess of Angus;[2] to the

Countess Dowager of Huntly,[3] the widow of the Earl who fell at Corrichie, as her enemies affirmed, a trafficker with witches;[4] to her daughter,

against the King, which, in 1594, ended in his forfeiture and flight from Scotland. After wandering through Europe, earning a precarious and disreputable livelihood by practising feats of arms, telling fortunes, and professing the art of necromancy, he died at Naples in 1612, of grief, so it was believed, for the death of Prince Henry. His grandson, who served as a trooper in the wars of the Covenant, suggested the Bothwell of Old Mortality.—(Sir W. Scott's Prose Works, vol. vii. pp. 181-186.)

Unless I misread the mouldering cyphers on Crichton Castle, they tell that Francis Stewart, Earl Bothwell, and his wife, Dame Margaret Douglas, built the finest portion of the pile—the arcade, the grand staircase, and the eastern gallery—

'The court-yard's graceful portico,
Above whose cornice, row on row,
Of fair hewn facets richly show
Their pointed diamond form.'

Its date, therefore, must lie between 1580 and 1594.

[1] Pp. 105, 106, 108, 119 : 'A Madame de Mar;' pp. 106, 107 : 'Aus dames de Mar,' etc.

Annabella Murray, daughter of Sir William Murray of Tullibardine, married, in 1557, John fifth Lord Erskine, who in 1565 became Earl of Mar. She is mentioned, in August 1566, as one of the Queen's three favourites who excited the King's jealousy; the others being the Countess of Argyle and the Countess of Murray. She survived till 1603.—(Letter from the Earl of Bedford, August 1566, in Principal Robertson's History of Scotland, app. no. xvii.; Works, vol. ii. p. 343.)

Knox calls her 'a verray Jesabell,' 'a sweatt morsall for the devillis mouth.' On the other hand, Sir James Melville describes her as 'wyse and schairp.' Mr. James Melville speaks of the young King 'walking vpe and down in the auld Lady Marrs hand,' discoursing of knowledge and ignorance, as 'the sweitest sight in Europe that day' [October 1574]. Another orthodox divine, in recording her death, writes : 'Feliciter vitam cum morte commutavit, omni-

bus grata, nemini exosa.' The King's own sense of her services to himself was such that he chose her to be governess to Prince Henry, and placed upon the record of the statute-book a grateful acknowledgement that, in her charge as well of himself as of his son, 'she hes done his Maiestie and the haill cuntrie trew thankfull worthie and guid service without spott negligence or reproche.'—(Knox's History of the Reformation, vol. ii. pp. 128, 380. Sir James Melville's Memoirs, p. 262. Mr. James Melville's Diary, p. 38. Archibald Simson's MS. Annales, quoted in the Countess of Mar's Arcadia, p. 9. Edinb. 1862. Acts of the Parliaments of Scotland, vol. iv. pp. 186, 187.)

[2] P. 105.

Mary, only daughter of John fifth Lord Erskine, Earl of Mar, by his marriage with Annabella Murray, became, in 1573, the wife of Archibald eighth Earl of Angus.

[3] P. 119 : 'A Madame de Hontelay.'

Elizabeth Keith, sister of William fourth Earl Marischal, married, about 1535, George fourth Earl of Huntly. We learn from her daughter's marriage-contract that she could not write. Her niece was the wife of the Regent Murray.

[4] 'The Erle [of Huntly], immediatlie after his Accusations of witchcraft and magic : the Countess Dowager of Huntly; tacken, departed this lyiff without any wound . . . . and so, becaus it was laitt, he was cassen over-thorte a pair of crealles, and so was caryed to Abirdene, and was laid in the tolbuyth thairof, that the response whiche his wyffis wyttches had gevin mycht be fulfilled, whay all affirmed (as the most parte say) that that same nycht should he be in the tolbuyth of Abirdene without any wound vpoun his body. When his lady gatt knowledge thairof, sche blamed hir principale witche, called Janet; but sche stoutlie defended hir self (as the devill can ever do), and affirmed that she geve a trew answer, albeit sche speck nott all the treuth; for she knew that he should be thair dead : but that could nott proffeit my lady. Scho was angrye and sorye for a seassone, but the devill, the messe,

the young and comely wife who, a few months afterwards, was divorced from Bothwell with such scandalous haste ;[1] to her daughter-in-law, the Countess of Huntly,[2] the only Hamilton to whom the Queen vouchsafes a token of regard, with the exception of Lady Seton,[3] the wife of the ever loyal First Master of the Household ; and to the Queen's bastard cousin Lady Livingston,[4] the

John Knox.

and wyttches have als great credyte of hir this day (12 Junij 1566) as thei had sevin yearis ago.'—(Knox's History of the Reformation, vol. ii. pp. 357, 358.)

Imputations of witchcraft and sorcery were among the commonplaces of controversy in that age. The Reformer himself had his full share of them : 'Quacumque iter faceret secum aliquot mulieres circumducebat . . . donec magicis artibus allectam filiam Comitis Ochiltriae pro vxore habuit. Erat enim magus, vt in multis per totam vitam apparuit.'—(Davidis Camerarii De Scotorum Fortitudine, pp. 276, 277. Paris. 1631. Cf. Nicol Burne's Disputation, foll. 102, 144, 175. Paris, 1581. R. Bannatyne's Journal, pp. 309, 310.) The accusation, it is said, was firmly believed by King James : 'Knoxium (quem Beza Apostolum Scotiae vocat) non impium modo fuisse, sed magnum, serenissimus Britanniarum Rex saepe magnis argumentis asseruit.'—(Joannis Barclaii Paraenesis ad Sectarios, p. 38. Romae, 1617.)

In Knox's case, the charge of sorcery may have received credit the more easily that he made public claim to the gift of foretelling future events. His belief that he himself possessed miraculous powers must, at the same time, have disposed him to believe more readily in the supernatural powers ascribed to others.

[1] P. 110: 'A Madame de Boduel.'

Bothwell's divorced wife.

Jane Gordon, daughter of George fourth Earl of Huntly, was born in 1545, and married, in February 1566, James fourth Earl Bothwell. She was divorced from him in May 1567, and in 1573 married Alexander eleventh Earl of Sutherland, after whose death (in 1594) she married the widowed husband of one of the Four Marys, Alexander Ogilvy of Boyne. She died in 1629.

Her son, the Knight of Gordonston, has drawn her character with an affectionate hand : 'Shoe wes vertuous, religious, and wyse . . . comlie . . . judicious, of excellent memorie, and of great vnderstanding above the capacitie of her sex. . . . Shoe alwise managed her effairs with so great prudence . . . that the enemies of her familie culd never prevaile against her, nor mowe . . . the cheiff ruellers of the state . . . to doe anything to her prejudice. . . . Amidst all these troublesome stormes

. . . shoe still injoyed the possession of her joynture . . . out of the Earldome of Bothwell, and keiped the same vntill her death, yea although that earldome hath fallen tuyse into the King's hands by forfaltur. . . . Shoe wes the first that caused work and labour the colehugh besyd the river of Broray, and wes the first instrument of making salt ther . . . And as shoe lived with great credit and reputation, so shoe dyed happelie, and wes (according to her own command) bureid by her sones . . . in the cathedrall church of Dornogh, in the sepulchre of the Earles of Southerland.'—(Sir R. Gordon's Genealogical History of the Earldom of Sutherland, pp. 145, 168, 169, 409.)

Her portrait, painted in old age, is at Dunrobin, and was engraved for private circulation by the late Duke of Sutherland. The features, large but well-shaped, have a firm, thoughtful, and placid expression. The cross and rosary which she holds in her hand, show that she kept her first faith to the end. One of her books—a beautiful copy of the Legenda Aurea, printed in 1470—is still preserved.

[2] P. 119: 'A la ieusne Contesse de Hontelay.'

Lady Anne Hamilton, daughter of James second Earl of Arran, and first Duke of Chatelherault, married, in 1558, George Lord Gordon, afterwards fifth Earl of Huntly. Her marriage contract shows that she could not write.

[3] P. 113: 'Aus dames de Ceston,' etc.

Isabel Hamilton, the daughter of Sir William Hamilton of Sanquhar, married, about 1552, George fifth Lord Seton. She died in 1606, having outlived her husband by twenty years.

[4] Pp. 106, 109, 120: 'A Madame de Leuinston ;' pp. 106, 107, 113: 'Aus dames de Leuinston,' etc.

Agnes Fleming, second daughter of Malcolm third Lord Fleming, married, about 1553, William sixth Lord Livingston.

She was the elder sister of Margaret Fleming, Countess of Atholl, one of the Queen's ladies of honour ; and of Mary Fleming, one of the Queen's Four Marys, the wife of Secretary Lethington.

Their father fell at Pinkie in 1547. Their mother, Janet Stewart, an illegitimate daughter of King James

wife of a noble not less eminent for his fidelity, and with herself in after years the companion of the Queen's captivity.[1]

Bequests to the Earl of Argyll, and the Earl of Mar.

The Privy Councillors, not already named, to whom the Queen makes bequests are, the Earl of Argyll,[2] the husband of her bastard sister; the Earl of Mar,[3] regarded by the extreme Reformers as the leader of a reaction, which, in the enjoyment of the spoils of the Reformation, laughed at its policy and discipline as a pious dream;[4] the Earl of

Janet Lady Fleming and King Henry II. of France.

IV. appears, with three of her daughters, in the earliest roll of the Queen's servants which I have seen. She accompanied Mary to France in 1548, and there had an intrigue with King Henry II., by whom, in 1551, she became the mother of Henry of Angouleme (or, as he was sometimes called, Henry of Valois), Grand Prior of France.—(M. Francisque-Michel, Les Ecossais en France, t. i. pp. 474, 503-6, t. ii. pp. 2, 3. Mr. Riddell's Stewartiana, pp. 48-51.)

Marriage feast in the Queen's Park.

There was another Lady Fleming (p. 71), to whom the Queen gave a devant of cloth of gold, etc., for her wedding-dress, in May 1562. This was Elizabeth Ross, the wife of John fifth Lord Fleming. They held their marriage feast in the open air : ' The bankett was made in the Parke of Holyroudhous, under Arthur's Seatt, at the end of the loche, quher grate triumph wes made, the Quein's Grace being present, and the King of Suethland's embassador, with many other nobles.'—(G. Marioreybanks, Annals of Scotland, p. 14. Diurnal of Occurrents, p. 72.)

[1] Lord and Lady Livingston shared the Queen's prison at Carlisle and at Bolton in 1568, and at Tutbury in 1569. The name of ' My Lady Leuiston, dame of honour to the Queen's Majesty,' is the first on the roll of Mary's servants at Sheffield in 1571. It contains also the name of her husband, ' My Lord Leuiston.' They seem to have been separated from the Queen in September 1571.—(G. Chalmers' Life of Queen Mary, vol. i. pp. 441, 442. Mr. T. Wright's Queen Elizabeth and her Times, vol. i. pp. 311, 394, 395. Lodge's Illustrations of British History, vol. i. p. 520, edit. 1838. Bishop Lesley's Diary, in the Miscellany of the Bannatyne Club, vol. iii. p. 153.)

Lord Livingston's father was one of the two lords specially intrusted with the keeping of the young Queen from 1544 to 1548.—(Registrum Secreti Sigilli, vol. xxii. fol. 15. MS. Register House.)

[2] P. 113 : ' Au Conte dArguilles.'

Archibald Campbell, fifth Earl of Argyll, succeeded his father the fourth Earl, in 1558, became Lord Chancellor in January 1573, and died in September 1575. He commanded the Queen's forces at Langside. His wife was the sister of the Regent Murray, who, with his brothers, the Commendators of Kelso, Holyrood, and Coldingham, contributed to the payment of her dowry of 5000 merks.

[3] P. 112 : ' Au Conte de Mar.'

John, fifth Lord Erskine, succeeded his father, the fourth Lord, in 1552, was made Earl of Mar in 1565, and Regent of Scotland in 1571. He died in October 1572.

His father was one of the two lords intrusted with the keeping of the young Queen from 1544 to 1548.

His sister was one of the concubines of King James V., by whom, about 1531, she became the mother of the Regent Murray.

[4] ' Some approved it, and willed the samyn have bene sett furth be a law. Otheris, perceaving thair carnall libertie and worldlie commoditie somewhat to be impaired thairby, grudged, insomuche that the name of the Book of Discipline became odious unto thame. Everie thing that repugned to thair corrupt affectionis was termed in thair mockage ' devote imaginationis.' . . . The cheaf great man that had professed Christ Jesus, and refuissed to subscrive the Book of Discipline, was the Lord Erskyn ; and no wonder, for besydis that he has a verray Jesabell to his wyffe, yf the poore, the schooles, and the ministerie of the Kirk, had their awin, his keching wald lack two parttis and more of that which he injustlie now possesses. Assuredlye some of us have woundered how men that professe godlynes could of so long continewance bear the threatnyngis of God against theavis and against thair housses, and knowing thame selfis guyltie in suche thingis as war openlie rebucked, and that thei never had remorse of conscience, neather yitt intended to restore any thingis

Atholl,[1] one of the three nobles who had raised a voice in Parliament against the new doctrines, protesting that he would believe as his fathers had believed ;[2] the turbulent, licentious Earl Bothwell, the worst man in the court, but the loudest in professions of zeal for the purer faith ;[3] his wife's brother, the Earl of Huntly,[4] now Lord Chancellor of the realm ; Bishop Lesley of Ross,[5] already distinguished by his defence of the old religion, and soon to be more widely known for the admirable devotion with which he gave

Bequests to the Earl of Atholl, the Earl Bothwell, the Earl of Huntly, and the Bishop of Ross.

of that whiche long thei had stollen and reft.'—(Knox's History of the Reformation, vol. ii. p. 128.)

Buchanan draws a very different character :—

'Si quis Areskinum memoret per bella ferocem,
Pace gravem nulli, tempore utroque pium ;
Si quis opes sine fastu, animum sine fraude, carentem
Rebus in ambiguis suspicione fidem ;
Si quod ob has dotes saevis jactata procellis
Fugit in illius patria fessa sinum ;
Vera quidem memoret, sed non et propria : laudes
Qui pariter petet has unus et alter erit.
Illud ei proprium est, longo quod in ordine vitae
Nil odium aut livor quod reprehendat habet.'

(Miscellaneorum Liber, xxv. : 'Joanni Areskino, Comiti Marriae, Scotorum Proregi.')

[1] P. 113 : 'A Conte dAtel.'

John Stewart, fourth Earl of Atholl, succeeded his father the third Earl in 1542, became Lord Chancellor in March 1578, and died in April 1579, as was suspected, of poison. He was the brother-in-law of Secretary Maitland of Lethington. The French ambassador describes him, in 1565, as 'très grand Catholique, hardy et vaillant et remuant, comme l'on dict, mais de nul jugement et expérience.'—(M. Teulet, Papiers d'Etat relatifs à l'Histoire de l'Ecosse, t. ii. p. 76.)

[2] 'Our Confessioun was redd . . . and the vottis of everie man war requyred accordinglie. Of the temporall estate onlie voted in the contrair, the Erle of Atholl, the Lordis Somervaill and Borthwick ; and yit for thair disassenting thei produced no bettir reassone, but 'We will beleve as oure fatheris beleved.'—(Knox's History of the Reformation, vol. ii. p. 121.)

[3] Pp. 113, 122 : 'Au Conte Boduel.'

Bothwell's religious scruples.

'Upon Sonday [10th February 1565-6], the Order [of the Cockle] is [to be] given [to the King.] . . . Divers Lords have bene . . . requyred to be at the masse that daye. Some have . . . refused. . . . and of them all Bothwell is the stoutest but worst thought of.'—(Randolph to Cecil, 7 February 1565-6, in Mr. T. Wright's Queen Elizabeth and her Times, vol. i. p. 220. Cf. Calderwood's History, vol. ii. p. 325.)

'Soon after [24th February 1565-6] the Earle Bothwell was married unto the Earle of Huntley his sister. The Queen desired that the marriage might be made in the chappell at the masse ; which the Earle Bothwell would in no wise grant.'—(Knox's History of the Reformation, book v. vol. ii. p. 520.)

We have mention of Bothwell's refusal to attend mass, 'albeit in great favour with the Queen,' in November and December 1565. His intercourse with Knox has already been referred to (pp. xxxvi., xxxvii., note 2.) He was among the lords who would not enter the Chapel Royal at Stirling, at the Prince's baptism, in December 1566, 'becaus it was done against the poyntis of thair religioun.' And, not even to secure the grand prize of his ambition and reward of his crimes, would he consent to be married to the Queen otherwise than by a Reformed minister after the Reformed rites : 'toda la cerimonia fue à la Calvinista.' —(M. Teulet, Papiers d'Etat relatifs à l'Histoire de l'Ecosse, vol. iii. p. 31 ; Lettres de Marie Stuart, p. 111. Knox's History of the Reformation, vol. ii. pp. 514, 539, 555. Diurnal of Occurrents, pp. 104, 111. Miss Strickland's Lives of the Queens of Scotland, vol. v. p. 291. Sir James Melville's Memoirs, pp. 178, 179.)

[4] P. 113 : 'Au Conte Hontelay ;' p. 123 : 'A Monssieur de Hontelay.'

George Gordon, son of George fourth Earl of Huntly, was restored to the forfeited honours of his father in 1565, held the office of Lord Chancellor from March 1566 till August 1567, and died suddenly at Strathbogie in October 1576.

[5] P. 113 : 'A lEsuesque de Lendors.'

John Lesley, the illegitimate son, it would seem, of Gavin Lesley, parson of Kingussie, commissary general of Murray, was born in 1527, became parson of Oyne in 1559, a Lord of Session in 1564, Commendator of the Abbey of Lindores in 1565-6, Bishop of Ross in 1566, and Bishop of Coutances (in France) in 1593. He died at Brussels in May 1596. It is a

himself to the service of the Queen; and Sir James Balfour,[1] the most corrupt person, as some have judged him, of that corrupt age,[2] but so scrupulous in his regard for the creed of Luther that he could not hold communion with the disciples of Calvin.[3] Each gets a finger-ring; and there are further legacies of a jewel, containing eleven diamonds and a ruby, to Bothwell, and of a jewel, containing five diamonds and a pearl, with an enamelled chain, to his brother-in-law, Huntly.

The Queen is careful to remember her attendants and servants of all ranks.

There are costly bequests to her Four Marys[4]—ladies of her own name

---

melancholy token of the general immorality of his age that such a man—the most estimable of the Scottish prelates—appears to have been the father of three illegitimate children.—(Genealogy of the Leslies, in Macfarlane's Genealogical Collections, MS. Advocates' Library, Edinburgh. James Gordon's History of Scots Affairs, vol. i. p. [xiii.], note †. Extracts from the Council Register of the burgh of Aberdeen, 1570-1625, pp. 192, 193.)

The Queen, it will be seen, mistakes the name of his abbey for the name of the see to which he had just been presented. He sat in the Privy Council as Commendator of Lindores on the 11th, and as Bishop of Ross on the 15th of April 1566. He describes himself as still only Bishop Elect on the 12th of March 1566-7, and would seem never to have been consecrated to the see of Ross.—(Registrum Secreti Concilii : Acta, 1563-7, pp. 192, 196. MS. Register House. Register of Deeds, vol. vii. foll. 263, 398, 399. MS. Register House.)

[1] P. 113 : 'A Iemes Balfour.'

Sir James Balfour, son of Michael Balfour of Montquhany, became parson of Flisk about 1560, a Lord of Session in 1561, a Privy Councillor in 1565, Clerk Register in 1566, Governor of Edinburgh Castle in the spring or summer of 1567, and Lord President of the Court of Session in December of the same year. He was forfeited for his adherence to the Queen's cause in 1571, and passed the latter years of his life in exile or obscurity, dying, it is supposed, about the year 1583.

[2] 'Sir James Balfour, the most corrupt man of that age.'—(Principal Robertson's History of Scotland, book vi. vol. ii. p. 40.)

[3] Knox, who had been chained to the same galley with him in France, writes : ' We have heard that the said Maister James [Balfour] alledgeis that he was never of this our religioun ; but that he was brought up in Martine's opinioun of the Sacrament, and tharefoir he can nott communicat with us.'—(History of the Reformation, vol. i. pp. 202, 228.)

[4] P. 113 : 'Aux quatre Maries ;' p. 124 : 'Aus quatre Maries.'   The Four Marys.

A.D. 1548. 'The Quene being as than betuix fyve and sax yearis of aige . . . wes embarqued in the Kingis awin gallay, and with her the Lord Erskyn and Lord Levingstoun quha had bene hir keparis, and the Lady Fleming hir fader sister, with sindre gentilwemen and nobill mennis sonnes and dochteris, almoist of hir awin aige ; of the quhilkis thair wes four in speciall, of whome everie one of thame buir the samin name of Marie, being of four syndre honorable houses, to wyt, Fleming, Levingstoun, Setoun, and Betoun of Creich ; quho remanit all foure with the Quene in France, during her residens thair, and returned agane in Scotland with hir Majestie in the yeir of our Lorde i^m v^c lxi yeris.'—(Bishop Lesley's History of Scotland, pp. 209, 297. Cf. Leslaei De Rebus Gestis Scotorum, p. 494.)

The Four Marys have a place in the roll of the beauties of the court of King Henry II. and Queen Catharine of Medicis : ' Mesdamoiselles de Flammin, de Ceton, Beton, Leviston, Escossoises.'—(Brantôme, t. v. p. 74.)

Nor are they forgotten in the verse of Buchanan :—

  ' Alma Salus, reduci tibi Nymphae haec vota dedere
    Quattuor.'

(Miscellaneorum Liber, xxxv. : 'Ad Salutem in Nup-

and age, who, having been chosen to accompany her to France, had returned with her to Scotland, and lingered in her court to the last, even after they had found other homes — the lovely Mary Livingston,[1] whose marriage with a younger son of the Lord Sempill, conspicuous for his grace or vigour in dancing, had disturbed the equanimity of Knox;[2] Mary

Bequests to Mary Livingston.

tiis Reginae.') Elsewhere, in his Masque of the Gods, he makes Jupiter extol to Diana the charms and virtues of Five Marys, counting the Queen as one of them :—

> 'Quinque tibi Mariae fuerant, sed quinque Dearum
> Instar erant forma, moribus, ingenio.
> Quinque Deum dignae thalamis, si jungere taedas
> Mortali superos ferrea fata sinant.'

(Epigrammatum lib. iii. : 'Pompa Deorum in Nuptiis Mariae.')

[1] Pp. 111, 120, 121 : 'A Lesuiston lesnee ;' pp. 116, 117 : 'A Leuinston laysnee.'

Mary Livingston—or, as she herself writes her name, 'Marie Leuiston' (pp. 115, 121)—the daughter of Alexander fifth Lord Livingston, married, on Shrove Tuesday (6 March) 1564-5, John Sempill of Beltreis, son of Robert third Lord Sempill. The Queen is a party to the marriage contract, names the marriage day, and gives a dowry of L. 500 a year in land. The bride's brother, Lord Livingston, adds 100 merks a year in land, or 1000 merks in money. The bridegroom gives as a jointure the Place of Beltreis, with lands and fishings taxed to the crown at L. 18, 16s. 8d. a year. The marriage contract, dated at Edinburgh on the 3d of March 1564-5, is subscribed by the Queen, and witnessed by John Lord Erskine, Patrick Lord Ruthven, and Secretary Maitland of Lethington. The Queen, beside other gifts (pp. 31, 70, 72), gave the bride her wedding-dress, and furnished the bridal masque. It was the first marriage among her Four Marys, and as such seems to have attracted unusual attention. 'Elle a commencé à marier ses Quatre Maries,' so the French ambassador wrote to Catharine of Medicis, 'et dict qu'elle veult estre de la bande.' Mary Livingston—or, as she was frequently called after her marriage, 'Madamoiselle de Sempill,' or 'John Sempill's wife'—seems to have been alive in April 1592. Her husband died in April 1579.—(Register of Deeds, vol. xix. foll. 359-361, vol. xl. fol. 268. MS. Register House. Registrum Secreti Sigilli, vol. xxxiii. foll. 5, 6, 14, 15. MS. Register House. Acts of the Parliaments of Scotland, vol. ii. pp. 559, 560 ; vol. iii. pp. 245, 246. Compotum Thesaurarii Reginae Scotorum, Mar. 1564-5. MS. Register House. M.

Teulet, Papiers d'Etat relatifs à l'Histoire de l'Ecosse, t. ii. pp. 32, 121, 167.)

[2] 'It wes weill knawin that schame haistit mariage betwix Johne Sempill, callit the Danser, and Marie Levingstoune, surnameit the Lustie.'—(Knox's History of the Reformation, vol. ii. pp. 415, 416.)

Polemical scandal : Mary Livingston :

I must believe this aspersion to be as groundless as any of the aspersions made on Knox's own chastity by his theological adversaries. See the Register of the Town Council of Edinburgh, 18th June 1563, in Kirkton's History of the Church of Scotland, pp. 22 ; Nicol Burne's Disputation, foll. 102, 143, 144 ; Dr. John Hamilton's Facile Traictice, p. 60, Lovaine, 1600 ; Davidis Camerarii De Scotorum Fortitudine, p. 276.

John Knox.

So little haste was there in Mary Livingston's marriage, that the despatches of the French and English ambassadors speak of preparations for it two months before it was celebrated. I need not add that they give no countenance to the scandal reported by Knox, and, so far as I can discover, reported by no one else. — (Letter from Randolph to Cecil, 9 January 1564-5, in Calendar of State Papers relating to Scotland, vol. i. p. 204. Letter from Randolph to the Earl of Bedford, in Miss Strickland's Lives of the Queens of Scotland, vol. iv. p. 95. Letter from Paul de Foix to Catharine of Medicis, January 1564-5, printed by M. Teulet in his Papiers d'Etat relatifs à l'Histoire de l'Ecosse, t. ii. p. 32.)

If there had been any blot on Mary Livingston's marriage, in March, we may be assured that Buchanan would not, in July, have made it the turning point of a masque at Holyrood, in which the Goddess of Chastity plays the chief part. The first lines of the piece are spoken by Diana to Jupiter :—

Buchanan's Masque of the Gods.

> 'Quinque mihi fuerant Mariae, pater alme, ministrae,
> Et decus, et nostri gloria prima chori.
> Hoc numero comitum coelo caput alta ferebam :
> Sumque aliis nimium visa beata Deis.
> Nam Venus et Juno successibus invida nostris,
> Unam de numero surripuere meo :
> Et nunc orba cohors numero sibi displicet, uno
> Pleiadum languet ceu minor igne chorus.' . . .

Beton,[1] the wife of Alexander Ogilvy of Boyne, the daughter of a house distinguished for its ability, and, it would seem, the scholar of the court,
since it is to her that Mary bequeaths her French, English, and Italian books ;[2]
Mary Fleming,[3] one of the Queen's bastard cousins, the betrothed of Secre-

Apollo breaks in :

' Juno vocat, Mariasque tuas jubet esse maritas
Castaque legitimi jura subire tori.'

The answer of Jupiter has been already quoted (pp.
xlvi., xlvii., note 4). The pageant closes with a speech
from the herald Talthybius :

' Alter Hymen laetis jam vocibus aethera pulset,
Sit Maria ut taedis altera juncta novis.
Connubio quantum sociat Venus aurea, tantum
Detrahitur numero, casta Diana, tuo.' . . .

—(Epigrammatum lib. iii. : ' Pompa Deorum in
Nuptiis Mariae.')

[1] Pp. 117-119, 124 : ' A Beton.'

Mary Beton—or, as she herself wrote her name,
' Marie Bethune'—was the niece of the Lady of Branksome of the ' Lay of the Last Minstrel,' and the daughter of Robert Beton of Creich, one of the Masters of
the Queen's Household, by his wife Dame Jeanne de
la Runvelle. She married, in May 1566, Alexander
Ogilvy of Boyne. The Queen named the marriage
day. The bride had a dowry from her father of 3000
merks, and a jointure from her husband yielding
150 merks and 30 chalders of grain yearly. The
marriage contract is signed by the Queen, the King,
and the Earls of Huntly, Bothwell, Argyll, Murray,
Angus, and Atholl. The bridegroom and the bride's
father subscribe themselves, after the fashion of the
time, by their territorial styles of ' Boyne' and
' Creycht.'—(Miscellany of the Maitland Club, vol. i.
pp. 39-49. Register of Deeds, vol. viii. foll. 322-324.
MS. Register House.)

The worth and beauty of Mary Beton are commemorated by Buchanan in four sets of verses on her
election as Queen of the Twelfth Night revels at Holyrood :—

' Regno animus tibi dignus erat : tibi regia virtus :
Et poterant formam sceptra decere tuam.
Fortuna erubuit sua munera sola deesse :
Quae tibi nunc plena dat cumulata manu.'

(Epigrammatum lib. iii., Valentiniana, 6-9 : ' Ad
Mariam Betonam pridie Regalium Reginam sorte duc-
tam.') It need scarcely be added that Buchanan's
' pridie Regalium' is the eve of the Epiphany, or
Twelfth Day—' les Rois,' or ' la fête des Rois,' as it was
called by the French,—' Uphaliday,' as it was glossed

in the Scottish calendar of that age, ' when Christ vas
reueled first to the Gentiles be the starre whilk guydit
the Thre Kingis to Bethleem.' ' Habits de Masque
faicts en la veille des Roix' appear in the Inventory
of the Queen's wardrobe at Chartley in 1586. Selden
speaks as if the ' chusing kings and queens on
Twelfth Night' was still in use in England in his day.
The choice was made by a bean hidden in a cake,
whence the person chosen was called King or Queen
of the Bean.—(Adam King's Cathechisme, kalend.
6. Jan. Paris, 1588. Prince Labanoff, Lettres de
Marie Stuart, t. vii. p. 236. Selden's Table Talk, voce
' Christmas ;' Opera, vol. iii. col. 2018.)

Mary Beton—or, as she was commonly called after
her marriage, ' the Lady Boyn,' or ' Madame de
Bouyn'—would seem to have survived to the year 1606.
A painting at Balfour House in Fife, shown as her
portrait, figures a very fair beauty, with dark eyes and
yellow hair. A letter, written by her in June 1563 to the
wife of Sir Nicholas Throckmorton, the English ambassador to France, and afterwards to Scotland, is in the
State Paper Office. Her wit and charms seem to have
fascinated his predecessor in the Scottish embassy,
Sir Thomas Randolph, who writes to Queen Elizabeth
and the Earl of Leicester how, for four days, he sat
next her at the Scottish Queen's table at St. Andrews,
tells the Earl of Bedford how he had her for his part-
ner at biles against Mary and Darnley, and, in describing the Twelfth Night reign of another of the Four
Marys, assures the Earl of Leicester that, ' if Beton
had lyked so short a tyme, so worthie a rowme,
Flemyng to her by good right should have given place.'
Mary Beton's husband outlived her, and married in
his old age the wife whom Bothwell had divorced,
the venerable Countess Dowager of Sutherland.—
(Mr. T. Wright's Queen Elizabeth and her Times,
vol. i. p. 188. G. Chalmer's Life of Queen Mary,
vol. i. p. 191. Calendar of State Papers relating to
Scotland, vol. i. p. 208, vol. ii. p. 825. Miss Strickland's Lives of the Queens of Scotland, vol. iv. p. 106.)

[2] P. 124.

[3] Pp. 116, 120 : ' A Flamy.'

Mary Fleming—or ' Marie Flemyng,' as she herself
wrote her name—was the fourth daughter of Malcolm

tary Maitland of Lethington,[1] and still in favour at Holyrood, although her lover was proscribed for his share in the death of Riccio; and Mary

third Lord Fleming (by his wife Janet Stewart, a natural daughter of King James IV.), and the youngest sister of Lady Livingston, and of the Countess of Athole.

Mary Fleming as Queen of the Bean. A letter from the English envoy in Scotland gives a glimpse of her as mistress of the Twelfth Night sports at Holyrood in 1563: 'You . . . should have seen . . . here upon Tuesday [5. January] . . . the great solemnity and royall estate of the Queen of the Beene. Fortune was so favourable to faire Flemyng that, if shee could have seen to have judged of her vertue and beauty, as blindly shee went to work and chose her at adventure, shee wold sooner have made her a Queen for ever, then for one only day, to exalt her so high and the nixt to leave her in the state shee found her . . . That day yt was to be seen, by her princely pomp, how fite a match she wold be, wer [shee] to contend ether with Venus in beauty, Minerva in witt, or Juno in worldly wealth, haveing the two former by nature, and of the third so much as is contained in this realme at her command and free disposition. The treasure of Solomon, I trowe, was not to be compared unto that which hanged upon her back . . . The Queen of the Been wes in a gowne of cloath of silver; her head, her neck, her shoulders, the rest of her whole body, so besett with stones, that more in our whole jewell house wer not to be found. The Queen herselfe [was] apparelled in collours whyt and black, [no other] jewell or gold about her, bot the ring that I brought her from the Queen's Majestie hanging at her breast, with a lace of whyt and black about her neck.'—(Letter from Randolph to Lord Robert Dudley, 15th Jan. 1563, in the Miscellany of of the Maitland Club, vol. ii. pp. 390-393.)

Buchanan laid the ready tribute of his verse at the feet of the mimic sovereign of a night:

> 'Regia, Flaminia, jamdudum sceptra teneres,
> Si genus aut virtus regia sceptra daret.
> Si det sceptra decus, dominaeque potentia formae,
> Non decor aut forma est dignior ulla tua.
> Si studiis hominumque favent bona numina votis,
> Jam tibi regna hominum vota precesque dabant.'

—(Epigrammatum, lib. iii., Valentiniana, 2-5: 'Ad Mariam Flaminiam sorte Reginam.')

When the Queen, after Chastellard's outrage in February 1563, deemed it unsafe to sleep alone, she chose her kinswoman Mary Fleming for her bedfellow.

Lethington in love. [1] Lethington's courtship of one of the Four Marys began as early at least as the autumn of 1564, when she

was about two-and-twenty, and he a widower of about forty. 'The Secretary's wife is dead'—so Kirkcaldy of Grange writes to Randolph, in September—'and he is a suitor to Mary Fleming, who is as meet for him as I am to be a page.' A month afterwards Randolph tells Cecil that Lethington is now believed to favour the Earl of Lennox, 'for the love he beareth to Mary Fleming.' In February 1564-5, we have Lethington himself confessing his passion in the grave ear of Cecil: 'The common affairs do never so much trouble me but that at least I have one merry hour of the four-and-twenty. . . . Those that be in love are ever set upon a merry pin.' A month later, the English envoy in Scotland writes to Sir Henry Sidney, who had himself been an admirer of Mary Fleming: 'She hath found another whom she doth love better. Lethington now serveth her alone, and is like for her sake to run beside himself. Both day and night he attendeth, he watcheth, he wooeth, his folly never more apparent than in loving her, where he may be assured that, how much soever he make of her, she will always love another better.' In June, Randolph tells Leicester that Riccio is in such favour with the Queen that 'Lethington hath now both leave and time to court his mistress, Mary Fleming.' He seems to have made use of his opportunity, for, in October, we find Randolph writing to Cecil: 'My old friend Lethington hath leisure to make love; and in the end, I believe, as wise as he is, will show himself a very fool, or stark, staring mad.' The murder of Riccio separated the lovers for six months, from March till September 1566, when Lethington was restored to the Queen's favour. In December he had a gift of one of her dresses of cloth of gold (p. 69). He was married to Mary Fleming on the 6th of January 1566-7, at Stirling, where the Queen kept the last Twelfth Tide she was to see beyond the walls of a prison. —(Calendar of State Papers relating to Scotland, vol. ii. p. 825, vol. i. pp. 201, 207, 212, 223, 238, 242. Bishop Keith's History of Scotland, vol. ii. p. 241. Miss Strickland's Lives of the Queens of Scotland, vol. iv. pp. 107, 131. Mr. Tytler's History of Scotland, vol. v. pp. 495-496.)

However her husband might waver or fail in his loyalty, Mary Fleming—or, as she was often called after her marriage, 'Madame de Lethington,' or 'the Secretary's wife'—remained unshaken in her devotion to her mistress. When Mary was a prisoner in Loch-

Bequest to Mary
Seton. Seton,[1] extolled by the Queen as the finest dresser of hair in Christendom,[2] and the only one of the Four Marys who never married. She had vowed herself to a

Ring sent to
the Queen in
Lochleven.

leven, means were found to convey to her a ring with a motto encouraging her to hopes of escape. Buchanan, in his Chamaeleon, says, that it came from Lethington. He may have been in the secret, but the token would appear to have been sent by Mary Fleming. 'The Quene said scho gat ane ring and thre wordis of Italianis in it'—so one of her attendants deponed on his examination after her flight—'I iudget [it cam fra the] Secretar, becaus of [the] langage. Scho said, 'Na, it was ane woman.' All the place saw hir weyr it. . . . Cursall' [one of the Queen's bedchamber women] 'show me the Secretaris wiff send it, and the vreting of it was ane fable of Isop betuix the Mouss and the Lioune, hou the Mouss for ane plesour done to hir be the Lioun, efter that, the Lioune being bound with ane cord, the Movss schuyr the corde and lut the Lioune louss. This far I hard suirlye ; and that the Quene said plainlye scho lipnit in him' [Lethington] 'that he fauorit hir and lamentit hir cace.'—(MS. Fragment in the Register House.) In May 1581, we find the Queen in her prison at Sheffield longing for the society of Mary Fleming.—(Prince Labanoff, Lettres de Marie Stuart, t. v. p. 222.)

Lethington died in June 1573. His widow, by her moving appeal to his old friend Burleigh, rescued his corpse from the shame and ignominy with which it was threatened by the Scottish law of treason. See above, pp. xxii. xxiii., note 3. In February 1583-4 she obtained a reversal of his forfeiture ; and in May 1584, the Parliament extended the benefits of the pacification of Perth in 1572, to her and to her children, whom she seems to have brought up in the old faith. Her only son is last heard of at Brussels in 1620, when he writes a Latin letter to Camden in vindication of his father's memory. The extinction of Lethington's male issue by the death of this son, in poverty and exile, was believed by many to fulfil the Knox's prophecies against
Lethington. prophetic imprecations to which Knox gave way when stung by the jeers of that remarkable man who, in diplomacy, had held his own against Cecil and the Cardinal of Lorraine, and, in theology, had shown himself as formidable in dispute with the preachers of Geneva as with the doctors of the Sorbonne.—(Knox's History of the Reformation, vol. ii. pp. 89, 363, 421, 460. Scot of Scotstarvet's Staggering State of Scots Statesmen, pp. 56-57. Kirkton's History of the Church of Scotland, p. 23. Registrum Magni Sigilli, lib. xxxvi. no. 571. MS. Register House. Acts of the Parliaments of Scotland, vol. iii. p. 313. G. Camdeni Epistolae, pp. 305, 306.)

A letter in French from Mary Fleming to her sister-in-law, Isabel Maitland, wife of James Heriot of Trabroun, is printed in Letters from Lady Margaret Burnet to John Duke of Lauderdale, p. 83. Edinb. 1828: Bannatyne Club. It is without date, but shows itself to have been written between 1567 and 1581.

[1] P. 118 : 'A Ceston.'

Mary Seton—or, as she herself wrote her name, 'Marie de Seton'—was the only daughter of George fourth Lord Seton, by his second wife Mary Pyeres or Pieris, a Frenchwoman who came to Scotland in the train of the Queen's mother in 1538.

When the Queen, after her surrender at Carberry, was hurried on foot, in her night-gown, through the streets of Edinburgh, her steps were supported by Mary Livingston and Mary Seton. We find her attended by Mary Seton in her captivity at Carlisle and at Bolton in 1568, at Chatsworth in 1570 and 1572, and at Sheffield in 1570, 1574, 1577, and 1582. They seem to have been separated before 1584, when Mary Seton retired to France. In October 1586, she is found at Reims, whence she writes to the French ambassador at Holyrood, of her long absence from Scotland, and of her sorrow to hear that new troubles had befallen the Queen her mistress. The allusion is to Babington's conspiracy.—(Sir Richard Maitland's History of the House of Seyton, p. 42. Glasg. 1829 : Maitland Club. M. Teulet, Papiers d'Etat relatifs à l'Histoire de l'Ecosse, t. ii. p. 167. Prince Labanoff, Lettres de Marie Stuart, t. vii. p. 123, t. iii. p. 116, t. iv. pp. 215, 239, 341-344, 377-381, 389, 390, 401, 402, t. v. pp. 436, 437. M. Laing's History of Scotland, vol. ii. p. 114. G. Chalmers' Life of Queen Mary, vol. i. pp. 441, 442. J. Hunter's History of Hallamshire, p. 66. Calendar of State Papers relating to Scotland, vol. ii. pp. 933, 1014. Miss Strickland's Lives of the Queens of Scotland, vol. vii. pp. 266-271, 441.) A French letter by Mary Seton, without date or address, is printed in Letters from Lady Margaret Burnet to John Duke of Lauderdale, pp. 81, 82.

Mary Seton had an elder sister Marion—one of the three daughters of her father's first marriage with Dame Elizabeth Hay—who appears among the attendants of Queen Mary of Guise in 1548, and became the wife of John Earl of Menteith.

[2] Sir Francis Knollys writes to Cecil, from Carlisle, on the 28th June 1568: ' Now here are six waiting women, although none of reputation, but Mistress Mary Mary Seton.
' the finest
busker' of
hair in Europe.

life of celibacy, and when, about the age of thirty-five, she reluctantly consented to seek release from her vow, her suitor, the Queen's Master of Household, suddenly died.[1]   Not long afterwards, when she had shared her mistress's prison for more than fifteen years, she withdrew to France, and entering the convent of St. Peter's at Reims, then under the rule of the Queen's aunt, ended her days there.

There are legacies of less price to three elder ladies of honour, the Countess of Atholl,[2] another of the Queen's bastard cousins, believed by the

Bequest to the Countess of Atholl.

Seaton, who is praised by this Queen to be the finest busker, that is to say, the finest dresser of a woman's head of hair that is to be seen in any country; whereof we have seen divers experiences, since her coming hither. And, among other pretty devices, yesterday and this day, she did set such a curled hair upon the Queen, that was said to be a perewyke, that showed very delicately. And every other day she hath a new device of head dressing, without any cost, and yet setteth forth a woman gaylie well.' — (G. Chalmers' Life of Queen Mary, vol. i. pp. 443, 444.)

Mary Seton's love affair.

[1] The story is told by the Queen in two letters, from her prison at Sheffield, to the Archbishop of Glasgow, her ambassador at Paris, the one written in January, the other in November 1577. Mary Seton's lover was the Archbishop's brother, Andrew Beton. He was the younger son of a younger son of the house of Balfour; and although Brantôme (t. v. p. 98) tells us that it was regarded as a 'fort bonne maison' — it had recently given a cardinal and two archbishops to the church—there was question if he were a fit match for a daughter of the proud house of Winton. 'On s'arrête beaucoup à la différence des tiltres et qualités,'—so Mary wrote to the Archbishop—'jusques à m'alléguer pour exemple la faulte qu'elle a ouï trouver au mariage des deux soeurs Levingston, seulement pour avoir espousé les puînés de leurs semblables; et craint on que les parens, au pays où telles formalités se gardent, n'en aient pareille opinion, comme elle dit qu'ils ont eue par ci-davant. Mays, comme Royne de l'un et de l'autre, j'ay offert de prendre la charge sur moy pour y remédier de tout ce que je pourray.'—(Prince Labanoff, Lettres de Marie Stuart, t. iv. pp. 341-344, 377-381, 389, 390, 401, 402.)

The Livingston sisters, to whom allusion is made, were Mary Livingston, who married a younger son

of the Lord Sempill, and Magdalene Livingston, who married a younger son of the Lord Erskine.

[2] P. 108: 'A Madame dHatel.'

Margaret Fleming, third daughter of Malcolm third Lord Fleming, married, first, Robert Master of Graham (or Montrose), slain at Pinkie in 1547; second, Thomas, Master of Erskine, who died in 1551; third, John fourth Earl of Athol. Her last marriage contract, dated on the 1st April 1557, stipulates that the Earl shall instantly 'wed and handfast' Margaret Fleming, Mistress of Montrose and Erskine; shall send to Rome, with all possible despatch, for dispensation for their marriage, notwithstanding the impediment of consanguinity; shall, within forty days, seise her for life in lands yielding 300 merks a year (reckoning the boll of grain at 13s. 4d.); and shall, before Martinmas next, marry her solemnly in face of the church. The bride's brother, James Lord Fleming, gives her a dowry of 2000 merks.

Handfasting.

She appears as a lady of honour in the earliest as well as in the latest roll of the Queen's household which I have seen.

She was the sister of Agnes Fleming, wife of William, sixth Lord Livingston, and of Mary Fleming, wife of Secretary Maitland of Lethington. A letter from her to Lady Livingston, written from Blair, in September 1560, is printed in Law's Memorialls, pp. xxv. xxvi. It shows that the Countess was a diligent worker in embroidery, and that Athol whisky was then in request in good houses in Lothian.

Knox's secretary records an instance of her power as an enchantress: 'On Tuysday the 3 of Julij 1571, Andro Lundie beand at dener with my maister, in a place of the lard of Abbotthalla, called Falsyde, openlie affirmet for treuth, that when the Quene was lying in leasing of the King, the Ladie Athole, lying thair lykwayis, bayth within the Castell of Edin-

The Countess of Atholl's incantations.

Bequests to the
Dowager Lady
Seton, and to
the wife of the
Laird of Criech.

Reformers to be endowed with strange powers of enchantment; Madame de Briante,[1] the French mother of Mary Seton, and herself grown grey in the service of the Queen and her mother; and Madame de Cric,[2] as Mary calls

burgh, that he come thair for sum busines, and called for the Ladie Reirres' [Margaret Beton, daughter of the Laird of Criech, aunt of Mary Beton, and wife of Arthur Forbes of Reres], 'whome he fand in hir chalmer, lying bedfast, and he asking hir of hir disease, scho answrit that scho was never so trubled with no barne that ever scho bair, ffor the Ladie Athole had cassin all the pyne of hir childbirth vpon hir.'—(R. Bannatyne's Journal, p. 238.)

Atholl would seem at all times to have been in bad repute for its witches: 'maleficiis mulierum semper Atholia erat infamis.'—(G. Buchanani Rerum Scoticarum Historia, lib. x. cap. 58.)

[1] P. 106: 'A Madame de Briante.'

Dame Mary Pyeres (or Pieris), a Frenchwoman who came to Scotland with Queen Mary of Guise in 1538, married, first, George fourth Lord Seton, who died in 1549; second, before 1555, Pierre de Cluise, Seigneur de Briante, who died in 1570. She continued, after her second marriage, to write herself 'Lady Seytoun,' but was, perhaps, more commonly known as Madame de Briante. She appears under that name in the list of the Queen's ladies of honour, in July 1562, and in February and March 1567.

In the deposition of French Paris, we have a glimpse of her in the Queen's chamber on the morning after the King's murder: 'Le Lundy matin, entre neuf et dix heures, ledict Paris dict qu'il entra dans la chambre de la Royne, laquelle estoyt bien close, et son lict tendu du noyr en signe de dueil, et de la chandelle allumee dedans la ruelle, la ou Madame de Bryant luy donnoyt à desieusner d'ung oeuf frais, la ou aussy Monsieur de Boduel arryve et parle à elle secretement soubz courtine.'—(Anderson's Collections relating to Mary Queen of Scots, vol. ii. p. 202. M. Laing's History of Scotland, vol. ii. pp. 287, 288. M. Teulet, Lettres de Marie Stuart, p. 102.)

In August 1570, we find her writing to the Queen from Dunkeld, where she had gone to be present, with the Countess of Atholl and Mary Fleming, at the council of the Queen's friends, which became known as the gathering of 'the witches of Atholl.' Her letter, which shows her anxious about the health of her daughter, Mary Seton, was intercepted; and its reflections on public affairs subjected the writer and her son to a brief imprisonment and an abortive trial.

—(Diurnal of Occurrents, pp. 185, 186. Pitcairn's Criminal Trials, vol. i. p. 14. R. Bannatyne's Journal, pp. 37, 53. M. Francisque-Michel, Les Ecossais en France, t. ii. pp. 68, 70, where her name is misprinted 'Pyenes.')

She returned to her own country in 1574, with letters from the Queen commending her to the favour and protection of the Archbishop of Glasgow and the Cardinal of Lorraine: 'Madame de Briante est retournée en France où elle pourra avoir beaucoup d'affayres, spécialement avesques son beau-frère, pour son douayre. . . . C'est une bonne et vertueuse dame et ancienne servante de la feue Royne, ma mère, et de moy; et sa fille, qui tous les jours me fayct service très-agréable, vous sçavez assez sa vertueuse vie et ses merites.'—(Prince Labanoff, Lettres de Marie Stuart, t. iv. pp. 238, 239.) Three months afterwards, the Queen renews her recommendations, in a letter to the Archbishop of Glasgow: 'J'avoys oublié de vous dire que je vous avoys écrit par ci-devant pour vous prier d'aider la bonne dame de Seyton, en toutes ses affaires, de ma faveur et de mon nom.'—(Id. p. 269.) She died within two years after her return to France.

[2] P. 106: 'A Madame de Cric;' p. 113: 'Aus dames de Cric,' etc.

'Jene de la Runuelle,' as she wrote her name, married, first, Robert Beton of Criech, who died in 1567; second, John Hay, Commendator of the Abbey of Balmerino, who died in 1573. She continued, after her second marriage, to write herself 'Lady of Creicht.' She appears as one of the Queen's ladies of honour in the rolls of the household in July 1562, and in February and March 1567. She died in 1576.

Her first husband is said to have accompanied the Queen to France in 1548, and to have returned with her to Scotland in 1561. He was in attendance as one of the Masters of the Household, when the murderers of Riccio burst into the Queen's cabinet. His last will bequeaths his wife and children to the Queen's protection: 'that scho be haill mantenare of my hous as my houpe is in hir Maiestie vndir God.' His family was peculiarly a court one. Its founder, his grandfather, was first Comptroller, then Treasurer to King James IV. His aunt was one of the concubines of King James V., by whom she

the French mother of Mary Beton, and wife of the Laird of Criech, one of her Masters of Household. The younger Mary Erskine,[1] although not counted among the Four Marys, receives as much as any of them. Her kinsman, Alexander Erskine of Gogar,[2] one of the Queen's equerries, or Masters of the Stables, gets a gold heart, garnished with three diamonds, a ruby, and a pearl. A jewel, containing a sapphire and a pearl, is left to his younger brother and colleague in office, Arthur Erskine of Blackgrange,[3] the equerry behind whom Mary took her seat when she made her midnight escape on horseback from the murderers of Riccio.[4]

was the mother of the Countess of Argyll. His sister, the wife of Arthur Forbes of Reres, was a favourite of Queen Mary, and wet-nurse to her son. His wife was one of her ladies of honour; his eldest daughter one of her Four Marys; his second daughter one of her maids of honour. He himself was one of her Masters of Household, Keeper of her Palace of Falkland, and Steward of her rents in Fife.

[1] P. 118: 'A Marie Ersquin;' pp. 120, 124: 'A Marie Arsquin.'

The name of 'Madamoiselle d'Asquin' appears in lists of the Queen's ladies of honour in February and March 1567. I have not observed it in any earlier roll. She may have been the Mary Erskine, afterwards Countess of Angus, daughter of John fifth Lord Erskine, Earl of Mar; or the Mary Erskine, afterwards, it is said, wife of Sir Dugald Campbell of Auchinbreck, daughter of Alexander Erskine of Gogar, Master of Mar. In the former case, she could not have been more than eight or nine; in the latter, not more than ten or eleven years of age at the date of the Queen's bequest.

[2] P. 123: 'A Alexandre Ersquin.'

Alexander Erskine—styled 'of Cagnor,' 'of Gogar,' and 'Master of Mar'—was the second son of John fourth Lord Erskine. He was born about 1521, and married in 1555 Margaret, daughter of George fourth Lord Home, who brought him a dowry of 2000 merks.

On the death of his brother, the Regent Mar, in 1572, he was placed in charge of the young King. Sir James Melville describes him as 'a nobleman of a trew, gentill nature, weill loued and lyked of euery man for his good qualities and gret discretion, in na wayes factious nor enuyous, a lover of all honest men, and desyred euer to haue sic as wer of gud conuersa-

tion to be about the Prince, rather then his awen nerer frendis gif he thocht them not sa meit.'—(Memoirs, p. 262. Calendar of State Papers relating to Scotland, vol. i. pp. 367, 371.)

[3] P. 123: 'A Artus Asquin.'

Arthur Erskine of Blackgrange was the son of John fourth Lord Erskine, and the brother of John fifth Lord Erskine, Earl of Mar, of Alexander Erskine of Gogar, Master of Mar, and of Margaret Erskine, mother of the Regent Murray.

He was in attendance on the Queen when she made her first entry into Edinburgh, in September 1561. Along with the silver keys of the city, a bible and a psalm-book, bound in purple velvet, were delivered to her. 'But when the bible was presented,' says Knox, 'sche began to frown: for schame she could not refuise it; but she did no better, for immediatelie sche gave it to the most pestilent Papist within the realme, to wit, to Arthure Erskyn.'—(History of the Reformation, vol. ii. p. 288.)

He had grants from the Queen of the lands of Blelak and others in Cromar, in December 1564, and of part of the escheat of Robert Lord Boyd, in November 1565. In January or March 1566, he married Magdalene Livingston, one of the Queen's 'filles damoiselles,' the sister of one of the Four Marys, and the daughter of Alexander fifth Lord Livingston. He died before July 1570.—(Registrum Secreti Sigilli, vol. xxxii. foll. 127, 128; vol. xxxiii. fol. 132; vol. xxxv. fol. 14. MS. Register House. Registrum Magni Sigilli, lib. xxxvi. no. 2. MS. Register House.)

[4] 'All men beinge gone to their lodgings, and no suspicion taken of anye that ether she wolde departe or not performe the promes to the Lords, abowte xij. of the clocke at nyghte she convoide her self a privie

Riccio's brother, Joseph[1]—a lad of eighteen, with little or none of his brother's ability, although the Queen had promoted him to his brother's place—

waye owte of the howse. She, her howsbonde, and one gentlewoman came to the place whear Arthur Ersken and the captaine of her garde keapte the horses, and so roode her waye behynde Arthur Ersken untyll she came to Seton. Ther she tooke a horse to her self, and roode to Dombarr to the castle, wheather resorted unto her the Lords Huntlye and Bothewell, and so divers of the whole countrie.'—(Letter from the Earl of Bedford, and T. Randolph, to the Privy Council of England, 27th March 1566, in Sir H. Ellis' Letters illustrative of English History, vol. ii. p. 214.)

Arthur Erskine was in attendance on the Queen when Riccio was dragged from her cabinet and murdered. He was about to lay hands on Lord Ruthven when the rest of the assassins crowded into the room, and made resistance hopeless. Fifteen months afterwards, he was in waiting in an ante-chamber with Sir James Melville, when the Queen, being alone in her cabinet with Bothwell, 'was so disdainfully handled, and with such reproachful language,' that she cried out for a knife to kill herself. It was on the second day after their marriage.—(Lord Ruthen's Relation of the Death of David Rizzi, in Scotia Rediviva, pp. 341, 342. Sir James Melville's Memoirs, p. 180. Letter from Du Croc to Queen Catharine of Medicis, 18th May 1567, printed by Prince Labanoff, in his Lettres de Marie Stuart, t. vii. pp. 110-112.)

[1] Pp. 113, 122, 123. Joseph Riccio is said to have come to Scotland in the train of the French envoy, Michel de Castelnau, sieur de Mauvissière. He was made the Queen's private secretary within ten days after his brother's murder. The appointment was ill taken, as we learn from the despatch of the French ambassador: 'Et non contante de cela, a faict desterrer le corps dudict David du cimetierre où il estoit, et l'a remis dedans l'esglise en une sépulture honorable, au rang des Roys. D'où les malveillans prennent occasion de mesdire, comme aussi pour avoir receu en l'estat de Secrétaire son frère, monstrant le vouloir beaucoup advancer, encores qu'il ne soit que un jeune homme de XVIII ans et de nulle suffisance.'—(Letter from Paul de Foix to Catharine of Medicis, printed by M. Teulet, in his Papiers d'Etats relatifs à l'Histoire d'Ecosse, t. ii. p. 119. Letter from Randolph to Cecil, 25th April 1566, in Principal Robertson's History of Scotland, app. no. xvi. ; Works, vol. ii. p. 342.)

He is spoken of by the English envoy as growing apace into favour with the Queen, in June 1566, about the date of the bequests in the text. But he seems, not long afterwards, to have fallen under suspicion of purloining a pair of the Queen's bracelets, and of borrowing money on false pretences from his countryman Timotheo Cagnioli, the court banker.—(Mr. Tytler's History of Scotland, vol. v. pp. 374-376, 387, 388, 509-513, where a letter from him is printed. Prince Labanoff, Lettres de Marie Stuart, t. i. pp. 392-394. Miss Strickland's Lives of the Queens of Scotland, vol. v. pp. 107-110, 195, 196.)

'Joseph, Davy's brother,' as he is called, was denounced by the Earl of Lennox as one of the King's assassins. He might not unnaturally be thought desirous of avenging his brother's murder upon the chief murderer, whose last hours, it was said, were troubled by the recollection which the Queen brought to his mind that it was about that time twelvemonth that her secretary was butchered. But I have not seen any evidence of Joseph Riccio's presence at the tragedy of the Kirk of the Field, in the judicial examinations which have been preserved. On the contrary, they seem to show that there was some difficulty in persuading him to leave Scotland before the meeting of the Parliament in April 1567. One of the last questions put to French Paris was about his flight : 'Estant interrogué, S'il savoyt pourquoy Joseph s'en alla de ce pays? Respond, Que la Royne lui dict : "Paris, il fault que tu controuves quelque chose en ton esprite pour faire peur à Joseph, affin qu'il s'en aille." Et voyant qu'il ne pouvoyt rien faire, elle luy dict : "Je feray faire une lettre que tu perderas derrier luy pour luy faire peur." Mais luy ne pouvant ce faire, elle le feist dire par le Justice Clerk, comme il peust, qu'il eust à comparoistre au Parlement ; chose qu'il l'affroyast grandement, et courut çà et là demandant son congé. Enfin la Royne baille neuf vingtz escus à Paris, pour les bailler à Joseph, affin qu'il s'en allast, ce qu'il feist ; et ainsy ayant receu la dict somme, il s'en alla.'—(M. Laing's History of Scotland, vol. ii. p. 289. M. Teulet, Lettres de Marie Stuart, p. 104.)

One of the letters said to have been addressed by Mary to Bothwell—the earliest of the series, supposed to have been written from Glasgow about the 24th of January 1567—would seem to show that the King was anxious about Joseph Riccio's dismissal : 'The King send for Joachim yisternicht, and askit at him . . . gif I

has three bequests. One is of a jewel, containing ten rubies and a pearl, which *Jewel given to the Queen by David Riccio.* Mary had accepted as a gift from the murdered Italian.[1] The others are of

Roll of the Queen's Household, drawn up by Joseph Riccio.

had maid my estait ? gif I had takin Paris and Gilbert to wryte to me ? and that I wald send Joseph away ? I am abaschit quha hes schawin him sa far ; yea, he spak evin of the marriage of Bastiane.'—(Goodall's Examination, vol. ii. pp. 4, 5. M. Teulet, Lettres de Marie Stuart, pp. 6, 7.)

Joachim, Paris, Gilbert, and Bastian were valets of the Queen's chamber. Bastian's marriage took place on the 9th of February 1567. The question which, in the Scottish translation (the French original is not extant), is rendered, 'gif I had maid my estait ?' runs in the Latin version by Buchanan, 'an familiae catalogum fecissem ?' It was the subject of a controversy in which Lord Hailes, Whitaker, and Malcolm Laing took part. M. Teulet, without observing its conclusive bearing on the dispute, has recently published, from the original in the Imperial Library at Paris, what is obviously the very 'estait' referred to—'Estat des gaiges des dames, damoiselles, gentilzhommes et autres officiers domesticques de la Royne d'Escosse, Douairère de France, pour une anneé commençant le premier jour de Janvier M Vᵉ LXVI et finissant le dernier jour de Décembre ensuivant, mil cinq cens soixante-sept.' It is dated at Edinburgh, on the 13th of February 1567, and is authenticated by the sign-manual of the Queen and by the subscription of Joseph Riccio, showing that, on this occasion at least, neither Paris nor Gilbert had been called in to play the secretary's part, and that Joseph Riccio had not yet been sent away. The 'estat' was transmitted to France for payment from the Queen's French dowry, and thus found its way to the Imperial Library.—(M. Teulet, Papiers d'Etat relatifs à l'Histoire de l'Ecosse, t. ii. pp. 121-137.)

Joseph Riccio is named in another of the letters said to have been addressed by Mary to Bothwell—that in which she shrinks from likening herself to Medea— supposed to have been written from Glasgow in the last days of January 1567 : 'I durst not wryte this befoir Joseph, Bastiane, and Joachime, that did bot depart evin quhen I began to wryte.'—(Goodall's Examination, vol. ii. pp. 36, 37. M. Teulet, Lettres de Marie Stuart, p. 45.)

René Benoist, confessor of Mary Stewart, and of Henry IV. of France.

The roll of the Queen's household, authenticated by Joseph Riccio's signature in February 1567, shows that he had a brother or brother-in-law for a colleague : 'René Bonneau, frère dudict Joseph.' If we suppose the name of René Bonneau to be the same

which is elsewhere written René Benoist, we have an additional reason for the unpopularity of David Riccio— his relation to the distinguished divine who was chosen by the Cardinal of Lorraine to accompany the Queen to Scotland, and had not been many weeks at Holyrood before he challenged Knox to controversy.—(Epistola Renati Benedicti ad Johannem Knox atque alios in Scotia ministros, 19. Novemb. 1561, reprinted in Mr. David Laing's Tracts by David Ferguson, pp. 81-88. Edinb. 1860 : Bannatyne Club.) The confessor of Mary Stewart published other two pamphlets against the Reformed doctrines, before he returned to France to acquire the name of the Pope of the Markets, from his popularity as a preacher among the shopkeepers of Paris ; to incur suspicions of heterodoxy which stopped his promotion to the bishopric of Troyes ; and to become the confessor of King Henry IV., whose conversion he is said to have helped.—(Niceron, Mémoires pour servir à l'Histoire des Hommes Illustres, t. xli. pp. 1-49.)

Jean Damyot, the necromancer who warned David Riccio of his fate.

In 'Jehan Damyte, notaire'—another of the secretaries enumerated in Joseph Riccio's roll in February 1567—we may recognise the French chaplain, a reputed adept in sorcery, who was said to have warned David Riccio of his fate, telling him to beware of the bastard. It is added that the Italian (who was himself reputed no mean necromancer) gave no heed to the hint, thinking that it pointed to the Earl of Murray, then an exile in England. But the prophecy was believed to have its fulfilment, when the first of more than fifty wounds, by which the poor Italian was mangled, was dealt by the King's uncle, a bastard of the house of Angus—George Douglas, the Postulate of Murray.—(G. Buchanani Historia Rerum Scoticarum, lib. xvii. cap. 62.)

[1] P. 123 : 'A Iosef que son frere mauoyt done.'

David Riccio's wealth ;

I have not observed any other trace of this gift. Riccio had grown rich during his short term of power : 'Of the greate substance he had ther is myche spoken ; some saye in gold to the value of £2000 sterling. . . . We heare of a juell that he had hanginge abowte hys necke of some price that cane not be hearde of.'— (Letter from the Earl of Bedford and T. Randolph to the Privy Council of England, 27th March 1566, in Sir H. Ellis' Letters illustrative of English History, vol. ii. p. 218.)

the nobles cringe to him.

Buchanan speaks of his 'opes non mediocres,' and tells how the nobles fawned upon him : 'Alebat hanc

an emerald ring,[1] enamelled in white, and a jewel containing twenty-one diamonds.[2]   They are to be carried to one whose name the Queen has spoken in her new Secretary's ear, but does not trust herself to write.   It would be idle now to seek to pry into the mystery, which was thus anxiously guarded.

There are bequests to four maids of honour — Lucrece Beton,[3] Mademoiselle de Thoré,[4] Magdalene Livingston,[5] and Barbara Sondre-

vanissimi hominis insaniam magnae partis nobiliorum adulatio, qui amicitiam ejus captabant, salutando, orationi ejus subserviendo, foribus obambulando, exitus
reditusque ejus observando.'   It is added that, at one time, he used to share Darnley's bed : 'in eumque familiaritatis gradum pervenerat, ut lectum, cubiculum, secretosque sermones communicaret.'—(Historia Rerum Scoticarum, lib. xvii. cap. 44.)

Sir James Melville, who describes him as 'a merry fellow and a good musician,' says that 'when he grew sa gret that he presented all signatours to be subscryuit be hir Maieste, some of the nobilite wald glowm vpon him, and some of them wald schulder him and schuyt hym by, when they entrit in the chamber, and fand him alwais speaking with hir Maieste ; and some again that had turnis to be helpit, new infeftmentis to be tane, or that desyred to preuaill against ther ennemys in court or session, addressit them vnto him, and dependit vpon hym ; whereby in schort tym he becam very rich.'—(Memoirs, pp. 131, 132.)

Buchanan says that Murray stood aloof from the crowd of flatterers ; and we know that Queen Elizabeth ascribed his first disgrace at the Scottish court to a plot which Mary was told he had formed against Riccio's life, at least four months before the Italian was assassinated.   But even Murray had to stoop at last. Shortly before Riccio's death, as Sir James Melville relates, 'my Lord of Murray sutted him very ernestly, and mair humbly then any man wald haue beleued, with the present of a faire dyamont, inclosed within a lettre full of repentance, and faire promyses fra that tym fourth to be his frend and protectour.'—(Memoirs, p. 147.   M. Teulet, Papiers d'Etat relatifs à l'Histoire de l'Eccosse, t. ii. p. 93.)

[1] P. 113 : 'A Iosef pour porter a celui que ie luy ay dit.'

[2] P. 122 : 'A Iosef pour bailler a que ie lui ay dit dont il ranuoir aquitance.'

[3] P. 119 : 'A Lucresse.'

Lucrece Beton—or as she herself writes her name,

'Lucresse Bethune'—was the daughter of Robert Beton of Criech, one of the Queen's Masters of Household.   She was the younger sister of Mary Beton, one of the Four Marys.

She appears as 'la jeune Bethon' in the list of the Queen's 'filles damoiselles' in July 1562, as 'Lucresse de Beton' in the list of February 1567, and as 'Lucresse' in the list of March 1567.   She married, after 1575, Andrew Wyshart of Muirton.   She survived him ; and, settling near her elder sister, made her last will, on the shores of the Boyne, in November 1623, leaving all that she had to Alexander Abercromby, of Birkenbog, and his daughter Mary.—(Original in the Register House.)

[4] P. 118 : 'A Tore.'

The name of 'Thore' appears among the 'filles damoiselles' in the list of the Queen's household in July 1562.   It is absent from the roll of February 1567.   She had married six months before.   There was a payment from the Treasury, on 30th August 1566, by command of the King and Queen, of £68, 15s. for 'xiij elnis iij quarteris of violat weluote (the elne v pundis) to be ane gowne to Madame Torrie to hir marriage.'—(Compotum Thesaurarii Reginae Scotorum. MS. Register House.)   She may have been of the family of M. de Thoré, mentioned by Brantôme, t. ii. pp. 447-449 ; t. v. p. 71.

[5] P. 111 : 'A Lesuiston la ieusne ;'   p. 117 : 'A Leuiston la ieusne ;'   p. 123 : 'A la ieusne Leuiston.'

Magdalene Livingston was the daughter of Alexander fifth Lord Livingston, and the younger sister of Mary Livingston, one of the Four Marys.   She appears as 'la jeune Leuiston' among the 'filles damoiselles' in the list of the Queen's household in July 1562.   Her name is absent from the roll of February 1567.   She married one of the Queen's equerries, Arthur Erskine of Blackgrange, in January or March 1566, when the Queen made her a gift of a vasquin of cloth of gold (p. 69).   She may be the 'Madame dAsquin' who appears in a list of the Queen's ladies of honour in March 1567.   Her husband died before

land[1]—and to their governess, Mademoiselle de la Souche.[2]   The largest share

falls to Magdalene Livingston, who had lately married the Queen's favourite

equerry, Arthur Erskine of Blackgrange.   A diamond ring, enamelled in

white and red, is left as a token of remembrance to Mademoiselle la Contine,

one of Mary's attendants at the French court, it would seem, who had not

followed her to Scotland.[3]

To Margaret Carwod,[4] her favourite bedchamber woman, the Queen

leaves, among other things, a miniature of herself set with diamonds, and a

Bequests to the
Mistress of the
Maids ;

to Mademoiselle
la Contine ;

to Margaret Car-
wod.

July 1570, and we hear of her intention to marry again in August 1577. 'Le mariage de Magdelaine Leving-ston me déplaist infiniment'—so the Queen writes to the Archbishop of Glasgow at Paris—'et je ne veulx, jusqu'à ce que j'en soit mieulx esclaircie, que vous luy envoyez ce que je vous ay mandé. —(Prince Labanoff, Lettres de Marie Stuart, t. iv. p. 389.) The cause of the Queen's displeasure does not appear. Mary Liv-ingston is said to have taken John Scrymgeour of Glaster for her second husband.

[1] P. 124 : ' A Sonderland.'

'Barbera Sonddrelland' appears in the earliest list of the Queen's household which I have seen. She is not in the lists of July 1562, or of February 1567. But the name of 'Sondrelan' occurs among the 'filles damoiselles' in the list of March 1567.

[2] P. 113 : 'Il sen fault vne chesne que vous naues pas ecrite esmaylle de blanc et rousge que ie laysse a Madamoyselle de la Souschee.'

The name of 'Madamoiselle de la Souche, gouver-nante des filles damoiselles,' appears on the rolls of the Queen's household in July 1562, and in February and March 1567.

[3] P. 112 : 'A la Contine pour souuenance.'

It appears from a marginal note on the Inventory of the Queen's Jewels made at her leaving France in August 1561, that some of them were given to Madamoiselle la Contine (p. 12). Her name does not occur in the lists of the household in 1562 or 1567.

[4] Pp. 117, 123: ' A Marguerite ;' pp. 123, 124 : ' Margaret Carwod.'

Margaret
Carwod.Margaret Carwod, one of the coheiresses of Carwod in Lanarkshire, probably owed her place at court to the Countess of Atholl, the Lady Livingston, or some other member of the house of Fleming, of which the Carwods seem to have been vassals. She appears as

one of the Queen's bedchamber women in May 1564, and in September 1565 (pp. 147, 158, 159.) In May or June 1566, the date of the bequests in the text, she seems to have had charge of the jewels in the Queen's cabinet (pp. 111, 119, 123.) She is spoken of by Buchanan as being, three or four months after-wards, 'omnium secretorum conscia,'—'ane woman priuie of all hir [the Queen's] secreitis.' One of the let-ters said to have been addressed by the Queen to Both-well—the most obscure of the series, supposed to have been written in the end of January or beginning of Febru-ary 1567—was described when first published as 'ane uther letter to Bothwell, concerning the departure of Margaret Carwod, quha wes preuie and ane helper of all thair lufe.' It complains of her folly, of her ingra-titude to the Queen, and of the offence which she has given to Bothwell. 'And quhen scho salbe maryit' —it proceeds—'I beseik yow giue me ane [vther], or ellis I will tak sic as sall content yow for thair conditiounis ; bot as for thair toungis or faithfulnes towart yow, I will not answer.'—(Anderson's Collec-tions relating to Queen Mary, vol. ii. pp. 8, 150, 151. M. Teulet, Lettres de Marie Stuart, pp. 46, 48.) A French copy of the letter in the State Paper Office is indorsed 'anent the depesche of Margaret Carwod quhilk wes before hir marriage.'—(Calendar of State Papers relating to Scotland, vol. ii. p. 865.)

The marriage of Margaret Carwod took place at Holyrood (the Queen giving the bridal feast) on Shrove Tuesday (11th of February) 1567, two days after the marriage of Bastian Pages, a valet of the Queen's chamber, to whose bridal masque at Holy-rood, on the night of Sunday the 9th of February, Mary hurried from her husband's bedside at the Kirk of the Field, an hour or two before his mur-der. It has been supposed by Malcolm Laing, Prince Labanoff, M. Mignet, and others, that as Margaret

little silver box, perhaps the memorable casquet marked with the crowned cypher of King Francis the Second, in which her accusers affirmed that they found the letters and sonnets produced by them as proofs of her criminal love for Bothwell, and of her guilty knowledge of his conspiracy against her husband's life.[1]

These are the only servants whom the Queen names. But the rest are not forgotten. Each of her twelve maids is to have a gold finger-ring;[2] her linen

---

Carwod and Bastian Pagez were both servants of the Queen, and both married about the same time, they married one another ; and some scandal and more romance have been built upon an assumption which a closer scrutiny would have shown to be groundless. The wife of Bastian Pagez was Christilly Hogg ; Margaret Carwod's husband was John Stewart of Tullypowreis in Atholl.—(Lodge's Illustrations of British History, vol. i. p. 520. Register of Deeds, vol. xvii. foll. 281, 282. MS. Register House.)

On the 8th of February 1567, the Queen granted a pension of 300 merks a year from the lands of Kinclevin in Perthshire, to ' hir louit familiare seruitrice Margaret Carwod.' On the same day, so French Paris affirmed, she sent him to the King's lodging at the Kirk of the Field, to fetch a furred coverlet ('une couverture de martres') to the Queen's chamber at Holyrood. On the 10th of February there was a payment from the Treasury, by the Queen's command, to Margaret Carwod, for her marriage dress, of £125, 6s. Her name is not included in the roll of the Queen's household made up three days afterwards. Her departure or dismissal had then taken place. But her absence, whatever may have been its cause, was only for a few weeks. On the 23d of March, the Queen orders eighty yards of fine linen to be delivered to ' her servitrice,' Margaret Carwod, who, three days afterwards, acknowledges their receipt, subscribing her name by the hand of a notary.—(Registrum Secreti Sigilli, vol. xxxvi. fol. 7. MS. Register House. Compotum Thesaurarii Reginae Scotorum, 8-10 Feb. 1566-7. MS. Register House. M. Teulet, Papiers d'Etat relatifs à l'Histoire de l'Ecosse, t. ii. pp. 121-137. Treasury Warrant and Acquittance, in the Register House.)

In November 1579, Margaret Carwod and her husband, John Stewart of Tullypowreis, sell their half of Carwod, for 500 merks, to her sister and coheiress,

Janet Carwod, and her husband, John Fleming of Persellands. In March 1584-5, they lend £1000 on mortgage at £10 per cent., to Francis Hay, Master of Erroll.—(Register of Deeds, vol. xvii. foll. 281, 282 ; vol. xxiii. foll. 242, 243. MS. Register House.)

[1] The casquet bequeathed by the Queen to Margaret Carwod in 1566, is described as ' vne petite boyt dargent' (p. 124).

The casquet said to have been given by the Queen to Bothwell, and to have been seized in the hands of his servant, in 1567, is described by the Regent Murray in 1568 as ' a silver box ;' by the Privy Council in 1568 and 1571 as ' ane silver box owergilt with gold ;' more fully in the Scottish version of Buchanan's ' Detectioun,' printed at St. Andrews in 1572, as ' ane small gylt coffer not fully ane fute lang, being garnischit in sindrie places with the Romane lettre F. under ane Kingis crowne ;' and in Buchanan's History, printed in 1582, as ' arculam argenteam literis undique inscriptam, quae indicarent eam aliquando Francisci Regis Francorum fuisse.'—(Anderson's Collections relating to Queen Mary, vol. ii. pp. 92, 257, 259. G. Buchanani Rerum Scoticarum Historia, lib. xviii. cap. 51.)

The Queen's handwriting, said to have been found in the casket, is described as ' Romane,'—that is, the character which we should now call Italic, then scarcely known in Scotland, except among those who had been educated abroad, and only beginning in France to displace the old Middle Age or Gothic character. Shakespere, writing about 1602, makes Malvolio in the Twelfth Night speak of ' the sweet Roman hand' of the letter by which he was befooled. The difference between the two styles will be seen by a glance at the facsimile of the Testamentary Inventory, where the Gothic of the Queen's secretary contrasts with the Roman of the Queen herself.

[2] P. 113 : ' Aus filles.'

is to be shared among her three bedchamber women;[1] and her plate and furniture is to be sold, that the price may be divided among her valets, grooms, tapestry-men, ushers, and others.[2]

In a postscript written with her own hand, Mary leaves her Greek and Latin books to be the beginning of a library[3] for the University of St. Andrews. The legacy would have been no inconsiderable one if it had taken effect; but the Queen's praiseworthy design for the advancement of learning in the ecclesiastical capital of her kingdom, was left to be fulfilled fifty years afterwards by her son, King James, and her grandchildren, Prince Henry, Prince Charles, and the Princess Elizabeth.[4]

Bequest of the Queen's Greek and Latin books to the University of St. Andrews.

The Testamentary Inventory of Mary's Jewels is followed by lists of articles delivered from the wardrobe at Holyrood in each month, from August 1561, when the Queen landed at Leith, until June 1567, when her marriage with Bothwell arrayed her nobles in arms against her.[5]

Inventories of things given out from the Wardrobe, from August 1561 till June 1567.

---

[1] P. 124: 'Ie laysse mon linge entre mes troys fammes.'

[2] P. 124: 'Ie laysse. . . ma chambre et la vay-selle de mes cofres entre les vallets de fourieres tapissiers et huissiers pour etre vandu a leur profit et des troys filles qui la guardent.'

'Chambre' seems to be used here to signify not the Queen's chamber, but its furniture. 'Le mot *chambre*,' says M. Douët-d'Arcq, 'ne s'entend pas d'une pièce faisant partie d'un appartement, mais du lit et de la tenture d'une chambre à coucher.'—(Comptes de l'Argenterie des Rois de France, p. 358.)

'Vayselle' appears to mean what we should now call plate. 'Cette expression,' says M. le Comte de Laborde, 'répond à l'idée qu'on se faisait encore, il y a soixante ans, du mot argenterie . . . Elle se composait de vases de toutes sortes (vaissels), plats, etc.' —(Notice des Emaux, par. ii. 'Glossaire,' p. 531.)

Not only plate, but cloth, dresses, and jewels were kept in the coffers of the Queen's chamber, as we learn from the 'Memoyre de tout ce que je [Servais de

Conde] prin dens les coffres de la chambre tant durant le temps que la Royne estoict a Loclin que depuys comansant en Jullet mil v[e] lxvii,' printed from the original (formerly in the Scottish College at Paris) in Illustrations of the Reigns of Queen Mary and King James VI., pp. 12-19. Maitland Club: 1834.

[3] P. 124: 'Ie laysse mes liuures qui y sont ceulx en Grec ou Latin a luniuersite de Sintandre pour y commancer vne bible.'

[4] The University Library of St. Andrews was founded in 1612, by King James VI., *ne sint magistri sine libris*, as he said. Lists of the volumes presented by him, by Prince Henry, Prince Charles, Queen Anne, and the Princess Elizabeth, are printed in the Miscellany of the Maitland Club, vol. i. pp. 322-326. Among them are copies of some of the books bequeathed by Queen Mary, such as the 'Commentarii Linguae Graecae' of Budaeus, the 'Commentarii Reipublicae Romanae' of Wolfgangus Lazius, etc.

[5] Pp. 125-176.

They are printed for the first time from the origi-

; Fool.

One of the first entries is of canvas for a bed to a female Fool, Nichola, or La Jardiniere,[1] whom the Queen brought with her from France. The poor creature lingered in Scotland, until the gates of an English prison had closed for ever upon her mistress, when the bounty of the Regent Lennox enabled her to make her way back to her own country.[2] She was not the only one of her unfortunate class in the Scottish court. A few days after the marriage which made Darnley a King, we find a dress of green velvet, and two blue bonnets with plumes given to his Fool.[3] Elsewhere we have record of payments from the treasury to other Fools of both sexes.[4]

Mary's French escort were shocked, like herself, by the signs of want and rudeness which they saw among her people. But there was one exception to the prevailing poverty, and even to eyes familiar with what the wealth of France and the renascent art of Italy had done for Amboise and for Fontaine-

---

nals in the Register House. The account of every year is authenticated by the Queen's sign manual. The account of the year 1566 shows itself to have been made up and authenticated on the 31st of May 1567.

Many of the entries have numbers (printed within parentheses) referring to corresponding numbers in older Inventories printed in the text.

The Inventory of the Queen Regent's moveables delivered to Servais de Conde, in September 1561 (pp. 18-27) is referred to at p. 127 (94) ; p. 129 (78) ; p. 130 (50) ; p. 131 (88), (46) ; p. 132 (82), (84), (85), (92), (93), (83) ; p. 137 (29) ; p. 138 (72), (73), (75), (76), (79) ; p. 139 (87) ; p. 140 (81) ; p. 142 (90), (50. 51. 52), (53. 54) ; p. 151 (96), (55) ; p. 152 (96), (91) ; p. 156 (80. 74), (89) ; p. 158 (86) ; p. 168 (10) ; p. 176 (81).

The Inventory of the Queen's moveables in Holyrood, in November 1561 (pp. 28-48) is referred to at p. 137 (50) ; p. 139 (120) ; p. 140 (51) ; p. 151 (144) ; p. 152 (119) ; p. 153 (17) ; p. 155 (118) ; p. 156 (125), (117) ; p. 157 (37. 38), (55. 99. 102. 100), (50) ; p. 161 (146) ; p. 162 (128) ; p. 163 (128), (143), (126), (142), (127) ; p. 164 (122) ; p. 165 (58) ; p. 167 (23), (121) ; p. 168 (58. 59) ; p. 169 (23) ; p. 174 (21).

The Inventory of the Earl of Huntly's moveables brought to Holyrood in December 1562 (pp.

49-56) is referred to at p. 165, (9 H) ; and p. 166 (9 H).

[1] Pp. 125-127, 130, 137, 142, 143, 146, 64.

[2] In August 1570, there was a payment from the Treasury of £15 'be the Regentis speciale command to Nichola the Fule to mak hir expensis and fraucht to France.'

Jacqueline Critoflat, the bedchamber woman charged with the custody of Nichola la Jardiniere (pp. 126, 127, 130, 137, 143-145, 147), had prepared for her departure three years before. In August 1567, there was a payment from the Treasury of £10 to 'Critoflat, keipar of the Quenis grace Fule, to pay her dettis to pas to France.' But payments continued to be made 'to Nichola the Fule and hir keipar,' until Christmas 1569.

[3] P. 156.

[4] There are payments from the Treasury to Janet Musche, fool, in April 1562 ; to 'Foysir the fule,' and 'to the man that keipis him,' in August 1565 ; to James Geddie, fool, in September 1565, May 1567 and September 1569 ; to 'Conny,' in January 1565-6, for a dress the same as that given at the same time to La Jardiniere ; to Jane Colquhoun, fool, in October 1566 and April 1567 ; and to George Steiwin or Geordie Styne, fool, in February 1566-7.—(Compota Thesaurariorum Reginae Scotorum. MS. Register House.)

bleau, Holyrood seemed a fine building.[1] We see from the accounts in the text, that it had a richly furnished chapel,[2] a ball-room glowing with heraldry,[3] a well-filled library carpeted with green cloth ;[4] and that among the Queen's private apartments were a hall or dining-room, hung with black velvet,[5] and a cabinet or drawing-room draped with green and crimson cloth.[6] The sense of insecurity which threw its shadow over these refinements, is shown by what we learn elsewhere, that the chief entrance to the Palace lay across a drawbridge, through a ponderous iron gate, fastened by two great bolts and a huge bar of iron ; that even the windows of the state-rooms had iron gratings; and that in the very heart of the pile, the passage which led from the royal chambers on one floor to the royal chambers on another floor, was guarded by a gate of iron.[7] Holyrood, doubtless, looked all the fairer to its French visitors, that it was built in the new style of French architecture. King James the Fifth seems, early in his reign, to have had French masons in his pay ; he brought one of them back from Orleans, when he returned from France with his first bride ;[8] the Duke

---

[1] ' L'Abbaye de l'Islebourg . . . est certes un beau bastiment, et ne tient rien du pays.'—(Brantôme, t. v. p. 95.)

Dr. Alexander Ales, who wrote an account of Edinburgh in Sebastian Munster's Cosmography, printed at Basle in 1550, describes Holyrood as ' palatium amplissimum et superbissimum.'—(The Bannatyne Miscellany, vol. i. p. 188.)

[2] Pp. 157, 36, 40, 41.

In February 1561-2, there was a payment from the Treasury of £10 to William Makdowale, the Master of Works, as a reward for the recovery of a pair of organs which had been carried away. They seem to have been bought for the Palace Chapel in August 1557, at the price of £36.

[3] P. 145.

[4] P. 126.

[5] P. 126.

[6] P. 126.

[7] The accounts of the Masters of Works at Holyrood in 1529-30, show payments for ' an gret irne yeit for the principall entress and draw brig of the new toure with twa gret boltis for the closing of the sloit of the said irne yeit and the greit bar of the samyn ;'

for ' ane irne bar to the treyne dure wythout the irne yet ;' for ' mendyng the lok of the litill irne yet vndyr the Kingis Grace awine chalmir in the southt tour ;' for ' ane irne yet in ane passage betuix the Kingis Grace over chalmeris and nethir chalmeris ;' for ' maid irne werk in a draw bar to the inner chalmer dure ;' for ' xxij stanis and ane half maid irne werk in ane gret bvnde window in the gret chalmer of the tour,' etc.

We have no contemporary picture of the Holyrood of Queen Mary. But the French features of the building, before it was altered and rebuilt by King Charles II. nearly as we now see it, are obvious enough in the drawings of James Gordon, parson of Rothiemay, engraved in Holland about 1647, and reproduced in the Bannatyne Miscellany, vol. i. p. 188 ; and in the Liber Cartarum Sancte Crucis, pref. p. lxxvi.

[8] By a writ dated at Orleans, on the 1st December 1536, King James v. appointed Mogin Martyne, Frenchman, sometime master mason of Dunbar Castle, to be master mason to the King, during his Grace's pleasure, with a salary of £60 a year, besides the ordinary wages of other masons, when employed on the King's works.—(Registrum Secreti Sigilli, t. xi. fol. 1. MS. Register House.)

of Guise, the father of his second, sent him six others ;[1] and Frenchmen held
the office of master masons to the Crown, and continued to work on the Scottish palaces throughout the reign of Mary.[2]   The traces of their art, now all
but obliterated at Holyrood, may still be perceived at Linlithgow, which
Mary of Guise is said to have praised as one of the most princely piles which
she had seen ; and they are yet more conspicuous at Falkland and at Stirling.
Nor was it in building only that French taste showed its influence in Scotland.
Frenchmen were employed to lay out our gardens ;[3] we gave work to French

French masons
in Scotland :
Thomas French ;

The name of Martyne's predecessor in office,
Thomas French, would seem to show that he too was
a Frenchman, or of French extraction. He is found
at work at Linlithgow in 1532.   Three years later,
he was made master mason to the King, for life, with
a salary of £30 a year.   One of his sons, turning his
steps northwards, built the south transept of the
cathedral of Aberdeen, and the fine bridge of seven
arches over the neighbouring Dee.—(Waldie's History
of Linlithgow, pp. 63, 64.   Registrum Secreti Sigilli,
t. x. fol. 6. MS. Register House.   Kennedy's Annals
of Aberdeen, vol. ii. p. 346.)

John Morow ;

An inscription of about the year 1500 still remains
to attest that John Morow, a native of Paris, had
charge of the mason-work of the cathedrals of St.
Andrews and Glasgow, the abbeys of Melrose and
Paisley, and the churches of Nithsdale and Galloway.
—(Proceedings of the Antiquaries of Scotland, vol.
ii. pp. 166-175.)

King James IV., as we see from his Treasury accounts, had an Italian mason in his pay, in the last
years of his reign.

Six French ma-
sons sent to Scot-
land by the Duke
of Guise ;

[1] Letters from the Duchess of Guise to her daughter Queen Mary of Guise, quoted by M. Francisque-
Michel, in his Les Ecossais en France, t. i. pp. 430,
431.

In July 1539, there was a payment from the Scottish
Treasury of £10, 'for the vj masonis quhilk the Duke
of Gwyse send to the Kingis Grace ;' and of £15 'for
the fraucht of jm speris with the said masonis furtht
of France to Leith.'—(Compotum Thesaurarii Regis
Scotorum. MS. Register House.)

Nicholas Roy ;

[2] By a writ, dated at Falkland in April 1539, King
James V. appointed Nicholas Roy, Frenchman, to be
master-mason to the King, during his Grace's pleasure,
with a salary of £80, besides the ordinary wages of
other masons, when employed on the King's works.

—(Registrum Secreti Sigilli, t. xiii. fol. 29. MS.
Register House.)

In January 1541-2, there was a payment from the
Treasury of £4, 6s. 8d. 'to the Frenche maister
masoun.'—(Compotum Thesaurarii Regis Scotorum.
MS. Register House.)   The name of 'Mr Nicholas
Roy, macon,' appears in a roll of the Queen's house-
hold about the year 1548.

John Roytell.

By a writ dated at Stirling, in March 1556-7, John
Roytell, Frenchman, was made principal master mason
to all the Queen's works, for life, with a salary of £50
a year.   He still held his office in November 1565.
He was made a burgess of Edinburgh in September
1550, at the request of the Prior of Holyrood, who
had feasted the provost and baillies the day before :
'ad requestum Prioris monasterii Sancte Crucis qui
prepositum et balliuos in dicto monasterio predie exis-
tentes eosdem bene tractabat.'—(Register of the Guild
of Edinburgh, vol. i., 10 Dec. 1550. MS. in the City
Archives.   Registrum Secreti Sigilli, vol. xxviii. fol.
62. MS. Register House.   Compota Thesaurarii Reginae Scotorum, Septemb.-Novemb. 1565. MS. Register House.)

French gardeners
in Scotland.

[3] By a writ, dated at Stirling, in August 1536, King
James V. made Bertram Galawtre, Frenchman, principal gardener of the King's yards and gardens, for
life, with a salary of £50 a year.—(Registrum Secreti
Sigilli, t. x. fol. 142. MS. Register House.)

A year or two later we find a French gardener,
brought to Scotland by the Cistercians of Kinloss, in
great repute throughout Murray.—(J. Ferrerii Historia Abbatum de Kynlos, p. 48. Bannatyne Club :
1839.)

King James IV. had a French gardener in his
pay in 1503 and 1504.—(Compotum Thesaurarii
Regis Scotorum 1502-4, foll. 110, 158. MS. Register
House.)

wrights, to French smiths, to French plasterers;[1] we followed French fashions at our tables, in our dress, in our manners;[2] French words made their way into our speech; French leeches dressed our wounds;[3] French dances were to be seen at our country fairs and on our village greens;[4] and Knox had to lament that in the masques and pageants which welcomed Mary's entry into her capital, the Reformed burghers—'fools,' as he calls them—aped the style of France.[5]

[1] Compotum Thesaurarii Regis Scotorum, 1502-4, foll. 113, 123, 145, 155. MS. Register House.

French fashions in Scotland.

[2] 'Here it is to be remembred,' says the Bishop of Ross, writing of the marriage of King James V. with Magdalene of France in 1537, 'that thair wes mony new ingynis and devysis, alsweill of bigging of paleicis, abilyementis, as of banquating and of menis behaviour, first begun and used in Scotland at this tyme, efter the fassione quhilk thay had sene in France. Albeit it semit to be varray comlie and beautifull, yit it wes moir superfluows and volupteous nor the substaunce of the realme of Scotland mycht beir furth or susteine; nottheles, the same fassionis and custome of coistlie abilyements indifferentlie used be all estatis, excessive banquating and sic lik, remanis yit to thir dayis' [the Bishop wrote about 1569], 'to the greit hinder and povartie of the hole realme.'—(Bishop Lesley's History of Scotland, p. 154. Cf. Sir James Melville's Memoirs, pp. 392, 393.)

French surgeons in Scotland.

[3] Compotum Thesaurarii Regis Scotorum 1502-4, foll. 129, 132. MS. Register House.

Queen Mary of Guise brought with her a French midwife and a French surgeon. The surgeon, Master John Cardelle, had letters of naturalization in 1558. The services of the midwife were secured by liberal pensions to her son and daughter in France.—(Registrum Magni Sigilli, lib. xxxii. no. 247. MS. Register House. Etat de Finances de notre petit filz le Duc de Longueville, 1539-1540. MS. Register House.)

The French gardener of Kinloss had some skill in surgery, gained probably by his loss of a limb in the wars of King Francis I. His leechcraft stood him in good service in Scotland: 'est etiam peritus chirurgiae, ut qui multos juverit in obligandis vulneribus toto hoc quinquennio per universam Moraviam.'—(J. Ferrerii Historia Abbatum de Kynlos, p. 48.)

Neither physicians nor surgeons were too plentiful in Scotland in the middle of the sixteenth century; but the younger Scaliger, who was at Holyrood in 1566, has greatly exaggerated the deficiency: 'Lors que mon frere fut en Escosse, il n'y avoit qu'un mede-

cin qui estoit medecin de la Reyne; et de mon temps en Angleterre, il n'y avoit gueres de medecins. En Escosse un menuisier saignoit, et il y avoit des barbiers qui tondoient seulement.'—(Scaligerana, pp. 365, 366, edit. 1695.)

It may be enough to say in answer to this, that a chair of medicine was founded in the University of Aberdeen in the reign of King James IV.; that King James V. had a physician, a surgeon, and an apothecary in his household, all of them Scots (the physician, it may be added, a son of the same old northern house which gave birth to Dr. John Arbuthnott, the friend of Pope and Swift, and the physician of Queen Anne); that Queen Mary had two physicians, a surgeon, and an apothecary; that the surgeons and barbers of Edinburgh were incorporated in 1505, and had an extension of their privileges from Queen Mary; that the barbers or 'leechers' of Aberdeen were incorporated in 1537; that, in 1568, a treatise on the plague was published at Edinburgh by Dr. Gilbert Skene; that, in 1579, the Earl of Atholl, who died at Kincardine in Perthshire, was attended by two doctors of medicine, both physicians to the King (Mr. Gilbert Moncreiff, who had a fee of £40, and Dr. Alexander Preston, who had a fee of £30), and by an 'Ireland leche,' one of the hereditary doctors of the Highlands, who had a fee of £10.—(Register of Confirmed Testaments in the Commissariot of Edinburgh, vol. viii. 26. Dec 1580. MS. Register House. Registrum Secreti Sigilli, vol. vi. fol. 7; vol. vii. fol. 6; vol. ix. fol. 116; vol. xix. fol. 44; vol. xxxviii. fol. 23. MS. Register House. M. Teulet, Papiers d'Etat relatifs à l'Histoire de l'Ecosse, t. ii. p. 126. Kennedy's Annals of Aberdeen, vol. ii. p. 173. Rotuli Scaccarii Regum Scotorum, no. 382. MS. Register House.)

[4] 'Auld lightfute thair he did forleit,
    And counterfuttet Fransss.'

—(Christis Kirk on the Grene, stanza v.)

[5] 'Great preparationis war maid for hir enteress in the town. In ferses, in masking, and in other prodigalities, faine wold fooles have counterfooted France.

When the Queen came to Scotland, the Court was still in full mourning for her husband, the King of France. It went into half mourning [1] on the first anniversary of his death, a day which seems to have been solemnly kept. Mass was said for his soul's repose in presence of the Queen, who made an offering of a great wax candle trimmed with black velvet; [2] and although few or none of her nobles attended, no point of the accustomed obsequies was omitted. [3] Mary would appear to have delighted in these more picturesque rites of her religion. We see her carrying tapers at Candlemas; [4] and washing the feet of the poor on Maundy Thursday. [5] This

Obsequies of King Francis II.

Candlemas.

Maundy Thursday.

—(Knox's History of the Reformation, vol. ii. pp. 287, 288.)

The plays and pageants which moved the Reformer's scorn, are described by an admiring hand, in the Diurnal of Occurrents, pp. 67-69.

[1] P. 129.

[2] P. 129 : 'Plus je deliure a Henry clerc de chapelle demi quartier de velours noir pour mettre a cierge de la Royne le jour du bout de lan du feu Roy.'

[3] Randolph, writing to Cecil on the 7th December 1561, says that the French ambassador, Paul de Foix, ' being admonished by some friend, came not unto the *Dirige* or mass upon Friday and Saturday [the 5th and 6th December] last, to the great misliking of the Queen. Moret [the ambassador from the Duke of Savoy] was there at both. She observed the old manner in all her doings ; she could not perswade nor get one Lord of her own to wear the deule for that day, not so much as the Earl Bothwell. . . . This [Sunday] is another day of mirth and pastime [running at the ring] upon the sands of Leith, where the Queen will be herself, to signify the sorrow of her heart after her soul mass.'—(Bishop Keith's History of Scotland, vol. ii. pp. 122, 123.)

[4] P. 131.

Carrying candles at Candlemas.

In 1565-66, Randolph tells Cecil that ' upon Candlemas daye, there carryed their candles with the Quene, her husbande, th'Earle of Lennox, and Earle Atholl.'—(Mr. T. Wright's Queen Elizabeth and her Times, vol. i. p. 220. Cf. Calendar of State Papers relating to Scotland, vol. ii. p. 835.)

Among schoolboys in the north, the observance survived the signing of the Covenant : ' Vpone the second of Februar [1643], being Candlemes day, the barnis of the Oldtoun [of Aberdeen] gramar scooll . . .

with candles lichtit in there handis, crying, reioysing, and blyth aneuche . . . about sex houris at night, cam . . . vp the yet to the Cross, and round about gois diuerss tymes, clyms to the heid thairof, and set on ane burning torche thairvpone . . . Attour thay went doun fra the Cross, convoying Johne Keith, brother to the Erll Marschall, who wes there King, to his lodging in the Channonrie, with licht candles.'—(Spalding's Memorialls of the Trubles, vol. ii. p. 229, edit. Aberd. 1851.)

[5] The day before Good Friday—the ' Coena Domini' of the Latin Church, the ' Maundy Thursday' and ' Shere Thursday' of England, ' le jour de la Cene' of France—was known in Scotland as ' Skyre Thurisday,' or ' Skir Furisday' (p. 52). As many poor maidens, as there were years in the Queen's age, had their feet washed by her, and were each of them presented with five quarters of linen, at 5s., 6s., or 6s. 8d. a yard, and with two yards of white kersey, at 15s. or 16s. a yard. The Queen had an apron and towel of cambric, at 40s. or 45s. a yard ; her attendants had aprons and towels of holland, at 20s. or 22s. a yard. In 1566, the King took part in the ceremony, having, like the Queen, an apron and towel of cambric. On this occasion, besides the twenty-four maidens whose feet were washed by the Queen, the King seems to have washed the feet of thirteen poor virgins, and to have given to each of them three and a-half yards of fine red cloth, at 24s. a yard. In 1567, when the Queen held her last Maundy at Holyrood, she was attended by nine ladies and maids of honour, seven maids and their governess, seven bedchamber women, eleven masters of household and gentlemen (including a doctor of theology, a physician, a secretary, an apothecary, a comptroller, an al-

Washing the feet of the poor on Maundy Thursday.

latter ceremony, indeed, passed into the Reformed Church ;[1] it was performed in person by Queen Elizabeth, and by more than one of her successors on the English throne ; and not much more than a century has elapsed since the

moner, etc.), nine valets of her chamber, one usher of her chamber, and ten officers (including two purveyors, an equerry, a barber, etc.) The first lady of honour was waited on by two maids ; the masters of household by three gentlemen ; the purveyors by two servants. The charge for two and a half yards of ' toille baptiste' or cambric was £5 ; for forty yards of holland, £40 ; for forty-four yards of ' small' or ' Scotch' linen, £14, 13s. 4d. ; for fifty yards of white kersey, £40 ; for forty yards of ' toille de Bretaine,' ' Bartane claithe,' or cloth of Brittany (used, it would seem, for carpeting), £20 ; in all, £119, 13s. 4d.—(Compota Thesaurariorum Reginae Scotorum, Mar. 1561-2, Apr. 1565, Apr. 1566, Apr. 1567. MS. Register House. Memoire du linge necessaire pour le jour de la Cene faict la ij^me d'Aprill mil v^e soixante sept. MS. Register House.)

Mary had made preparation for a Skyre Thursday which she was not suffered to keep. ' Certen clothe bought at Chartley for her intended Mawndye,' in 1586, was found in her rooms at Fotheringhay, after her execution. The observance was stopped by Sir Amias Poulet, the same stern jailer who tore down her cloth of state.—(Prince Labanoff, Lettres de Marie Stuart, t. vii. p. 272. Calendar of State Papers relating to Scotland, vol. ii. p. 986.)

[1] It seems, however, to have early become unpopular in Scotland. Robert Bowes, the English ambassador at Holyrood, writes to Sir Francis Walsingham, in April 1583, that the people of Edinburgh are raging against M. Meyneville, the French envoy, ' to see both his priest kept amongst them, and (as they think) saying mass, and also himself keeping his Maundy solemnity like a king, and passing to holy saints and wells on pilgrimage ; which thing they think to be done in such contempt against the religion of their laws, as the King is busily occupied to suppress their passions.' Walsingham, in reply, instructs Bowes to advise the King of Scots of the inconvenience of M. Meyneville's ' stout and insolent speeches, and his observance of the ceremonies of the Romish religion, especially in the late keeping of the Maundy, a thing very offensive to the subjects of the King of Scots.'—(Correspondence of Robert Bowes of Aske, p. 399. Surtees Society : 1842. Calendar of State Papers relating to Scotland, vol. i. p. 439.)

Two years afterwards, we find the King giving ' nynetein gownis of blew claith, nynetein pursis, and in ilk purse nynetein schillingis to nynetein aigit men, according to the yeiris of his Hienes aige.' But the bounty was given, not on the Thursday before Easter, but on the King's birthday in June.—(Compotum Thesaurarii Regis Scotorum, Jun. 1585. MS. Register House.) *King James the Sixth's Maundy.*

In the sixth century, the monks of Iona washed the feet of strangers who visited their monastery.—(Dr. Reeves's Adamnan's Life of St. Columba, pp. 27, 345.) *Maundy at Iona.*

In the same age, if we may trust a writer of the twelfth century, the Apostle of Strathclyde kept his Maundy yearly at Glasgow : ' in Coena Domini, post confectionem sacri crismatis et olei, prius multitudinis pauperum, et postea leprosorum, pedes propriis manibus cum lacrimis lavans, et capillis tergens ac crebris osculis demulcens, ad mensem postea ipse diligenter illis ministrabat.'—(Jocelin of Furnes, Vita S. Kentegerni, c. xvii., in Pinkerton's Vitae Antiquae Sanctorum Scotiae, p. 231.) *St. Mungo's Maundy.*

We have record of the Maundy of the Scottish Kings—' Mandatum in Coena Domini '—towards the end of the eleventh century. The Bishop of St. Andrews describes its religious observance by St. Margaret and her husband King Malcolm : ' inter haec trecentos pauperes in Regiam aulam consuetudo erat introduci ; quibus per ordinem circumsedentibus, cum Rex et Regina ingrederentur, a ministris ostia claudebantur ; exceptis enim capellanis quibusdam religiosis et aliquibus ministris, illorum eleemosynae operibus interesse nulli licuerat. Rex ex una, Regina vero ex altera parte, Christo in pauperibus servierunt : magnaque cum devotione cibos et potum, specialiter ad hoc praeparatos, obtulerunt.'—(Turgot, Vita S. Margaretae, cap. iii. §§ 18, 21-23, in the Acta Sanctorum, Jun. t. ii. pp. 332, 333.) *St. Margaret's Maundy.*

The example of St. Margaret was followed by her daughter ' the good Queen Maud,' the wife of King Henry I. of England. Her brother, King David of Scotland, told St. Aelred of Rievaux, how, on entering her chamber one evening, he found her washing the feet of lepers : ' ecce domus plena leprosis, et Regina in medio stans, depositoque pallio, cum se linteo praecinxisset, posita in pelvi aqua, coepit lavare *Queen Matilda's Maundy.*

i

Archbishop of York, as the substitute of King George the Second, discharged the duty in the chapel-royal at Whitehall.[1]

There is repeated mention of the Queen's borrowed ringlets, or perukes,[2] as they are called, which she wore of different colours.[3] At first she seems to have used them only in compliance with the fashion of the day; but what had been merely an ornament, became a necessity when sorrows had whitened and sickness had thinned her hair. The auburn tresses which she laid upon the block at Fotheringhay, were not her own; and when her head dropped from them

---

pedes eorum et extergere, extersosque utrisque constringere manibus, et devotissime osculari.'—(Aelred, Genealogia Regum Anglorum, in Twysden's Historiae Anglicanae Scriptores Decem, col. 368.)

In 1490, King James IV. kept his 'Skyr Thurisday' at Holyrood, and gave 'xviij gray gownis and xviij payre of schone and dublaris [dishes] and coppis [cups] to xviij pure men,' and 'to ilk ane of the xviij men xviij penneis.' The grey gowns were changed into blue at least as early as 1537.—(Compota Thesaurariorum Regum Scotorum. MS. Register House.)

In 1526, King James V., girt with a linen apron, celebrated his Maundy at Holyrood, giving bread, beer, and salt herrings, cod and salmon, to the poor with his own hands: 'per manus Domini Regis in seruicio pauperum.'—(Excerpta e Libris Domicilii Jacobi V., pp. 53, 54, 79. Bannatyne Club: 1836.)

[1] Brand's Popular Antiquities, vol. i. pp. 142-150. edit. 1849.

The Sovereign still gives Maundy alms to an allotted number of poor persons on both sides of Tweed. The dole in London, distributed as of old on Maundy Thursday, is a purse with as many silver pennies as there are years in the Queen's age, some woollen and linen clothing, and a small sum in lieu of the food which was at one time given. Edie Ochiltree in the Antiquary has made every one familiar with the Queen's bedesmen in Scotland. They are now all but extinct. In the Civil Service Estimates for 1862-3 there is a sum of £10 'for alms to Her Majesty's only remaining bedesman, the expense of furnishing him with a gown,' etc.

The observance of Maundy, it seems, is still maintained by one of the Reformed communions in Scotland. The Glassites are said to 'hold by the most literal interpretation of Scripture rules, as concerning the kiss of charity, and the washing of the feet of fellow-disciples'—(Chambers's Encyclopaedia, vol. iv. pp. 784, 785. Lond. 1862.)

[2] P. 130: 'Vne aulne de toille pour acoustrer les perruques de la Royne;' p. 141: 'demie aulne de toille pour faire des ataches pour des perruques pour la Royne;' p. 145: 'vne aulne de toylle pour friser de perruque pour la Royne.'

In October 1567, Servais de Conde sent to the Queen at Lochleven 'plusieurs perruques et aultres telles choses y servant.' In July 1568, he sent to her at Carlisle, after her flight into England, 'ung paque de perruque de cheveux.'—(Illustrations of the Reigns of Queen Mary and King James VI., pp. 14, 16.)

It was at Carlisle that Mary Seton, to the surprise of Sir Francis Knollys, 'among other pretty devices, did set such a curled hair upon the Queen, that was said to be a perewyke, that showed very delicately,' (see above, pp. L, li. note 2). Sir Francis speaks of the peruque in a way which shews that it was then a novelty in England; indeed it is said to have been unknown there until the reign of Queen Elizabeth, who at one time had as many as eighty peruques. But coiffs of Venice gold, 'with ther perukes of here hanging to them, and long labells of coleryd lawne,' are mentioned in the first year of King Edward VL.—(Archaeologia, vol. xxvii. p. 72.)

[3] Nicholas White, who saw the Queen at Tutbury in February 1569, writes to Cecil: 'She is a goodly personage, . . . hath withall an alluring grace, a pretty Scottish accente, and a searching wit, clouded with myldnes . . . Her hair of itself is black, and yet Mr. Knollys told me that she wears hair of sundry colors.' —(Mr. T. Wright's Queen Elizabeth and her Times, vol. i. p. 311.) Brantôme, on the other hand, who last saw Mary at Holyrood in October 1561, describes her hair as fair—'si beaux, si blonds et cendrez' (t. v.

in the executioner's hands, its only covering was seen to be a few short grey hairs on either temple.[1]

We hear of the Queen's hunting gear,[2] of her riding habits,[3] of her mule-litter,[4] of her head-dress of cloth of silver for the Parliament which was broken up by the murder of Riccio.[5] But we miss any trace of the High- The Queen's High-
land dress. land garb[6] which, as we learn elsewhere, was made ready for her journey into Argyll in the summer of 1563. It was an attire of which she would seem to have been fond. She had herself painted in it, and, if she did not wear it in France, must have worn it before she was two months in Scotland; for Brantôme says that he had seen her in it, and that she looked like a goddess.[7]

The Queen's Scottish accent. p. 111.) But he agrees with White in praising her Scottish accent : 'sa langue naturelle, qui de soi est fort rurale, barbare, mal sonnante et seante, elle la parloit de si bonne grace, et la façonnoit de telle sorte, qu'elle la faisoit trouver très belle et très agreable en elle, mais non en autres' (t. v. p. 85). Much of the charm, no doubt, was in her voice, which Brantôme tells us, was 'très douce et très bonne' (t. v. p. 86).

[1] The contemporary French report of the Queen's execution describes her head-dress as 'un voile de linomple, fort beau et blanc . . . un couvrechef fait de linomple en manière de coiffe, et par là-dessous une perruque de cheveux fort bien scéante.' It is added that, when the executioner held up the head, 'il tomba soudainement de ses mains, pour ce qu'il ne l'avoit prise que par la peau de ses cheveux faux.' In a following paragraph we are told that 'la teste estoit nue de cheveux devant et derrière, et razée exprès pour y appliquer quelque cataplasme, et en chaque costé petits cheveux gris, mais non pas beaucoup.'—(M. Teulet, Papiers d'Etat relatifs à l'Histoire de l'Ecosse, t. ii. pp. 879, 881, 883.) We learn from Brantôme that Mary's hair turned grey at thirty-five (t. v. p. 111).

[1] R. Winkfield, an eye-witness, in his letter to Burleigh, from Fotheringhay, 11th February 1586, observed "her borrowed heire auburne," her own hair being "polled verie short," as appeared when the severed head was held forth by the executioner, denuded of its coverings.'—(Mr. Albert Way, Cata- logue of the Museum of the Archaeological Institute, at Edinburgh in 1856, pref. p. xxiv.)

[3] Pp. 146, 150.

[2] Pp. 157, 158.
[4] P. 150.

The Queen's litter. Among the articles in the Castle of Edinburgh, belonging to the King and his mother, in 1578, was 'ane littare lynnit with crammosie satyne and steikit with the harnissing thairto and tua litle chyres in it and a cordoun of silk and gold.'—(Mr. Thomson's Collections of Inventories, p. 239.)

[5] P. 163.

[6] 'The Queen, the Parliament now ended, hath made her Highland apparel for her journey into Argile.'—(Letter from Randolph to Cecil, in Bishop Keith's History of Scotland, vol. ii. p. 201.) There is mention of this journey in the text (p. 138).

King James the Fifth's Highland dress. It appears that when King James v. went to hunt in the Perthshire Highlands, he had 'ane schort Heland coit of variant cullorit veluet,' lined with green taffeta; hose of 'Heland tertane ;' and 'syde Heland sarkis of holland claith.'—(Compotum Thesaurarii Regis Scotorum, Aug. 1538.) John Taylor, the Water Poet, who was at a grand hunt in Braemar in 1618, tells us, in an often quoted passage, that the Highland garb was worn by every one 'as if Licurgus had been there, and made lawes of equality,' adding that, 'as for their attire, any man of what degree so- ever that comes amongst them, must not disdaine to weare it ; for if they doe, then they will disdaine to hunt.'—(The Pennylesse Pilgrimage, cited in the Transactions of the Iona Club, vol. i. part ii. pp. 39, 40.)

[7] 'Estant habillée à la sauvage (comme je l'ay vetie) et à la barbaresque mode des sauvages de son pays, elle paroissoit, en un . . . habit barbare et grossier,

Bishop Lesley describes the dress, which he assures us was very becoming, as a long loose cloak of damask, over a gown which reached to the ankles, and was generally embroidered.[1] Of such Highland mantles, as they were called, the Queen had three, one white, another blue, a third of black frieze, pasmented with gold, and lined with black taffeta.[2] There is here no appearance of tartan, nor does that stuff seem in that day to have been generally worn by the Wild Scot of either sex. The Highlandmen who figured in the pageants at the Prince's baptism at Stirling, in 1566, were clad in goat hides;[3] and a book of costumes, published at Paris in the following year, represents even Highland women as dressed in skins.[4]

une vraye déesse. Ceux qui l'ont veüe habillée le pourront ainsi confesser en toute vérité ; et ceux qui ne l'ont veüe en pourront avoir veu son portrait, estant ainsi habillée.'—(Brantôme, t. v. p. 85.) The 'savages' of Scotland, it need scarcely be added, were the Highlanders,—the ' Wild Scots,' or ' Scoti Sylvestres,' as they were called, both in Britain and on the Continent. See below, p. lxx. note 1.

Dress of Highland women. [1] ' Mulierum autem habitus apud illos decentissimus erat. Nam talari tunicae, arte phrygia vt plurimum confectae, amplas chlamydes quas iam diximus [illas quidem demissas ac fluxas, sed in sinus tamen quosdam, vbi volebant, decenter contractas], atque illas quidem polymitas, superinduerunt. Illarum brachia armillis, ac colla monilibus, elegantius ornata, maximam habent decoris speciem.'—(Bishop Lesley, De Rebus Gestis Scotorum, p. 58.)

Martin, writing at the end of the seventeenth century, describes the costume as not then wholly extinct among the Western Islanders : ' The ancient dress wore by the women, and which is yet wore by some of the vulgar, called *arisad*, is a white plade, having a few small stripes of black, blew, and red ; it reached from the neck to the heels, and was tied before on the breast with a buckle of silver or brass, according to the quality of the person. I have seen some of the former of an hundred marks value ; it was broad as any ordinary pewter plate, the whole curiously engraven with various animals, etc. There was a lesser buckle which was wore in the middle of the larger, and above two ounces weight ; it had in the center a large piece of chrystal, or some finer stone, and this was set all round with several finer stones of a lesser size. The plad being pleated all round, was tied with a belt below the breast ; the belt was of leather, and several pieces of silver intermix'd with the leather like a chain. The lower end of the belt has a piece of plate about eight inches long and three in breadth, curiously engraven ; the end of which was adorned with fine stones, or pieces of red corral. They wore sleeves of scarlet cloth, clos'd at the end as men's vests, with gold lace round 'em, having plate buttons set with fine stones. The head dress was a fine kerchief of linen strait about the head, hanging down the back taper-wise ; a large lock of hair hangs down their cheeks above their breast, the lower end tied with a knot of ribbands.'—(Description of the Western Islands of Scotland, pp. 208, 209, edit. 1703. Cf. the Reverend John Lane Buchanan's Travels in the Western Hebrides from 1782 to 1790, pp. 97-89.)

The Queen's Highland mantles. [2] ' Ane Hieland mantill of blak freis pasmentit with gold and lynit with blak taffetie ; ane blew Hieland mantill ; ane quheit Hieland mantill.'—(Inventair of Jowellis, etc., within the Castell of Edinburgh, pertening to our Soverane Lord and his Hienes derrest Moder, 1578, printed in Mr. Thomson's Collection of Inventories, p. 231.)

Highlanders wear skins. [3] ' For twenty aucht gaitt skynnis quhairof was maid four Hieland wyld mens claithingis from heid to fute price of the peice iiij schillingis summa v pundis xij schillingis.'—(Expensis of Fyreworkis at the Baptisme of my Lord Prince in Striueling, December 1566. MS. Register House.)

[4] I know this book only in the pages of M. Francisque-Michel, who describes it as rare : ' Recueil de la diversité des habits qui sont de present en usage,

There is notice of a velvet glove for the Queen's favourite pastime of shooting at the butts.[1] Nor was archery the only outdoor sport which she practised. Knox tells us that, when summoned to the interview in which she asked his good offices to reconcile the Countess and the Earl of Argyll, he found her hawking on the shores of Lochleven.[2] We hear from an eye-witness how she gave the signal for letting a hound loose upon a wolf during a great hunt in the forest of Athol, when, although the herd broke through the tinchel, about three hundred and sixty deer, five wolves, and a number of wild

The Queen's sports: archery, hawking, hunting.

tant ès pays d'Europe, Asie, Affrique, et Isles sauvages. A Paris, 1567.' Under the engraving of the Highlandwoman is written :

> ' C'est la Sauvage au pays Escossoys
> De peaux vestue encontre la froidure.'

—(Les Ecossais en France, t. ii. pp. 123, 124.)

This may be compared with one of the earliest descriptions of the Highland dress which we have, that of Dr. John Mair, published in 1521 : 'A medio crure ad pedem caligas non habent, chlamyde pro veste superiore, et camisia, croco tincta, amicimtur . . . Tempore belli . . . in panno lineo multipliciter intersuto aut caerato aut picato cum cervinae pellis coopertura vulgus Sylvestrium Scotorum corpus tectum habens in praelium prosilit.'—(Joannes Major, De Rebus Gestis Scotorum, p. 34.)

Highlanders' waxed or tarred shirts.

We hear little more of the common Highlander's upper garment of hides or skins. It would seem to have been disused as woollen stuffs became more plentiful. But his large linen shirt, ornamented with needlework, and smeared with wax, tallow, or tar, long survived. It is mentioned in 1578 by the Bishop of Ross : 'Ex lino quoque amplissima indusia conficiebant, multis sinibus, largioribusque manicis, foris ad genua vsque negligentius fluentia. Haec potentiores croco, alii autem adipe quodam, quo ab omni sorde diutius manerent integra illinebant . . . In his conficiendis, ornatus aut artis omnino cura non videbatur neglecta : siquidem filo cerico, viridi potissimum, aut rubeo, indusiorum singulas partes artificiosissime continuabant.'—(Bishop Lesley, De Rebus Gestis Scotorum, p. 58.)

The tarred shirt seems to have been worn as late as the end of the seventeenth century. It is mentioned by Colonel Cleland in his description of the Highland Host in 1678 :

> ' It's marvelous how in such weather,
> Ov'r hill and hop they came together ;

> How in suche stormes they came so farr ;
> The reason is they're smeared with tar,
> Which doth defend them heel and neck,
> Just as it doth their sheep protect.'

—(Collection of Several Poems and Verses composed upon Various Occasions, p. 13. Printed in the year 1697.)

Lord Macaulay, interpreting this passage, as I think, too literally, has described the Highlanders as 'smeared with tar like sheep.'—(History of England, c. xiii. vol.' iii. p. 306. edit. 1855.)

[1] P. 149.

In April 1562, Randolph writes to Cecil, from St. Andrews, how the Queen and the Master of Lindsay shot at the butts in her privy garden against Mary Livingston and the Earl of Murray. In February 1567, Drury writes to Cecil from St. Andrews, how the Queen and Bothwell won a dinner at Tranent in a shooting match against the Earl of Huntly and Lord Seton. The Queen had butts in her south garden at Holyrood.—(G. Chalmers' Life of Queen Mary, vol. i. p. 109. Miss Strickland's Lives of the Queens of Scotland, vol. iv. p. 95. Mr. Tytler's History of Scotland, vol. v. pp. 390, 516. Compotum Thesaurarii Reginae Scotorum, 27. Mar. 1567. MS. Register House.)

The Queen's shooting matches.

[2] Knox's History of the Reformation, vol. ii. pp. 373-379.)

The Reformer tells us that the Queen spoke to him of ' the offering of a ring to her by the Lord Ruthven' (see above, p. xii. note 1), adding that she did not like his lordship, because, she said, ' I know him to use enchantment.' When at their first interview, in 1561, the Queen told Knox 'that it was said to hir, that all which he did was by necromancye' (see above, pp. xlii., xliii., note 4), the Reformer's answer was a protestation how earnestly he had preached against it : ' And whare they sclander me of magick, nycro-

: goats were slain in one day.[1]   As an instance of her indifference to the King's fate, her adversaries affirmed that, a few days after his murder, she was seen playing golf[2] and pallmall[3] (or croquet as we should now call it) in the fields

mancie, or of any other arte forbidden of God, I have witnesses (besydis my awin conscience) all congregationis that ever heard me, what I spake both against suche artis, and against those that use suche impietie.' —(History of the Reformation, vol. ii. pp. 278, 280.)

[1] 'Anno enim redemptionis nostrae sexagesimo tertio supra sesquimillesimum, Comes Atholiae, ex regio sanguine princeps, venationem ingenti apparatu et magnis sumptibus, optimae atque illustrissimae Reginae Scotiae exhibuit, cui ego tunc adolescens interfui (cuiusmodi venationem *regiam* nostrates appellare solent). Habebat autem Comes ad duo millia Scotorum Montanorum, quos vos hic Scotos Syluestres appellatis, quibus negocium dedit ut ceruos cogerent ex syluis et montibus Atholiae, Badenachae, Marriae, Morauiae, aliisque vicinis regionibus ; atque ad locum agerent venationi destinatum. Illi vero, vt sunt valde pernices et expediti, ita dies noctesque concursarunt, vt intra bimensis tempus amplius duo millia ceruorum cum damis et capreis vnum in locum compulerint : quos Reginae principibusque in valle considentibus, et caeteris qui vna aderant omnibus, visendos venandosque proposuerunt. Sed ita, mihi crede, omnes illi cerui velut agmine composito incedebant (haeret, enim, haerebitque semper id animo spectaculum meo) vt ducem vnum et rectorem cerneres praeeuntem, quem alii quoquo iret subsequebantur : is autem

'Ceruus erat forma praestanti et cornibus ingens.'

Qua ex re non mediocrem animo Regina cepit voluptatem : cepit mox et timorem, vbi ad eam Atholius, qui talibus a pueritia venationibus assnetierat, 'Vides,' inquit, 'ducem illum cornigerum qui turmam praeit ? Periculum nobis ab illo est. Si enim aliquis eum furor timorue ab isto montis dorso in hanc planiciem compulerit, nostrum sibi quisque prospiciat : nemo certe ab iniuria tutus erit, quandoquidem caeteri eum sequentur confertim, et viam sibi ad hunc, qui a tergo est montem, nobis proculcatis statim aperient.' Cuius sententiae veritatem alius illico eventus patefecit. Laxatus enim Reginae iussu atque immissus in lupum insignis admodum ac ferox canis, dum fugientem insequitur, ita ceruum illum ductorem exterruit, vt retro vnde venerat fugam capesseret : cunctique cum eo regressi eruperunt ea parte qua Montanorum corona arctissime cingebantur : ipsis vero Montanis nihil spei, nihil refugii reliquum fuit, nisi vt strati in erica pronos

se proculcari, aut praeteriri paterentur : quorum nonnullos cerui transiliendo vulnerarunt, alterum quoque aut tertium peremerunt, vt statim Reginae nunciatum fuit. Et vero ita glomerati euasissent omnes, ni homines illi venatus peritissimi ipsos e uestigio sequuti, arte quadam extremos ab ipso agmine distraxissent qui mox Reginae et nobilium canibus in praedam cessere. Confecti autem eo die fuerunt circiter trecenti sexaginta, cum quinque lupis et capreis aliquot.'—(Dr. William Barclay, De Regno et Regali Potestate adversus Buchananum, Brutum, Boucherum et reliquos Monarchomachos, lib. ii. pp. 279, 280. edit. Hanov. 1612.)

The writer, a son of the house of Gartley, was born in Aberdeenshire in 1546, became Professor of Law at Angers, and died in France in 1605. Himself a scholar of mark, he was the father of a much more distinguished son, John Barclay, the author of the long famous romance of Argenis, written in Latin which won the admiration of Grotius, and was preferred by Coleridge to the Latin of Livy and of Tacitus.

[2] We first hear of golf in Scotland in 1457, when *Golf.* it was forbidden by Parliament as an unprofitable pastime, which drew the people away from archery and other warlike sports. The prohibition was renewed in 1471, and again in 1491.—(Acts of the Parliaments of Scotland, vol. ii. pp. 48, 100, 226.) Golf was played by Queen Mary's grandfather, King James iv., and by her grandsons Prince Henry and King Charles i. There was a payment from the Treasury, in February 1504, of nine shillings for 'golf clubbes and balles to the King that he playit with.' It is told of Prince Henry that, as he raised his golf-club to strike the ball, a bystander cried out, 'Beware that you hit not Master Newton' (his tutor) when the Prince dropped his club, with the remark, 'Had I done so, I had but paid my debts.'—(Strutt's Sports and Pastimes of the People of England, p. 103. edit. 1830.) It is said that King Charles i. was playing golf on Leith Links when tidings of the Irish rising of 1641 were brought to him.

[3] 'Palemaille' or 'paille-maille' is described by *Pallmall.* Cotgrave in 1611, as 'a game, wherein a round box bowle is with a mallet strucke through a high arch of yron (standing at either end of an alley one) which he

beside Seton.[1]   Among her in-door amusements we find cards,[2] chess[3] (which The Queen's sports : cards, chess, tables.
her son thought too wise and philosophical[4]), tables or backgammon,[5] and a
company of puppets.[6]   These last-named toys had recently been brought to Her puppet show.

that can do at the fewest blowes, or at the number
agreed on, winnes.'

[1] 'Few dayes eftir the murthir remaining at Haly-
rudehous, she past to Seytoun, exercing hir one day
richt oppinlie at the feildis with the palmall and goif.'
—(Articles given in by the Earl of Murray to Queen
Elizabeth's Commissioners at Westminster, on the 6th
December 1568. Hopetoun MS.)

Mr. Malcolm Laing, who had never seen these
Articles, has an argument of some length to show that
they were 'undoubtedly the same' with Buchanan's
Detection. Camden, with better information, had
rightly distinguished between the two documents.—
(M. Laing's History of Scotland, vol. i. pp. 161, 169,
241-243, 309.)

Cards.

[2] 'Be the Quenis Grace speciale command to
Robert Makesone ane of the virlottis of hir Grace
chalmer to gif hir Maiestie to play at the cartis, fyftie
pundis.'—(Compotum Thesaurarii Reginae Scotorum,
30. Nov. 1565. MS. Register House.)

When King James IV. waited on his bride, the
Princess Margaret of England, at Newbattle, he found
her playing cards. They were a favourite amusement
at his court, as well as at the court of his son, King
James V., as we learn from the verse of Sir David
Lindsay.

Chess.

[3] There is more than one set of chess pieces in the
Inventory of the Jewels and other articles in the Castle
of Edinburgh belonging to the King and his Mother,
in 1578 : 'Ane quhite polk of greit chas men of
bane ; ane litle grene polk with sum chas men ; ane
quhite buist with chas men in personages of woid.'—
(Mr. Thomson's Collection of Inventories, pp. 238,
240.)

Sir Frederic Madden has exhausted the antiquities
of chess in Europe, in his admirable paper on the
fine chess men carved in walrus tusk, supposed
to be of the twelfth century, found in the island of
Lewis, and now divided between the British Museum
and Lord Londesborough.—(Archaeologia, vol. xxiv.
pp. 203-291.) The game was so popular in Scotland
in that age that we discover a maker of chessmen
and tablemen (or backgammon men) in a hamlet near
Melrose in 1166. He worked in deer horn and bone.
—(Reginaldi Dunelmensis Libellus de Beati Cuthberti
Virtutibus, pp. 185-188. Surtees Society : 1835.)

'The chesse,' or, 'the chesses' appears to have
been a favourite game of King James I.—(Cronycle of
the Death of James Stewarde, Kynge of Scotys, in
Pinkerton's History of Scotland, vol. i. pp. 466, 467.)

[4] 'As for the chesse, I thinke it ouer fonde, be- King James VI. on games and pastimes.
cause it is ouer wise and philosophicke a follie.'—
(BAΣIΛIKON ΔΩPON, or His Maiesties Instrvctions
to his dearest sonne, Henry the Prince, p. 125. edit.
1603.) The King recommends 'archery, palle maille,
and suche like faire and pleasant field games.' 'As for
hawking,' he says, 'I condemne it not ; but I must
praise it more sparinglie, because it neither resembleth
the warres so neere as hunting doth in making a man
hardie and skilfullie ridden in all grounds, and is
more vncertaine and subject to mischances, and
(whiche is worst of all) is there-through an extreame
stirrer vp of passions.' He will not join in the cen-
sure of all games of hazard : 'when it is foule and
stormie weather, then, I say, may ye lawfully play at
the carts or tables.'

[5] Mr. Thomson's Collection of Inventories, p. 241 : Tables.
'Ane polk with table men.'

King James I. played at 'the tables' on the night
of his murder at Perth in 1437. The Treasury Accounts
show us King James IV. playing at 'the tables,' in
Montrose, with old Earl Archibald Bell the Cat.

[6] P. 139 : 'deux chanteaux de damas gris broche Puppets.
dor pour faire vne robbe a vne poupine ;' 'trois
quartz et demi de toille dargent et de soye blanche
pour faire vne cotte et aultre chose a des poupines.'

It would appear from the Inventory of 1578 that the
set, when complete, had been of thirty-eight pieces,
half of one sex and half of the other : 'Ane coffer
quhairin is contenit certane pictouris of wemen callit
pippenis, being in nomber fourtene mekle and litle,
fyftene vardingaill for thame, nynetene gownis kirtillis
and vaskenis for thame, ane packet of sairkis slevis
and hois for thame, thair pantonis, ane packet with ane
furnist bed, ane uther packett of litle consaittis and
triffilis of bittis of crisp and utheris, tua dussane and
ane half of masking visouris :' 'Ane litle buist grene
paintit on the cover with nynetene portratouris of
men on horsbak and utheris fantaseis of evir bane and
woid :' 'Ane creill with sum bulyettis of tymmer and
pippennis.'—(Mr. Thomson's Collection of Inventories, pp. 238, 240.)

great perfection in Italy, and were then and for a century afterwards in especial favour in high places.[1]

The Queen's masques.

We have more interest in those frequent Masques,[2] or Triumphs, as they were called, in which Knox appears to have seen nothing but folly or sin,[3] although Murray approved them by more than his presence, and Buchanan adorned them with the fruits of his genius and the spoils of his learning. Scarcely any feast or solemnity seems to have been thought complete without them. In some cases, the Queen and her court played the chief parts; in others, the valets of her chamber, or, if she were the guest of the city, the young burghers, were the actors. In every instance there was an attempt, by dress or otherwise, to personate character. Occasionally the performance was only dumb show, but more frequently the performers sang or recited verses, with or without the help of music from one or more instruments. At times the skill of the carpenter was tasked for machinery, and the craft of the painter for some sort of decoration.

Her entry into Edinburgh.

The first Masques of which we hear were on the great day of the Queen's entry into her capital, a fortnight after her return from France. Leaving Holyrood, Mary rode along the terrace on which Princes Street now stands, and winding up the green bank which was washed by the North Loch, passed into the Castle. The cannon thundered as she left its gates, after dining with her nobles at noon, and rode down the Castlehill, where she was met by an escort of fifty young citizens, in the guise of Moors, with jewelled rings in their mouths, and gilded chains on their necks and limbs. The Queen now took her place under a pall of purple velvet, with fringes of gold and

---

[1] M. Charles Magnin, the learned and amusing historian of the puppet show, writing of the reign of King Lewis XIV. of France says: 'Les marionnettes étaient alors un plaisir royal, que recherchaient, par imitation, la noblesse et la bourgeoise.'—(Histoire des Marionnettes en Europe, p. 189. edit. 1862.)

[2] Pp. 73, 127, 128, 133, 136, 138, 141, 144, 145, 162, 167, 185, 186.

[3] Knox's History of the Reformation, vol. ii. pp. 287, 288, 314, 319, 362, 363, 370, 381, 416, 417. It does not appear, however, that Knox was against all dramatic representations. We are told of his presence at a marriage masque or play which figured the fulfilment of one of his prophecies, and the hanging of two or three of his enemies.—(Diary of Mr. James Melvill, p. 22.)

silk, borne by twelve of the gravest burghers, clad in long gowns of black velvet, black velvet coats, crimson satin doublets, and velvet bonnets ; and the procession moved onwards to the Upper or Butter Tron, at the head of the West Bow, where a wooden arch, painted in bright colours and hung with coats of arms, had been raised. It was surmounted by a company of children singing ; and, as the Queen passed through, a cloud or globe descended on her path, and bursting asunder disclosed a boy in the guise of an angel, who delivered to her the keys of the town, with a bible and a psalter bound in purple velvet. Having spoken certain verses[1] in praise and welcome of the Queen and in honour of Holy Scripture, the angel was received back into his tabernacle, and the procession passed on to the Tolbooth—the Heart of Midlothian, as it was called in a later day—where, on a stage of two tiers, stood four fair damsels, in costly raiment, representing Fortitude, Justice, Temperance, and Prudence. After another address here, the Queen reached the Cross, which poured wine from all its spouts, while healths were drunk, and glasses were broken, and more allegory was acted by four fair maidens gorgeously apparelled. There was another stage with another address at the Lower or Salt Tron. Some zealous Reformers had here devised the representation of a priest burned at the altar in the act of elevating the host. But this was forbidden by the Earl of Huntly, who bore the Sword of State in the procession, and the destruction of Korah, Dathan, and Abiram was figured instead, to the seeming content of both sides ; the Reformers regarding it as an example of God's vengeance upon idolatry, the Roman Catholics as an example of God's vengeance upon those who took the priesthood upon themselves without authority. The fifth and last stage was built at the Netherbow, the boundary of the city on the east. Here an

---

[1] They were sent by Randolph to Cecil, and are now in the State Paper Office. If they may be judged by the opening stanza, they are sorry doggerel :

'Welcome, oure Souueraine, welcome, oure natyue Quene,
Welcome to vs your subiects greate and smalle,
Welcome, I saye, even from the verie splene,
To Edinburghe, youre syttie principall.'
—(Calendar of State Papers relating to Scotland, vol. i. p. 174.)

address was spoken by a dragon, who was then set on fire and burned, during the singing of a psalm. On reaching Holyrood, certain children, who had followed the procession in a cart, made a speech against the old religion, and sung another psalm. Then the burghers, who had carried the Queen's pall, took from the cart a cupboard of gilt plate, bought from the Earl of Morton and Sir Richard Maitland of Lethington for two thousand merks, and presented it to the Queen in the outer chamber of the Palace.[1] Like gifts welcomed her entry into Perth, Dundee, Aberdeen, and other towns, and helped to fill her treasury or added to the splendour of her table.[2] We see her bequeathing gold and silver work which had come to her in this way, to her aunt the Abbess of St. Peter's at Reims.[3]

[1] Diurnal of Occurrents, pp. 67-69. Letter from Randolph to Cecil, 7th Sept. 1562, in Mr. T. Wright's Queen Elizabeth and her Times, vol. i. pp. 73, 74. Knox's History of the Reformation, vol. ii. pp. 287-289. Register of the Town Council of Edinburgh, vol. iv. foll. 14, 15. MS. in the City Archives.

I have corrected what seems to be a mistake, and supplied an obvious deficiency in the description (in the Diurnal of Occurrents) of the allegorical personages on the stage at the Tolbooth, from the contemporary account of the entry of Anne of Denmark, thirty years afterwards, when not a few of the devices which had welcomed Queen Mary were acted over again : ' At her Grace's comming to the Tolbooth, there stood on high the four Virtues, as first Justice, with the balance in one hand, and the sword of justice in the other ; then Temperance, having in one hand a cup of wine, and in the other a cup of water ; Prudence, holding in her hand a serpent and a dove, declaring that men ought to bee as wise as the serpent to prevent daunger, but as simple as the dove eyther in wrath or malice ; the last is Fortitude, who held a broken pillar in her hand, representing the strength of a kingdome.'—(The Receiving of King James and his Queene, in Papers relative to the Marriage of King James VI., p. 41. Bannatyne Club : 1828.) Justice and her fellow Virtues, Temperance, Prudence, and Fortitude, were old stock-pieces of Edinburgh pageants. They appear in the entry of the Princess Margaret, the bride of King James IV., in 1503.—(Relation of John Younge, Somerset Herald, in Leland's Collectanea, vol. iv. pp. 289, 290.)

The escort of Moors, which figured in 1554, as well as in 1561, has a conspicuous place in ' The Discription of the Qveenis Maiesties maist honorable entry into the Tovn of Edinbvrgh, vpon the 19 day of Maii 1590, by Iohn Bvrel,' a poem, printed in Papers relative to the Marriage of King James VI.

[2] In January 1562, the town council of Aberdeen, in respect of the ' prencely propynis giffin to the Quenis Grace in Edinburght and Dunde and vther townis,' voted 2000 merks ' for the preparatioun and decoratioun of the toun and to be propynit to hir Grace, as wse hes bene, in tymes bypast to be done to Kingis and Princes of this realme at thair first entre.'— (Extracts from the Council Register of Aberdeen, 1398-1570, pp. 339, 340, 346, 347. Spalding Club : 1844.)

[3] P. 124 : ' Il y a deus cueurs dor de mes entrees auuesques vne comme vne rose et vn hault goubellet couuert et vn bouclier et quelque Notre Dames que ie veus etre enuoyees a ma tante de St Piere.' Cotgrave gives as one of the meanings of entrée, ' a present or gratuitie bestowed on a prince, etc., at his first entrie into a place.'

One of the two gold hearts bequeathed by the Queen was given to her at her entry into Perth, in September 1561 : ' At St. Johnston's she was well received, and presented with a heart of gold full of gold, I know not to what value ; she lik'd nothing the pageants there, they did too plainly condemn the errors of the world.' —(Letter from Randolph to Cecil, 24th September 1561, in Bishop Keith's History of Scotland, vol. ii. p. 86.)

The Queen's entry into Aberdeen.

The Queen's entry into Perth.

The first masque of which we hear at Holyrood was in October 1561, at Masque at Holyrood in October 1561. the Queen's farewell banquet to her uncle, the Grand Prior of the Knights of St. John of Jerusalem, in France.[1] It must have been witnessed by Brantôme and by Chatellard; and among the performers were two valets of the Queen's chamber,[2] and a son of the Duke of Montmorency, the Seigneur de Damville, who was believed to be so enamoured of Mary, that he had followed her to Scotland, although forbidden to aspire to her hand by the young wife whom he left at home.[3] It would appear to have been for this, or for some

---

[1] Francis of Lorraine (seventh son of Claude, first Duke of Guise), Grand Prior of the Knights of the Hospital of St. John of Jerusalem, in France, and General of the French galleys, commanded the ships which bore Queen Mary to Scotland in August 1561. He left Holyrood, on his return to France, on the 9th of October in the same year. He died of over-exertion at the battle of Dreux, in March 1563, at the age of twenty-nine. Brantôme, who accompanied him to Scotland, has written his life.—(Vies des Grands Capitaines François, disc. lxxvi.; Oeuvres, t. iii. pp. 146-158.)

[2] P. 127.

[3] P. 128.

M. Damville's love of the Queen.

[4] 'Depuis qu'elle fut vefue jusques à son retour en Escosse, il est vray qu'elle souffrit les inclinations de quelques seigneurs de la cour, et entr'autres du Sieur de Damville, depuis Mareschal, Duc de Montmorency et Connestable de France, et qu'elle declara qu'elle l'épouseroit, si par la mort de sa femme Antoinette de la Marck fille du Duc de Bouillon, ou autrement, il r'entroit en liberté de se remarier. Cette passion le fit embarquer auec elle pour la conduire en son royaume, où il enuoya vn gentil-homme de sa part nommé Chastellard, qui en deuint si espris qu'il s'oublia soy-mesme aussi bien que le seruice de son maistre, et se monstra si obstiné dans sa folie qu'elle fut obligée d'en faire vne victime à son honneur.'—(Additions aux Memoires de Messire Michel de Castelnau, par Monsieur le Laboureur, in Jebb, De Vita Mariae Scotorum Reginae, t. ii. p. 476.) Damville took his departure from Holyrood, along with the Grand Prior of France, on the 9th of October 1561, carrying with him a letter from the Queen to his father the Constable of France. See above, p. xxxviii. note 1; Prince Labanoff, Lettres de Marie Stuart, t. i. pp. 111, 112.

Damville's passion for Mary is glanced at by Cecil in a letter, written from Westminster, on the 7th February 1562-3, to Sir Thomas Smith, the English envoy in Paris : 'Captain de Hayss, the trafficquer for D'Anville, is returned, and pretendeth that D'Anville intendeth to come hyther with conditions for peace ; but I guess his comming hyther is but for a passadg into Scotland, where they saye his hart is.'—(Mr. T. Wright's Queen Elizabeth and her Times, vol. i. p. 122.)

The story of Damville's retainer, the unfortunate Chatellard, appears in a new light in a lately published despatch from Perrenot de Chantonnay, the Spanish ambassador at Paris. He writes from that capital, on the 3d May 1563, to his sovereign, King Philip II., that Chatellard, on being put to the torture, confessed that he had been suborned by the wife of the Admiral Coligny and other enemies of the house of Guise, to endeavour, by every possible means, to cast such a stain on the Scottish Queen's honour as should hinder her marriage with the King of Sweden, the Archduke Charles, or any other princely suitor : 'Confessó muy claramente que Madama de Curosot, y otros enemigos de la casa de Guisa, le avian persuadido de passar en Escocia y procurar por todas las vias possibles de hazer alguna cosa con la qual la honrra de la dicha Reyna viniesse á disputa, para estorvar que el Rey de Suecia ni el Archiduque, ni otro principe quisiesse casar con la dicha Reyna.'—(M. Teulet, Papiers d'Etat relatifs à l'Histoire de l'Ecosse, t. iii. p. 5.)

Story of Chatellard.

It is certain that Chatellard was a follower of the Reformed faith, and that he left the service of M. Damville rather than bear arms against the Huguenots.—(Brantôme, t. v. p. 123.) His religious zeal, indeed, would seem to have been so conspicuous as to gain him a page in the history of French Protestantism.—(M. Francisque-Michel, Les Ecossais en France, t. ii. p. 49,

other festivity soon after the Queen's arrival in Scotland, that Buchanan devised a masque, in which, with a glance probably at his own circumstances, he made Apollo and the Muses march in procession before the throne, telling, in Latin verse, how, being driven by war from their old abodes, they had taken their flight to the lettered court of the Queen of the Scots :

'Sedibus extorres bello, ad te fugimus, una

Musarum caste quae pia sacra colis.

Non querimur : magna exilium mercede levatur,

Si fruimur vultu nocte dieque tuo.'

Each Muse, as she passed, addressed a few words of compliment to Mary. The lines put into the mouth of Melpomene sound strangely now :

'Sit procul a tragico semper tua vita cothurno,

Et mihi fas hostes sit celebrare tuos.'[1]

One of Mary's uncles, the Marquis of Elbeuf, still tarried in Scotland, and took part in an equestrian masque before the Queen, in November 1561. He was one of six, disguised as Stranger Knights, who ran at the ring against the Commendator of Holyrood, the Commendator of Coldingham, and four others,

---

quoting 'un article intéressant sur Pierre de Bocsozel, sieur de Chastelard, dans *la France Protestante*, de MM. Haag, t. iii. pp. 354-357.') Had he been of another creed, the stern Scottish Reformer would have written in another way of the last moments of one who died with the verses of Ronsard upon his lips, and the image of Mary Stewart in his heart.—(Knox's History of the Reformation, vol. ii. p. 369.) Buchanan is so often content to copy Knox, that his omission of the story of Chatellard (which the Reformer tells with scandals, so far as I have observed, told by no one else) may be regarded as significant.

Randolph wrote to Cecil, that when Chatellard returned to Scotland, he presented to the Queen 'a book of his own making written in metre,' probably the volume of 'Frenche sonnatis in writt' which appears among the Queen's books in 1578.—(Bishop Keith's History of Scotland, vol. ii. pp. 180, 181. Mr. Thomson's Collection of Inventories, p. 244.) During his first visit to Holyrood, as we learn from one who was with him there, he wrote verses to the Queen, which the Queen answered in verse : 'La

Reyne donc, qui aimoit les lettres, et principalement les rithmes, et quelquefois elle en faisoit de gentilles, se plut à voir celles dudit Chastellard, et mesme elle luy faisoit response ; et, pour ce, luy faisoit bonne chere et l'entretenoit souvent.'—(Brantôme, t. v. pp. 122, 123.) One of Chatellard's poems to the Queen may be seen in Jebb, De Vita Mariae Scotorum Reginae, t. ii. pp. 497, 498, and in M. Mignet's History of Mary Queen of Scots, app. n. vol. ii. p. 123. English translat. edit. 1851.

[1] G. Buchanani Epigrammatum lib. iii. : 'Pompae : Apollo et Musae Exules.'

Ruddiman, who believed that Buchanan did not return to Scotland until 1563, conjectured that this masque was written for the Queen's marriage in 1565. But we now know that Buchanan was in Scotland in the Queen's service, in the summer or autumn of 1561. In February 1561-2, a payment of £125 was made from the Treasury 'be the Quenis Grace speciale command to Maister George Buchquhannan for the Mertimes terme jm ve lxj yeris bigane.'—(Compotum Thesaurarii Reginae Scotorum. MS. Register House.)

who rode in women's attire.[1] Grotesque matches of this kind seem to have been the fashion of the day. Not many months before, during Mary's brief reign in France, her uncle, the Grand Prior, and the Duke of Nemours ran at the ring, before the court at Amboise, both in women's apparel; the Prior in the guise of an Egyptian, with a she ape, swaddled like a baby, on his arm; the Duke in the guise of a burgher's wife, with a huge pouch and a bunch of more than a hundred keys at his girdle.[2]

In January 1562, the Queen's bastard brother, Lord John Stewart, Commendator of Coldingham, married Bothwell's sister. Mary was at the wedding feast at Crichton, and we may be sure that a masque was among the good sport and many pastimes which delighted the English ambassador.[3] Four weeks afterwards, the nuptials of another of the Queen's bastard brothers, Lord James Stewart, afterwards Earl of Murray, were celebrated at Edinburgh with a splendour such as had seldom been seen in Scotland. On the day before the marriage, he was belted Earl of Mar. The marriage was in St. Giles' Church, and Knox preached the sermon. A long train of nobles witnessed the rites, and escorted the bridegroom and bride to Holyrood, where the Queen gave a grand banquet and masque. Then came dancing, and fireworks, and running at the ring, and the making of twelve knights,[4] and so the first day, Sunday, closed. The next night Mary was enter-

Masque at Crichton Castle.

Masques at the Earl of Murray's marriage.

---

[1] 'We fell in talk of the pastimes that were the Sunday before, where the Lord Robert, the Lord John, and others ran at the ring, six against six, disguised and apparelled, the one half like women, the other like strangers, in strange masking garments. The Marquis that day did very well; but the women, whose part the Lord Robert did sustain, won the ring. The Queen herself beheld it, and as many as listed ... This [Sunday] is another day of mirth and pastime [running at the ring] upon the sands of Leith, where the Queen will be herself.'—(Letter from Randolph to Cecil, 7th December 1561, in Bishop Keith's History of Scotland, vol. ii. pp. 119, 120, 123, 125.)

'Quod reliquum fuit ejus anni [1561], dimissis

honorifice Gallis, qui Reginam officii gratia comitati fuerant, ludis et conviviis transactum.'—(G. Buchanani Rerum Scoticarum Historia, lib. xvii. cap. 11.)

[2] Brantôme, t. iii. pp. 154, 155.

[3] See above, p. xl. note 3.

[4] Their names are upon record : 'Collyne Campbell of [Glenurchy], Johnne Gordone of Descfurde, Johnne Wischart of Pettarrow, Mathow Campbell of Lowdoune, Patrik Lermonth of Darsye, George Haliburtoun of Petcur, William Kirkcaldy of Grange, Johne Ogilvy of Inuerquarite, Andro Murray of Ardingosk, Alexander Dunbar of Cumnok, Johnne Stewart of Traquhare, and Johnne Stewart of Mynto.'—(Register of Decreets, vol. xxxv. foll. 160, 161. MS. Register House.)

Knights made at the Earl of Murray's marriage.

tained at a banquet, in what had been Cardinal Beaton's house in the Black
Friars' Wynd, a company of the young burghers being in attendance to perform
a masque, and to escort the Queen back to Holyrood.   The third night saw
another banquet at the Palace, when Mary drank to the English Queen, and
sent the cup (it was of gold, and weighed twenty ounces) to the English
ambassador.[1] We need not question what Knox says of the offence which
these festivities gave to many of the more austere Reformers ; but when he
adds that the masques which continued to disquiet him during Mary's reign,
had their beginning in Murray's marriage,[2] he does obvious injustice to one
who happened at the time to have incurred his displeasure, by withstanding
an act of intolerance,[3] which the majority of the Scottish Reformers condemned,
and not even Calvin ventured to approve.[4]   Many godly men, we are told,

---

[1] Diurnal of Occurrents, pp. 70, 71 (where the list of the knights is imperfect, and 'merschance' and 'masry' are miswritten for 'mumchance' and 'maskry.')   Knox's History of the Reformation, vol. ii. pp. 313-315.   Letter from Randolph to Cecil, 12th February 1561-2, in Mr. Tytler's History of Scotland, vol. v. p. 216.

On the 31st of January 1561-2, there was a payment from the Treasury of £20, 16s. 4d. for thirty-eight yards of red and white taffeta delivered to the Queen's French tailor 'to be maskin claithis.'

[2] 'The greatness of the bancquett, and the vanitie used thairat, offended many godly. Thair began the masking, which from year to year hath continewed since.'—(Knox's History of the Reformation, vol. ii. p. 314.) Buchanan blames the excess of the banquets, but is silent as to the masques : 'Quibus in nuptiis, epularum magnificentia, aut verius immoderata luxuria, omnium amicorum animos graviter offendit, et invidis maledicendi materiam suppeditavit : eoque vehementius, quo ille in omni superiore vita se temperantius gesserat.'—(Rerum Scoticarum Historia, lib. xvii. cap. 26.)

[3] 'Whill that Papistis war so confounded, that none within the realme durst more avow the hearing or saying of messe, then the theavis of Lyddesdaill durst avow thair stowth in presence of ane upryght judge, thair war Protestantis found, that eschamed not at tables, and other open places, to ask, " Why may nott the Queyn have hir awin messe, and the forme of hir religioun ? What cane that hurte us or our religioun ?"

. . . When preparatioun began to be maid for . . . the messe . . . in the chapell . . . the Lord Lyndesay (then but Maister), with the gentilmen of Fyiff and otheris, plainlie cryed in the close " The idolater preast should dye the death," according to Goddis law . . . But the Lord James (the man whom all the godlye did most reverence) took upoun him to keap the chapell door . . . that nane should have entress to truble the preast.'—(Knox's History of the Reformation, vol. ii. pp. 265, 266, 270, 271.)   Two years later, the question of the appropriation of the church lands and revenues led to such a rupture between Murray and Knox, that 'familiarlie after that tyme thei spack nott togetther mor then a year and half.'—(Id. vol. ii. pp. 381-383, 461.)

[4] 'Tranquillitatem . . . interturbavit adventus Reginae, nam, triduo postquam illa appulerat, erectum est rursus idolum illud missalicum. Semetipsos opposuerunt viri, etsi pauci, graves et authoritate clari . . . Verum quia major pars etiam eorum qui nobiscum adhuc in doctrina consentiunt, diversum suasit, vicit tunc impietas quae et bodie sibi vires acquirit. Habent posteriores quod indulgentiae suae praetextant, affirmare, scilicet, Reginam, omnes verbi ministros, (et te quoque), in hac esse sententia quod nobis non licet prohibere quominus illa suam religionem aperte profiteatur. Quem rumorem tametsi ego ut falsissimum subinde reprehendo, radices tamen in multorum cordibus sic egit ut ego revellere non possum [l. possim], nisi ex te sciam an hujus modi questio ad ves-

Knox and Calvin.

grieved at the excess of the Good Regent's nuptial banquet, and the vanity of
the sports which followed; but that the banquet was made and the sports
played upon a Sunday, does not appear to have given any offence. Sunday,
indeed, in that age, was the day generally chosen for mirth and revel. It
was on a Sunday that the Reformed Commendators of Holyrood and Coldingham, both of them Lords of the Congregation, rode at the ring in women's
clothes.[1] It was on a Sunday that the Reformed municipality of Edinburgh gave
its grand banquet to the Queen's French kinsfolks.[2] Knox travelled on a
Sunday,[3] wrote letters on a Sunday,[4] and had the Duke of Chatelherault and
the English ambassador to sup with him on a Sunday.[5] The Gaelic translator
of Knox's 'Forms of Prayers,' the Reformed Superintendent of Argyle and
Bishop of the Isles, feasted the Queen and the ambassador of Savoy on a Sunday.[6] For more than twenty years after Knox was in his grave, Robin Hood
plays were acted on Sundays, and the King of May held his gambols on Sundays,
in Scotland;[7] as in England masques and interludes continued to be performed
before the court on Sundays, throughout the reigns of Elizabeth and James.[8]

tram ecclesiam proposita sit, et ad illam quoque quid
responderint fratres?'—(Letter from Knox to Calvin,
24th October 1561, printed from the original (in the
possession of M. Feuillet de Conches), by M. Teulet,
in his Papiers d'Etat relatifs à l'Histoire de l'Ecosse,
t. ii. pp. 12-14, where a facsimile of the letter is given.)

It is not easy to reconcile this letter with what Knox
tells us in his History. He not only conceals that he
had written to Calvin, but he affirms that Secretary
Maitland prevented him from writing. When his assertion, that he had not written, became known (in June
1564), he was again asked to write, but refused.—(History of the Reformation, vol. ii. pp. 291, 292, 459, 460.)

[1] See above, p. lxxvii. note 1.
[2] Diurnal of Occurrents, pp. 66, 67. See above,
p. xxxvii. note 1. On the 26th of August 1561, the
town council of Edinburgh ordered 'that thair be ane
honorabile banquet maid to the Princes hir Graces
cousingis [uncles] vpoun Sonday nixt.' Only two days
afterwards the council imprisoned Mr. Alexander
Skene, advocate, 'for taking and ressauing of the
diabolicall idoll callit the preistis sacrament at Pasche
last in the contempt of the religioun and the glorie of

God now establisched.'—(Register of the Town
Council of Edinburgh, vol. iv. foll. 10, 14. MS. in the
City Archives.)
[3] Diurnal of Occurrents, p. 94.
[4] Calendar of State Papers relating to Scotland,
vol. i. pp. 115, 116.
[5] Letter from Randolph to Cecil, 30. November
1562, in Selections illustrating the Reign of Queen
Mary, p. 106. (Maitland Club : 1837.)
[6] Cecil's or Murray's Diary, in M. Laing's History
of Scotland, vol. ii. pp. 87, 88.
[7] Booke of the Universall Kirk of Scotland, Aug.
1574, Oct. 1576, Apr. 1578, July 1591, March 1596 ;
part i. pp. 312, 375 ; part ii. pp. 407, 410, 784 ; part
iii. p. 874 (Bannatyne Club: 1839-1845). Acts of the
Parliaments of Scotland, Nov. 1579, vol. iii. p. 138.
[8] Mr. J. P. Collier's Annals of the Stage, vol. i. pp.
208, 237, 242, 243, 248, 252, 253, 257, 377, 442.
'The day,' says Bishop Percy, 'originally set apart
for theatrical exhibition appears to have been Sunday ;
probably because the first dramatic pieces were of a
religious cast.'—(Reliques of Ancient English Poetry,
vol. i. pp. 266, 267. edit. 1823.)

Masques for the meeting of the Scottish and English Queens.

Great things were hoped from a meeting between Mary and the English Queen at Nottingham in the summer of 1562. The interview was first postponed, and then abandoned; but so far were the preparations carried that Cecil had revised the masques. They were conceived in that spirit of dull pedantic allegory which disfigured the literature, and tainted the art of the age. The first night was to show a prison, called Extreme Oblivion, with Argus or Circumspection for its jailer. A lady, personating Pallas, was to ride into the hall on a unicorn, bearing a banner, on which were to be painted two ladies' hands, one grasping the other, with the word FIDES above in letters of gold. Next, two ladies were to enter together, one representing Prudentia, riding on a golden lion, the other representing Temperantia, riding on a red lion, both lions having crowns of gold on their heads. These were to be followed by six or eight ladies in masques leading captive Discord and False Report, with ropes of gold about their necks. All these having marched round the hall, Pallas on her unicorn, turning to Queen Elizabeth, was to say in verse that the gods, hearing of the memorable meeting of two such Queens, had commanded her to tell them how Prudentia and Temperantia had long and earnestly prayed Jupiter to deliver up False Report and Discord, to be punished as they should think good; how Jupiter at length had granted their prayer; and how they had now determined to commit the two offenders to the prison of Extreme Oblivion. The jailer, Argus or Circumspection, was then to receive from Prudentia a lock inscribed IN ETERNUM, and from Temperantia a key inscribed NUNQUAM; and when he had thus locked up False Report and Discord, the trumpets were to blow, and the English ladies were to lead the Scottish nobles to the dance.

The scene of the second night was to be a castle, named the Court of Plenty, with two porters at its gates, one called Ardent Desire, the other Perpetuity. Peace, entering in a chariot drawn by an elephant with Friendship on his back, was to march round the hall, followed by six or eight lady masquers.

Friendship, addressing the English Queen in verse, was to set forth that Pallas had told the gods how worthily the night before Prudentia and Temperantia had shut up False Report and Discord in the prison of Extreme Oblivion ; and that now the gods, understanding that Prudentia and Temperantia were sojourning in the Court of Plenty, had sent Peace to dwell with them for evermore. The Court of Plenty was then to pour forth streams of all sorts of wines, and the English lords were to masque with the Scottish ladies.

The third and greatest night was to open with the entry of Disdain riding on a wild boar, and Malice Prepense, in the likeness of a huge serpent, dragging after them an orchard with six or eight lady masquers, seated under trees laden with apples of gold. Disdain, directing his speech to Queen Elizabeth, was to show in verse how his master Pluto, the lord of hell, mightily incensed by what had passed on the two preceding nights, had sent his chief captain, Malice Prepense, to demand either that Discord and False Report, his master's faithful servants, shall be set free from the prison of Extreme Oblivion, or that Peace, his master's deadliest enemy, shall be delivered up to him by the porters of the Court of Plenty. Here Discretion was to come in, leading the good horse Boldness, with Hercules or Valiant Courage on his back, followed by six or eight lords in masques. Discretion, turning to the English Queen, was to declare in verse, that Jupiter, foreseeing the mischievous intent of Pluto, has sent Valiant Courage to overthrow his designs ; but that the fiends Disdain and Malice Prepense are such mighty warriors, that it will go hard with Valiant Courage unless he be encouraged by Prudentia and Temperantia ; and that therefore Jupiter has ordered Discretion, in the presence of the two Queens, to repair to the Court of Plenty, and there to demand of Prudentia how long she desires that Peace shall dwell between her and Temperantia, and of Temperantia, when Peace shall depart from her and Prudentia ? These questions are answered by Prudentia letting down from the battlements of the Court of Plenty a shield inscribed EVER, and by Temperantia letting down a sword of

l

steel inscribed NEVER.   With these arms, Valiant Courage sets upon Disdain and Malice Prepense, puts Disdain to flight, and slays Malice Prepense outright.   The six or eight lady masquers then leave their orchard, and the piece closes with their song of triumph.[1]

If the masques at the Scottish court ran in no better strain, we need not regret that our information about them should be so scanty.   Thus, of the masque at Lord Fleming's marriage in 1562, we discover no more than that it was acted on a Sunday in May, upon the greensward margin of a little lake in the Queen's Park, under the shadow of Arthur Seat.[2]   Of the masque at the marriage of the Commendator of St. Colm's Inch, with the sister of the Earl of Argyll, in 1563, we hear only that it was given on a Sunday at midwinter, in the mountain stronghold of Castle Campbell; that some of the company were masqued like shepherds, with white damask pouches; and that others played upon the lute.[3]   Of a masque in December 1563, all that we learn is, that three of the performers wore great Swiss bonnets of blue velvet.[4]   Of the masque at Mary Livingston's marriage on Shrove Tuesday 1565, we know nothing but that a painter was set to work in its preparation.[5]

We hear more of a Shrovetide masque at Holyrood in February 1564. It was given at a banquet, the grandest, we are told, which any man living had

[margin note: Masque in the Queen's Park.]

[margin note: Masque at Castle Campbell.]

[margin note: Shrovetide masque at Holyrood in 1564.]

---

[1] 'Devices to be shewed before the Queenes Majestie, by way of maskinge, at Nottingham Castell, after the metinge of the Quene of Scotts,' printed from the original (among the Lansdowne MSS. in the British Museum) endorsed by Cecil, 'May 1562,' in Mr. J. P. Collier's Annals of the Stage, vol. i. pp. 180-188.

[2] See above, pp. xliii., xliv., note 4.

[3] Pp. 136, 138.

Sir James Stewart (a grandson of the house of Avondale), Captain of Doune, and Commendator of St. Colm's Inch, joined the Reformers in 1560, was made Lord Doune in 1581, and died in 1590. He married, at Castle Campbell, on the 10th of January 1563, Margaret Campbell, eldest daughter of Archibald fourth Earl of Argyll. Their eldest son married, in 1580, the eldest daughter of the Regent Murray,

and became, in her right, Earl of Murray. He was 'the Bonny Earl' slain at Donybristle by the Gordons in 1592.

[4] P. 141.

The English ambassador bears witness to the gaiety of the Scottish court during the first two years after the Queen's return from France : 'Until the arrival of Monsieur le Croc . . . we did nothing but pass oure time in feasts, banquetting, masking, and running at the ring, and such like.'—(Letter from Randolph to Cecil, 15th May 1563, in Principal Robertson's History of Scotland, app. no. vii. ; vol. ii. p. 319.)

[5] On the 10th of March 1564-5, there was a payment from the Treasury of £12 'to the painter for the mask on Fastronis Evin to Marie Levingstonis mariage.'

seen in Scotland, except at the marriage of a prince. There were three courses, all served by gentlemen dressed, like the Queen and her attendants, in black and white.[1] A boy, with bandaged eyes, personating Cupid, came in with the first course, the servants singing an Italian sonnet,[2] probably written by Riccio.[3] *Italian verses, probably by Riccio.* The second course was ushered in by a fair young maid representing Chastity, and Latin verses by Buchanan[4] were sung in her praise. A child, in the *Latin verses by Buchanan.* character of Time, accompanied the third course, and again the servants sang Latin verses by Buchanan, foretelling that, so long as heaven and earth should endure, the mutual faith and affection of Mary of Scotland and Elizabeth of England should flourish green in remembrance :

> ' Durabit usque posteris
> Intaminata seculis
> Sincera quae Britannidas
> Nectit fides Heroidas.
>
> ' Rerum supremus terminus
> Ut astra terris misceat,
> Regina Scota diliget
> Anglam, Angla Scotam diliget.' [5]

In the multitude of vain prophecies, which rebuke the blindness and presump-

---

[1] Pp. 144, 145. Letters from Randolph to Cecil, 17th and 21st February 1563-4, in Miss Strickland's Lives of the Queens of Scotland, vol. iv. pp. 36-42.

[2] The English ambassador at Holyrood took care to send a copy of the verses to Whitehall :

> ' Quest'è colui che'l mondo chiama amore,
> Amaro come vedi et vedrai meglio
> Quando fia tuo, com'è nostro signore,
> Mansueto fanciulo et fiero veglio,
> Ben sa ch'il prova, et fiatl cosa piana,
> Anzi mill' anni e infin adhor ti sueglio.
> El nacque d'otio et di lascivia humana,
> Nutrito di pensier dolci et soavi,
> Fatto signor et dio da gente vana.
> Quale è morto da lui, qual co' più gravi
> Leggi, mena sua vita aspra et acerba,
> Sotto mille cathene et mille chiavi.'

—(Letter from Randolph to Cecil, 27th [*l.* 21st] February 1563-4, in Bishop Keith's History of Scotland, vol. ii. p. 220.)

[3] I conjecture the lines to be Riccio's, because he appears to have been the only Italian scholar in the court, with the exception of the Queen herself (see an Italian sonnet by her in M. Laing's History of Scotland, vol. ii. p. 220), and Secretary Maitland of Lethington (see above, pp. xlix., l. note 1.) If the lines had been Mary's, the English ambassador would not have failed to say so, when he sent them to Cecil. Lethington, again, although the son of a poet, and the brother of poets, does not seem to have numbered verse-making among his accomplishments.

Riccio was, doubtless, one of the ' gentlemen apparelled all in white and black, divers that could sing among them,' who, as the English envoy writes, served the courses and sang the verses.

[4] G.· Buchanani Miscellaneorum Liber, ii. : ' In Castitatem.' Letter from Randolph to Cecil, 27th [*l.* 21st] February 1563-4, in Bishop Keith's History of Scotland, vol. ii. p. 220.

[5] G. Buchanani Miscellaneorum Liber, xvi. : ' Mu-

tion of mankind, there are few of which the failure has been more signal or more melancholy.

In July 1565, the pen of Buchanan was tasked for the masques at the Queen's marriage with the son and heir of his feudal lord and chief. The festivities were prolonged through three days,[1] and there seems to have been a masque each day. In the first, five goddesses, and as many gods, were introduced. Diana complained to Jupiter, in Latin verse, that one of her bright band of Five Marys had been taken from her by the envious powers of love and marriage. Her lamentations were answered or derided by Juno and Venus, Ceres and Pallas, among the goddesses; and by Saturn and Mars, Mercury and Apollo, among the gods. The judgment of Jupiter dismissed the complaint, and the herald Talthybius exultingly proclaimed that the song and the torch were ready for the nuptials of another Mary.[2] The second masque was equestrian. A troop of Ethiopians, a troop of Knights of the North, a troop sent by Nep-

tuus Amor.' Letter from Randolph to Cecil, 27th [l. 21st] February 1563-4, in Bishop Keith's History of Scotland, vol. ii. p. 220.

It is obviously of these verses that the English ambassador speaks, when he tells Cecil how Mary having drunk to Elizabeth, he thanked the Scottish Queen in his sovereign's name, and, he continues, 'she gave me answer, "that it was more in heart than in outer show, and that shall these verses testify;" which she gave me in my hand, the selfsame that were sung, and willed me to do with them as I liked, which I trust your honour will present unto the Queen's Majesty.'—(Letter from Randolph to Cecil, 21st February 1563-4, in Miss Strickland's Lives of the Queens of Scotland, vol. iv. p. 42.)

[1] 'During the space of three or four days, there was nothing but balling, and dancing, and banquetting.'—(Knox's History of the Reformation, book v. vol. ii. p. 495.)

[2] G. Buchanani Epigrammatum lib. iii.: ' Pompa Deorum in Nuptiis Mariae.' See above, pp. xlvi., xlvii., xlviii., notes 4, 2.

M. Teulet has printed a contemporary account of the masques and pageants at the Queen's first marriage at Paris in 1558.—(Papiers d'Etat relatif à l'Histoire de l'Ecosse, t. i. pp. 292-303.) It was cele-

brated with great pomp throughout Scotland. The Queen Regent made proclamation that all the burghs should ' mak fyris and processioun generall for the completing and solemnizing of the mariage betuix oure Souerane Ladie and the Dolphine of France.' These burghal festivities are described by the Knight of Lethington in his verses ' On the Quenis Maryage to the Dolphin of France :'

' All burrows townis, everilk man you prayes
To mak bainefyres, farseis, and clerk playes;
    And, throw your rawis, carroul, daunce, and sing;
And at your croce gar wyne rin sundrie wayes;
As wes the custome in oure eldaris dayes,
    Quhen that they maid triumphe for ony thing:
And all your staires with tapestrie gar hing.
Castellis, schuit gunnis; schippis and galeays,
    Blaw up your trumpettis, and your drumis ding.'

—(Poems of Sir Richard Maitland of Lethingtoun, pp. 5, 6. Maitland Club: 1830.) At Edinburgh, the great bombard, Mons, was shot from the Castle, and we learn that her bullet reached Wardie moor. Among the payments from the city treasury, 'for the play maid at the Triumphe of our Souerane Ladyis mariage,' we find £4 to ' William Adamson for his travell takin in the play;' 25 merks to ' Walter Bynning, painter, for his painting and all his labouris;' £10 to ' William Lauder for his travell and lawbouris in setting

tune, and a troop of motley or party-coloured Knights, defiled before the Queen, reciting Latin verses, in which they extolled the renown of her virtues, and offered to serve her to the death, in peace or war, on land or sea : '

> ' Sunt animi, sunt dextrae animis servire paratae,
>
> Et mens imperium promta subire tuum.
>
> Si fortuna animis fuerit, si viribus aequa,
>
> Officiis in te non prior ullus erit.'

They were followed by a band of Knights bearing the badge of Pallas on their helmets, who threw down the gauntlet to a band of Knights, each of whom had a Cupid for his crest :

> ' Pallas adest, hasta metuenda et Gorgone saeva :
>
> Qui locus hic jaculis, parve Cupido, tuis !' [1]

We know nothing more of the third masque than that the Four Marys were introduced to offer oblations to the returning goddess of Health, in Latin verses written by Buchanan :

> ' Alma Salus, reduci tibi Nymphae haec vota dedere
>
> Quattuor, ut dominae conciliere suae,
>
> Ejus et aeternam statuas in pectore sedem :
>
> Non alia poteris sanctius aede coli.' [2]

In January 1566, a French envoy arrived at Holyrood to invest the young King with the Order of St. Michael. The ceremony was followed by a banquet, and the banquet by a masque, in which the Scottish lords were the performers. The next night saw another banquet, and another masque acted by the Queen, her Four Marys, and other three ladies of the court. The plot of

Masques at Holyrood, on the King's receiving the Order of the Cockle.

---

furthe of the play ; £5 to 'all the wrychtes quhilkis wrocht the play grayth for the tymmer and warkmanship ;' £4 to 'Patrik Dorane for making certane claythis ;' 6s. 8d. to 'Adam Smytht, takkisman of Andro Mowbrayis yarde for the dampnage and skaytht sustenit be him in tramping doun of his gers of the said yarde be the convoy and remanend playeris in the tyme of the Triumphe maid for oure Souerane Ladyis mariage.'—(Register of the Town Council of

Edinburgh, vol. ii. ad fin. MS. in the City Archives.)

[1] G. Buchanani Epigrammatum lib. iii. : 'Pompae Equestres.'

[2] G. Buchanani Miscellaneorum Liber, xxxv. : 'Ad Salutem in Nuptiis Reginae.'

'Nymphas,' says Ruddiman, 'hic vocat quatuor Mariae Scotae corporis ministras, quae etiam omnes Mariae nominabantur.'

the piece has not been preserved ; we know only that the Queen and her companions, disguised in men's apparel, presented the French ambassador and his attendants with richly ornamented Scottish daggers in black velvet sheathes.[1] On the third day, at noon, the Earl of Mar gave a banquet in the Castle ; and at night, the Queen, the King, and eight others, of whom Riccio was one, took part in a masque at Holyrood.[2]

Masque and fireworks at the Prince's baptism. The masque for the grand banquet at the Prince's baptism at Stirling in December 1566, was arranged, it would seem, by Buchanan, who supplied the Latin verses, and by Bastien Pagez, a French valet of the Queen's chamber,[3]

---

[1] P. 162 : 'Plus je delliure a vng coutellier iiij quartier de veloux noyr pour fairre viij fourreaux a des dacques dEcosse.'

'And the samin nycht [Sunday, 10. February], our Soueranis maid ane banket to the Ambassatour, in the auld chappell of Halyrudhous, quhilk wes reapparrellit with fyne tapestrie and hung magnificentlie, [and] the lordis maid the maskery efter supper in ane honourable maner. And vpoun the ellevint day of the said moneth, the King and Quene in lyik manner bankettit the samin Ambassatour ; and at evin our Soueranis maid the maskrie and mumschance, in the quhilk the Quenis Grace and all hir Maries and ladies wer all cled in men's apperrell ; and everie ane of thame presentit ane quhingar, bravelie and maist artificiallie made and embroiderit with gold, to the said Ambassatour and his gentilmen, euerie ane of thame according to his estate.'—(Diurnal of Occurrents, p. 87.)

Fifty years afterwards, the question of how far one sex is forbidden by Scripture to assume the dress of the other would appear to have been discussed in relation to the magnificent masques so common at Whitehall in the reign of King James VI. See, in Selden's Opera (t. ii. coll. 1690-1696), his learned letter to Ben Jonson on 'the literal sense and historical of the holy text [Deut. xxii. 5.] usually brought against the counterfeiting of sexes by apparell.'

[2] Letter from Randolph to Cecil, cited in Miss Strickland's Lives of the Queens of Scotland, vol. iv. p. 248. Diurnal of Occurrents, p. 87.

Scottish scene-painter, 1554-1566. There was a payment from the treasury of £4 'to Walter Bynning, painter, for painting of the King of Francis armys, and of our Souerane Lordis armys quhen his Maiestie ressauit the Ordour of the Cokle.'

—(Compotum Thesaurarii Reginae Scotorum, Jun. 1566. MS. Register House.)

Walter Bynning seems to have been much employed in the decoration of masques and pageants. In October 1554, he had a payment of £5 from the city of Edinburgh, 'for the making of the play graith and paynting of the handsenye and the playaris facis . . . providand alwyss that the said Walter mak the play geir vnderwrittin furthcummand to the town, quhen thai haif ado thairwith, quhilkis he hes now ressauit, *videlicet*, Aucht play hattis, ane kingis crowne, ane myter, ane fules hude, ane septour, ane pair angell wyngis, twa angell hair, ane chaplet of tryumphe.' In 1558, he got twenty-five merks 'for his painting and all his labouris takin be him in the tryumphe maid at our Souerane Ladyis mariage.' In 1561, the city treasurer was ordered 'to deliuer to Patrik Schang, wrycht, and Walter Bynning, tymmer, canves, and all vthir necessaris conveniente for the triumphis and fairssis at the Over Trone, Tolbutht, Croce, Salt Tron, and Nethir Bow' on the occasion of the Queen's entry.—(Register of the Town Council of Edinburgh, vol. ii. fol. 33, fol. ult. ; vol. iv. foll. 14, 15. MS. in the City Archives.)

[3] Buchanan, in his 'Detectio Mariae,' describes *Bastien Pagez.* his fellow-labourer in the masque at Stirling : 'Erat is Sebastianus Arvernus genere, homo et ob psallendi peritiam et sales Reginae admodum gratus ;' 'This Sebastiane was ane Aruernois, a man in greit favour with the Quene for his cunning in musike, and his merie jesting.' See above, pp. liv., lv., note 1 ; pp. lvii., lviii., note 4. We find forty yards of taffeta (at 26s. the yard) delivered to him on the 6th of December 1566, 'to be some preparlatifs for the baptesme :' his acquittance, in the Register House, shows that he

who devised the machinery. When the dishes were to be brought in, they were placed upon a table so constructed, that it seemed to move through the great hall of its own accord, accompanied by musicians in female attire, singing songs, and playing upon instruments. A procession of Rural Gods marched before, each groupe as it passed the dais reciting a few lines of Latin. The Satyrs, the Naiads, and the Oreads, addressed the Prince; the Nereids and the Fauns turned their speech to the Queen:

' Virtute, ingenio, Regina, et munere formae
    Felicibus felicior majoribus,
Conjugii fructu sed felicissima, cujus
    Legati honorant exteri cunabula:
Rustica quem donis reverentur Numina, silvis
    Satyri relictis, Najadesque fontibus.' [1]

The Satyrs, as we learn from an eye-witness, not content with playing the part assigned to them, chose to wag their long tails, in the hope, no doubt, of creating a laugh among their companions in the hall. But the retainers of the English ambassador fancying that it was done in their derision (there must have been Kentishmen among them), were so incensed that the Queen and the ambassador had difficulty in appeasing their wrath.[2] The masque, thus

wrote a fine Roman hand. He was imprisoned on suspicion of being an accomplice in the King's murder, but was released without a trial. He returned to the Queen's service, and continued in it to the end, following her body to the grave at Peterborough.—(Pitcairn's Funerals of Mary Queen of Scots, pp. 20, 23.) The Queen in her will, made the day before her execution, left 2000 francs to him, and 2000 francs to his daughter Mary Pages, the Queen's godchild.—(Prince Labanoff, Lettres de Marie Stuart, t. vi. p. 489; t. vii. pp. 250, 252, 253, 259, 260, 262, 265, 269.) Among other things bequeathed to him by the Queen, was ' a sewt of savage attire,' doubtless one of the habits in which he had figured in the masques at Holyrood and Stirling.

[1] G. Buchanani Epigrammatum lib. iii. : ' Pompae Deorum Rusticorum dona ferentium Jacobo VI. et Mariae matri ejus, Scotorum Regibus, in coena quae Regis baptisma est consecuta.'

One of the earliest, and not the least learned or least able of the Queen's many apologists, has pointed out the apparent inconsistency of the praises which Buchanan thus lavishes upon her, with the open immorality of which he elsewhere accuses her : ' Which are we to trust to? Buchanan in this epigram (on the 17th of December 1566) giving us the highest characters of the Queen's virtue, and rendring such a publick testimony to it in the presence of such an assembly, where the Queen's character and behaviour was so well known? or the same Buchanan, in his Detection, telling the Queen of England and her council, that, at this very time, Queen Mary was publickly known for a vicious monster, and expatiating before them on the subject, with all the fluency of his virulent pen?'—(Thomas Innes, Critical Essay on the Ancient Inhabitants of Scotland, vol. i. pp. 348-354.)

[2] ' During ther being in Stirling, ther wes daily banketing, dancing, and triumphe; and at the princi-

Buchanan's inconsistencies.

interrupted, was followed by a discharge of fireworks from a mimic fortress, the possession of which was contested by motley bands of Moors, Highlanders, Centaurs, Lanzknechts, and Fiends.[1]

The Queen's last masque at Holyrood.

.The last masque which Mary was to see at Holyrood was on Shrove Sunday 1567, at the marriage of a favourite valet, the Frenchman who, along with Buchanan, devised the masque for the Prince's baptism. The Queen was present at the wedding dinner in the Palace at noon. At four o'clock she supped with the Earls of Argyle, Huntly, Bothwell, and Cassilis at a farewell banquet given by the Bishop of the Isles to the Ambassador of Savoy. She rode to the Kirk of the Field at seven, and spent the evening with the King in the same chamber where Bothwell and other nobles were playing at dice. Her talk with the King seemed fond and cheerful, but she is said to have dropped one remark which sank deep in his mind—that it was about that time twelve-month that David Riccio was murdered. She rose hurriedly between ten and eleven, exclaiming, ' I have failed to Bastien, that this night of his marriage I promised him the masque, and to bed his bride.' With this she took leave of the King, kissing him, and putting a ring on his finger; and having called for

Masque of Satyrs at the Prince's baptism.

pall banket ther fell out ane gret eylest and gruge amang the Englismen ; for a Frenchman callit Bastien deuysed a nomber of men formed lyk Sattyres, with lang tailes, and whippis in ther handis, rynnyng befoir the meit, quhilk wes brocht throw the gret hall vpon ane trym engyn, marching as apperit it alain, with musiciens clothed lyk maidins, playing vpon all sortis of instrumentis and singing of musick. Bot the Sattiers wer not content only to red rown, bot pat ther handis behind them to ther tailes, quhilkis they waggit with ther handis, in siç sort as the Englismen supponit it had bene deuysed and done in derision of them, daftly apprehending that quhilk they suld not seam to haue vnderstand. For Mester Hattoun, Mester Ligniche, and the maist part of the gentilmen desyred to sowp before the Quen and gret banket, that they mycht se the better the haill ordour and cerimonies of the triumphe ; bot sa schone as they saw the Sattires waging ther tailes or romples, they all set down vpon the bair flure behind the bak of the burd, that they suld not see them selues scornit, as they thocht.

Mester Hatton said vnto me, Gif it wer not in the Quenis presens and hall, he suld put a dagger to the hart of that Frenche knaif Bastien, whom he allegit did it for dispyt, that the Quen maid mair of them then of the Frenchemen. I excused the matter the best I mycht, bot the rumour was sa gret behind the Quenis bak, wher hir Maieste sat, and my Lord of Bedford, that they hard and turnit about ther facis to wit what the matter menit. I schew them how that it was for the Sattiers ; sa that the Quen and my Lord of Bedford had baith anough ado to get them satisfied.'—(Sir James Melville's Memoirs, pp. 171, 172.)

[1] Expensis maid be Johne Chisholme comptrollar of the artailyarie wpoune the Fyreworkis at the Triomphe of the Baptisme of my Lord Prince in Stiruiling in December 1566. MS. Register House. Diurnal of Occurrences, p. 105. The display cost £190, 17s. 5d. Forty days were spent in its preparation, and help was asked from the Laird of Roslin in making ' sum waik poulder meit for mixing of fyre work.'

her horse, rode by torchlight to Holyrood, accompanied by Argyle, Huntly, Bothwell, and Cassilis. The marriage festivities had not long ceased in the Palace, when, about two hours after midnight, a crash like a thunderclap shook the city, and the headlong flight of armed men through the streets told that the King's murderers had done their work.[1]

The tragedy of the Kirk of the Field brought the revels of Mary's court abruptly to a close. Three months afterwards she married Bothwell; but at these hateful nuptials, says a chronicle of the day, 'there was neither pleasure nor pastime used as was wont to be used when princes were married.'[2] More than twenty years, it would seem, were to pass before Holyrood saw another masque. It came from England, a gift from Queen Elizabeth to King James the Sixth and his Danish bride,[3] and was perhaps the first example they beheld of a class of entertainments which, during their reign at Whitehall, was raised to its highest pitch of splendour by the art of Inigo Jones, the music of Lawes, and the learning and poetry of Ben Jonson.[4]

Masque for the marriage of King James VI.

Mary Stewart had a fondness for dogs which was inherited by more than

The Queen's dogs.

---

[1] Cecil's, or Murray's Diary, and Depositions of William Pourie, of Hay of Talla, of John Hepburn, of Thomas Nelson, and of French Paris, in M. Laing's History of Scotland, vol. ii. pp. 87, 88, 244, 254, 255, 257, 258, 267, 277, 278. Deposiciones for the Kingis slauchter, 11. Feb. 1567. Hopetoun MS. G. Buchanani Rerum Scoticarum Historia, lib. xviii. capp. 12, 13. Articles given in by the Earl of Murray to Queen Elizabeth's Commissioners at Westminster, on the 6th Dec. 1568. Hopetoun MS.

[2] Diurnal of Occurrents, pp. 111, 112.

[3] 'Quhilk [marriage] Monsieur du Croq, the Frenche ambassadour sa greitlie disdaynit, that, being ludgit within a very schort space to the Palace of Halyrude-hous, he wald not at the Quenis desyr pas to banket.' —(Articles given in by the Earl of Murray to Queen Elizabeth's Commissioners at Westminster on the 6th Dec. 1568. Hopetoun MS.) Compare Du Croc's despatches to Catharine of Medicis, published by Prince Labanoff, Lettres de Marie Stuart, t. vii. pp. 110, 112, and by M. Teulet, Lettres de Marie Stuart, pp. 110, 111.

[4] Mr. J. P. Collier's Annals of the Stage, vol. i. pp. 270, 271.

[5] 'The masque,' says Gifford, 'magnificently constructed, was not committed to ordinary performers. It was composed, as Lord Bacon says, for princes, and by princes it was played. The prime nobility of both sexes, led on by James and his Queen, took upon themselves the respective characters; and it may be justly questioned whether a nobler display of grace and elegance and beauty was ever beheld, than appeared in the masques of Jonson.'—(Gifford's Ben Jonson, vol. i., mem. pp. ccxxv., ccxxvi.)

Queen Anne of Denmark was an actor in Ben Jonson's Masque of Blackness in 1605, Masque of Beauty in 1607, Masque of Queens in 1609; and in Samuel Daniel's Masque of the Vision of the Twelve Goddesses in 1604, and Masque of Tethys's Festival, or the Queen's Wake, in 1610. 'I believe,' says Warton, 'that she is the first of our Queens that appeared personally in this most elegant and rational amusement of a court.'—(History of English Poetry, vol. ii. p. 540, note, edit. 1840.)

Masques at the English court of King James VI.

one generation of her descendants. There is mention in the text of ‘ blue velvet for collars to the Queen's little dogs.’[1] We learn elsewhere that, in ordering her household, a daily ration of two loaves was set apart for them ;[2] that they were under the charge of a keeper ;[3] and that some of them were occasionally sent to France.[4] The taste continued to the last. ‘ If my uncle’—she wrote from her prison at Sheffield, in 1574, to the Archbishop of Glasgow, her ambassador at Paris,—‘ if my uncle, the Cardinal of Guise, has gone to Lyons, I am sure he will send me a couple of pretty little dogs, and you will buy me as many more ; for, except in reading and working, my only pleasure is in all the little animals that I can get. They must be sent in baskets, well stowed, so as to keep them warm.’[5] A little dog followed her to the scaffold at Fotheringhay, and nestling among the clothes which she threw off as she bared her neck for the block, lay there until all was over and the clothes began to be gathered up, when it crept between the severed head and body, and would not leave them until it was taken away by force.[6]

Gifts by Mary to her kinsfolks, companions, and attendants appear

---

[1] P. 141.

[2] ‘ Pour les chains de la Royne, ij pains.’ — (Menu de la Maison de la Royne faict par Monsieur de Pinguillon 1562, p. 10, in Despences de la Maison Royale 1561-2. MS. Register House.)

[3] There were payments from the Treasury of £12, in January 1561-2, ‘ to Anthone Guedio for keiping of the Quenis Grace doggis ;’ and of £33 in March 1564-5, for liveries to the ‘ boy that keipis the doggis,’ and to a boy of the Queen's French tailor.

[4] P. 148.

There was a payment from the Treasury, in March 1565-6, of £6, ‘ be the Quenis Grace speciale command to George Temple, baxster in Leithe, for certane breid furneist be him to certane doggis passand in France.’

[5] Prince Labanoff, Lettres de Marie Stuart, t. iv. pp. 228, 229.

The Queen's dog on the scaffold at Fotheringhay.

[6] ‘ La Reyne d'Escosse avoit un petit chien avec elle sur l'eschaffaut, qui se tint tout ce tems-là assis, coy, ne se bougeant nullement d'auprès d'elle. Mais sistost que la teste fut tranchée et mise sur la place, on le vit remouvoir et crier, puis se mist en une place, qui estoit entre le corps et la teste, et se tint là jusques à ce que l'on le vinst oster ; ce qui fut fait par force, et estant mis près le sang tout chaud, refusa de le lescher, chose non contraire au naturel des chiens.’—(Le Vray Rapport de l'exécution faicte sur la personne de la Reyne d'Escosse, published by M. Teulet, in his Papiers d'Etat relatifs à l'Histoire de l'Ecosse, t. ii. p. 884.)

‘ One of the executioners pulling off her garters, espied her litle dogg which was crept under her clothes, which could not be gotten forth but by force, yet afterward wold not departe from the dead corpse, but came and lay betweene her head and her shoulders, which being imbued with her bloode, was caryed away and washed.’—(Reporte of the manner of the Execution of the Scottish Quene, in Sir H. Ellis' Letters illustrative of English History, second series, vol. iii. p. 117.)

‘ Fut trouuee vne petite chienne dedans sa robbe, qu'il l'auoit suiuie en bas, laquelle vne grande Princesse de France a voulut auoir pour l'amour de la deffunte.’ —(La Mort de la Royne d'Escosse 1589, reprinted by Jebb, De Vita Mariae Scotorum Reginae, t. ii. p. 641.)

in almost every page. There is a present of we know not what to the Duchess of Montmorency in France.[1] A little dog is sent to another French friend.[2] Silks and cloths of silver and gold are given to the Earls of Murray, Argyle, Huntly, and Bothwell,[3] for their dresses at the Prince's baptism. There is a present of linen to Mary Courcelles, a French bedchamber woman, who helped the Queen in her escape from Lochleven, and lived to be rewarded by her son when seated on the English throne.[4] A more famous but less fortunate servant, David Riccio, or Secretary David as he is called, has three gifts. At the Queen's marriage, which he is said to have done so much to bring about, he gets ten yards of black velvet brocaded with gold,[5] probably for a wedding garment. Five months afterwards he has four yards of black velvet;[6] and in January 1566, he receives as much cloth of gold figured with scales.[7] We are told elsewhere that the Italian, who affected princely state in his horses, and other appointments, strove to hide the defects of his person by the sumptuousness of his dress.[8] It is related, as an instance of his splendour, that, on the night of his murder—Knox gloried in calling it a 'just act, and most worthy of all praise,'[9]—he had on

Gifts to Riccio.

Knox and Riccio.

[1] P. 144.

[2] P. 148.

[3] P. 166.

[4] P. 141. Miss Strickland's Lives of the Queens of Scotland, vol. vi. p. 73, note 1. M. Francisque-Michel, Les Ecossais en France, t. i. p. 435. See above, pp. xlix., L, note 1.

[5] P. 155.

[6] P. 159.

[7] P. 161.

Riccio's ugliness. [8] 'Supellectili, cultu corporis, equorum et genere et numero, longe Regem superabat : quae res eo videbatur indignior, quod non faciem cultus honestabat, sed facies cultum destruebat.'—(G. Buchanani Rerum Scoticarum Historia, lib. xvii. cap. 55.)

A few weeks before his murder, he had a grant from the King and Queen, of £200 'for reparatiounis of his chalmer.' After his death, the Queen ordered inquiry to be made for his horses.—(Compotum Thesaurarii Reginae Scotorum, 31. Jan. 1565-6, 29. Maii 1566. MS. Register House.)

[9] 'That pultron and vyle knave Davie was justlie punished . . . by the counsall and handis of James Dowglas, Erle of Morton, Patrik Lord Lyndesay, and the Lord Ruthven, with otheris assistaris in thare cumpany, who all, for thare just act, and most worthy of all praise, ar now unworthelie left of thare brethrein, and suffer the bitterness of banishement and exyle.'—(Knox's History of the Reformation, vol. i. p. 235.) When the young wife of Knox's old age became a widow, she chose one of Riccio's murderers for her second husband—Andrew Ker of Faudonsyde, who is said to have held a pistol to the Queen's breast.

The murder of Riccio justified as a religious duty.

The fanaticism which inspired so many of the assassins of Riccio, had been inflamed by sermons and prayers protracted through a whole week, and was not to be appeased by the blood of one sacrifice. On the same night, and under the same roof, it sought and found another victim in a learned and zealous Dominican, Friar John Black, a professor in St. Mary's College at St. Andrews, who had publicly disputed against one of the most eminent of the Re-

Murder of Friar John Black.

a furred night-gown of damask, a doublet of satin, and hose of russet velvet.[1]

Bothwell's marriage with Lady Jane Gordon.

Mary appears to have taken unusual interest in Bothwell's marriage with the daughter of the Earl of Huntly, who fell at Corrichie.[2] She was a party

Riccio's oak at Melville.

Bothwell's wives: 1. Lady Jane Gordon;

formed divines.—(Goodall's Examination, vol. i. pp. 247-252. Mr. David Laing's note, in Knox's History of the Reformation, vol. ii., app. no. iv. pp. 592-595.)

[1] Letter from the Earl of Bedford and T. Randolph, 27th March 1566, in Sir H. Ellis' Letters illustrative of English History, vol. ii. p. 218.

Buchanan (lib. xvii. cap. 55) says that Mary wished to make the Italian a peer, and to put him in possession of one of the fairest baronies on the Esk. On the night of his murder, Lord Ruthven told the Queen that Riccio 'had caused her Majesty to put out the Lord Ross from his whole lands, because he would not give over the lordship of Melvin to the said Davie.' —(Scotia Rediviva, p. 341.) A tree in the park at Melville, near the site of the old castle, is still shown as 'Riccio's oak.'

[2] The worth, the beauty, and the accomplishments of Lady Jane Gordon (see above, p. xliii. note 1) would seem to have taken a strong hold on Bothwell. Secretary Maitland told Queen Mary after Carberry, that even after Bothwell became her husband, he wrote letters to his first wife, protesting his affection for her, and grossly disparaging the Queen : ' Et luy dict davantaige que le Duc avoit escript plusieurs fois à la Contesse de Bautuel, sa première femme, depuis qu'il a couché avec la Royne, par lesquelles il mande à ladicte Contesse la tenir pour sa femme et la Royne pour sa concubine.' Mary affected not to believe the story, but Lethington replied that the letters would speak for themselves. The French ambassador, who reports the conversation, adds : 'Mais nous ne doubtons point en ce royaulme qu'il n'aime mieux sa première femme que la Royne.'—(Letter from Du Croc to Catharine of Medicis, 17th June 1567, printed by M. Teulet, in his Papiers d'Etats relatifs à l'Histoire de l'Ecosse, t. ii. p. 170.) The letters and sonnets which Mary is said to have written to Bothwell are full of jealousy of his Countess. The sixth sonnet alludes to her learning, and we know otherwise that she could read the Legenda Aurea in the original Latin.—(M. Laing's History of Scotland, vol. i. p. 346, note.) It would appear from the fourth sonnet that Bothwell was not her first lover.

Buchanan (lib. xviii. cap. 30) affirms, that when Bothwell, after his divorce from Lady Jane Gordon, married the Queen, he had other two wives still living : 'duas uxores, adhuc vivas, haberet, tertiam ipse nuper, suum fassus adulterium, dimisisset.'

One, doubtless, was Dame Anna Rostung, daughter of a wealthy Norwegian, Christopher Throndson Rostung. She was known in Norway as 'the Scottish lady,' in August 1565 ; and two years afterwards, when Bothwell in his flight from Scotland was brought captive to Bergen, she claimed him as her husband. The contemporary diary of Absolon Pedersen Beyer, reader of theology in Bergen, relates that, on the 17th of September 1567, she 'upraided the Earl Bothwell that he had taken her from her native country, and would not treat her as his lawful wife, although he had pledged himself to [her parents] and herself, by hand, mouth, and letters, which she caused to be read before him. And whereas,' the diary continues, ' he has three wives still living, first herself, second another in Scotland [i.e., Lady Jane Gordon] from whom he has bought himself, and lastly Queen Mary : therefore, said Dame Anna, he was good for nothing. Then he promised her a yearly rent from Scotland of a hundred dollars, and gave her a ship, with anchor, ropes, and other appurtenances.'—(Notices of James, Earl Bothwell, by Professor P. A. Munch of Christiania, read to the Society of Antiquaries of Scotland, 3d June 1850. MS. in the Library of the Society. Cf. Les Affaires du Conte de Boduel, 1568, app. pp. xxxv. xxxix. Bannatyne Club : 1829.) This is obviously the lady mentioned by De Thou : ' cum accusatus esset ab amicis cuiusdam nobilis virginis Noruegicae, quam ante plures annos, pacto matrimonio violatam, alia superinducta deseruerat.'— (Thuani Historiarum Sui Temporis, lib. xl. t. i. p. 819, edit. 1625.)

The other may have been the heroine of 'the Lay of the Last Minstrel,' Dame Janet Beton, widow of Sir Walter Scott of Branksome. In an action against her, in April 1559, it was pleaded ' that James Erle Boithuell, schiref principale of Edinburgh, within quhais jurisdictioun the said Dame Jonet now dwellis is suspect to be juge . . . in the said mater ; the said Erle and scho, as . . . is informitt, being quyetly mariit or handfast, or, at the leist, sik vtheris caussis of suspicione being betuix tham that the said Erle is suspect to be juge in ony causs to be movit aganis hir be ony personnis, as is notourlie knawin.'

2. Dame Anna Rostung.

3. Dame Janet Beton, Lady of Branksome.

to the marriage contract,[1] and gave the bride her marriage dress (it was of cloth of silver, lined with white taffeta).[2]   The bride was of the old faith, and the

—(Register of Acts and Decreets, vol. xix. foll. 346, 347. MS. Register House.)   In September 1560, Randolph wrote to Cecil of a report that the Earl Bothwell was married.—(Calendar of State Papers relating to Scotland, vol. i. p. 163.)   The Lady of Branksome's name was associated with Bothwell's in a placard, affixed on the door of the Tolbooth of Edinburgh, six days after the King's murder, accusing the Queen of 'assenting thairto, throw the perswasioun of the Erle Bothwell, and the witchecraft of the Lady Buckcleugh.' —(Anderson's Collections relating to Queen Mary, vol. ii. p. 156.)   The Lady of Branksome frankly confessed that she had fallen, but not with Bothwell, before her first marriage.—(Liber Officialis S. Andree, p. 86. Abbotsford Club : 1845.)   But that her sister, Lady Reres, was a paramour of Bothwell ('inter pellices Bothuellii fuerat'), appears to rest only on the authority of Buchanan's 'Detectio Mariae,' and other works of that kind.

If we can trust the paper known as Bothwell's Testament or Confession, he declared, on his death-bed, 'that all the frendship which he had of the Quene, he gatt alwayes by witchcraft, and the inventions belanginge thereunto, specially by use of sweete water ;' or, as it runs in the French version, 'par enchantement, auquel dès sa jeunesse, à Paris et ailleurs, il s'estoit beaucoup addoné.'   He confessed, also, 'comme il avoit débauché deux filles d'un grand seigneur de Danemarque, les menants en Escosse, et deux autres d'un grand seigneur de la ville de Lubecque, soubs ombre de mariage avec leurs filles, et tant d'autres filles nobles, tant en France que Danemarque, Angleterre et Escosse.'—(Prince Labanoff, Pièces et Documents relatifs au Comte de Bothwell, pp. 44, 47. Bishop Keith's History of Scotland, vol. iii. pp. 304, 305.)   He was reputed guilty of still worse things. See the Earl of Bedford's letter to Cecil, 6th April 1565, in G. Chalmers's Caledonia, vol. ii. p. 459, note

m. ; and the first deposition of French Paris, in M. Laing's History of Scotland, vol. ii. p. 274.

[1] It is dated at Edinburgh, on the 9th of February 1565-6.   The bridegroom settles on the bride the lands and castle of Crichton, etc.   But they are heavily mortgaged ; and the bride's dowry of twelve thousand merks is to be applied to the redemption of the mortgages.   The contract is signed by the Queen, with whose 'aduiss and express counsale' the marriage is contracted ; by the Earl of Huntly, the bride's brother, who undertakes to pay her dowry ; by the Countess Dowager of Huntly, who, as she cannot write, subscribes, 'with my hand led on the pen be the Lord Bischope of Galloway ;' by the bride, 'Jane Gordoun with my hand ;' by the bridegroom, 'James Erle Boithuille,' as in the facsimile given below of his subscription to another deed ; and by George Lord Seton, Alexander Lord Hume, David Lord Drummond, and Laurence Master of Oliphant, who are sureties for payment of the bride's dowry.   The witnesses to the contract are the Earl of Atholl, the Earl Marischal, the Bishop of Galloway, the Commendator of Lindores (John Lesley, afterwards Bishop of Ross), Mr. James Balfour, parson of Flisk (afterwards Sir James Balfour, Lord President of the Court of Session), and Mr. David Chalmer, chancellor of Ross.—(Register of Deeds, vol. viii. foll. 232-234. MS. Register House.)

It appears that Bothwell's chief creditor was an Edinburgh merchant, James Barron, an eminent Reformer, the friend of Knox, and a representative of the Scottish capital in the first General Assembly.   It was he who brought Bothwell and Knox together in 1562, (see above, pp. xxxvi. xxxvii. note 2) ; and their first meeting was in his house.—(Register of Deeds, vol. v. fol. 370 ; vol. viii. fol. 352. MS. Register House. Knox's History of the Reformation, vol. i. pp. 246, 268 ; vol. ii. pp. 322, 323.)

[2] P. 162.

Bothwell's marriage contract with Lady Jane Gordon.

Queen wished the nuptials to be solemnised in the Palace Chapel according to the old rites. But no entreaties could overcome Bothwell's tender regard for the Protestant religion ;[1] the conscience which smiled at murder and adultery, was appalled by the forms of a heterodox belief ;[2] and the marriage vows which he was to break almost as soon as they were made, were blessed by a Protestant preacher in the face of a Protestant congregation.[3] The Queen gave the marriage banquet, which, according to the custom of the time, was upon a Sunday ; and justing, and running at the ring, and making of knights prolonged the festivities, it is said, through five days.[4]

The Queen's marriage with Bothwell.

Of Mary's own infatuated marriage with Bothwell,[5] little more than a

The Fleshly Gospellers.

[1] See above, p. xlv. note 3.

[2] We learn from the Knight of Lethington's verses 'On the Miseries of the Tyme,' that men such as Bothwell, 'quha in thair wordis appeiris rycht godlie, bot yit thair warkis the plaine contrair declaris,' were known by the name of 'the Fleschlie Gospellaris :'—

   'Thai think it weill—an thay the Paip do call
     The Antechryst ; and mess, idolatrie ;
   And syne eit flesche upon the Frydayes all—
     That thai serve God rycht than accordinglie,
   Thocht in all thingis thai leif maist wicketlie.'

—(Poems of Sir Richard Maitland of Lethingtoun, p. 33.)

[3] Diurnal of Occurrents, p. 88. Principal Robertson's History of Scotland, app. no. xx. ; Works, vol. ii. p. 346.

[4] History of Scotland by R. Lindsay of Pitscottie, p. 394. edit. 1749.

Had the Queen issue by Bothwell ?

[5] One who has been cited as a contemporary writer, although he was not born till nearly forty years after Mary's death, affirms that by her marriage with Bothwell she had a daughter, who was carried to France, and became a nun in the convent of Notre Dame at Soissons.—(Jean Le Laboureur, Additions aux Memoires de Michel de Castelnau, in Jebb, De Vita Mariae Reginae Scotorum, t. ii. p. 610.) The story does not seem to have received much or any credit until of late years, when Dr. Lingard and Prince Labanoff gave it their sanction. The grounds on which belief is claimed for it, are very ably and fairly stated by Earl Stanhope in the Quarterly Review, vol. lxxvii. no. cliii. pp. 141-144. If I remain unconvinced, I may appeal, not only to the contemporary chronicle of George Marjoreybanks of Edinburgh,

which expressly declares that the Queen had no issue by Bothwell (Annals of Scotland, p. 19), but to the decisive authority of Mary herself. The birth of her supposed daughter is placed in February 1568 ; but the Queen, writing to her aunt and mother-in-law, in July 1570, calls King James 'zoure littil sonne [*i.e.,* grandson, *petit-fils*], and my *onelie* childe.'—(Letter to the Countess of Lennox, in Principal Robertson's Dissertation on King Henry's murder, appended to his History of Scotland, vol. ii. p. 273, note b., edit. Oxf. 1825 ; and in Prince Labanoff's Lettres de Marie Stuart, t. iii. p. 78.) Mary, indeed, would seem to have prided herself on giving birth to but one child. One of her favourite devices showed a lion and its whelp, with the legend VNVM QVIDEM SED LEONEM.—(Anderson's Diplomata Scotiae, pl. clxxvii. no. 4. Letter to Ben Jonson, 1. July 1619, in the Works of Drummond of Hawthornden, p. 137, edit. 1711.)

The story of Le Laboureur, it may be added, is not the only one of its kind. Bishop Burnet gave currency to the still more unlikely tale that Mary, during her imprisonment in Lochleven, became by George Douglas the mother of a son, who was the father of Robert Douglas, a famous Covenanting divine, who preached at the coronation of King Charles II. at Scone in 1651.

The wife whom Bothwell divorced to marry Mary, was, by her second husband, the mother of five sons and two daughters. But she bore no child to Bothwell. Nor does it appear that, of all the marriages and all the amours of that licentious Earl, there was any issue beyond one bastard son, to whom Bothwell's divorced mother bequeathed all her property. The bastard's mother is unknown, but he seems to

twelvemonth afterwards, the text preserves only one notice—the delivery from her wardrobe in May 1567 of some Spanish furs (which had belonged to her mother) to make a night-gown for my Lord Duke of Orkney.[1]   There are

have inherited his father's lawlessness and turbulence.—(The Bannatyne Miscellany, vol. iii. pp. 304, 423.)

[1] Pp. 176, 26.

Bothwell was made Duke of Orkney on the 12th of May 1567 (three days before his marriage with Mary), by a patent, which the Queen, in her marriage-contract, undertook to ratify in Parliament. It seems to have passed the Great Seal, but was not recorded. He carried it with him to Denmark. It was ignored by the Scottish Parliament, which attainted him simply as Earl Bothwell.—(Registrum Secreti Sigilli, vol. xxxvi. foll. 92, 93, 46. MS. Register House. Goodall's Examination, vol. ii. p. 59. Les Affaires du Conte de Boduel, app. no. ii. pp. xxxvi., xl. Acts of the Parliaments of Scotland, vol. iii. pp. 5-10.)

The house of Hepburn fatal to its benefactors :

The most scholarly and accomplished of our older genealogists, contemplating the rise and fall of the Hepburns, remarked two things as memorable in their history : (1.) The ruin which they brought upon their benefactors ; (2.) The hereditary gallantry or natural arrogance which prompted four generations of their chiefs to aspire to the love of as many widowed Queens. 'This house,' says Sir George Mackenzie, 'was a fatal house to their retainers ; for they arose by the Dunbars in the decay of the English power in Scotland, Reg. Dav. II., the first being ane mean captive, thereafter a follower of the house of March. At the first banishment of the Dunbars, Reg. Rob. III., they followed the Douglasses. This was the second step of their rising. The third went by the forfalture of the Earl of Douglas, whereby they got many lands, and were made Lords of Parliament [A.D. 1456-7]. The fourth was by the forfalture of the Duke of Albany, and the slaughter of King James III. at Bannockburne, at which time they were made Earls [A.D. 1488]. It was hereditary to the house of Hailes to be kind to the widdow Queens, as Patrick [first Lord Hailes] to Queen Jean, widdow of James I. ; his son [Adam, Master of Hailes] to Queen Mary of Gelderland [widow of James II.] ; Patrick [third] Earl Bothwell, to Queen Mary of Lorrain, widow of King James V. ; his son [James, fourth Earl Bothwell] to Queen Mary.'—(Genealogical Collections, MS. Advocates' Library.)

Four of its chiefs aspire to the love of four widowed Queens :

1. Queen Jane Beaufort.

The widow of King James I., the heroine of 'the King's Quair,' stooped to marry a knight's younger son, who was still living, although in exile, when she fled to the castle of Dunbar, while it was held by the first Lord Hailes against the crown. The amour of the heroic Queen Mary of Gueldres with the Master of Hailes, has been doubted by Sir David Dalrymple, but, it is to be feared, upon no sufficient grounds. As to Queen Mary of Guise, we have the solemn affirmation of Earl Patrick, or 'the Fair Earl,' as he was called, that she 'promest faithfullie, be hir hand writ, at twa sindre tymis, to tak the said Erle in mariage, hir taiking deliuerit to him thairupoun, and day assignit thairto,' and, he might have added, 'his wife divorced therefor.'—(Short Chronicle of the Reign of King James II., pp. 7, 37, 38. J. Major, de Rebus Gestis Scotorum, lib. vi. capp. 15, 19. G. Buchanani Rerum Scoticarum Historia, lib. xi. cap. 23, lib. xii. cap. 18, lib. xv. cap. 12. Lord Hailes, Remarks on the History of Scotland, ch. viii., in Annals of Scotland, vol. iii. pp. 69-71. Pinkerton's History of Scotland, vol. i. pp. 199, 252. The Bannatyne Miscellany, vol. iii. pp. 279, 414, 415.)

2. Queen Mary of Gueldres ;

3. Queen Mary of Guise.

Nothing is recorded of the personal appearance of Patrick, the first Lord Hailes, or of his son Adam, Master of Hailes. Lindsay of Pitscottie describes Patrick, the third Earl Bothwell, as 'fair and whitely, something hanging-shouldered and going forward, but of a gentle and humane countenance.' Patten, the English historian of the battle of Pinkie, says, that he was 'of a right comely port and stature.' Sir Ralph Sadler adds, that he is 'the most vain and insolent man in the world, full of pride and folly.'

I have already spoken of the ungainly looks of his son, Queen Mary's Bothwell (see above, pp. xxvi., xxvii., note 5). As I write, a portrait (painted by Otto Bache in 1861), of what is shown as his mummy at Faareveille, is presented by Mr. Horace Marryat to the Society of Antiquaries of Scotland ; and if he can be judged by this, Brantôme assuredly did him no injustice when he called him one of the ugliest of men. 'I defy any impartial Englishman,' says Mr. Marryat, 'to gaze on this body without at once declaring it to be that of an ugly Scotchman. It is that of a man about the middle height ; and, to judge by his hair, red mixed with grey, of about fifty years of age. The forehead is not expansive ; the form of the head behind denoting bad qualities, of which Bothwell, as we all know, possessed plenty : high

Bothwell's mummy.

no traces of the gifts which her accusers affirmed that she made to him of the clothes, armour, and horses of the King whom he had murdered,[1] and of more than twenty thousand crowns' worth of her own jewels.[2]

The next Inventory is of the furniture which was placed, by the Keeper of the Queen's Wardrobe, in the house prepared for the King at the Kirk of the Field, and perished with him in the explosion that left scarcely one stone of the pile standing upon another.[3]

cheek-bones ; remarkably prominent, long, hooked nose, somewhat depressed towards the end (this may have been the effect of emaciation) ; wide mouth, hands and feet small, well-shaped, those of a high-bred man.'—(Residence in Jutland, vol. i. pp. 417-419.) The British chaplain at Copenhagen, who was present at the opening of the tomb, in May 1858, says, 'the skeleton was that of a strong, square-built man, from 5 feet 5 inches to 5 feet 7 inches long ; light hair mixed with grey remained attached to the skull ; the forehead was low and sloping ; the cheek-bones high ; the nose prominent ; and the hair and teeth agreed with Bothwell's age.'—(Account of the latter years of James Hepburn, Earl of Bothwell, by the Rev. R. S. Ellis, in the Archaeologia, vol. xxxviii. p. 313.) The church of Faareveile is close by the castle of Drachsolm, where Bothwell, it would seem, died on the 14th of April 1578, not in the castle of Malmoe, in 1575 or 1576, as was believed in Scotland at the time.

[1] 'Alswa she disponit hir said vmquhile husbandis horss, clething, armour, and quhatsoeuir wes his, to Boithuell his cheif murtherar and vtheris his knawin vnfreindis.'—(Articles given in by the Earl of Murray to Queen Elizabeth's Commissioners, at Westminster, on the 6th Dec. 1568. Hopetoun MS.)

'Bona defuncti, arma, equos, vestem, reliquamque supellectilem, ac si fuissent redacta in fiscum, Regina, aut interfectoribus, aut paternis inimicis, divisit. Haec ut palam gererentur, ita multorum dictis palam incessebantur : adeo ut quidam opificum, qui vestem Regiam Bothuelio ad corporis modum adaptabat, ausus sic dicere, "Hic se jus et morem patrium libenter agnoscere, cum spolia defuncti cedant carnifici." '—(G. Buchanani Rerum Scoticarum Historia, lib. xviii. c. 21.)

' Bodwell rode upon the courser that was the King's, when he rode to the assize.'—(Letter from Drury to Cecil, 15th April 1567, in Mr. Tytler's History of Scotland, vol. v. pp. 520, 521.)

[2] In answer to questions by Cecil in November 1573, the Earl of Morton affirmed that Bothwell had delivered to him of the Queen's jewels to the value of 20,000 or 30,000 crowns.—(G. Chalmers' Life of Queen Mary, vol. iii. p. 82.)

Mr. Chalmers characteristically calls the assertion a 'deliberate falsehood, for the obvious purpose of calumnious deception, by a miscreant, who was very capable of asserting any lie, or committing any villany.' —(Id. vol. iii. p. 85.) But the assertion was not first made by Morton, nor does it rest only on his authority. Sir Robert Melville of Murdocairny, in his examination before the Justice-Clerk and others, on the 19th October 1573, deponed that 'ane suldert namyt John Hythe . . . quha . . . wes with the Erll Boithuile quhen he fled away to Orknay, shew to this d[eponair] that the Erll Boithuile said thay had gottin of his within the Castell [of jowellis quhilk the] Quene had gevin him better nor xx^m crownis.'—(Hopetoun MS.)

[3] Pp. 177, 178.

It is printed for the first time from the original, authenticated by the Queen's subscription, in the Register House.

Many of the entries have numbers (printed within parentheses), referring to corresponding numbers in older inventories printed in the text.

The Inventory of the Queen Regent's moveables, delivered to Servais de Conde, in September 1561 (pp. 18-27), is referred to at p. 177 (7.)

The Inventory of the Queen's moveables in Holyrood, in November 1561 (pp. 28-48), is referred to at

Long before the Scottish capital had spread itself to either side of the steep and narrow ridge stretching from the Abbey to the Castle, the height from which the University now looks down upon the Cowgate was crowned by a church known from its site and dedication as St. Mary's, or Our Lady Kirk in the Fields. It was founded before the close of the thirteenth century, when it would seem to have been served by the Austin Canons of Holyrood, in whose patronage it was.[1] Early in the sixteenth century, it appears as a collegiate church, with an hospital or bedehouse, and endowments for a provost, prebendaries, and choristers, whose manses formed a small close or quadrangle, called ' the Priests' Chambers,' having the ' Provost's Place' or house on the south side, and a draw-well in the middle. The city wall, which was extended round the buildings after Flodden, did not save them from the fury of the English arms in 1544. Ten years afterwards, the ruined hospital, standing about a spear-cast to the north, passed into the hands of the Duke of Chatelherault,[2] who built on its site a mansion, which, at the time of the King's murder, was inhabited by the Archbishop of St. Andrews, the Duke's bastard brother, and the ablest man of all the Hamiltons. It is told by a partisan of the rival house of Lennox, that, on the night which made the name of the Kirk of the Field for ever memorable in our annals, the Duke's Lodging, as it was called, was filled with armed men, who watched as if for some expected event, and that the lights which gleamed in its windows suddenly disappeared before Arthur Seat and the Crags had ceased to echo the peal which told that the tragedy was completed.[3]

p. 177 (7. 45), (91. vj piece), (6) ; p. 178 (35), (84), (167).

The Inventory of the Earl of Huntly's moveables, brought to Holyrood in December 1562 (pp. 49-56), is referred to at p. 177 (2 ʜ), (18 ʜ) ; p. 178 (18 ʜ).

[1] Decimae tam Religiosorum quam Cleri in Archidecanatu Laudonensi, circa A. D. 1295, in the Correspondence, Inventories, Account Rolls, etc., of the Priory of Coldingham, pp. cxi., cxii. Surtees Society : 1841.

[2] Registrum Domus de Soltre, etc., pp. xxxiv-xlii. 261-272. Bannatyne Club : 1861. This volume contains a facsimile of a rude drawing and plan of the Kirk of the Field, at the moment of the King's murder, sent by the English envoy in Scotland to the court at Whitehall, and now in the State Paper Office.

[3] G. Buchanani Rerum Scoticarum Historia, lib. xviii. cap. 15. Ane Admonitiovn to the Trew Lordis, 1571, reprinted in Dr. Irving's Memoirs of Buchanan, pp. 338, 339.

The King was brought to the Provost's Place on Saturday the first, and was murdered on the morning of Monday the tenth of February. The house, which is said to have stood waste for some time, had only two months before come into the possession of the brother of Sir James Balfour, one of Bothwell's most trusted associates.[1] It seems to have been a building of two storeys, containing six or seven rooms. It had three doors. One on the north side, opening from the close or quadrangle, led to the rooms on the ground floor, and to the turnpike or spiral stair by which the second floor was reached. Another door opening from the city wall, on which the south gable of the house abutted, led into a cellar on the ground floor. A third door, on the east side, opened into a garden, to which we are told that the Queen, although the season was the dead of winter, used to pass with Lady Reres at night, to sing and take her pastime. It was through this door that the conspirators, who had false keys to all the locks, brought in the gunpowder by which the house was blown up.[2]

The Provost's Place contained a hall, two chambers or bedrooms, a cabinet, a wardrobe, and a cellar, besides a kitchen, apparently under another roof.[3] Of these rooms, only three or four seem to have been furnished from Holyrood.[4] The rest either stood empty, or more probably were left with the furniture which was found in them.

The hall was hung with five pieces of tapestry, part of the plunder of

[1] Registrum Secreti Sigilli, 9. Dec. 1566, vol. xxxv. foll. 95, 96. MS. Register House.
[2] Nelson's deposition, in Anderson's Collections relating to Queen Mary, vol. iv. pp. 164-168. Depositions of French Paris and of Hay of Talla, in M. Laing's History of Scotland, vol. ii. pp. 270-290, 252-255.
[3] A letter from the Privy Council of Scotland to Catharine of Medicis, written on the day of the murder, describes the building as consisting ' d'une salle, deux chambres, cabinet, et garderobe.'—(M. Laing's History of Scotland, vol. ii. pp. 94, 95.) The cellar appears in Nelson's deposition : ' that dur, quhilk passit throuch the sellare and the toun wall.' The first

deposition of French Paris mentions the kitchen : ' Je m'en vins à la petite cour, et entre à la cuisine demandant une chandelle au cuysynier.' The hall (perhaps including the wardrobe), is probably to be identified with 'the litill gaylery,' spoken of in Nelson's deposition, as leading ' derrit to sowth oute of the Kingis schalmir, havand ane windo in the gawill throw the toun wall.' It was separated from the King's chamber by a stone wall, which saved Nelson and two others who slept with him in the gallery, from the explosion which destroyed everything on the other side of the wall.
[4] P. 177 : ' Et y auoict vne chanbre salle et garderobe garnye ainsy quil sensuyct.'

Strathbogie.[1] It had a high chair or chair of state, covered with leather,[2] and The Kirk of the Field: a dais or cloth of state of black velvet, fringed with black silk.[3]

The walls of the King's chamber, on the upper floor, were hung with six The King's Chamber; pieces of tapestry, which, like the hangings of the hall, had been spoiled from the Gordons after Corrichie.[4] The floor had a little Turkey carpet.[5] There were two or three cushions of red velvet,[6] a high chair covered with purple velvet,[7] and a little table with a boardcloth or cover of green velvet brought from Strathbogie.[8] The bed, which had belonged to the Queen's mother, was given to the King in August 1566. It was hung with violet-brown velvet, pasmented with cloth of gold and silver, and embroidered with cyphers and flowers in needlework of gold and silk. It had three coverlets, one being of blue taffeta quilted.[9] A bath stood beside the bed, having for its lid one of the doors of the house taken from its hinges for the purpose.[10] It was in this room that the Queen sat talking with the King, on the Sunday night before his murder, while Bothwell, having seen the sacks of gunpowder emptied on the floor of the chamber below, played at dice with Argyle, Huntly, and Cassilis.

The wardrobe, which seems to have been on the upper floor, was hung The Wardrobe; with six pieces of tapestry figuring a rabbit hunt.[11] Here there was a canopy of yellow shot taffeta, fringed with red and yellow silk.[12]

In a chamber on the ground floor, directly under the King's chamber, The Queen's Chamber. there was a little bed of yellow and green damask,[13] with a furred coverlet,[14] in which the Queen slept on the nights of Wednesday and Friday, and in-

---

[1] Pp. 177, 51.
[2] P. 177.
[3] Pp. 177, 29.
[4] Pp. 177, 51.
[5] P. 177.
[6] P. 36.
[7] P. 177.
[8] Pp. 177, 49.
[9] Pp. 177, 19, 31, 34.
[10] 'Befoir . . . the Quenis lying in the Kingis Lugeing . . . sche causit tak doun the uttir dour that closit the passage towart baith the chalmeris, and causit use the samyn dour as a covir to the bath fatt quherin he wes baithit: and sua ther wes na thing left to stope the passage into the saidis schalmeris bot only the portell durris. As alsua sche causit tak doun the . . . new blak bed, sayand it wald be sulyeit with the bath.'—(Nelson's deposition in Anderson's Collections relating to Queen Mary, vol. iv. p. 166.)
[11] Pp. 177, 39.
[12] Pp. 178, 33.
[13] Pp. 177, 178, 45.
[14] M. Teulet, Lettres de Marie Stuart, pp. 87, 88.

tended to sleep on the very night on which the King was murdered.[1] It was in this room, which had a window looking into the close,[2] and a door opening into the passage to the garden,[3] that the murderers placed the gunpowder by which the building was hurled into the air; the Queen's bed, it was said, being moved to one side of the chamber, so that the powder might be heaped up right under the King's bed.[4] Two of the murderers, Young Talla and John of Bowton, were locked into the room, and lay concealed there for more than three hours, when, having fired the match, they escaped from the house by the door opening into the garden, where they found Bothwell and the rest of his accomplices impatient for the explosion.[5]

In the articles of accusation which the Regent Murray preferred against the Queen before the English commissioners at Westminster, it was affirmed that, on the Friday before the murder, she ordered a bed and some tapestry of value to be carried back from the Kirk of the Field to Holyrood, and to be replaced by others of less worth.[6] Nelson, one of the valets of the King's

[1] 'Sche sett upe ane grein bed for hir self in the . . . laich chalmir [undir the King] quherin sche lay . . . tua nychtis [*videlicet* the Wednisday and Fraday befoir his murthour], and promist alsua to haif biddin thair upoun the Sounday at nycht.'—(Nelson's deposition in Anderson's Collections relating to Queen Mary, vol. iv. p. 166.)

[2] Deposition of John Hepburn, called John of Bowton, in Anderson's Collections relating to Queen Mary, vol. ii. pp. 186.

[3] Articles given in by the Earl of Murray to Queen Elizabeth's Commissioners, at Westminster, on the 6th December 1568. Hopetoun MS.

[4] 'Comme le dit Paris voulloyt dresser le lict de la la Royne en sa chambre qui estoyt droyt soubs la chambre du Roy ainsi que Monsieur de Boduel luy avoyt commandé . . . le dict Sieur de Boduell deffendist au dit Paris de ne dresser le lict de la Royne droict soubz le lict du Roy, "Car je y veulx mettre la pouldre en cest endroyt là," ce dit-il.'—(Second deposition of French Paris in M. Laing's History of Scotland, vol. ii. p. 284.)

[5] Depositions of John Hay, younger of Talla, and of John Hepburn, called John of Bowton, in Ander-

son's Collections relating to Queen Mary, vol. ii. pp. 181, 182, 186.

[6] 'At hir cuming to Edinburgh, she convoyit the King to the appoynted ludging . . . quhilk was vnmeit in all respectis for ony honest man to luge in ; setuat in a solitar place at the outmest parte of the towne ; ruynous, waist, and not inhabite be ony of a long tyme before . . . Bot to abuse the warld be apperance of that new reconsiliatioun betuix hir and [him] . . . she lay in the hous vnder the King, quhair also thaireftir the pulder wes placit, being ane vnmeit place for a Prince to ludge in, twa nychtis, *videlicet*, the Wednisday and Fryday before his murther . . . Vpon the Sonday at nycht . . . the Quene past vp the way to that same hous, and gaif the King all maner of intertenement, to colour the act quhairof the executioun followit sa neare, for she said she wald ly thair all nycht. Howbeit, in the meanetyme, Parice, hir familiar servand in hir chalmer, was in the laich hous quhair she lay the nychtis preceding, and oppynit the dur thairof takand in the pulder and the murtherars thairat, for he kepit the key that oppynnyt to that entres of the garding. And becaus thair wes a bed and sum tapestre of valour in that ludging sett vp for

chamber, deponed that the bed which was taken away was a new one of black The Kirk of the Field: figured velvet, and that the bed which was substituted for it was an old one of purple.[1] This may mean the bed of violet-brown velvet described in the text. But the text is silent as to any change of one bed for another. It is equally silent as to any change of tapestry, nor is such a change spoken of by Nelson or by any other witness, although French Paris asserted that, on the Saturday before the murder, he was sent by Margaret Carwod to fetch a furred coverlet from Coverlet said to have been taken back to the Queen's chamber.[2] Buchanan gives a place in his history to the story of Holyrood. the bed, but affirms that it was the Queen's, not the King's bed, which was changed,[3] so contradicting not only the evidence of the King's valet Nelson,

Margaret Car-wod's marriage.

the King, befoir his cuming thairto, she causit remove the samin be the Kepaires of hir Gardrop to Halyrud-hous, on the Fryday preceding the murther, and ane vther wors wes sett vp in the place thairof quhilk she thocht guid anewch to be wairit in sic vse, seing it wes destinat for the same. The pulder being laid in the laich hous quhairat Boithuile in proper persoun wes present, he come thairfra in to the Kingis chalmer. And eftir he had plaid at the dice a quhile with the vtheris lordes quhilkis attendit thair on the Quene, Parice come vp out of hir chalmer and gaif ane signe that all wes preparit ; quhilk sa sone as she persauit (being kissand and familiarlie interteneand the King, at quhilk tyme she pat ane ring on his fingar) she said " I have faillit to Bastian, that this nycht of his mariage promisit him the mask." And swa incontinent [she] cryit for hors and departit toward Halyrudehous, Boithuile being in hircumpany . . . Vpoun the morne eftir the murther quhilk wes Twysday, the ellevint day, Margret Carwod, the Quenis familiar and se-crete servand (quhais gret credite in all thingis is not vnknawin to our aduersaires) was mariet within the Quenis Palace, and the banket maid on the Quenis charges, quhilk declarit that the dule schortlie for the King decayit : and thair wes the dayis following mair travell for the inquisitioun of certane money stowin fra the said Margret, nor for the Kingis murther re-cently committit.'—(Articles given in by the Earl of Murray to Queen Elizabeth's Commissioners, at West-minster, on the 6th December 1568. Hopetoun MS.)

[1] 'The Quene . . . convoyit him to the . . . hous, and at his cuming thairto, the schalmir wes hung, and ane new bed of blak figurat welwet standing

thairin . . . Sche causit tak doun the said new blak bed, sayand it wald be sulyeit with the bath, and in the place thairof sett upe ane auld purple bed that wes accustomat to be carit.'—(Nelson's deposition in Anderson's Collections relating to Queen Mary, vol. iv. pp. 165, 166.)

The new black bed spoken of by Nelson seems to be the 'bed of blak figurit veluat . . . all enrichit with pasmentis of gold and siluir, and freinyeit with gold and siluir,' which came into the Queen's posses-sion, with other spoils of Strathbogie, in December 1562. It was sent to her at Hamilton, during the ten days that she kept court there in May 1568, between her escape from Lochleven and her defeat at Lang-side (p. 49).

[2] Nicolas Hubert's first deposition in M. Laing's History of Scotland, vol. ii. p. 276, with the note and correction by M. Teulet in his Lettres de Marie Stuart, pp. 87, 88.

[3] 'Caetera quidem circumspecte, et callide provisa videbantur : in re tamen levi, non levia vestigia, ad scelus deprehendendum, relinquebantur. Lecto enim, in quo Regina noctes aliquot cubitaverat, inde ablato, viliorem in ejus locum substituerunt, in tanta famae prodigalitate, exiguae pecuniae parci.'—(G. Buchanani Rerum Scoticarum Historia, lib. xviii. cap. 13.)

Earl Stanhope, assuming the bed to have been changed, contends that the fact should be received as a token of the Queen's innocence. 'Can we conceive any woman,' he asks, 'much less a sovereign, pausing on the verge of an atrocious murder to secure some household furniture from damage, and incurring the risk of suspicion on that account ? There is a pre-

but the Regent's articles of accusation, in the preparation of which he himself is believed to have helped.[1]

Inventory of part of the Queen's books, church vestments, masquerade dresses, and pictures, in 1569.

The last Inventory in the volume is of part of the Queen's library, the vestments of her Chapel Royal, her masquing habits, and paintings, delivered up to the Regent Murray, eighteen months after her flight into England.[2] We have elsewhere an inventory of another and larger portion of her library kept in the Castle in 1578.[3] Both inventories, unfortunately, are so inaccurate and imperfect that it is impossible to identify many of the works which they enumerate. Nor have we any means of knowing how far they should be received as lists of all the Queen's books. It has been seen that these were kept at Holyrood in a room carpeted with green cloth;[4] and that they were catalogued under three divisions, Greek, Latin, and Modern Languages.[5]

Greek books.

In Greek, we find Homer, Herodotus, Sophocles, Euripides, Isocrates; all Plato, with a volume of commentaries besides; Demosthenes; Ptolemy's Geography; two copies of Lucian; Athenaeus; the Poemander of Hermes

---

cedent of King Frederick the Second—Thiebault, we think, tells the story—who, seeing his nephew and presumptive heir fall from his horse in battle, cried out, "There is the Prince of Prussia killed! Let his saddle and bridle be cared for!" But where shall we find another case of a Queen exclaiming, "Strangle my husband in his bed, but spare, oh spare, the curtains and the coverlet."'—(The Quarterly Review, vol. lxvii. no. cxxxiv. pp. 339, 340.)

[1] G. Buchanani Rerum Scoticarum Historia, lib. xix. cap. 16. M. Laing's History of Scotland, vol. i. pp. 147, 161, 169, 241-244.

[2] Pp. 179-187.
It is printed, for the first time, from the original in the Register House, authenticated, in November 1569, by the signatures of the Regent Murray and his secretary, Mr. John Wood of Tilliedavy.
It would appear that, with the exception of four or five volumes, all the books in this list were lost before the end of March 1578, when a new catalogue was

made, without any regard to the threefold classification of the earlier inventory.
At some time between 1568 and 1573, a box of the Queen's books, some of them 'merkit with the Quene and King of Frances armes,' passed into the hands of Lord Torphichen. They would seem to have been rescued from the wreck of the Queen's moveables at Holyrood, 'quhilkis wer all disparsit, dismemberit, and spilt, be sogeouris and harling thame on sleddis throuch the foule muris.'—(Mr. Thomson's Collection of Inventories, pp. 182-192.)

[3] It is printed, in the Appendix to the Preface, No. II., from the original in the Register House. It is included in Mr. Thomson's Collection of Inventories, pp. 242-248; and is reprinted, with bibliographical notes, to which I have to acknowledge myself much indebted, in the Miscellany of the Maitland Club, vol. i. pp. 3-12.

[4] Pp. lxi, 126.

[5] Pp. xlviii, lix, 124, 179-183.

Trismegistus; the Praeparatio Evangelica of Eusebius of Caesareia; St. Chrysostom's Homilies on the Epistles of St. Paul; the Dictionary of Hesychius; the Progymnasmata of Aphthonius, a common text-book for rhetoric in Queen Mary's days;[1] the Greek Grammar of Clenardus, then, perhaps, in the height of its popularity in the schools; and the Commentarii Linguae Graecae of that great scholar of whom Buchanan wrote:

> 'Gallia quod Graeca est, quod Graecia barbara non est,
> Utraque Budaeo debet utrumque suo.'[2]

There is a copy of the Epistles of St. Ignatius, but whether in Greek or in the Latin version, does not appear.

There are Latin translations of Diodorus Siculus; Diogenes Laertius; and the Geography of Ptolemy, perhaps the fine edition recently published at Lyons by the unfortunate Servetus,[3] containing his remarkable estimate of the national character of the Scotch.[4] There are French translations of Herodotus; the Cyropaedia of Xenophon; Aristotle's Ethics; the Timaeus, and the Symposium of Plato;[5] the Olynthiacs of Demosthenes;[6] Hippocrates; part of Plutarch, doubtless in the admired version of Amyot; Herodian; the

Latin and French translations from the Greek.

---

[1] It was in use at Edinburgh in 1628.—(Professor Dalzel's History of the University of Edinburgh, vol. ii. p. 377.)

[2] G. Buchanani Epigrammatum lib. ii. no. 7: 'Gulielmo Budaeo.'

[3] Clavdii Ptolemaei Alexandrini Geographicae Enarrationis Libri Octo, ex Bilibaldi Pirckeymheri tralatione, sed ad Graeca et prisca exemplaria à Michaële Villanouano iam primum recogniti. Adiecta insuper ab eodem Scholia quibus exoleta urbium ad nostri seculi morem exponuntur. Lvgdvni, 1535. fol.

[4] 'Scoti ad iram paullo propensiores . . . Gallis amicissimi, Anglorumque regi maxime infesti . . . Indiscreti Scotorum habitus, indiscreta fere omnia, eadem fere lingua, ijdem mores, subita ingenia, et in ultionem prona, ferociaque. In bello fortes, inediae, uigiliae, algoris patientissimi, decenti forma sed cultu negligentiori: inuidi natura ac caeterorum mortalium contemptores: ostentant plus nimio nobilitatem suam, [ita], ut, in summa egestate, suam genus ad regiam stirpem referant: necnon dialecticis argutiis sibi

Servetus' character of the Scotch.

blandiuntur: gaudent mendacio, nec pacem colunt ut Angli.'—(Europae Regionvm traditio recens Michaelis Villanouani: De Britannia et Hybernia.)

There is no trace of Servetus ever having been in Scotland. But his practice as a physician may have led him into camps, and almost every camp in that age swarmed with Scotch. Or he may have written, as Sir James Mackintosh supposed, from the knowledge which he gathered in the monasteries and colleges, where the poor scholars of all Europe were mingled.—(Dissertation on the Progress of Ethical Philosophy, p. 365, note i. edit. 1853. History of England, vol. ii. p. 39, note †, edit. 1831.)

[5] Le Timée de Platon, traitant de la nature du monde et de l'homme; ensemble les trois Olynthiaques de Demosthene; le tout translaté du Grec, avec l'exposition des lieux difficiles, par Louis le Roi. Paris, 1551. 4to.

Le Sympose de Platon, ou de l'amour et de beauté, traduit du Grec par Louis le Roi, avec trois livres de commentaires du même sur ledit Sympose, extraits

Aethiopica of Heliodorus, bishop of Tricca;[1] and the Περὶ Βασιλείας of Synesius, bishop of Ptolemais.[2]

Latin books.

Latin literature is less favourably represented. We have account only of the Offices of Cicero, three volumes of his works, printed on vellum, and nine in gilt binding; two copies of Virgil, with a volume of commentaries on his Georgics; Horace; Livy, with a copy of the Annotations of the Swiss scholar, Henricus Loritus; the De Viris Illustribus of Cornelius Nepos, in the epitome of Aemilius Probus; the De Arboribus of Columella; St. Augustine, with a volume of commentaries upon his Epistles; Vegetius; and two works of Boethius, his De Consolatione Philosophiae, and his book on the Topica of Cicero. There are two French and Latin Dictionaries, and what served for a time as a sort of Latin dictionary, the Cornucopia sive Linguae Latinae Commentarii of Nicolas Perotti, bishop of Siponto.[3]

Middle Age and Modern Latin prose.

There are a good many volumes of medieval and modern Latin prose, of which it may be enough to name the De Corpore et Sanguine Domini of Bertram, or Ratramn, the monk of Corbey; the Vita Christi of Ludolph of Saxony; the De Sphaera of Joannes de Sacrobosco; the Scriptum super

de toute philosophie, et recueillis des meilleurs auteurs tant Grecs que Latins, dans lesquels les passages des poëtes sont mis en vers François par Joachim du Bellay. Paris, 1559. 4to.

[1] P. 180: 'The Historie of Ethiopia be Diodore.'
Histoire Aethiopique d'Heliodorus, traitant des loyales et pudiques amours de Théogenès et de Chariclée, traduite du Grec en François. Paris, 1547, fol.

The high repute in which this romance was held in Scotland, may be seen from the praise bestowed upon it by the poetical Earl of Stirling about 1630: 'The Aethiopian History of Heliodorus, though far inferiour to the Cyrus of Xenophon for the weight and state of the matter, as fitted to instruct greatness; yet above it for the delicacy of the invention and variety of accidents, strange, yet possible, leading the curious reader by a baited appetite, with a methodical intricateness, through a labyrinth of labours, entertaining his expectation, till he come unto the end, which he must seek that he may understand the beginning: A work

whereof the author, though he had loss thereby (being a bishop), needed not to be ashamed, his chief person doing nothing that was not worthy to be imitated.'—(Anacrisis, in the Works of W. Drummond of Hawthornden, p. 161.)

[2] P. 180: 'The Institution of ane Christiane Prince be the Beshope Senesorie.'
Institution d'un Prince Chretien, traduite du Grec de Synese, par Daniel d'Auge. Paris, 1555. 8vo.

The recognition of this work is not the only service of the same kind for which I have to thank Mr. Halkett of the Advocates' Library. I am under like obligations to Mr. David Laing of the Signet Library.

[3] The first Principal of the University of Aberdeen, writing about 1530, makes room in his Scottish History for a few words in praise of Perotti's schoolbooks: 'Nicolaus Perotus Sipontinus episcopus, multo sudore annixus vt in disciplinis tradendis rudis aboleretur vetustas et adolescentes bonis artibus eleganti sermone rite instituerentur.'—(H. Boethii Scotorum Historiae, lib. xviii. fol. 382. edit. 1575.)

materia Concilii Generalis of Nicolaus de Clamangiis; the Chronica Chroni-
corum, as the Nuremberg Chronicle was called; the De Genealogia Deorum
of Boccacio; the Commentarii Reipublicae Romanae of Wolfgangus Lazius;
and the Roma Instaurata of Flavius Blondus, which the younger Scaliger,
niggard of praise as he was, confessed to be a good book, although, as he added,
there is nothing in it which you will not find elsewhere.[1]

We recognise only four volumes of modern Latin poetry—the Carmina of
the Italian, Petrus Angelus Bargaeus; the Elegy on King Henry the Second of
France, by the biographer of Budaeus, Louis Leroy;[2] the Epithalamium on
the Queen's marriage with Darnley, by the youthful pen of one who, in older
years, amid his great practice as a lawyer, still found leisure for Latin verse,
Sir Thomas Craig of Riccarton, the variously accomplished author of the
Jus Feudale;[3] and Buchanan's translation of the Psalms, inscribed to Mary
in lines which, perhaps, on one bank of Tweed, although they are no longer
on every grammar schoolboy's lips, may still be thought unsurpassed by all the
verse that has been lavished upon her during three hundred years by poets
of almost every nation and language of Europe:

Modern Latin poetry:

Sir Thomas Craig's Epithalamium;

Buchanan's Psalms.

> ' Nympha, Caledoniae quae nunc feliciter orae
> Missa per innumeros sceptra tueris avos ;

---

[1] Scaligerana, p. 61.

[2] P. 181 : ' Ludouici Regii Consolatio.'

Ad Illust. Reginam D. Catharinam Medicem Francisci II. Franciae Regis matrem Consolatio, in morte
Henrici Regis ejus mariti. Paris, 1560. 4to.

The author was a friend of Buchanan.—(Iambon
Liber, 14 : 'Ad Ludovicum Regium.')

[3] Henrici illvstrissimi Dvcis Albaniae Comitis
Rossiae etc. et Mariae serenissimae Scotorum Reginae
Epithalamium. Per Tho. Craigvm. Impressvm Edin-
bvrgi per Robertvm Lekprevik. Anno 1565. 8vo.

The copy in the University Library at Edinburgh
is the only one now known. But the poem has been
twice reprinted, first, by Mr. David Laing, in facsimile,
at Edinburgh, in 1821 ; and again, with a translation
into English verse, in a privately printed work, ' Epithalamia tria Mariana, infelicibus eheu! avibus conscripta, plures abhinc annos Anglice vertit, et (amicis

perpaucissimis donanda) prelo nunc primum mandat
Franciscus Wrangham. Cestriae, 1837.' The other
Epithalamia in Archdeacon Wrangham's tract are
on the Queen's first marriage—the one by our own
Buchanan, the other by the illustrious Michel de
l'Hôpital, chancellor of France. 'It would not be
difficult,' says the accomplished translator, ' even if
no names had been prefixed to them, to assign, from
internal evidence, to the scholar and the statesman,
their respective verses. Perhaps a finer panegyric was
never penned, even by the mighty Wizard of the North
himself, than that paid to the " quiver'd Caledonians"
by their classical compatriot, in the lines beginning

" Illa pharetratis est propria gloria Scotis,
Cingere venatu saltus, superare natando
Flumina, ferre famem, contemnere frigora et aestus ;
Nec fossa et muris patriam, sed Marte tueri,
Et spreta incolumem vita defendere famam ;
Polliciti servare fidem," etc., etc.'

Archdeacon Wrangham's ' Epithalamia tria Mariana.'

Quae sortem antevenis meritis, virtutibus annos,

　　Sexum animis, morum nobilitate genus ;

Accipe (sed facilis) cultu donata Latino

　　Carmina, fatidici nobile regis opus.

Illa quidem, Cirrha procul et Permesside lympha,

　　Pene sub Arctoi sidere nata poli :

Non tamen ausus eram male natum exponere foetum,

　　Ne mihi displiceant quae placuere tibi :

Nam quod ab ingenio domini sperare nequibant,

　　Debebunt genio forsitan illa tuo.'[1]

Italian and French translations from the Latin.

We find Italian versions of Sallust and of Ovid's Metamorphoses ; and French versions of Sallust, Ovid's Epistles (the metrical translation of Octavien de Saint Gelais), Valerius Maximus (whom Darnley is said to have translated into English),[2] Lucan, Suetonius, and part of Orosius. Of Latin works, written in the middle ages, or after the revival of letters, we have French translations of the Speculum Humanae Salvationis, the Legenda Aurea of Jacobus de Voragine, the Chronicon Summorum Pontificum of Martinus Polonus, the De Vitis Pontificum of Platina, the Moriae Encomium of Erasmus, the Cosmographia of Petrus Apianus.

Italian books.

The Italian books are the Triumphs of Petrarch ; the Decameron of Boccacio ; the Orlando Furioso of Ariosto, which may have been commended

Buchanan's ' Nympha, Caledoniae.

[1] This famous dedication seems to have fascinated Scottish writers of Latin verse. It left its mark, almost in the moment of its birth, on Sir Thomas Craig's Epithalamium on the Queen's second marriage. It suggested a dedication to her, during Buchanan's lifetime, by one who lived to win higher titles to distinction, Alexander Seton, Earl of Dunfermline, whose fine taste and skill in building made Fyvie and Pinkie what they now are.—(Bishop Lesley's De Rebus Gestis Scotorum, p. 282.) It was obviously in the mind of Mark Alexander Boyd when he wrote the dedication of his Epistolae Heroidum to King James vi.—(Delitiae Poetarum Scotorum, vol. i. p. 142.) It inspired Thomas Dempster's dedication of his Latin version of the Cherry and the Slae, to Captain Alexander Bruce of Kincavell.—(Cerausum et Sylvestre Prunum, p. 2. edit. 1696.) Its influence may be traced in two dedications by Arthur Johnstone, the dedication of his Psalms to the Countess Marischal, and the dedication of his Song of Solomon to King Charles I.—(A. Jonstoni Poemata, pp. 422, 423.) And its echoes linger in the graceful lines in which Dr. Francis Adams of Banchory inscribed to Lord Aberdeen the pages meant ' to show that the Muses of Greece and Rome vouchsafe still, as in Arthur Johnstone's days, an occasional visit to the banks of the Dee and its sister stream, as well as to those of the Isis and the Cam.' —(Arundines Devae, pp. ii. xiii. Edinb. 1853.)

[2] ' The King's father translated Valerius Maximus into English.'—(The Workes of James, King of Great Britaine, pref. by Bishop Montagu of Winchester. Lond. 1616.)

to Mary by the lines believed to celebrate her father's praise ;[1] a poem on the Siege of Troy ; the Asolani of Bembo ; the three. octavos of Lettere Volgari de diversi nobilissimi Huomini, printed at Venice in 1564 ; and Italian versions of Sallust, Ovid's Metamorphoses, the romance of. Ogier the Dane, and the Marcus Aurelius of Antonio de Guevara, bishop of Cadiz. There are French translations of the Orlando Innamorato of Boiardo ; of the Vite de Santi of Pietro Natali of Venice ; and of the De Gestis Francorum of Paolo Emili of Verona, better known, perhaps, as Paulus Aemilius.

There are two Spanish books—a volume of Chronicles, and an edition of the Cancionero de Romances, probably that of Antwerp in 1555. There is a copy, either in the original Spanish, or in an Italian or French version, of a book which Ronsard presented to. King Charles the Ninth of France, with some verses by himself[2]—the Dialogues on Love, of Leon the Hebrew. There are French translations of the. popular romance of Palmarin, and of the still more popular romance of Amadis de. Gaul. The Italian translation of that ' golden book,' as it was called, the Marco Aurelio of Guevara has already been spoken of ; and there is a copy of the second edition of the French translation, printed at Paris in 1555, with the title of L'Horloge des Princes. Spanish books.

The books in French, as might have been expected, far outnumber the books in any other language. . Passing by translations and merely ephemeral works, we have, in history, the Chronicles of Froissart, with their. stories of Scottish chivalry gathered in the castles. of the Douglasses ;[3] the Chronicles of Monstrelet ; the work in which the poet and historian, Jean Lemaire of Belges, traced the descent of the Franks from the son of Hector of Troy ; La Mer des Histoires, printed at Paris in 1536 ; a Life of Charlemagne, printed at Poitiers in 1546 ; the History of the First Crusade under French books : History.

---

[1] History of Scotland, by W. Drummond of Hawthornden, p. 348. edit. 1681.

[2] Oeuvres de Pierre de Ronsard, vol. i. pp. 541, 542. edit. 1623.

[3] ' A mon retour . . . en Avignon, je trouvai un chevalier et deux écuyers d'Ecosse de l'hôtel du Comte de Douglas lesquels je reconnus, et ils me reconnurent par les vraies enseignes que je leur dis de leur pays. Car de ma jeunesse, je, auteur de cette histoire, je chevauchai tout partout le royaume Froissart at Dalkeith.

Godfrey of Bouillon, by Philip Aubert of Massoigne; the Genealogy of the Kings of France, by Jean Bouchet, printed at Paris in 1537; the Discourse on the History of Lorraine and Flanders, by Charles Estienne; a Chronicle of the Emperors and Kings of Austria; the Chronicle of Scotland by Denis Sauvage, the historiographer of King Henry the Second; the History of his Own Time, and the Chronicle of Savoy,[1] by Guillaume Paradin; the Ecclesiastical History of his Own Time, by the Franciscan friar, Simon Fontaine; Charles du Moulin's Origin and Progress of the Realm of France, printed at Paris in 1561; the Mirror of Politics, by Guillaume de la Per-

rière. In prose fiction we have the romances of Jason, Lancelot du Lac, Gyron the Courteous, Gadifer and Perceforest,[2] and the endless sequels of Amadis de Gaul; and one or more of the later books of Rabelais, who, among other references to Scottish affairs, remembers the capture of Inchkeith[3] by the

French under Montalembert in the summer of 1549. In poetry we have the works of Alain Chartier, whom the Princess Margaret of Scotland, the hapless wife of the Dauphin, who became King Lewis the Eleventh, stooped to kiss as she passed through the hall where he had fallen asleep; the poems of the Queen of

---

d'Ecosse, et fus bien quinze jours en l'hôtel du Comte Guillaume de Douglas, père de ce Comte James, dont je parle présentement, en un châtel, à cinq lieues de Hamdebourch, que on dit au pays Dalquest; et ce Comte James, je l'avois vu jeune fils et bel damoisel, et une sienne soeur que on appelloit Blanche; si fus informé des deux parties, et tout en la saison que la bataille avoit été . . . Je ne sçais à qui la terre de Douglas est retournée. Car quand je, auteur de cette histoire, fus en Ecosse, et en son châtel à Dalquest, vivant le Comte Guillaume de Douglas son père, ils n'étoient que deux enfants, fils et fille.'—(Les Chroniques de Jean Froissart, liv. iii. chapp. 117, 121; t. xi. pp. 387, 388, 422. edit. Buchon, 1825.)

[1] P. 179 : 'The Corniclis of Sauoy.'
Cronique de Savoye. Par Maistre Guillaume Paradin Chanoyne de Beauieu. A Lyon, par Jean de Tovrnes et Gvil. Gazeav. 1552. fol.

This volume was among the Queen's books in the Castle in 1578, and is now, with a volume which belonged to Bothwell, in the fine library of Mr. James T. Gibson-Craig. It is in the original brown calf binding, stamped with the arms of Scotland, and the crowned cypher of the Queen.

[2] 'The Saxt and Last Volume of the Auld Cronicles of England in French.'
Le Sixiesme et Dernier Volume des Anciennes Croniques d'Angleterre auquel est contenu lacheuement des aduentures merueilleuses dudit pays mises a fin par le preux cheualier Gulifer yssu de sang du noble roy Perceforest nouuellement imprime a Paris. 1528.

[3] 'Et pense que, a ce matin, ayt esté lisle des Cheuaulx prez Escosse par les seigneurs de Termes et Dessay saccagee et sacmentee, auecques tous les Angloys qui lauoyent surprinse.'—(Rabelais, liv. iv. chap. 67.)

The capture of the Horse Island, as the French called Inchkeith, in the summer of 1549, by André de Montalembert, sieur de Dessé, is related in Bishop Lesley's History of Scotland, pp. 226-229, and in the Diurnal of Occurrents, p. 48. The victor — 'le magnanime et vertueux d'Essé,' as Du Bellay calls him— immediately afterwards returned to France, leaving the command of the French forces in Scotland to Paul de Thermes.

Navarre, 'Les Marguerites de la Marguerite des Princesses ;' the poems of Cle- French books :
Poetry ; ment Marot, containing verses on the first nuptials of King James the Fifth of Scotland ; two copies of a work which, printed at least as early as 1527, ran through many editions, ' Le Jardin de Plaisance et Fleur de Rhetorique, con- tenant plusieurs traités en rime Francoys,' among which is a ballad of two Scot- tish soldiers of fortune, in the broken French of their nation ; the poems of Marc Claude de Buttet, who attempted to bring the Greek and Roman metres into use in the poetry of France ; one of the poems of Olivier de Magny ; the second edition of the Olive of one of the Queen's three favourite poets, Joachim Joachim du Bellay ; Du Bellay, the author of some pleasing verses in her praise ;[1] his Recueil de Poesie ; his David and Goliath ; the translations from Greek and Latin poets into French verse, which he contributed to Leroy's translation of Plato's Sym- posium ; his prose Defence of the French Language ; Aubert's Elegy upon his Death in 1560 ; two copies of the poet Ronsard's Discourse on the Miseries of his Ronsard. Time ; his Answer to the Calumnies of the Preachers and Ministers of Geneva ; his prose Abbreviate of the Art of French Poetry ; his Nouvelles ; and the First Book of his Poems, dedicated to the Queen, and filled with verses in her praise, which she requited by a gift of two thousand crowns' worth of plate inscribed A RONSARD L'APOLLON DES FRANCOIS.[2] The French Apollo is said to have received his first lessons in verse from a Scottish scholar and poet, who taught him to read Virgil and Horace during the two years and a half which he passed at Holy-

[1] Les Oevvres Francoises de Ioachim Dv Bellay, foll. 481, 482, 485. edit. Rouen, 1597. At foll. 476-479, there are verses for a tilting match in which the Queen's first husband figured : ' Entreprise dv Roy Davphin povr le tovrnoy, sous le nom des Chevaliers Auantureux.'

The Queen's gift
of plate to Ron-
sard.

[2] ' Le Premier Liure des Poëmes,' writes Ronsard's commentator, P. de Marcassus, ' est addressé à la plus belle Princesse qui fust iamais, Marie Stuard vefue de François II. et mere de Iacques Roy de la Grande Bretaigne. Ceste Princesse cherissoit grande- ment nostre poëte, et l'estimoit, comme elle le tes- moigna bien par le buffet de vaiselle d'argent, de la valeur de deux mille escus, qu'elle luy enuoya, auec ceste inscription : A RONSARD L'APOLLON DES FRANCOIS.'—(Oeuvres de Ronsard, vol. ii. p. 1171.)

Ronsard's biographer, Claude de Binet, tells the story somewhat differently : ' Ceste belle Royne d'Escosse, toute prisonniere qu'elle estoit, laquelle ne se pouuoit saouler de lire ses vers sur tous autres, en recompense desquels et de ses loüanges y parsemées, l'an 1583 elle luy fit present d'vn buffet de deux mille escus qu'elle luy enuoya par le Sieur de Nau son secretaire, auec vn inscription sur vn vase qui estoit elabouré en forme de rocher, representant le Parnasse, et vn Pegase au dessus. L'inscription portoit ces mots : A RONSARD L'APOLLON DE LA SOVRCE DES MVSES.'—(Oeuvres de Ronsard, vol. ii. p. 1652.)

rood as page to King James the Fifth.[1]   He left Scotland at the age of sixteen, but revisited it on a political mission some years afterwards, before his growing deafness finally determined him to devote himself to a life of letters.   His fame was probably at its height when he was called to teach the young Queen of Scots to write French verses.[2]   He deplored her return to Scotland in an elegy[3] which she was often seen to weep over in days when leaving France was yet her heaviest sorrow.   When greater afflictions had wrung her heart, the pages of Ronsard beguiled the weary years of her long captivity.[4]   Nor was he unmindful of her regard.   When the publication of the Sonnets to Both-well filled her friends with alarm, her old master was ready to avow his belief that verses so coarse and rugged could never have been written by her.[5]

English books.

It was not until she had ceased to reign, and had left Scotland for ever, that she set herself seriously to the study of English;[6] and among her books, it would seem that only three in that tongue are to be recognised with certainty

---

Ronsard at Holy-rood.

[1] ' Il fut donné page a Monsieur d'Orleans : auec lequel ayant demeuré quelque temps, il receut commandement de suiure le Roy d'Escosse, qui estoit lors [A.D. 1537] deçà la mer, et l'accompagner en son royaume : ce qu'il fit, et y sejourna deux ans et demy, pendant lesquels il apprit les particularitez et la langue de la prouince.   Or ce fut là premierement qu'il commença à prendre goust à la poesie.   Car vn gentilhomme Escossois, nommé le Seigneur Paul, tres bon poëte Latin, se plaisoit à luy lire tous les iours quelque chose de Virgile ou d'Horace, le luy interpretant en François, ou en Escossois : et luy qui auoit desia jetté les yeux sur les rymes de nos anciens autheurs, s'efforçoit de le mettre en vers le mieux qu'il luy estoit possible.'—(Oraison Fvnebre svr la mort de Monsievr de Ronsard, prononcée en la Chapelle de Boncourt, l'an 1586, par Monsievr dv Perron, depvis Cardinal etc., in the Oeuvres de Ronsard, vol. ii. p. 1670.)

It would be hard to recognise under any name like Paul, any Scottish writer of Latin verse in the reign of King James v.; and, indeed, another biographer not only informs us that he was assured by the poet's friend, Baif, that Seigneur Paul was a Piedmontese, but shifts the scene to the French court.—(Claude de Binet, in the Oeuvres de Ronsard, vol. ii. p. 1641.)

[2] M. Francisque-Michel, Les Ecossais en France, vol. i. p. 494.)

[3] Elegie sur le despart de la Royne Marie retournant à son royaume d'Escosse.   A Lyon, 1561. 8vo. It is reprinted, but with many changes, in the Oeuvres de Ronsard, vol. ii. pp. 1178, 1179.

' Surtout elle aymoit la poësie et les poëtes, mais surtout M. de Ronsard, M. du Bellay, et M. de Maison Fleur, qui ont faict de belles poësies et elegies pour elle, et mesmes sur son partement de la France, que j'ay veu souvent lire à elle mesme en France et en Escosse, les larmes à l'oeil, et les souspirs au coeur.' —(Brantôme, t. v. p. 84.)

[4] Oeuvres de Ronsard, vol. ii. p. 1652.   See above, p. cix. note 2.

[5] Ronsard's opinion on the Sonnets to Bothwell.

' Elle se mesloit d'estre poëte, et composoit des vers, d'ont j'en ay veu aucuns de beaux et très bien faictz et nullement ressemblans à ceux qu'on luy a mis à sus avoir faicts sur l'amour du Comte de Bothwel : ils sont trop grossiers et mal polis pour estre sortis de sa belle boutique.   M. de Ronsard estoit bien de mon opinion en cela, ainsi que nous en discourions un jour, et que nous les lisions.'—(Brantôme, t. v. p. 84.)

[6] Letter from Nicholas White to Cecil, 26th Feb. 1568-9, in Haynes' Collection of State Papers, p. 509.

—a Catechism; the Acts of Parliament of Queen Mary of England; and the Acts of Parliament of King James the Fifth of Scotland. This last work, Scottish books. printed at Edinburgh, in 1541, and Sir Thomas Craig's Epithalamium, printed at Edinburgh, in 1565, appear to be the only books from a Scottish press, unless we hold the Catechism to be the Catechism of Archbishop Hamilton, printed at St. Andrews in 1552. Other two works may be claimed for Scotland, but both were printed abroad. Buchanan's Psalms were published at Paris. The work described as the Astrology of James Bassantine, may be either his Explication de l'Astrolabe, or his Discours Astronomiques, both written in the language of his adopted country, and both published at Lyons, the former in 1555, the latter in 1557. It was believed that, within a twelvemonth after the Queen's return from France, the author foretold her captivity and ruin, and the succession of the King of Scots to the crown of England.[1]

Mary was too deeply interested in the great ecclesiastical revolution of her Controversial divinity. age to neglect its literature. The Reformed doctrines, indeed, had been made the subject of her school exercises; and among the themes which she had to turn from French into Latin, was a make-believe letter from Mary Queen of Scots to John Calvin, rebuking his denial of purgatory, out of the mouths of

---

Bassantine's prediction of the Queen's fate.

[1] The story is reported by Sir James Melville. 'This puttis me in remembrance,' he writes, 'of a taill that my brother Sir Robert tald me, the tym that he wes busyest dealing betwen the twa Quenis, to interteny ther frendschip, and draw on ther meting at a part besyd York [A.D. 1562]. . . . Ane Bassentin, a Scottis man, that had bean trauelit, and was learnit in hich scyences, cam to him and said: "Gud gentilman, I hear sa gud report of yow that I loue yow hartly, and therfore can not forbear to schaw yow, how that all your vprycht dealing and your honest trauell wilbe in vain, wher ye beleue to obtean a weall for our Quen at the Quen of Englandis handis. Ye bot tyn your tym; for first, they will neuer meit togither; and nyxt, ther will neuer be bot discembling and secret hattrent for a whyll, and at lenth captyuite and vtter wrak for our Quen be England." My brother's answer again was, that he lyked not to heir of sic deuelisch newes, nor yet wald he credit them in any sort, as false, vngodly, and vnlawfull for Christiens to medle them with. Bassentin answerit again: "Gud Mester Meluill, tak not that hard oppinion of me. I am a Christien of your religion, and feares God, and purposes neuer to cast my self in any of the vnlawfull artis that ye mean of, bot sa far as Melanthon, wha was a godly theologue, has declaired and wreten anent the naturell scyences, that ar laufull and daily red in dyuers Christien vniversites; in the quhilkis, as in all vther artis, God geues to some les, to some mair and clearer knawlege then till vthers; be the quhilk knawlege I haue also that at lenth, that the kingdome of England sall of rycht fall to the crown of Scotland, and that ther are some born at this instant that sall bruk landis and heritages in England. Bot alace, it will coist many ther lyues, and many bludy battailes wilbe fochten first or it tak an satteled effect; and be my knawlege," said he, "the Spaniartis wilbe helpers, and will tak a part to themselues for ther labours, quhilk they wilbe laith to leaue again."'—(Sir James Melville's Memoirs, pp. 202, 203.)

Controversial
divinity.

Socrates and Plato.[1] Nor did her shelves show only one side of the controversy. We find the four folios of Luther's *Enarrationes in Genesim*; the *Harmoniae Evangelicae* of the elder Osiander; the *Simplex ac Pia Deliberatio qua ratione Christiana ac in verbo Dei fundata Reformatio instituenda sit*, of Herman, Archbishop and Elector of Cologne; the *De Coena Domini* of Peter Martyr; the French version of Calvin's Institutes; and his fatal Defence of the burning of Servetus.[2] Among works on the other side, we recognise two written at Holyrood, and published at Paris in 1562, by René Benoist, the doctor of the Sorbonne, who accompanied the Queen from France, and afterwards became the confessor of King Henry the Fourth[3]—his *Necessarius atque Certus Modus tollendae Religionis Discordiae*, and his *Triomphe et Excellente Victoire de la Foy*. We miss a book which the English envoy presented to Mary in October 1561—the Oration of Theodore Beza at that famous conference at Poissy, which, it was vainly hoped, would reconcile the religious differences of France.[4] But we have the Oration made on the same

---

[1] Latin Themes of Mary Stuart, Queen of Scots, published, for the first time, from the original manuscript in her own handwriting, in the Imperial Library at Paris, by M. Anatole de Montaiglon, pp. xiii.-xv., 22, 23. Warton Club: 1855.

Calvin's defence
of the burning of
Servetus.

[2] *Defensio Orthodoxae Fidei de Sacra Trinitate, contra prodigiosos errores Michaelis Serueti Hispani : vbi ostenditur haereticos iure gladii coercendos esse, et nominatim de homine hoc tam impio iuste et merito sumptum Geneuae fuisse supplicium.* Per Iohannem Caluinum. Oliua Roberti Stephani, 1554. 8vo.

'I am more deeply scandalised,' writes the greatest of historians, 'at the single execution of Servetus, than at the hecatombs which have blazed in the auto da fés of Spain and Portugal.'—(Gibbon's History, chap. liv., note 36. Cf. his Miscellaneous Works, vol. v. pp. 400-404. edit. 1814.) Mr. Hallam has avowed his belief, that 'the death of Servetus has perhaps as many circumstances of aggravation as any execution for heresy that ever took place.'—(Introduction to the Literature of Europe, vol. ii. p. 109, note. edit. 1839.)

Calvin and Knox.

If nothing can be said in extenuation of the burning of Servetus, it may at least be remembered, to Calvin's credit, that, a few years afterwards, he appears to have withheld his sanction from Knox's intolerant denial to

the Queen of the same liberty of conscience which he claimed for himself. See above, p. lxxviii., note 4. We may please ourselves with the belief, that still less would the apostle of Geneva have approved of the praise which the Scottish Reformer bestowed upon the murder of Riccio—'an event,' as Sir James Mackintosh has called it, 'sufficient to dishonour a nation, and to characterise an age.'—(History of England, vol. iii. p. 78.)

[3] See above, p. lv., note.

[4] 'I advertised the Lord James . . . before that The Colloquy of I would desire audience of the Queen's Majestie, his Poissy. sovereign . . . to know of him, whether that the Queen would take it in no evil part, if I presented to her Grace, at my next coming unto her, the Accord at the Assembly at Poissy in the controversy upon the Sacrament. He encouraged me boldly to it, thereunto assuring me that she would accept it well. The Oration of Beza that I gave unto her Grace before, she read (as he saith) to the end. . . . I thought best to give his lordship the copy [of the Accord] . . . That night, after supper, he presented it unto her. She doubted first of the sincerity thereof; I was alleged to have received it from your honour. Many disputes, I heard say, rose that night upon it. The Queen said

occasion by Beza's adversary, the Queen's uncle, the Cardinal of Lorraine. There is a book of devotion by another Cardinal of the house of Guise, the Queen's granduncle, that splendid but licentious prelate of whom the story ran that a blind beggar in the streets of Rome was so startled by the munificence of his alms, as to exclaim—' Thou art either the Christ, or the Cardinal of Lorraine.'

Among the few Manuscripts enumerated, we discover a copy, in the Queen's handwriting, of the famous Latin speech in defence of learned women, which, when no more than thirteen, she delivered in the hall of the Louvre, in presence of King Henry the Second, Catharine of Medicis, and the whole French court.[1]

Manuscripts: The Queen's Latin speech at the Louvre.

she could not reason, but that she knew what she ought to believe. The Marquis [of Elbeuf] affirm'd that he never thought Christ to be otherwise in the sacrament than it was there written ; but yet doubteth not but the mass is good. Against that much was said, but little good done. . . . She asked whether her uncle the Cardinal's Oration was printed : I said that I lookt daily for it.'—(Letter from Randolph to Cecil, 24th October 1561, in Bishop Keith's History of Scotland, vol. ii. pp. 94-96, 101.)

' The Accord at the Assembly at Poissy,' was a short statement of the doctrine of the Eucharist, approved by Beza and his colleagues on one side, and by the Cardinal of Lorraine on the other, but afterwards repudiated by the Cardinal's colleagues. It ran in these words : ' Confitemur Jesum Christum in Coena nobis offerre, dare, et vere exhibere substantiam sui corporis et sanguinis, operante Spiritu Sancto : nosque recipere et edere spiritualiter et per fidem, verum illud corpus quod pro nobis mortuum est, ut simus ossa de ossibus ejus, et caro de carne ejus : ut eo vivificemur, et ea quae ad salutem nostram necessaria sunt, percipiamus. Et quoniam fides innixa verbo Dei res perceptas facit praesentes ; per illam verum et naturale corpus et sanguinem Jesu Christi per virtutem Spiritus Sancti comedi et bibi fatemur, eoque respectu praesentiam corporis et sanguinis Christi in Sancta Coena agnoscimus.'—(Vita T. Bezae, in Melchior Adam's Vitae Theologorum Exterorum, pp. 110, 111. edit. Francof., 1705.)

[1] ' Elle s'estoit faicte fort sçavante en Latin. Estant en l'aage de treize à quatorze ans, elle declama devant le Roy Henry, la Reyne, et toute la court, publiquement en la salle du Louvre, une oraison en Latin qu'elle avoit faicte soubstenant et deffendant, contre l'opinion commune, qu'il estoit bien seant aux femmes de sçavoir les lettres et arts liberaux. Songez quelle rare chose c'estoit et admirable de voir cette sçavante et belle Reyne ainsi orer en Latin, qu'elle entendoit et parloit fort bien ; car je l'ay veu là : et fut si curieuse de faire faire à Antoine Fochain, de Chauny en Vermandois, et l'addresse à ladite Reyne, une rethorique en François que nous avons encore en lumiere, afin qu'elle l'entendist mieux et se fist plus eloquente en François, comme elle a esté, et mieux que si dans la France mesme eust pris sa naissance.'—(Brantôme, t. v. pp. 83, 84.)

The text-book referred to by Brantôme is the La Rhetorique Françoise d'Antoine Fouquelin de Chauny en Vermandois. A tresillustre princesse Madame Marie Royne d'Ecosse. A Paris, 1555. 8vo. The author speaks of the high hopes which the Queen awakened : ' De quoy vous me semblates donner un certain presage, alors qu'en la presence du Roy, accompaigné de la pluspart des Princes et Seigneurs de sa cour, vous soutenies par une oraison bien Latine, et defendies contre la commune opinion, qu'il estoit bien seant aus femmes de savoir les lettres et ars liberaus. Au quel endroit je diroy en quelle admiration d'un chacun vous auriez esté ouye, quel jugement auroit esté fait, et quelle esperance auroit esté conceüe de vous par toute cette si noble compaignie, si je le pouvoi dire sans soubçon de flatterie. . . . Que pleut à Vôtre Majesté que j'eusse peu finer de céte tant elegante oraison, ou plûtôt de la Françoyse traduction, qu'il vous en pleut faire quelque temps apres : il ne m'eut esté besoin chercher si loing des exemples, etc.'

I give this passage as it is quoted by M. Francisque-

Manuscripts :
French sonnets,
probably by Cha-
tellard ;

In the volume described as a manuscript of French Sonnets, we should, perhaps, recognise the volume of his own verses which Chatellard presented to the
Queen on his infatuated return to Scotland in 1562.[1] The parchment manuscript on the 'Government of Princes' was, perhaps, a work of the same class
as the De l'Institution d'un Prince, compiled by Budaeus for the use of the

The Queen's book
of French verses
on the Institution
of a Prince.

Queen's first husband, King Francis the Second, and as the 'book of verses, in
French, of the Institution of a Prince,' written by the Queen for the use of
her son, King James, and kept by him in a cover of her needlework as
one of his most cherished heirlooms.[2] There are some other manuscripts

The Queen's Latin
themes.

Michel in his Les Ecossais en France, vol. i. p. 493.
M. Anatole de Montaiglon, who first brought it to
light, in his edition of the Latin Exercises written by the
Queen in 1554, writes : 'Much has been said on the
early learning of Mary. The great credit she has received on this account will be perhaps a little destroyed
by this publication ; for the reader will see her knowledge of the Latin to be not very sound nor firm, and
some blunders are of such a nature as to render us
somewhat incredulous as to her learning at this period
of her life. The admiration, inspired by the praise
bestowed by Brantôme on the famous Latin speech delivered in the French court, will be somewhat impaired
by the thought that it was a little after our themes,
which perhaps were given to her as a first preparation
towards this subject, and show us that she was certainly
not unaided in the composition of her speech. . . .
It had been said by one of the court, . . . that women
had nothing to do with learning ; and by way of jus-
tification for himself and encouragement to his pupils,
the preceptor fills fifteen letters (xxvi.-xl.) with the
names of learned girls and women. His learning was
easy ; numerous were the books on illustrious women,
and perhaps he did not even seek so far. In one
place (letter xxxv.), he speaks of a certain Cassandra
Fidelis as praised by Politianus in some one of his
Epistles ; and when we refer to them, this letter of
Politianus, the thirteenth in the third book, is found
to be on the subject of learned women, and with the
commentary of Franciscus Silvius in the Parisian
edition of 1523, it contains almost all the names used
by the preceptor.'—(Latin Themes of Mary Stuart,
Queen of Scots, pref. pp. xvii., x., xii.)
Mr. Leopold Massey (writing from Paris in Novem-
ber 1862) affirms that the French versions of these
Latin Themes are 'in a Scotch hand, and Scotch-

French, the hand and the French of John Lesley,
afterwards Bishop of Ross, who took the degree of
doctor of laws in the University of Paris, not many
years before these letters are dated.'—(The Gentleman's Magazine, vol. ccxiii. p. 758.)
The dates of the Themes run from the 25th of
August 1554 to the 5th of January 1554-5. Can it be
shown that Lesley was then in France ? It has
hitherto been supposed that he returned to Scotland
in April 1554.
[1] 'Chastelet . . . is well entertained by the Queen,
and hath great conference with her. He rideth upon
the soar gelding that my Lord Robert gave unto her
Grace. He presented a book of his own making,
written in meeter : I know not what matter.'—(Letter
from Randolph to Cecil, 18th Nov. 1562, in Bishop
Keith's History of Scotland, vol. ii. pp. 177-180.)
The book must have been manuscript, for Chatellard
seems to have printed nothing : 'Il fit plusieurs
rithmes tres belles, que j'ay veues escrites en main ;
car jamais elles n'ont esté imprimées, que j'aye veu.'—
(Brantôme, t. v. p. 123.)
[2] 'The Queene his Maiesties mother wrote a booke
of verses in French of the Institution of a Prince, all
with her owne hand, wrought the couer of it with her
needle, and is now of his Maiestie esteemed as a most
pretious jewell.'—(The Workes of James, King of
Great Britaine, pref. by Bishop Montagu of Winchester. Lond. 1616.)
'Queen Mary of Scotland wrote a book of verses
in French of the Institution of a Prince, all with her
own hand, wrought the cover with her needle, which
the King kept as a relick of her memory, as I have
seen.'—(W. Sanderson, Lives of Queen Mary and
King James VI., p. 262. Lond. 1656.)
Among the books which Drummond of Hawthorn-

which it may be difficult or impossible now to identify;[1] but we need not hesitate to recognise in what is described as 'a great Diet Book of the Duke,' a large finely written folio of the Household Expenses of the Regent Arran in the year 1546, still preserved among the public records of Scotland.[2]

Manuscripts: Household book of the Regent Arran.

The catalogue, which enumerates in all about two hundred and forty works,[3] closes with a note of six Mass Books burned by the Regent Murray.[4] It might be supposed that they were no common volumes which were cast into the fire by such illustrious hands,—that if the governor of a nation stooped to do a hangman's work, it was because the superstitious vulgar shrank from destroying what had been adorned by kings or hallowed by saints of old. But, in truth, the passions of that age ran so high, that when offences against religion were to be punished, it was accounted meritorious in the best and noblest to share in offices which, in ordinary times, are abandoned to the meanest of mankind. Thus, at Paris, in a procession which inaugurated the burning of six Huguenots, King Francis the First marched on foot, carrying a torch in his hand;[5] at Westminster, the Parliament of King Edward the Sixth commanded all the Roman Catholic ritual books to be openly burned by the Reformed archbishops and bishops, their chancellors or commissaries;[6] and in Scotland, before the Reformation was six months old, the church books and vestments

Service books burned by the Regent Murray.

den gave to the University of Edinburgh in 1626, was one by Queen Mary, 'Tetrasticha, ou Quatrains à son Fils. MS.'—(Avctarivm Bibliothecae Edinburgenae, p. 23. Edinb. 1627.)

[1] E.g., 'Ane Epistle to the Quene writtin in Frenche be Diodet Sairell ;' 'Ane Oratioun buik in write.'

[2] Liber Emptorum et Expensarum Domicilij Jacobi domini de Hammiltoun comitis Arranie necnon Protectoris et Gubernatoris tocius regni Scocie: Wilhelmo Coluill commendatario de Culros gerente et exercente officium Rotulatoris anno nostre salutis millesimo quingentesimo quadragesimo sexto. MS. Register House.

[3] The catalogue of King Francis the First's library at Fontainebleam, showed 1781 manuscripts and 900 printed books.—(M. Edmond Werdet, Histoire du Livre en France, par. i. p. 344. Paris, 1861.) But the

Queen's kinswoman, Louise of Lorraine, wife of King Henry III. of France, seems at her death in 1601 to have had no more than 83 works. They were for the most part in morocco bindings, and were valued in all at about 160 livres. There were 7 in Latin, and 5 in Italian. Demosthenes was the only Greek author.—(Le Prince Augustin Galitzin, Inventaire des Meubles Bijoux et Livres estant a Chenonceaux le huit Janvier 1603, pp. 10-16. Paris, 1856.)

[4] P. 187: 'Item mair tayne be my Lordis Grace hym self vj syndrie buikis. Item tane be my Lordis Grace and brint vj Mess Buikis.'

[5] Le Père Daniel, Histoire de France, t. iii. coll. 298, 299. edit. 1713.

[6] Act 3 and 4 Edward VI., 4. Nov. 1549; Statutes of the Realm, vol. iv. pp. 110, 111.

Library of King Francis I. of France

Library of Louise of Lorraine, Queen Dowager of France.

at Dalhousie were given to the flames, by the Earl of Arran and Lord James Stewart.[1] It is impossible not to regret the service books of the Chapel Royal destroyed by the Regent. We may reasonably grieve for them as fair examples of the Scottish art of that age,—interesting proofs of the skill and taste of the monks of Culross and the canons of St. Andrews.[2] But it is not necessary to think that they must have had still higher claims to our regard, or to deplore their loss as if they were the venerable books of which the confessor of St. Margaret relates, that her husband, the rude unlettered King Malcolm, would kiss and fondle them for her sake, or take them away that he might bring them back to her glittering with gold and gems.[3]

The library which the Queen's predecessors had gathered at Holyrood was lost in the first years of her reign, when the Palace was sacked and burned by the English.[4] Her books, therefore, it would seem, must have been collected for her own use, and may be looked upon as showing, in some sort, the bent of her reading and the measure of her learning. We see at once how her shelves were filled by what Sir James Melville tells us of her fondness for history,[5]

The Queen's love of History.

Church vestments and books at Dalhousie, burned by the Earls of Arran and Murray.

[1] 'The Laird of Dalhousy is in ward in the Castell of Sanctandrois, becaus he gaif thre or four puir Friars meat in his Place. My Lord of Arran and my Lord James seirchit all his Place, and gatt thame not; but thai brunt all the bukis and mess-claiths that wes in the Place.'—(Letter from T. Archibald to the Archbishop of Glasgow, 18th Dec. 1560, in Bishop Keith's History of Scotland, vol. iii. pp. 7, 8, note 2.) It is probably of this baron of Dalhousie that Drummond of Hawthornden tells, that when asked by the Regent Murray how he liked a preacher to whom they had been listening, he answered, 'Passing well; purgatory he hath altogether ta'en away; if, the morn, he will take away hell, I will give him half the lands of Dalhousie.'—(Archaeologia Scotica, vol. iv. pp. 79, 80.)

Service books written at St. Andrews and at Culross.

[2] Payments were made from the Treasury of £14, 8s. to the bedell of St. Andrews for a Breviary to King James IV. in 1502-4; of £14 to the monks of Culross, for books to the Franciscans of Stirling, in 1502-4; and of £24 'to Dene Mychaell Donaldsone, monk of Culross, for an grete Antiphonall buke,' for the Chapel Royal, in 1538-9. In recording that Abbot Thomas who died in 1535 gave a Missal and a

Gradual to his monastery of Kinloss, his biographer is careful to add that both were written at Culross.— (Ferrerii Historia Abbatum de Kynlos, p. 35.) A Psalter, it would seem, of the fifteenth century, now in the Advocates' Library at Edinburgh (18. 8. 11), is inscribed ME FIERI FECIT RICARDUS MERCHEL QUONDAM ABBAS DE CULENROS.

St. Margaret's books.

[3] 'Libros, in quibus ipsa vel orare consueverat, vel legere, ille, ignarus licet litterarum, saepe manuversare solebat et inspicere; et dum ab ea quis illorum esset ei carior audisset, hunc et ipse cariorem habere, deosculari, saepius contrectare. Aliquando etiam advocato aurifice ipsum codicem auro gemmisque perornari praecepit, atque perornatum ipse Rex ad Reginam, quasi suae devotionis indicium, referre consuevit.'— (Turgot, Vita S. Margaretae, c. ii. § 11, in the Acta Sanctorum, Jun. t. ii. p. 330.)

Holyrood burned in 1544.

[4] 'Also, we brent thAbbey called Holy Rodehouse, and the Pallice adioynynge to the same.'—(The Late Expedicion in Scotlande, vnder the Erle of Hertforde, 1544, p. 7, reprinted in Dalyell's Fragments of Scotish History. Edinb. 1798.) Cf. Archaeologia Scotica, vol. iv. pp. 1, 2, 13, 14.

[5] Sir James Melville told Queen Elizabeth in 1564,

and by what Brantôme and others tell us of her love of French poetry.[1] *The Queen's love of French poetry.* Her two or three volumes of Spanish are in keeping with what is related of her slender knowledge of that speech.[2] She had better store of Italian

The Queen's French verses.

that when the Scottish Queen 'had leaser fra the affaires of hir contre, sche red vpon gud bukis, the historeis of dyuers contrees.'—(Memoirs, p. 124.)

[1] 'Surtout elle aymoit la poësie et les poëtes, mais surtout M. de Ronsard, M. du Bellay, et M. de Maison Fleur . . . Elle se mesloit d'estre poëte, et composoit des vers, d'ont j'en ay veu aucuns de beaux et très bien faictz . . . Elle en composoit bien de plus beaux et de plus gentils, et promptement, comme je l'ay veüe souvent, qu'elle se retiroit en son cabinet, et sortoit aussi tost pour nous en monstrer à aucuns honnestes gens que nous estions là. . . . La Reyne donc, qui aimoit les lettres, et principalement les rithmes, et quelquefois elle en faisoit de gentilles, se plut à voir celles dudit Chastellard, et mesme elle luy faisoit response.'—(Brantôme, t. v. pp. 84, 85, 123.)

French verses by her now lost.

Neither Chatellard's verses nor the lines which the Queen wrote in answer, have been preserved. The 'Quatrains à son Fils,' or metrical 'Institution of a Prince,' which she composed for the instruction of King James, although long treasured by him as a choice relic, and extant in more than one copy, so late as 1627, has since disappeared. Even by those who believe that she wrote the twelve Sonnets to Bothwell, it is now admitted that the French originals have been lost.—(M. Teulet, Lettres de Marie Stuart, pp.

Verses by her now extant.

65, 66.) It would seem that no more than six pieces, containing in all not quite three hundred lines, which can be shown to have been written by her, are now known to exist:

(i.) Her lines in French (eleven stanzas, of six lines each) on the death of her first husband, King Francis II., printed by Brantôme, t. v. pp. 88-90.

(ii.) A sonnet, in two versions, Italian and French, sent by her to Queen Elizabeth, apparently soon after her flight to England in 1568, printed by M. Laing, in his History of Scotland, vol. ii. pp. 220, 221.

(iii. and iv.) A sonnet in French, and a poem of a hundred lines in the same language, ' Meditation faite par la Royne d'Escoce, Dovairiere de France, recueillie d'vn Livre des Consolations Divines, composez par l'Evesque de Rosse,' written in 1572; printed by Bishop Lesley in his Piae Afflicti Animi Consolationes, Paris, 1574, and reprinted in D. Home's Lettres et Traitez Chrestiens, Berger., 1613, and in the Bannatyne Miscellany, vol. i. pp. 341-348.

(v.) A sonnet in French, beginning ' Que suis je, helas, et de quoi sert ma vie,' supposed to have been written at Fotheringhay, preserved in the State Paper Office, and printed in Walpole's Royal and Noble Authors, vol. v. pp. 43, 44. edit. 1806. There are also preserved in the State Paper Office, two stanzas in French, beginning ' Celuy vraiment n'a poinct de courtoisie,' supposed to be ' written by the Queen of Scots, lamenting her condition,' about 1582.—(Calendar of State Papers relating to Scotland, vol. ii. p. 935.)

(vi.) Fourteen scraps of French verse, containing fifty lines in all, written on the margins of an illuminated Book of Hours, now in the Imperial Library at St. Petersburg, printed by Prince Labanoff, in his Lettres de Marie Stuart, t. vii. pp. 346-352. A description of the book, and facsimiles of two of its pages, are given in the Proceedings of the Society of Antiquaries of Scotland, vol. iii. part iii. pp. 394-403.

Verses wrongly ascribed to the Queen.

The touching lines, beginning ' Adieu, plaisant pays de France,' supposed to be written by her as she set sail for Scotland, and first published (as ' tirée du manuscrit de Buckingham') in the Anthologie Françoise in 1765, have been proved by M. Philarète Chasles and others to be the avowed composition of Anne-Gabriel Meusnier de Querlon, a French journalist, who died in 1780.—(M. Edouard Fournier, L'Esprit dans l'Histoire, pp. 157-163. edit. 1860.) Warton has shown that two English lines said to have been written by her on a pane of glass at Fotheringhay, are part of a poem printed in 1557.—(History of English Poetry, vol. iii. p. 62.) The ' Mutuus Amor,' cited by a recent biographer as a proof of the ease with which she could write Latin poetry, is by Buchanan.—(Miscellaneorum Liber, xvi.) Nor does there seem to be any sufficient authority for ascribing to her the Latin lines beginning ' O Domine Deus ! speravi in te,' printed as hers in Walpole's Royal and Noble Authors, vol. v. p. 45.

[2] ' In optimis quibusque Europae linguis perdiscendis plurimum studij locabat ; tanta autem erat suauitas sermonis Gallici, vt in eo facunda doctissimorum iudicio haberetur ; nec Hispanicum, aut Italicum neglexit, quibus ad vsum magis, quam ad ostentationem, aut volubilitatem, vtebatur ; Latinum intelligebat melius, quam efferebat ; ad Poetices leporem plus a natura, quam ab arte habuit. Literarum formas pingebat scite, et, quod in muliere rarum, velociter.'—(G. Conaei Vita Mariae Stvartae, 1624, in Jebb, vol. ii. p. 15.)

Her knowledge of languages.

Her handwriting.

That Mary was a swift writer, is likely enough ;

The Queen's knowledge of Italian and Latin.

books, for that was a tongue which she could both read and write.[1] Her early proficiency in Latin may perhaps have been overrated at the French court; but she had Buchanan for her master after she returned to Scotland,[2] and, when in her twentieth year, read Livy with him every day after dinner.[3] Nothing seems to be recorded as to her acquaintance with Greek;[4] but with the Greek books which we see in her possession,[5] it is hard to believe that her studies did not extend to that language, more especially when it is remembered that she lived in an age of learned sovereigns, and was bred in the most learned court of Europe.

Did she know Greek?

Her own court of Holyrood was probably the most accomplished which Scotland ever saw. She herself was confessed by every one to be the most charming princess of her time.[6] Her large sharp features might perhaps

The Queen's person.

but for the rest, some may be tempted to hold with honest Pepys, who, on Evelyn's showing him a few of her letters, exclaimed, 'Lord! how poorly, methinks, they wrote in those days, and on what plain uncut paper.'—(Diary, 24th Nov. 1665, vol. iii. p. 126. edit. 1851.)

[1] See above, p. lxxxiii. note 2; p. cxvii. note 2; G. Chalmers's Life of Queen Mary, vol. ii. p. 265.

[2] 'Ther is with the Quene, one called Mr George Bowhanan, a Scottishe man, verie well lerned, that was schollemaster unto Monsieur de Brisack's sone, verie godlye and honest.'—(Letter from Randolph to Cecil, 30. Jan. 1561-2, in G. Chalmers's Life of Ruddiman, p. 319, note.) See above, p. lxxvi. note 1.

The Queen and Buchanan:

[3] 'The Queen readeth daily, after her dinner, instructed by a learned man, Mr George Bowhanan, somewhat of Lyvie.'—(Letter from Randolph to Cecil, 7. Apr. 1562, in G. Chalmers's Life of Queen Mary, vol. i. p. 105.) She had been trained to habits of reading at the French court: "Tant qu'elle a esté en France, elle se reservoit tousjours deux heures du jour pour estudier et lire: aussi il n'y avoit gueres de sciences humaines qu'elle n'en discourust bien.'—(Brantôme, t. v. p. 84).

She reads Livy with him daily.

[4] Con praises her Latinity, but says nothing as to her Greek. See above, p. cxvii. note 2. A still earlier biographer gives her credit for five languages, but Greek is not one of them: 'Latine, Gallice, Scotice, Anglice, Hispanice, docta.' — (Adam Blackwood, Martyre de Marie Stvart, 1587-1589, in Jebb, vol. ii. p. 177.)

It may be questioned if the distinction of Scotch and English into two languages, is one which Mary herself would have made. 'Les Escossois et Anglois,' said the younger Scaliger, who had travelled in Britain, 'parlent mesme langage Saxon, vieux Teutonique, ils se servent de mesme Bible, et ne different pas plus que le Parisien d'avec le Piccard.'—(Scaligerana, pp. 365, 366, 68.)

Scotch and English one language.

[5] A good many translations from the Greek appear among the Queen's books; and we know that she used translations as a help to acquire the knowledge of at least one language. 'She harde the Englishe sarvice with a booke of the Psalmes in Englishe in hir hand . . . When sarvice was done, hir Grace fell in talke with me of sundry matters . . . beginning first to excuse her ill Englishe, declaring hir self more willing then apt to lerne that language; howe she used translations as a meane to attayne it.'—(Letter from Nicholas White to Cecil, 26th February 1568-9, in Haynes' Collection of State Papers, p. 509.)

The Queen studies English by translations.

[6] 'Num studiis, genere, atque opibus, num denique forma
Inuenient aliam quae se huic componere possit?'

—(In Francisci Illvstriss. Franciae Delphini, et Mariae Sereniss. Scotorvm Reginae Nvptias, Ampliss. Viri M[ichaelis] H[ospitalii] Carmen. Paris. 1560. 4to.)

'Toy qui as veu l'excellence de celle
Qui rend la ciel sur l'Escosse enuieux,
Dy hardiment, contentez-vous mes yeux,
Vous ne verrez iamais chose plus belle.'

—(Joachim Du Bellay, 'La Royne-Davphine,' in his Oeuvres Françoises, foll. 481, 482.)

The Queen's beauty.

have been thought handsome rather than beautiful but for the winning vivacity The Queen's features ;
and high joyous spirit which beamed through them. It has been questioned
whether her eyes were hazel or dark grey,[1] but there is no question as to their her eyes ;
starlike brightness.[2] Her complexion, although fresh and clear, would seem her complexion.
to have been without the brilliance so common among our island beauties.[3] Her

---

' Ipsam quatuor regnorum insignia ornavere ; sed forma, cui parem ea aetate fuisse nullam memorant, digna Europae totius imperio habebatur.'—(F. Strada, De Mariae Scotorum Reginae Vita et Morte, in Jebb, vol. ii. p. 105.)

> . . . . 'vne Royne si belle,
> Belle en perfection : car toute la beauté
> Qui est, et qui sera, et a iamais esté,
> Pres de la sienne est laide, et la mere Nature
> Ne composa iamais si belle creature.
>
> Que ne viuent encor les Palladins de France !
> Vn Roland, vn Renaud ! ils prendroient sa defense,
> Et l'accompagneroient et seroient bien heureux
> D'en auoir seulement vn regard amoureux.'

—(Ronsard, ' Regret a l'Hvillier, pour Marie Stvard, Royne d'Escosse,' in his Oeuvres, vol. ii. pp. 1177, 1178.)

' Encore qu'elle n'eust ny sceptre ny couronne, sa seule personne et sa divine beauté valoient un royaume. . . . Le feu Roy Charles, son beau frere . . . je l'en ay veu tellement amoureux, que jamais il ne regardoit son pourtraict qu'il n'y tint l'oeil tellement fixé et ravy, qu'il ne s'en pouvoit jamais oster ny s'en ressasier, et dire souvent que c'estoit la plus belle princesse qui nasquit jamais au monde.'—(Brantôme, t. v. pp. 87, 90, 91.)

' Estant donc arriué en Escosse, ie trouuay cette Princesse en la fleur de son âge, estimée et adorée de ses sujets, et recherchée de tous ses voisins ; en sorte qu'il n'y auoit grande fortune et alliance qu'elle ne pûst esperer ; tant pour estre parente et heritiere de la Reyne d'Angleterre, que pour estre doüée d'autres graces et plus grandes perfections de beauté, que Princesse de son temps.'—(Memoires de Michel de Castelnau, in Jebb, vol. ii. p. 460.)

' Audiui a multis, iisque sane in hoc genere bene lynceis, quicquid viderant in Anglia, Gallia, Italia, Germania, Flandria pulchri et venusti, id totum, quantum et quantulum erat, prae hac conformatione membrorum, hac venustate, hac maiestate, hac huius Reginae suauitate penitus sorduisse.'—(Maria Stvarta Regina Scotiae innocens a caede Darleana, vindice O. Barnestapolio, 1588, in Jebb, vol. i. p. 385.)

' Inter omnes suae aetatis Reginas admirabili atque incomparabili corporis pulchritudine praedita.'—(Martyre de Marie Stvart, par Adam Blacuod, in Jebb, vol. ii. p. 177.)

' Etiam post taediosi carceris molestiam, pristinum oris decus ac pulchritudo, quo tot homines in sui amorem rapuerat, integre adhuc relucebant . . . de cetero obesior solito, quasi jam valetudine minus firma.' — (Thuani Historiarum Sui Temporis lib. lxxxvi. cap. 13 ; t. iv. p. 435. edit. 1733.)

[1] G. Chalmers's Life of Queen Mary, vol. i. pp. xviii, xix. Mr. Albert Way's Catalogue of the Archaeological Museum at Edinburgh in 1856, p. 205. The preponderance of authority appears to be in favour of grey, and Lord Byron has ruled accordingly :

> . . . . 'blue eyes or gray—
> The last, if they have soul, are quite as good,
> Or better as the best examples say :
> Napoleon's, Mary's (Queen of Scotland), should
> Lend to that colour a transcendent ray.'

[2] ' Quand vos yeux estoilez, deux beaux logis d'amour,
> Qui feroient d'vne nuict le midi d'vn beau iour
> Et penetraient les coeurs' . . . .

—(Ronsard, ' Regret, a Marie Stvard, Royne d'Escosse,' in his Oeuvres, vol. ii. p. 1172.)

> ' Aspice quantus honos frontia, quae gratia blandis
> Interfusa genis, quam mitis flamma decoris
> Fulguret ex oculis.' . . .

—(G. Buchanani Silvae, iv : ' Francisci Valesii et Mariae Stuartae, Regum Franciae et Scotiae, Epithalamium.')

' Le premier soir que nous feusmes embarquez, le Seigneur de Chastellard, qui despuis fust execute en Escosse, . . . (qui estoit gentil cavallier et homme de bonne espée et bonnes lettres), ainsi qu'il vist qu'on allumoit la fanal, il dict ce gentil mot : " Il ne seroit point besoing de ce fanal, ny de ce flambeau, pour nous esclairer de mer, car les beaux yeux de ceste Reyne sont assez esclairans et bastans pour esclairer de leurs beaux feux toute la mer, voire l'embrazer pour un besoing." '—(Brantôme, t. v. p. 94.)

[3] Ronsard speaks of her alabaster brow and ivory bosom : ' vostre front d'albastre,' ' cet yuoire blanc qui enfle vostre sein.'—(Oeuvres, vol. ii. p. 1172.) But Sir James Melville admits that her complexion

The Queen's hair ;   hair appears to have changed with her years from a ruddy yellow to auburn, and from auburn to dark brown or black, turning grey long before its time.[1]

her figure ;   Her bust was full and finely shaped, and she carried her large stately figure with majesty and grace.[2] She showed to advantage on horseback,[3] and still more

her voice ;   in the dance.[4] The charm of her soft sweet voice is described as irresistible ;[5] and she sang well, accompanying herself on the harp, the virginals, and still

---

was not equal to Queen Elizabeth's : 'the Quen of England was whytter, bot our Quen was very lusome.' —(Memoirs, p. 124.)

[1] See above, p. lxvi. note 2 ; G. Chalmers's Life of Queen Mary, vol. i. p. xix ; Mr. Albert Way's Catalogue of the Archaeological Museum at Edinburgh in 1856, pp. 204-206, 210, 211. Brantôme, who last saw Mary in the autumn of 1561, assures us that her hair was what in Scotland we should perhaps have called ' blind fair': ' si beaux, si blonds, et cendrez.' Ronsard, who had known her from a girl, writing at the moment of her departure from France, speaks of her golden ringlets :

'Quand vostre front d'albastre, et l'or de vos cheueux, Annelez et tressez.'. . . .

—(' Regret, a Marie Stvart, Royne d'Escosse,' in his Oeuvres, vol. ii. p. 1172.) Sir James Melville, on being pressed by Queen Elizabeth to say whether her hair (which he tells us was ' golden coloured,' ' reder then yellow') or the Scottish Queen's was the fairest, evaded the question by the answer, that ' the fairnes of them baith was not ther worst faltes.'—(Memoirs, p. 123.) This was in 1563. Six years afterwards, Nicholas White wrote to Cecil that Mary's hair was black. Brantôme tells us that it was grey in 1577. She wore borrowed tresses of auburn on the scaffold at Fotheringhay.

[2]   . . . . ' Quam conspirarit amico, Foedere cum tenera gravitas matura juventa, Lenis et augusta cum majestate venustas.'

—(G. Buchanani Silvae, iv : ' Francisci Valesii et Mariae Stuartae Regum Franciae et Scotiae, Epithalamium.')

' Quand vostre belle taille et vostre beau corsage Qui resemble au pourtraiß d'vne celeste image.' . . .

—(Ronsard, ' Regret, a Marie Stvart, Royne d'Escosse,' in his Oeuvres, vol. ii. p. 1172.) We learn from Sir James Melville that she was taller than Queen Elizabeth.—(Memoirs, p. 124.)

' Elle estoit d'une belle charnure et grâce : la poitrine ronde.'—(La vray rapport de l'execution faicte sur la personne de la Reyne d'Escosse, printed by M. Teulet, in his Papiers d'Etat relatifs à l'Histoire de l'Ecosse, t. ii. p. 883.)

[3] ' Equum conscendere et domare, quantum ad iter,   The Queen's aut venationem qua delectabatur, necessarium erat,   horsewoman- studuit, reliquam illius exercitationis curam ad viros,   ship. non mulieres, spectare dictitans.'—(G. Conaei Vita Mariae Stvartae, in Jebb, vol. ii. p. 15.)

[4] ' Ad numeros probe ob miram corporis agilitatem   Her dancing. saltabat, venuste tamen et decenter, nam tacito humilique membrorum motu quamlibet chordarum harmoniam exprimebat.'—(G. Conaei Vita Mariae Stvartae, in Jebb, vol. ii. p. 15.) No one who has seen Mr. Charles Kirkpatrick Sharpe's inimitable drawing at Abbotsford (it is engraved in Mr. Mark Napier's Memorials of Dundee, vol. i. p. xvi.), will need to be reminded how Sir James Melville, on being pressed by Queen Elizabeth to say whether she or Queen Mary was the better dancer, answered that the Scottish Queen ' dancit not sa hich and disposedly' as her English sister.— (Memoirs, p. 125.)

[5] ' Elle avoit encore ceste perfection pour faire mieux embrazer le monde, la voix très douce et tres bonne.'—(Brantôme, t. v. p. 86.)

' Quand vos sages propos, quand vostre douce vois Qui pourroit esmouuoir les rochers et les bois, Las ! ne sont plus icy.'

—(Ronsard, ' Regret, a Marie Stvart, Royne d'Escosse,' in his Oeuvres, vol. ii. p. 1172.)

' Such styncken pryde of wemen as was sein at that Parliament [May 1563], was never sein befoir in Scotland. Thre syndrie dayis the Quene raid to the Tolbuyth. The first day sche maid a paynted orisoun ; and thair mycht have been hard among hir flatteraris, " Vox Dianae ! The voce of a goddess (for it could not be Dei) and not of a woman ! God save that sweat face ! Was thair ever oratour spack so properlie and so sweitlie !"'—(John Knox, History of the Reformation, vol. ii. p. 381.)

oftener on the lute, which set off the beauty of her long, delicate, white hand.[1] The Queen's hand; The consciousness how that hand was admired, may have made it more diligent in knitting and in embroidery, in both of which she excelled.[2] Her manner was *her address, accomplishments, etc.* sprightly, affable, kindly, frank perhaps to excess, if judged by the somewhat austere rule already beginning to prevail among her Scottish subjects. She spoke three or four languages, was well and variously informed, talked admirably,[3]

The Queen's skill in music

[1] 'Ad cantus excellentiam multum ei profuit natura quaedam non adscita vocis inflexio ; testudinem, lyram, et clauicymbalum quod vocant, apte pulsabat.'—(G. Conaei Vita Mariae Stvartae, in Jebb, vol. ii. p. 15.) 'Thre bukis of musik' appear in the catalogue of the wreck of her library in 1578.

Sir James Melville told Queen Elizabeth in 1564, that the Queen of Scots 'somtymes wald play vpon lut and virginelis.' On being asked if she played well, he answered 'Reasonably, for a Queen.' He confessed afterwards that on the virginals she did not play so well as the English Queen.—(Memoirs, pp. 124, 125.) A fine miniature of Mary, in Lord Fitzhardinge's possession, shows her playing on a lute. In December 1566, she ordered £10 to be paid 'for luit stryngis, and the carynge of the lutis and raparis of thame.'—(Treasury Warrant. MS. Register House.) 'Two lutes, and two lute bookes, covered with velvet,' appear in her Fotheringhay Inventory.

'Elle chantoit très bien, accordant sa voix avec le luth, qu'elle touchoit bien joliment de ceste belle main blanche, et de ces beaux doigts si bien façonnez, qui ne devoient rien à ceux de l'Aurore.'—(Brantôme, t. v. p. 86.)

Ronsard speaks more than once of the beauty of her hand. Thus in his Regret :

'Quand vostre longue et gresle et delicate main.'

And again in his Fantaisie :

'Et vostre main des plus belles la belle,
N'a rien sinon sa blancheur naturelle,
Et vos longs doigts, cinq rameaux inégaux.'

—(Oeuvres, vol. ii. pp. 1172, 1174.)

Her knitting and needlework.

[2] 'Quod reliquum erat in gynaeceo inter matronas ancillasque lucubrantes transigebat, aut texens, aut acu pingens : variae adhuc [A. D. 1624] in Gallia ab ea miro artificio elaboratae operae cernuntur, quas Diuum altaribus sacrauit, in eo potissimum monasterio, in quo post recentem in regnum illud appulsum enutrita fuit.'—(G. Conaei Vita Mariae Stvartae, in Jebb, vol. ii. p. 15.)

'I asked hir Grace,' says Nicholas White, in describing his interview with the Queen at Tutbury in February 1568-9,—'I asked hir Grace, sence the wether did cutt of all exercises abrode, howe she passed the tyme within. She sayd that all that day she wrought with hir nydill, and that the diversitie of the colors made the worke seme lesse tedious, and contynued so long at it till veray payn made hir to give over. . . . Upon this occasion she entred into a prety disputable comparison between karving, painting, and working with the nydill, affirming painting in hir awne opinion for the most comendable qualitie.'—(Letter to Cecil, in Haynes' State Papers, pp. 509, 510.) One of her first requests, after the gates of Lochleven had closed upon her, was for 'an imbroiderer to draw forth such work as she would be occupied about.'

In 1619, Drummond of Hawthornden describes, *State-bed embroidered by the Queen, and bequeathed to her son.* in a long letter to Ben Jonson, 'the *impresas* and emblems on a bed of state wrought and embroidered all with gold and silk by the late Queen Mary, mother to our sacred Sovereign.' 'The workmanship,' he concludes, 'is curiously done and above all value.'—(Works, p. 137.) This was doubtless the bed, described as 'vncomplete, sewit be his Maiesties mother, of gold, silver and silk,' which, in September 1616, was ordered to be sent from Holyrood to England, 'thair to be mendit and prouidit with furnitour answerable,' and then to be sent back to Holyrood.—(Registrum Secreti Concilii : Acta 1615-1617, fol. 63. MS. Register House.) It is apparently the 'bedd wrought with needle woorke of silke, silver, and golde, with divers devices and armes, not throughlye finished,' found in the Queen's apartments after her execution, and bequeathed by her to her son King James.—(Fotheringhay Inventory in Prince Labanoff's Lettres de Marie Stuart, t. vii. p. 254. Cf. Calendar of State Papers relating to Scotland, vol. ii. p. 1021.)

[3] 'Toutesfois, quand elle devisoit avec aucuns, elle *Her conversation.* usoit de fort doux, mignard et fort agreable parler, et avec une bonne majesté, meslée pourtant avec une fort discrete et modeste privauté, et surtout avec une fort belle grace.'—(Brantôme, t. v. p. 85.)

and wrote both in prose and in verse, always with ease and sometimes with grace or vigour.[1]

The Queen's court.

In the ring of which she was the centre were statesmen like Murray and Lethington, soldiers like Kyrkcaldy of Grange,[2] men of letters like Buchanan, Lesley, Sir Richard Maitland, and Sir James Melville.[3] The first poet of France published verses deploring his absence from her brilliant court ;[4] Damville, the flower of French chivalry, repined at the fate which called him away from it so soon ;[5] Brantôme and the younger Scaliger,[6] delighted to speak in old age of the days which they passed beneath its roof. If Knox darkened its gates only to prophesy wrath and woe, his glowing eloquence melted hearts almost as bigoted as his own, and wrung admiration from minds which were shocked by the ferocity of his temper,[7] and by the arrogance and intolerance

---

The Queen's letters.

[1] See above, p. cxiii. note 1 ; p. cxvii. note 1. 'De plus, elle escrivoit fort bien en prose, surtout en lettres, que j'ay veües très belles et très éloquentes et hautes.' —(Brantôme, t. v. p. 85.)

Kyrkcaldy of Grange.

[2] 'That worthy champion . . . wha had done sic notable seruice in France . . . that I hard the King, Hendre II., point vnto him and said, " Yonder is ane of the maist vailyeant men of our tym " ' . . . and the Gret Constable of France wald not speak with him oncouerit . . . and England had proif of his qualites . . . wher he . . . be singular combat vincust the Lord Yuers brother, betuen the tua armyes of England and Scotland.'—(Sir James Melville's Memoirs, pp. 256, 257.)

Sir James Melville.

[3] 'Sir James Melville . . . whose Memoirs, now freed from all suspicion of interpolation, may be justly compared with the most valuable materials which British history affords.'—(Sir Walter Scott, History of Scotland, vol. ii. p. 93. edit. 1830.)

[4] ' O Liure donq' plus heureux que ton maistre,
    Tu vas au lieu auquel' ie voudrois estre,
    Voire où ie sui tousiours par le penser,
    Et si le corps pouuoit la mer passer
    Comme l'esprit, ie verrois à toute heure
    Le beau sejour où la Royne demeure,
    De qui les yeux luisent comme vn beau iour.

    En si plaisant et celeste sejour
    Vit la vertu, l'honneur, la courtoisie,
    Et la beauté, etc., etc.'

—(Ronsard, 'Envoy, a Marie Stvart, Royne d'Escosse,' in his Oeuvres, vol. ii. p. 1176.)

[5] See above, p. lxxv. note 3.

Joseph Scaliger at Holyrood.

[6] 'Marie Stuard, Reyne d'Escosse, avoit un beau mary, et delectabatur turpidis adulteris. (Apud Petronium sunt mulieres quae foenum ament.) Lors que j'y estois elle estoit en mauvais mesnage avec son mary, à cause de la mort de ce David. L'Histoire de Buchanan est tres-vraye, elle ne parloit point avec son mary : l'Ambassadeur qui fut envoyé, eut d'elle un buffet de 400 escus, et fit contribuer tous ceux qui estoient avec elle jusques aux valets. C'estoit une belle creature.'—(Scaligerana, pp. 255, 256.)

I have failed to find any other trace of Scaliger's visit to Holyrood. It must have been at some time between Riccio's murder in March 1566, and Darnley's murder in February 1567. The great scholar's recollections of what he saw or heard in Scotland are not always to be relied on. There can be no question, for example, as to the inaccuracy of what he says (pp. 200, 201) about the Queen's father : 'Le Roy d'Ecosse, Jacques V. estoit camard, ce qui estoit bien laid, quia nasus honestamentum faciei.'

Knox's violence.

[7] The Reformer's violent counsels and intemperate speech were remarkable, even in his own ruthless age. See above, pp. xviii. xlii. xliv. xlv. xlvii. l. lxiii. lxxii. lxxvi. lxxviii. lxxix. xci. cxii. 'John Knox,' says a careful reviewer of his writings, 'inculcated as a most sacred duty, incumbent on the civil government in the first instance, and, if the civil government is remiss, incumbent on the people, to extirpate completely the opinions and worship of the

of his creed.[1]   Nor, in the Holyrood of that day, were learning and accomplishments the gifts only of two or three.   It was no unlettered throng which acted or applauded masques in which the dialogue ran in Latin or Italian verse.   Even the contemptible King got credit for writing a ballad and translating Valerius Maximus.[2]   His murderer, the brutal debauched Both-

Catholics, and even to massacre the Catholics, man, woman, and child.'—(The Edinburgh Review, vol. xxvii. p. 167. Sept. 1816.)

Knox's intemperate language: 'As to Maister Knox,' wrote Buchanan, in the year in which the Reformer died, 'his Historie is in hys freindes' handes, and thai ar in consultation to mitigat sum part the acerbite of certain wordis.'—(Mr. T. Wright's Queen Elizabeth and her Times, vol. i. p. 429.) It was remarked, before the publication of this letter, that 'the extravagances of John Knox have received no splendid encomiums from the historical pen of Buchanan : he was too enlightened to applaud the fierce spirit of intoleration in men who had themselves tasted the bitterness of persecution.'—(Dr. Irving's Memoirs of Buchanan, p. 316.)

his History of the Reformation : It was long believed that the most offensive passages in the Reformer's History were unauthorized interpolations ; but this belief has been dispelled by Mr. David Laing's late elaborate edition, which places beyond doubt that what have been called 'the scurrile discourses in it, more fitting a comedian on a stage than a divine or minister,' 'the ridiculous toys and malicious detractions in that book,' are written by Knox himself. Lord Hailes has shown how little its statements are to be relied upon even in matters which were within the Reformer's own knowledge.— (Memorials of Scottish Councils, counc. 1549, in the Annals of Scotland, vol. iii. pp. 260-262, note. edit. 1819.) But with all its faults, the work has high literary merits ; and Mr. Grub scarcely says too much, when he calls it 'superior to anything previously to be found in the prose literature of Britain, and unequalled by any work which appeared in Scotland before the middle of the eighteenth century.'—(Ecclesiastical History of Scotland, vol. ii. pp. 185-188.)

his intolerance. [1] 'Knox's famous intolerance is well known. . . . In a conversation with Maitland he asserted most explicitly the duty of putting idolaters to death. Nothing can be more sanguinary than the Reformer's spirit in this remarkable interview. St. Dominic could not have surpassed him. It is strange to see men, professing all the while our modern creed of charity and

toleration, extol these sanguinary spirits of the sixteenth century.'—(Mr. Hallam's Constitutional History of England, vol. i. p. 138, note. edit. 1842.)

[2] See above, p. cvi. note 2.

Verses, etc., attributed to the King. In a letter to Queen Mary of England in 1554, Darnley says : 'It haith pleased your moste excellente Maiestie laithie to accepte a little plote of my simple penning, which I termed *Vtopia Nova* ; for the which it being base, vile, and maymed, your Maiestie haith given me a riche cheane of golde.'—(Sir H. Ellis, Letters Illustrative of English History, second series, vol. ii. pp. 249-251.) The letter has a strong savour of the schoolmaster ; and probably all that Darnley (who was then in his ninth year) had to do either with it or with the *Utopia Nova*, was to transcribe the copies set before him by his tutor, John Elder, a native of Caithness, who had studied at St. Andrews, Aberdeen, and Glasgow, and was the author of 'A Letter sent into Scotlande,' printed in 1555 ; and of a Letter to King Henry VIII., giving an account of the Scottish Redshanks or Highlanders, printed in the Bannatyne Miscellany, vol. i. pp. 3-18, and again in the Collectanea de Rebus Albanicis of the Iona Club, pp. 23-32. The 'Letter sent into Scotlande' was addressed to Darnley's uncle, Lord Robert Stewart, bishop of Caithness ; and along with it Elder sent some verses and adages written by Darnley, whom he praises as likely to prove 'a witty, virtuous, and an active well-learned gentleman.' His mother is said to have taken great pains in his education, 'lui ayant fait apprendre dés sa jeunesse à iouër du luth,' à dancer, et autres honnestes exercices.'—(Memoires de Castelnau, in Jebb, vol. ii. p. 462.) The singular beauty of his penmanship is attested by a letter to the Earl of Leicester, written from Dunkeld on the 21st February 1564-5, now in the British Museum.—(Addit. MSS. 19,401, no. 46, fol. 101.)

The Bannatyne Manuscript ascribes to 'King Henry Stewart' a ballad of eight stanzas, 'The Complaint, an Epistle to his Mistress on the force of Luve,' first printed by Allan Ramsay in The Evergreen, vol. i. pp. 108-111. edit. 1724, reprinted by Lord Hailes, in his Ancient Scottish Poems, pp. 220, 221, 316,

well, collected books and seems to have been fastidious as to their bindings ;[1]
and as he rode along his well-marshalled lines at Carberry,[2] abiding the
issue of his fate, he could remind the French ambassador of the story of him
who, having failed in his endeavours to mediate between the hosts of Scipio
and of Hannibal, withdrew to a spot from which he could scan the fortune of
the fight, and never in his life saw better sport.[3]

The list of the Queen's books is followed by an inventory of vestments of
the Chapel Royal, masquing habits, and paintings.[4] Among the vestments we
may recognise an altar cover of cloth of gold,[5] and a canopy of purple velvet,[6]

and again in Walpole's Royal and Noble Authors,
vol. v. pp. 24-31.

[1] Two volumes which belonged to Bothwell are
still known. Both have been handsomely bound in
calf, and bear the book stamp of his arms.

One volume is, Larismetique et Geometrie de
Maistre Estienne de la Roche dict Ville France,
nouuellement imprimee et des faultes corrigee, a la
qvelle sont adioustees les Tables de diuers comptes,
auec leurs Canons, calculees par Gilles Huguetan
natif de Lyon. A Lyon, 1538. fol. It came into the
possession of William Forbes of Tolquhon, in 1588,
the year before the completion of his fine Aberdeenshire castle, where it remained till the beginning of
the last century. It has been well kept, and now
stands, beside a book which belonged to Queen Mary,
in the library of Mr. James T. Gibson-Craig.

The other volume contains two books :—(i.) Les
Dovze Livres de Robert Valtvrin touchant la Discipline Militaire translatez de langve Latin en Fran-
coyse par Loys Meignet Lyonnois. A Paris, 1555.
fol. (ii.) Flaue Vegece Rene homme noble et illustre
du fait de Guerre et fleur de cheualerie quatre liures :
Sexte Jule homme consulaire des Stratagemes especes
et subtilitez de guerre quatre liures : Aelian de l'ordre
et instruction des batailles vng liure : Modeste des
Vocables du fait de guerre vng liure : Pareillement
cxx histoires concernans le faite de guerre ioinctes a
[V]egece. Traduicts fidellement de Latin en Francois :
et collationnez (par le polygraphe humble secretaire
et historien du parc dhonneur) aux liures anciens tant
a ceulx de Bude que Beroalde et Bade. A Paris,
1536. fol. It is now in the library of the University
of Edinburgh. The book stamp impressed upon it,
and upon the better-preserved volume in Mr Gibson-
Craig's library, is engraved on the title-page of Les

Affaires du Conte de Boduel, 1568. It shows his arms
(quarterly : first and fourth, a bend ; second and third,
on a chevron, a rose between two lions rampant respec-
tant : behind the shield, an anchor : supporters, two
lions : crest, a horse's head bridled : motto, KIIP
TREST), with the circumscription IACOBVS HEPBVRN·
COMES BOTHV· D· HAILLES· CRITHONE· ET LIDDES·
ET MAGN· ADMIRAL· SCOTLÆ·

A facsimile of an autograph French letter from
Bothwell (signing himself ' James duc of Orkinay') to
King Charles IX. of France, written from Copenhagen
on 12th Nov. 1568, is given by M. Teulet in his Papiers
d'Etat relatifs à l'Histoire de l'Ecosse, t. ii. p. 257.

[3] We have the testimony of the French Ambassador Bothwell at
to the skill with which Bothwell ordered his troops Carberry
on his last battle-field : ' Il fault que je dise que je vis
ung grand cappitaine parler de grande asseurance et
qui conduisoit son armée galliardement et sagement.'
—(Letter from Du Croc to King Charles IX., 17th
June 1567, printed by Prince Labanoff, in his Lettres
de Marie Stuart, t. vii. p. 119.)

[3] ' Il me dist qu'il ne falloyt donc plus parler, pour
ce qu'il voyoit ses ennemys qui s'approchoient et
avoient desjà passé le ruisseau ; que si je voullois
ressembler à celluy qui moyennoit une paix et amytié
entre les deux armées de Scipion et d'Annibal, ayant
leurs deux armées prest à se joindre comme ces deux
icy, ne pouvant rien faire, il ne se voullust rendre
partial d'ung costé ni d'autre, il print une place pour
juger, et au partir il eust an veue le plus grand
passe-temps qu'il vist jamais.'—(Letter from Du Croc
to King Charles IX., 17th June 1567, printed by
M. Teulet in his Papiers d'Etat relatifs à l'Histoire
de l'Ecosse, t. ii. p. 176.)

[4] Pp. 184-186.   [5] Pp. 184, 53 no. 35.
[6] Pp. 184, 53 no. 34, xxiii. note 6.

part of the cathedral ornaments of Aberdeen given in keeping to the Earl of Huntly, and seized by the crown among the rich spoils of his castle of Strathbogie.[1] The list of masquing habits reckons thirty-three dresses, for the most part of satin ; and we learn elsewhere that there were twelve breast-plates, twelve back-plates, and twelve helmets, all of cloth of gold or silver, with five coronets and as many coiffs.[2] The only portraits mentioned are eight panels of ' the New Doctors,' or, as they seem to be called in an earlier inventory, the Doctors of Germany.[3] The painted cloths enumerated were hangings for walls;[4] twenty-eight are distinguished as of large size and Flemish workmanship.

Masquerade dresses.

Paintings.

The dispersion of the treasures accumulated in the Queen's coffers, wardrobe, and jewelhouse, would seem to have begun, like other graver misfortunes, with her infatuated passion for Bothwell. In March 1567 she gave him three of her costliest church vestments of cloth of gold ; not long afterwards he had a gift of some of her mother's Spanish furs ; and, if her adversaries can be trusted, she bestowed upon him the horses, armour, clothes, and furniture of her murdered husband.[5] Early in May, on the eve of the marriage so fatal to both, she ordered the gold font sent by Queen Elizabeth for the Prince's baptism, to be turned into money (it weighed three hundred and thirty-three

Dispersion of the Queen's jewels, etc.

Gifts to Bothwell.

Gold font, the gift of Queen Elizabeth, ordered to be coined.

---

[1] See above, pp. xxv. xxvi.

[2] 'Fyve masking garmentis of crammosie satine freinyeit with gold and bandit with claith of gold. Sex maskenis of the same pairt of thame uncompleit. Tuentie foure scheildis of claith of gold for bak and foir. Tuelf heid peces of clath of silver claith of gold and crammosie satine. Ellevin pair of slevis of craip of silver bandit with claith of gold. Thre Egyptianis hattis of reid and yallow taffeteis. Sum uther bladdis of silver claith and uther geir meit for maskene. Fyve masking quaiffis for the hind heid. Fyve litle crownis for the foirheid.'—(Masking Claithis etc. within the Castell of Edinburgh pertening to Our Soverane Lord and his Hienes derrest Moder, 1578, in Mr. Thomson's Collection of Inventories, p. 237.)

[3] Pp. 186, 25 no. 71.

[4] 'La toile peinte était une des tentures les plus ordinaires pendant le moyen âge. On commençait par coucher un encollage assez épais sur le tissu, à peu près comme le font encore nos décorateurs de théâtres, et sur cet apprêt on peignait soit des sujets, soit des ornements.'—(M. Viollet-le-Duc, Dictionnaire Raisonné du Mobilier Français, pp. 278, 279.)

In a list of goods plundered by Scottish pirates, during Queen Mary's reign, from a bark bound from Dieppe to Dantzic, we find 'fyve paintit claythis of the Forlorne Sone.'—(Registrum Secreti Concilii : Acta 1563-1567, p. 42. MS. Register House.)

[5] P. 53, no. 32 ; pp. 176, 26 ; p. xcvi. note 1.

Painted cloths

ounces,[1] and yielded five thousand crowns), for the hire of mercenaries to quell the revolt for which, it was foreseen, that marriage would be the signal.[2] Before the middle of June, when they parted on Carberry Hill, never to meet again, she had lavished upon him jewels valued at more than twenty thousand crowns, or six thousand pounds sterling.[3]   Her last words to him were vows of fidelity ;[4] and next day, although closely imprisoned, and so wild with despair, that she refused all nourishment, and with bare bosom and hair streaming about her ears, showed herself at her chamber window, calling upon the people for help,[5] she is said to have found means of conveying to him a purse of gold, as a token of her faith and affection.[6]

Jewels given by the Queen to Bothwell.

[1] Historie of King James the Sext, p. 5. The Diurnal of Occurrents (p. 103) describes the font as of fine gold 'of twa stanes of weicht.'

[2] 'The Queen is come to the castle of Edinburgh, conveyed by the Earl Bothwell . . . She minds to levy five hundred footmen and two hundred horsemen. The money that she hath presently to do this, which is five thousand crowns, came from the font your lordship brought unto the baptism.'—(Letter from Kyrkcaldy of Grange to the Earl of Bedford, 8. May 1567, in Mr. Tytler's History of Scotland, vol. v. p. 409.) James Beton, writing from Edinburgh on the 17th June, for the information of the Archbishop of Glasgow at Paris, reports that the Confederated Lords found the font, not yet melted, in the Mint, upon the 12th of June.—(M. Laing's History of Scotland, vol. ii. p. 108.)

[3] See above, p. xcvi. note 2.

The Queen's parting from Bothwell.

[4] 'Elle feit partir Monsieur le Duc [d'Orkney], avecque grande angoise et doulleur de son cousté,' says a friendly eye-witness, 'et plus souventefois s'entrebèsserent au départir. Sur la fin, Monsieur le Duc luy demanda si elle ne voulloit de sa part garder la promesse de fidellité que elle luy avoit faicte ; de quoy elle luy assura. Là dessus, luy bailla sa main ainsi que il départoit,' etc., etc.—(Récit des événements du 7 au 15 Juin 1567, par le Capitaine d'Inchkeith, printed by M. Teulet, in his Papiers d'Etat relatifs à l'Histoire de l'Ecosse, t. ii. pp. 165, 166.)

The Queen after Carberry.

[5] 'L'on la mena souper au logis du Prévost. Mais, combien qu'elle n'avoit mangé de xxiiii heures paravant, ne voullut oncques rien goutter . . . Le lendemain ensuyvant, elle fust gardée comme une captive dans sa chambre, où n'y avoit nul de ses serviteurs qui eust entrée pour parler à elle. Et, par nuyt, elle

vient en une des fenestres de sa chambre et cria au secours. Et le lendemain, de cas pareille, devant tout le peuple, elle se meist à la fenestre, criant à l'ayde et au secours ; et se tint là un certain espace, jusques à ce que les seigneurs en furent advertis qui luy allèrent reconforter par bonnes parolles.'—(Récit par le Capitaine d'Inchkeith, in M. Teulet's Papiers d'Etat relatifs à l'Histoire de l'Ecosse, t. ii. p. 166.)

'Sche cam yesterday to ane windo of hir chalmer that lukkit on the hie gait, and cryit forth on the pepill quhow sche was halden in prison, and keepit be hir awin subjects quha had betrayit hir. Sche cam to the said windo sundrie tymes in sa miserable a stait, her hairs hingand about her loggis, and hir breist, yea the maist pairt of all her bodie, fra the waist up, bair and discoverit, that na man could luk upon hir bot sche movit him to pitie and compassion.'—(Letter from James Beton, to his brother Andrew, for the information of the Archbishop of Glasgow, 17. June 1567, in M. Laing's History of Scotland, vol. ii. p. 114.)

[6] 'And being in Edinburgh vpoun the xvj day of . . . Junij 1567 . . . the noblemen past to hir humlie requiring hir that she wald . . . be content that the pretendit and vnlawfull mariage quhairin she wes vnprouisitlie enterit tobe dissoulit for hir awin honour, the saulfgard of hir sone, and the quietnes of hir realme and subiectis.   To the quhilk na vther ansuer culd be obtenit bot rigorous minassing on the ane pairt, avowand tobe revengit on all thame that had schawin thame selffis in that cause ; and on the vther part offerand to leif and gif ower the realme and all, swa she mycht be sufferit to posses the murtherar of hir husband.   And in farther pruif of hir inordinat affectioun towardes him she convoyit a purs with gold

The Queen's last gift to Bothwell.

The jewels which the Queen had given to Bothwell, with most of her own moveables, were detained in the Castle, or fell into the hands of the Confederated Lords.[1] More than thirteen hundred ounces of her silver plate, according to one account, or twice that quantity according to another, were coined at once to meet the more urgent needs of the new government.[2] A few weeks afterwards, when Murray, before accepting the Regency, waited upon the Queen at Lochleven, she is said to have entreated him to take her diamonds and other valuables into his keeping as the only means of saving them for herself and her child.[3] The trust, it is added, was accepted unwillingly. It was certainly ill kept. The Regent needs little defence from the Queen's complaint that fear of offending him hindered Sir Robert Melville from delivering up a ring which had been sent to her by Queen Elizabeth as a pledge of affection, and which Mary now

Marginal notes:
Plate coined by the Confederated Lords.
Jewels, etc., given in charge to the Regent Murray.
The Regalia.

---

to him be Dauid Kintor the same xvj day.'—(Articles given in by the Earl of Murray to Queen Elizabeth's Commissioners at Westminster, on the 6th Dec. 1568. Hopetoun MS.)

[1] After the Queen was sent to Lochleven, on the 17th of June 1567, the Confederated Lords 'went doun to the Palace of Halyrudhous, and tooke up an inventar of the plait, jewells, and other movables. Upon the 24th day of June they threw doun sindrie things in the Queen's Chappell, where the Queene had her masse.'—(Calderwood's History of the Kirk of Scotland, vol. ii. p. 366.)

'Ces traistres abominables . . . toute la nuict se mirent à piller tous ses meubles, bagues et ioyaux, qu'elle auoit en son Palais, et ne luy laisserent chose quelconque, dont elle et son fils n'ont oncques peu retirer que bien peu.'—(Adam Blackwood, Martyre de Marie Stvart, in Jebb, vol. ii. p. 219.)

[2] 'Vpoun the xv and xvj dayes of Julij [1567], the [Confederated] Lordis causit streik the Quenis wark in xx shilling, xxx shilling, and x shilling peices, quhilk extendit to aucht stane wecht.'—(Diurnal of Occurrents, p. 117.)

'Thay spairit not to put violent handis upoun hir Majesties copburd, weyand saxtene stane weght, and meltit the same, and convertit all in coyne, wherby they forgeit a staff to brek hir heid with hir awin geir.'—(Historie of King James the Sext, p. 16.)

An order of the Confederated Lords for coining twenty-seven pieces of the Queen's plate (weighing seventy-four marks, or five hundred and ninety-two ounces), which were in the hands of Servais de Conde, is printed in the Appendix to the Preface, No. III., from a collation of two copies, one in Bishop Keith's History of Scotland, vol. i. pp. cv. cvi. ; the other in Selections illustrating the Reign of Mary Queen of Scotland, p. 194.

It is dated on the 10th of July 1567. Fourteen days afterwards, the Confederated Lords issued an order to Servais de Conde to deliver up 'the Crown, Sceptre, and Sword Royall of the realme' for the coronation of the Prince.—(Bishop Keith's History of Scotland, vol. i. p. cvi.)

[3] 'The Queen required him . . . to take her jewels, and things of value which were hers, into his custody . . . He shewed himself very unwilling to have the custody of her jewels . . . Since . . . she hath written a letter of her own hand unto the said Earl, requiring him to take her jewels, and all she hath of value, into his custody ; for otherwise she is sure neither she nor her son shall have good of them.'—(Letter from Throckmorton to Queen Elizabeth, 20. Aug. 1567, in Bishop Keith's History of Scotland, vol. ii. p. 738.)

On the 10th of September, Sir James Melville writes to Throckmorton, that 'the delivery of the Castle and jewels to the Regent has colded many of the stomachs' of the Hamiltons.—(Calendar of State Papers relating to Scotland, vol. ii. p. 845.)

Pearls sold by
Murray to Queen
Elizabeth.

wished to recover, in the vain hope that it would be a spell to summon
help from England.[1] But he has to answer a heavier charge. The jewels had
not been many months in his hands before he despatched an envoy to London
to sell some of the finest to the English Queen.[2] The transaction was so secret
that it would seem not to have reached Mary's ears.[3] But it did not

On the 13th of October, the Regent named commissioners to audit the account of all the gold and
silver received by the Earl of Morton from the Queen's
servants or otherwise, since the 10th of June.—
(Registrum Honoris de Morton, vol. i. p. 28.)
On the same day, a sum of 18s. 8d. was paid
' be my Lord Regentis Grace command for transporting of the Quenis Grace cofferris of Halierudehous to the Castell of Edinburght,' and a sum of 55s.
'for transporting of the haill tapestrie furtht of the
Abbay of Halierudehous to the Castell of Edinburght.'
—(Computum Thesaurarii Regis Scotorum, 1567. MS.
Register House.)

Plate deliver-
ed to the Re-
gent by the
Queen's Almo-
ner.

The Regent's acknowledgment of the receipt (on
the 13th of November 1567) of sixteen pieces of the
Queen's plate, from her almoner, Archibald Craufurd,
parson of Eglesham, is reprinted in the Appendix to
the Preface, No. IV., from Robertson's Topographical
Description of Ayrshire, pp. 431, 432. The original
is in the Craufurdland charter chest. There was a payment from the Treasury, in March 1567-8, for charging
' the Lard of Petfirren to deliuer certane siluer plaitis.'

The Queen's
horses.

It appears that the Queen was allowed to dispose
of her horses as she pleased. They were thirty-four
in number. See Appendix to the Preface, No. VII.

Ring given by
Queen Eliza-
beth to Queen
Mary, as a
pledge of suc-
cour in time of
need.

[1] ' Il vous souvient qu'il vous a plu me mander diverse
fois que vous entendiez, voyant la bague que m'avez
envoyée, me secourir dans toutes mes afflictions.
Vous sçavez comme mon frère de Mora a tout ce que
j'ay. Ceulx qui ont quelque chose sont convenu me
rien délivrer. Robert Melvin au moyns dit ne me
l'oser rendre, combien que je la lui avois baylié se-
grettemant comme mon plus cher joyau.' Parquoi je
vous supplie que voyant la présante, ayez pitié de
votre bonne soeur,' etc. etc.—(Letter from Mary to
Elizabeth, 1. May 1568, printed by Prince Labanoff,
in his Lettres de Marie Stuart, t. ii. pp. 67, 68.)

We have the other side of the story in the deposition of one of the Queen's attendants at Lochleven :
' The Quene desirit me sindry tymes ask ane ring fra
him [Sir Robert Melville] quhilk he had of her in
keping [that] scho gat fra the Quene [of] Ingland. I
raid to him at Disart, quhair he was at that present,
and schew the Quene desirit sic ane ring, bot, becaus

scho estemit [it] as ane jowall, I said I wald not cary
it. He anserit, And houbeit I wald, he wald nocht
gif it ; my Lord Regentis Grace knew of it, and he
wald nocht offend him ; he was the man he luffit best,
and had ane sufficient pruiff of the samyn baytht in hir
motheris tyme and in hir awin ; bot he wald vret ane
excuis. Quhilk he send to me within tua dayis with
ane precept to be subscrevit be the Quene of his pen-
sioune,' etc.—(MS. Fragment in the Register House.)

The ring was given up to the Queen during the
brief triumph which followed her escape : ' Item declaris that efter the Quenis cuming furth of Lochlevin
quhen sche wes in Hammyltoun she send for this
deponar and he deliuerit vnto hir a ring . . . quhilk
ring he hard sensyne that Johnne Betoun conveyit
agane fra the Quene to the Quene of England.'—(Examination of Sir Robert Melville, 19. Oct. 1573.
Hopetoun MS.)

It was in vain that Mary reminded Elizabeth of the
promises of which the ring was the token : ' Davantage la dicte dame se souvient que la Royne sa bonne
soeur, en tesmoignage et confirmation de l'amytié qui
estoit entre leurs Majestez, luy envoya une baggue avec
asseurance et promesse d'employer ses forces et
moyens en sa faveur quand Sa Majesté en auroit besoing, et que, pour signal de ce, la dicte baggue luy
seroit renvoyée ; laquelle sa dicte bonne soeur a depuis receue par les mains du feu seigneur de Beton,
soubz laquelle asseurance Sa Majesté est aussi venue
en ce pays.'—(Letter from Mary to Elizabeth, Sheffield, 14. Febr. 1571-2, in Prince Labanoff's Lettres
de Marie Stuart, t. iv. p. 29.)

[2] It appears by a letter to Catharine of Medicis,
from Bochetel de la Forest, the French ambassador at
London, that the jewels had been brought to London
for sale, in April 1568 : ' actendu qu'ilz tiennent ceste
affaire-cy secret.'—(M. Teulet, Papiers d'Etat relatifs
à l'Histoire de l'Ecosse, t. ii. p. 201.)

[3] A fortnight after the sale had been completed,
the Queen is found giving instructions to Lord Fleming to move the French king to forbid their sale if
they should be carried to France : ' Toucher un mot
au dit Seigneur Roy des bagues et joyaulx de la dite
Dame qu'elle a esté advertye avoir esté envoyez par

escape the watchful Queen Mother of France. Catharine of Medicis was eager to possess herself of pearls which she had admired or envied of old at Fontainebleau, and of which she now heard that they were confessed at Whitehall to be of matchless beauty. But she was too late. Before she could tell the French ambassador in England to give the price which was set upon them, they had been bought by Queen Elizabeth for twelve thousand crowns, or three thousand six hundred pounds sterling.[1]

les rebelles hors du pays pour vendre. Et s'il se trouvoit y en avoir aucuns en France, que le Roy veuille commander les arrester et cependant faire deffendre à tous quelz qu'ils soient de n'en acheter n'y ne s'en mesler et entremettre aucunement.'—(Instructions to Lord Fleming, 30. May 1568, in Prince Labanoff's Lettres de Marie Stuart, t. ii. p. 89.)

Her friends in France heard of the affair, but their information was so little accurate that they believed that the jewels which fell into Queen Elizabeth's hands, came to her by gift, not by purchase : 'le reste ayant esté baillé par le bastard Mourray à la Royne d'Angleterre et à ceux de son conseil, vendu en France et en Flandres.'—(Adam Blackwood, Martyre de Marie Stvart, in Jebb, vol. ii. p. 219.)

[1] The story is told in five letters from the French ambassador, Bochetel de la Forest, to King Charles IX. of France, to Catharine of Medicis, and to her secretary, written from London, on the 2nd, the 8th, and the 15th of May, and in two letters in answer from Catharine of Medicis, of the 21st May 1568, printed partly by M. Teulet, in his Papiers d'Etat relatifs à l'Histoire de l'Ecosse, t. ii. pp. 201, 202, 211, 214, 217, 218, and partly by Prince Labanoff, in his Lettres de Marie Stuart, t. vii. pp. 129, 130, 132, 133.

Catharine of Medicis and the Queen's pearls. It appears that Murray sent the jewels to London by his trusty dependant Nichol (or Michael) Elphinstone. They were shown to Queen Elizabeth on the 1st of May, in presence of the Earls of Pembroke and Leicester, 'qui les trouvèrent d'une beauté nompareille.' They seem to have been kept from the sight of the French ambassador, so that he could not describe them to Catharine except from the reports of others : 'Je me suys enquis particulièrement de ces bagues de la Royne d'Escosse qui sont par deçà. J'ay sceu que les grosses perles, dont m'escrivoit une foys Vostre Majesté, y sont, et, comme on me les a specifiées, il y en a six cordons, où elles sont enfilées comme patenostres, et, oultre cela, environ vingt cinq à part et séparées les unes

des aultres, encores plus belles et plus grosses que celles qui sont enfilées, la pluspart comme noix muscades. Elles n'ont pas été troys jours icy qu'on les a faict aprécier par divers marchans, ceste Royne [d'Angleterre] les voullant prendre pour la somme qu'elles seront évaluées ; c'est à sçavoir à la raison que les prendroit ung marchant qui voudroit gaigner dessus à les vendre. Elles ont été premièrement monstrées à troys ou quatre orfèvres et lapidaires de ceste ville [Londres] qui les ont estimées à troys milles livres sterlings, qui font dix mille escuz, s'offrant d'en bailler la dicte somme si on voulloit. Quelques marchans Italiens, qui les ont veues après, les ont prisée jusques à douze mille escuz, qui est environ le prix, ainsi qu'on m'a dict, pour lequel ceste Royne les prendra. Il y a un Genèvois qui les a veues après tous les aultres, qui les a estimées à seize mille, mais je pense qu'elles lui demeureront à douze . . . Le reste des dictes bagues n'approche pas de la valleur des perles, et n'en ay ouy spéciffier que une pièce de licorne qui est bien mise en oeuvre et fort enrichie.' On le 15th of May, the French ambassador writes to Catharine de Medicis, that his nephew will tell her about the sale of the jewels to Queen Elizabeth for 12,000 crowns : 'et mesmement de ces bagues, lesquelles, ainsy qu'il vous dira, ont esté icy envoyées fort secrétement, et enfin, comme j'ay cidevant escript, acheptées par ceste Royne pour la somme de douze mil escuz.'

The pearls spoken of seem to be those which Mary, in her Testamentary Inventory, divided between the Scottish crown and the houses of Guise, Aumale, and Elbeuf (pp. 96-98, 101, 102). The bit of what was Unicorn's horn. supposed to be the horn of a unicorn (probably part of the tooth of a narwhal) appears to be the 'pièce de licorne garnye dune chayne dargent,' which the Queen bequeathed to her nephew Francis Stewart (p. 110). The horn, regarded as an antidote to all poison, was fastened to a chain, so that it might be dipped into cups or dishes. In May 1574, Mary writes from Sheffield to the Archbishop of Glasgow at Paris : 'Je vous prie

The bargain may have been hastened by tidings that, on the day after the jewels were first shown to the English Queen, Mary escaped from Lochleven. Henceforth there was an end of any semblance even of trust or forbearance between the Queen and her brother. The Parliament which met a few months after Langside, passed an Act placing her diamonds at his

Murray's intended
sale of the rest of
the Queen's jewels,
stopped by Queen
Elizabeth.

disposal;[1] and he lost no time in preparing for their sale. Mary implored the interposition of the English Queen;[2] and Elizabeth's remonstrances led Murray to abandon his intention.[3] Except complaints by the dethroned princess that the cause of her adversaries was maintained by the treasure of which they had spoiled her,[4] we hear no more of her jewels during the Regent's life.

m'envoyer de la vraye terre sigillatée, si la pouvez recouvrer pour argent, sinon en demander à Monsieur le Cardinal mon oncle ; ou, s'il n'en a, plutost que n'en recouriez à la Royne, ma belle-mère, et au Roy, un morceau de fine licorne, car elle m'est bien nescessère.' Some such fragment—'une rouelle de licorne garnye d'or attachée à une chaisne d'or ;' 'a peece of an unicornes borne with a little pendant of gold'—which she had beside by her at Chartley and Fotheringhay, she left to her son, King James.— (Prince Labanoff, Lettres de Marie Stuart, t. iv. 170 ; t. vii. pp. 246, 254.) There was 'a pece of an unicornes borne not garnysshed weyinge iii quarters and a half scant,' among the jewels of King Henry VIII. Among the jewels of King James in the Tower in 1605, were 'one longe pece estemed for an unicorns borne,' and 'three other peces estemed likewise to be unicornes borne.'—(Antient Kalendars and Inventories of the Treasury of the Exchequer, vol. ii. pp. 263, 306.) The unicorn's horn is of frequent occurrence in French inventories of the fourteenth, fifteenth, and sixteenth centuries.—(M. le Comte de Laborde, Notice des Emaux du Louvre, par. ii. 'Glossaire,' pp. 359-365.)

Act of Parliament of 1568 concerning the Queen's jewels.

[1] Acts of the Parliaments of Scotland, 24. August 1568, vol. iii. p. 56 : 'Ane Act maid this day concerning the Queenis jowellis.' In the absence of the parliamentary record, the terms of the Act are to be gathered from contemporary notices. A letter written from Edinburgh, on the 31st of August, tells the English minister that the Scottish Parliament has sanctioned the Regent's 'intromission,' with the Queen's jewels.—(Calendar of State Papers relating to Scotland, vol. ii. p. 857.) On the 1st of September,

the Queen complains that the Scottish Parliament has ordered her jewels to be sold.—(Prince Labanoff, Lettres de Marie Stuart, t. ii. p. 172.) In February 1573-4, the Regent's widow, when sued for recovery of some of the Queen's diamonds before the Privy Council, appealed from its judgement, 'allegeing this caus aucht onelie to ressave tryell in Parliament, and befoir na uthir jugeis, in respect of ane Act of Parliament maid, as scho allegeit, committing the dispositioun of our said Soverane Lordis jowellis pertening sumtyme to his Hienes Moder, to umquhile James Erll of Murray, Regent of this realme for the tyme.'— (Mr. Thomson's Collection of Inventories, p. 197.)

[2] 'Je vous suplie de commander . . . que le reste de mes bagues ne soyent vandues, comme ils ont ordonné en leur parlemant ; car vous m'avés promis qu'il n'i auroit rien à mon presjudice. Je seroys bien ayse que les eussiés pour plus de seuretay, car se n'est viande propre pour traystres, et entre vous et moy je ne fays nulle diférance ; car je seroys joyeuse qu'il y en eût qu'eussiés agréable, les prenant de ma mayn ou de mon bon gré si les trouvés de votre goust.' —(Letter from Queen Mary to Queen Elizabeth, written from Bolton, on the 1st of Sept. 1568, printed by Prince Labanoff, in his Lettres de Marie Stuart, t. ii. p. 172.)

Mary's letter
to Elizabeth to
stop the sale of
what remained
of her jewels.

[3] On the 2nd of Oct. 1568, Queen Elizabeth wrote to Murray, advising him to forbear from the sale, or other disposition, of the jewels of the Queen of Scots. He answered, on the 6th, that he meant to obey her command.—(Calendar of State Papers relating to Scotland, vol. i. p. 267.)

[4] In December 1568, the Queen's Commissioners, in their answer to a protest by the Regent Murray,

In January 1570, the hand of Bothwellhaugh dealt to him the fate which he had conspired to inflict upon Riccio.[1] It then appeared that, among other crown diamonds of mark which he had bestowed upon his wife, was the famous Great Harry, presented to the Queen by her father-in-law, King Henry the

The Great Harry given by Murray to his wife.

charge him and his allies with 'maintening and setting furth' the accusation against the Queen,[1] 'with hir awin pois, jewellis, and substance, quhilk unjustlie and violentlie thay reft and spuilzeit, be thair tressounabill corruption of the keiparis thairof.'—(Goodall's Examination, vol. ii. p. 293.) In October 1568, the same Commissioners complained that Murray and his associates had 'intromettit with the haill strenthis, munitiounis, jewellis, and patrimonie of the crowne,' and that when the Queen escaped from Lochleven they made war upon her, 'be men of weir, quhilk they had wagit upon hir Grace's awin silver.'—(Goodall's Examination, vol. ii. pp. 128, 129, 338, 340.) The Queen, in an appeal to all the princes of Christendom, written at Carlisle in June 1568, says that the Confederate Lords, after Carberry, 'incontinente s'impadronirono delli castelli, case, artiglierie, monitioni, oro, argento, gioje, mobili, vasi, vestimenti et d'ogni cosa di Sua Maestà, convertendo tutto in loro benefitio particolare et in stabilimento della loro tirannica usurpation ;' or, as it runs in the French version, 'tout soudain après, se saisirent des chasteaux, maisons, artillerie, munitions, or, argent, baggues, joyaulx, meubles, habillemens et vaisselle de Sa Magesté, convertissans le tout à leur particulier proffict et establissement de leur tyrannicque usurpation.'—(Prince Labanoff, Lettres de Marie Stuart, t. vii. p. 318, t. ii. p. 91, t. iv. p. 30; M. Teulet, Papiers d'Etat relatifs à l'Histoire de l'Ecosse, t. ii. p. 245.)

Murray an accessory to the murder of Riccio.

[1] Murray's accession to the conspiracy against Riccio is placed beyond question by his subscription to the bond by which the conspirators oblige themselves 'to extirpe out of the realme of Scotland, or tak, or slay' every person whom the King 'sall pleis to command' as opposing his right of succession to the Scottish crown, in default of the Queen's issue. The bond, dated eight days before Riccio's murder, is printed in the Miscellany of the Maitland Club, vol. iii. pp. 188-191, from the original in the charter-room of the Earl of Leven and Melville. Murray's is the first signature; Knox's father-in-law's is the third. The object of the bond, obvious enough on its very face, is made quite certain (i.) by the explicit avowal of its author, Lord Ruthven, who, like Knox, went

to his grave in the firm persuasion that the murder was a 'just act, and most worthy of all praise ;' (ii.) by the counter-obligation granted by the King to the conspirators, in which 'an stranger Italian, called David,' is the only person named of those whom the conspirators are, 'in case of any difficulty . . . immediately to take them and slay them, wheresoever it happeneth,' even 'in presence of the Queen's Majesty, or within her Palace of Holyroodhouse.'—(Lord Ruthven's Relation of the Death of David Rizzi, in Scotia Rediviva, pp. 329-340. Goodall's Examination, vol. i. pp. 266-268. Mr. Tytler's History of Scotland, vol. v. pp. 338-341.)

Four months before the murder was accomplished, Queen Elizabeth told the French ambassador at Whitehall, that the reason of Murray's disgrace at Holyrood was the information which had reached Mary of his design against Riccio's life : 'Et sur ce que je pressoys ladicte dame de me dire d'où pouvoit estre advenu, sans quelque grand faulte dudict Comte de Moray, que la Royne d'Escosse, qui l'avoit auparavant tant aimé et honoré, l'eust en si grand hayne ? Elle, s'estant ung peu teue et secoué sa teste, me respondit que c'estoit pour ce que la Royne d'Escosse avoit esté informée que le Comte de Moray avoit voullu faire pendre ung Italien nommé David qu'elle aymoit et favorisoyt, luy donnant plus de crédit et authorité que ses affaires et honneur ne devoient.'—(Letter from Paul de Foix to King Charles IX. of France, 16. Oct. 1565, printed by M. Teulet, in his Papiers d'Etat relatifs à l'Histoire d'Ecosse, t. ii. p. 93.)

Murray's desertion of his fellow conspirators.

Murray's letters in the State Paper Office and elsewhere, show how desperate were his fortunes when he embarked in the conspiracy to murder a man, for whose favour he had humbled himself to sue with professions of repentance for past neglect and promises of friendship for the future.—(Calendar of State Papers relating to Scotland, vol. i. pp. 225-227. Registrum Honoris de Morton, vol. i. pp. 14, 15. Sir James Melville's Memoirs, p. 147.) He lies under the further imputation of deserting his fellow-conspirators, when the success of the common enterprise, achieved at the hazard of their lives, had restored him to prosperity and power. He formally commissioned Sir James Melville to tell the Queen 'how that he

Second of France, and bequeathed by the Queen to the Scottish Crown as a memorial of herself and of the prince who gave it to her.[1] Mary's anger kindled at the tidings, and from her prison at Tutbury she threatened Lady Murray with vengeance if all the Queen's jewels in her possession were not instantly given up to the Earl of Huntly and Lord Seton.[2] The Countess entreated Cecil to move Queen Elizabeth to intercede for her with Mary;[3] and, whether by reason of this intercession or otherwise, it is certain that neither Huntly, on behalf of Mary, nor the Earl of Lennox, as Murray's successor in the Regency,[4] was able to force the Great Harry from the grasp of the widowed Countess.[5] Lennox, it appears, was foiled about the same time in an attempt to recover some of the Queen's jewels and furs from Mary Livingston's husband, whom he cast into prison at Blackness, and for whose

had dischargit him self vnto them that had committed the lait odious crym, and wald promyse Hir Maieste never to haue do with them nor trauell for them.'—(Sir James Melville's Memoirs, p. 152.) It is to this obviously that Knox refers when, commending the murderers of Riccio for 'thare just act, and most worthy of all praise,' he complains that they 'ar now unworthely left of thare brethrein, and suffer the bitterness of banishement and exyle.'—(History of the Reformation, vol. i. p. 235.)

[1] Pp. 90, 93. Mr. Thomson's Collection of Inventories, pp. 265, 291, 307, 318.

[2] 'Albeit your late husband had so unnaturally and unthankfully offended us . . . we desired not his blood shed . . . but maun be sorry for his death, since the which, we are informed, ye have tane in possession certain of our jewels, such as our H of dyamant and ruby, with a number of other dyamante, ruby, perles, and gold work, whereof we have the memoir to lay to your charge. Which jewels, incontinent after the sight hereof, ye sall deliver to our right trusty cousins and counsellors the Earl of Huntley, our lieutenant, and my Lord Setoun, who will, on so doing, give you discharge of the same in our name, and will move us to have the more pity of you and your children. Otherwise, we assure you, ye shall neither bruik lands nor goods in that realm, but to have our indignation as deserves. Thus wishing you to weigh with good conscience, we commit you to God.' The Queen added, in her own hand, 'As I mynd to pitie yow in

your adversite, giff you doe your deuti, so be sur, iff you hald ani thing pertins me from me, yow and your birnes and meinteners schal feel my displesour heavilie. Nor is wrangous geir profitable. And so I will be to you as you schal deserve. MARIE R.'—(Letter from the Queen to the Countess of Murray, 28. March 1570, in Miss Strickland's Lives of the Queens of Scotland, vol. vii. pp. 62, 63.)

[3] On the 27th of October, the Countess of Murray wrote from Dunnottar to Queen Elizabeth, that 'she is now put at by so many that make actions against her and her bairns, that she sees no refuge from ruin but in her Majesty's protection and help.' On the 2d of November, the Countess wrote to Cecil, 'begging his mediation with the Queen of England . . . that her Majesty will cause the Queen of Scots to speak favourably to the Earl of Huntly, in respect to some jewels claimed of her as belonging to the said Queen of Scotland.' On the 13th of November, her entreaties were backed by Randolph in a letter to Cecil, 'requesting his favour towards the Countess of Murray, in respect to her persecution by Lord Huntly for the Queen of Scots' jewels.'—(Calendar of State Papers relating to Scotland, vol. i. p. 308.)

[4] 'Heidis sent to Mr. Randulphe for Ladie Countesse of Murray,' in Miss Strickland's Lives of the Queens of Scotland, vol. vii. pp. 104, 105.

[5] Mr. Thomson's Collection of Inventories, pp. 195-200.

release the Queen instructed the Bishop of Ross to plead with Queen Elizabeth.[1]

When Mary fled from her capital to begin the disastrous campaign which closed at Carberry, most of her jewels were in the Castle; and they remained there, along with great part of her apparel and tapestry, after the fortress was surrendered to the Regent Murray. He gave it in keeping to Kyrkcaldy of Grange, and when that mirror of Scottish knighthood, yielding to his own chivalrous impulses, and to the persuasive eloquence of Lethington, passed over to the Queen's side after Murray's death, the Castle and all that it contained passed with him. During the three years that it was held for the Queen, her diamonds were the garrison's chief source of credit. In the summer of 1570, when Grange was straining every nerve to strengthen its defences,[2] he seems to have sent some of the Queen's jewels, dresses, and hangings to be sold in London. But the watchful ministers of the English Queen not only stopped the sale, on the pretext that, as they affirmed, it was without Mary's consent, but ordered the articles to be detained.[3] The English market being thus closed against him, Grange turned elsewhere. It is related that, in the following spring, his brother appeared in Leith Roads in a little bark laden with munitions and stores,

The Queen's jewels etc. in the Castle, 1568-1573.

Jewels and furs & the keeping of Mary Livingston and her husband.

[1] 'We have understand that the Erle of Lenox . . . perswmes to spoilze ws of certane jowelles, yea of the best we have restand in sum particulare handes in keiping, whom he tormentis therfor be impresonement, bosting, and other unlefull regors. He hes impresoned Johne Sempill becaus he refused to delyver to him these that he keipis, and we knaw not be what tytills or raison he hes to crave the same. Ye sall mak the Quene oure good sister understand cleirly thir extortions conforme to the particulare adwises ye have receavit, etc., etc.'—(Letter from the Queen to the Bishop of Ross, 24. November 1570, in Prince Labanoff's Lettres de Marie Stuart, t. iii. pp. 124, 125.)

Among other acts of oppression urged against the Regent Lennox, it was said that 'he hes chairgit Johnne Simple to deliuer certane jowellis and furres of martrik, and sabels, perteining to the Quenis Maiestie of Scotland, quhilk the said Johnes wyfe hes hed in keiping; and becaus Johnne Simple wald not deliuer the same to the Erle, he hes caussit put him in prisoun within the castell of Blaknes.'—(R. Bannatyne's Memorials of Transactions in Scotland, p. 348. Bannatyne Club: 1836.)

[2] Diurnal of Occurrents (May and August 1570), pp. 174, 184.

[3] Calendar of State Papers relating to Scotland (5. August 1570), vol. ii. p. 890.

On the 10th of December 1570, Mary writes from Sheffield to Lethington and Grange: 'I cannot beleve, having na certenty . . . that ye have appointed with my meubelles at the Quene of England's procurement. I traist, if so be, it is rather for my advantage nor otherwise, and will mak no new alteration without my advise.'—(Prince Labanoff, Lettres de Marie Stuart, t. iii. p. 134.)

bought in France with the price of a parcel of the Queen's diamonds.[1] About a twelvemonth afterwards another parcel seems to have been sold to a secret agent of Queen Elizabeth for two thousand five hundred pounds.[2] Other parcels were at different times given in pledge to Edinburgh merchants, goldsmiths, and others, for moneys advanced by them to supply the needs of the garrison.

When at length the English cannon without, and want and mutiny within, forbade all hope of further resistance, and terms of capitulation began to be debated, one of the articles was, that Grange should account for all the Queen's jewels and other moveables.[3] But the implacable Morton, who had now succeeded to the Regency, would agree to nothing but unconditional surrender;[4] and rather than suffer what remained of the jewels to fall into his hands, the garrison seem to have hidden part of them in a crevice of the Castle rock, and to have delivered others to Sir William Drury, the commander of the English troops.[5] It was whispered that Grange carried some away concealed on his person, but to

[1] 'Upon Tuisday, the 8th of May [1571], hors and foot were sent doun to Leith, to bring up the provisioun, which Mr. James Kirkaldie brought out of France in a little barke . . . He tooke with him to France some of the Queen's jewells, sold them, and brought home three or foure last of powder, some croslets and rotchets of small ordinance, four or five tunne of wine, some bisket, bread, and suche other furniture.'—(Calderwood's History of the Kirk of Scotland, vol. iii. p. 74.)

[2] Calendar of State Papers relating to Scotland (29. March 1573), vol. ii. p. 371.

[3] 'Item, the Capten [Kyrkcaldy of Grange] desyris to mak compt and restitutioun of all the prencelie jowels and uther movable guds delyverit unto him at the acceptation of the hous, ather to the Queynis lieutenents, or to sik uther person or persons, as the nobilitie now assemblit sall decerne; and that he may have a sufficient discharge thareupoun be act of Parliament.'—(Historie of King James the Sext, pp. 121, 141. Diurnal of Occurrents, pp. 314, 333.) Sir William Drury's summons to surrender the Castle, on the 25th of April 1573, made special mention of the jewels and household stuff among its stores.—(Journal of the Siege, in the Bannatyne Miscellany, vol. ii. p. 73.)

[4] Sir James Melville's Memoirs, p. 253.

[5] 'In Grange's chambre sondry papers was founde, and lately the Crowne, Sword, and Sceptre, and hydden in a woodden chest in a cave, where the inventory was of the jewelles, which are many and riche, but the most parte in gage; some with the Lard of Fernihurst [Grange's son-in-law], some with my Lady Hume, some with my Lady Lydington, and many with sondry other persons, who be all knowen. Whereof the Regent hath recovered some already, and shall do more. Grange had sondry delyvered him by one Mosman, before his coming out of the Castle, which he put in his hose, as Mosman sayth, and declareth the parcelles which the Regent's Grace hath sent to the Generall, as also the note of such as be in the hands of the Ladye Hume and of Lydington, because they be in the Generalle's garde.—(Letter from Sir H. Killigrew to Lord Burghley, 13. June 1573, in Mr. T. Wright's Queen Elizabeth and her Times, vol. i. p. 482.)

A 'Memor of the Kingis Jowellis now being in the Marschell of Barwickes handes,' drawn up soon after the surrender of the Castle, is printed in the Appendix to the Preface, No. v., from the original in the State Paper Office (Scotland, Elizabeth, vol. xxv. no. 68).

this slander he gave an indignant denial, protesting, as he should answer to God, that he took nothing out of the Castle but the clothes upon his back and four crowns in his purse.[1]

The jewels hidden in the Castle were discovered without much difficulty, and among them were 'the Honours,' as the Crown, Sceptre, and Sword of State were fondly called among a people to whom they were dear, as the visible signs of a hardly-won national independence. It was not so easy to recover the spoil which had passed into the hands of the English commander. But Morton addressed himself to the English court,[2] and, although he had to contend against the claims of the Queen of Scots,[3] his influence and importunity seem at length to have been so successful, that we hear of the

Discovery of the Regalia and other jewels hidden in the Castle.

Jewels recovered from the English general.

Grange's declaration as to the jewels in the Castle.

[1] Declaration of Sir William Kyrkcaldy of Grange, 13. June 1573, printed in the Appendix to the Preface, No. VI., from a copy (authenticated by Sir William Drury, and endorsed by Lord Burghley) in the State Paper Office (Scotland, Elizabeth, vol. xxv. no. 69).

[2] An inventory of the jewels which had come into the possession of the English commander, appears to have been sent to the English ministers not long after the surrender of the Castle on the 29th of May 1573. On the 5th of August, Morton wrote to the Countess of Lennox, and to Killigrew, the English envoy in Scotland, 'to crave of the Marshal of Berwick [Sir William Drury] the jewels that are in his hands, which he is obliged in honour, and by indenture and promise made at the incoming of the Queen's Majesty's forces [of England], to deliver to the King's use.' On the 19th of August, he again wrote to the Countess of Lennox, with instructions and information as to the jewels in the possession of Sir William Drury and others.—(Mr. Tytler's History of Scotland, vol. vi. p. 478. Calendar of State Papers relating to Scotland, vol. i. pp. 378, 380.)

The Queen claims the jewels which had been in the Castle.

[3] We first hear of Mary's claim in a letter to La Mothe Fénélon, the French ambassador at London, written from Chatsworth, on the 3d of August 1573: 'Je vous prie de faire tous vos efforts envers la Reyne d'Angleterre affin qu'elle me fasse rendre mes pierreries et aultres hardes que j'avois dans le Chasteau de Lislebourgh.' On the 27th of September she again writes to him: 'Je vous prie solliciter l'inventaire de mes bagues, que ma dicte bonne soeur vous a dict qu'elle mandera à Morthon qu'il envoye, et qu'elles me soyent rendues, comme elle scait qu'elles sont à moy.' She returns to the subject, on the 30th of November, in a letter written from Sheffield: 'Je vous prie . . . surtout poursuivre l'inventaire de mes bagues et qu'elles me soyent rendues, suivant ce que ma dicte bonne soeur vous a cy devant dit estre son intention et maintenant n'avoir oublié d'en faire escrire à Morthon. Je les ay cy devant demandées assez instamment et ay à cette heure matière de presser plus que jamais sur la responce qui vous a esté faicte, par où il semble qu'il charge ceux, qui devant luy ont tenu le Chasteau de Lislebourg, de les avoir toutes quasi escartées ès mains de marchands et orfeuvres, ce qui n'est excuse pour luy servir d'acquit suffisant, ains pour le charger davantage et faire craindre qu'il les veut dérober. Car il a faict mourir ceux qui les avoient entre leurs mains et m'en debvoient respondre, ou pour le moins qui pouvoient tesmoigner de ce qu'il y avoit; en quoy se manifeste trop évidemment sa finesse et sa ruse. Mais puisque la dicte dame ma bonne soeur a tel pouvoir sur luy, je croy qu'elle ne vouldra luy suffrir faire ce larcin. Le Comte de Moray ne prétendit jamais qu'elles feussent gardées pour aultre que pour moy, ainsi qu'il a tousjours plainement déclaré devant sa mort, encore que Morthon luy a souvent voullu persuader, comme j'ay esté advertie, de les dissiper, affin d'en avoir sa part; ayant assez faict paroistre par aultres démonstrations qu'il n'i a imposture ou aultre meschanceté qu'il ne commette ou soit participant, où il y a espérance de butin et rapine.'—(Prince Labanoff, Lettres de Marie Stuart, t. iv. pp. 77, 83, 90, 91.)

detention only of some diamonds on which moneys had been advanced,[1] and of one jewel which had found its way into Queen Elizabeth's possession.[2]

Jewels recovered from pawn, etc.

Parliament had given the new Regent powers for the recovery of the Queen's diamonds and other moveables which had fallen into private hands,[3] and he hastened to proceed against all who had jewels or household stuff in their keeping, whether by gift, by purchase, in pledge for moneys lent, or otherwise. He recovered six jewels which had been pawned with the Provost of Edinburgh for twenty-six hundred merks,[4] and a pearl necklace and fifteen diamonds which had been pawned with Lady Home for six hundred pounds.[5] In neither case was payment made of the sums for which the gems had been pledged. Lord Torphichen, the secularised Prior of the Knights of St. John in Scotland, was called to account for books, tapestry, and furniture.[6] While the body of her husband, the marvellously gifted Lethington, lay yet unburied,[7] sentence was given against Mary Fleming for restitution of a chain of diamonds and rubies.[8] The gallant Grange, after reckoning for every jot and tittle

---

Jewels pawned with the English General.

[1] On the 3d of August 1574, Killigrew writes to Lord Burghley that the Regent means to claim certain jewels pawned to Sir William Drury for £600.—(Calendar of State Papers relating to Scotland, vol. i. p. 386.)

Jewel in the hands of Queen Elizabeth.

[2] On the 19th of August 1573, Alexander Hay, one of Morton's dependants, writes to Killigrew that the Regent has recovered some of the jewels, but not that piece which was in the hands of the Queen of England, and until she delivers it up she will find little favour.—(Calendar of State Papers relating to Scotland, vol. i. p. 380.)

Act of Parliament of 1573 concerning the Queen's jewels.

[3] 'Forsamekle as the jowellis houshald stuff mvnitionis and movable guidis quhatsumeuir, sumtyme pertening to the Quene our Soucrane Lordis moder, and now pertening to his Majestie sen his Hienes coronatioune, ar dispersit and fallin in the handes of diuers the subiectis of this realme and vtheris quhilkis hes the samyn, and dalie sellis and disponis, or hes sauld and disponit thairupoun . . . That thairfore . . . my Lord Regentis Grace caus persew the havaris, resettaris, sellaris, and intromettouris with the saidis jowellis, houshald stuff, mvnitionis, and movable guidis now pertening to our Soverane Lord . . . recovering and collecting of the same agane to his Hienes vse and

behalf,' etc., etc.—(Acts of the Parliaments of Scotland (26. Jan. 1572-3), vol. iii. p. 74.)

Jewels pawned with the Provost of Edinburgh.

[4] 'Twa garnessingis, the ane sett with xviij dyamontis and xviij orient perll or thairby, the vther sett with xviij dyamondis xviij rubeis or thairby ; togidder with vther foure seuerall peces sett in gold, quhairof twa wes rubeis, ane dyamont, and ane sapheir.'—(Registrum Secreti Concilii : Acta 1579-1581, pp. 577, 578. MS. Register House.)

Jewels pawned with Agnes Gray, Lady Home.

[5] 'Fyftene dyamontis all set in gold inammalit with quhyte, togidder with ane carcat of perll contenand sevin greit perle and aucht knoppis of small perle, every knop contenand fyftene small perle.'—(Mr. Thomson's Collection of Inventories, p. 195.)

[6] Mr. Thomson's Collection of Inventories, pp. 182-192.

[7] See above, pp. xxii. xxiii. note 3.

Lethington's body denied burial.

Calderwood seems to find pleasure in recording that 'he lay so long unburied, that the vermine came from his corps, creeping out under the doore of the hous where he was lying.'—(History of the Kirk of Scotland, vol. iii. p. 285.)

Jewels in the hands of Mary Fleming.

[8] 'Ane chayn of rubeis with twelf markes of dyamontis and rubeis and ane mark with twa rubeis.'—(Mr. Thomson's Collection of Inventories, pp. 193, 194.)

in his charge,[1] had been sent to the gibbet to appease the preachers who clamoured for his blood, that God's plague might cease in the land.[2] And now Sir Robert Melville, with the halter round his neck, had to answer for everything which had passed through his hands, as well as to reveal the secrets of the Castle during its long defence.[3] As hard a task as any yet remained. Murray's widow, now again a wife, still kept possession of the Great Harry. She had baffled Mary, Huntly, and Lennox, and did not yield to Morton without an obstinate struggle, in which the English Queen had to interpose again and again.[4]

The Great Harry recovered from Murray's widow.

Grange's life demanded by the ministers.

[1] Appendix to the Preface, No. VI.

[2] 'What offers were made on Grange's behalf for safety of his life, I send you herewith the copy, which, as you may consider, are large as meikle as possibly might have been offered. Yet, considering what has been, and daily is, spoken by the preachers, that God's plague will not cease quhill the land be purged of blood . . . I deliberated to let justice proceed as it has done.'—(Letter from the Regent Morton to Killigrew, 5. Aug. 1573, in Mr. Tytler's History of Scotland, vol. vi. pp. 477, 478. Cf. Calderwood's History of the Kirk of Scotland, vol. iii. p. 241.)

Semple, the preachers' poet, threatened Morton with the fate which befel the son of Kish for sparing the king of the Amalekites, and overtook the Regent Murray for not obeying the behests of Knox :

' Quhairfor put God the powar in zour hand ?

Spair neuer Agag for na brybe of geir.
Quhat come of Saull, with his fatt oxin thair ?
Ga, reid the Bybill, it will sone declair.

My Lord of Murray wes degradit sone
For not fulfiling of the Lordis desyre.'

—(The Sege of the Castel of Edinburgh, imprentit anno 1573, reprinted in Dalyell's Scotish Poems of the Sixteenth Century, pp. 297, 298.)

Deposition of Sir R. Melville as to the Queen's jewels.

[3] His examination, on the 19th of October 1573, in so far as it relates to the Queen's jewels and other moveables, is printed in the Appendix to the Preface, No. VII., from the Hopetoun MS. It has been so much injured by damp, as to be illegible in many places. The discharge granted to him by the Queen at Bolton, on the 15th of October 1568, to which he more than once makes reference in his examination, is printed in the Miscellany of the Maitland Club, vol.

iii. pp. 187, 188, and in Prince Labanoff's Lettres de Marie Stuart, t. ii. p. 218.

[4] On the 3d of February 1573-4, the Regent and Lords of Council gave judgment against the Countess and her second husband, the Earl of Argyle, for refusing to restore or even to produce ' thre greit rubyis and thre greit dyamontis with ane greit jowell in the forme of ane H set with dyamontis.' An appeal was at once taken to Parliament. On the 18th of July 1574, Killigrew writes to Walsingham as to the need of Queen Elizabeth's interference for my Lord of Argyle and his lady. On the 12th of August, we hear of the conditions upon which the Regent of Scotland, at the request of the Queen of England, will agree that the Earl and Countess of Argyle shall retain in their hands certain jewels belonging to the King of Scotland. Seven days afterwards the Earl and the Countess write to Queen Elizabeth, thanking her for her intercession with the Regent. On the same day the Earl writes to Killigrew that he means to agree to the conditions proposed to him and his Countess, in respect of the King's jewels, in regard of which they had been so extremely handled. A conference took place between the Regent and the Earl, but the result was unsatisfactory ; and on the 10th of September the Countess once more writes to Queen Elizabeth, complaining of farther demands made by the Regent respecting the King's jewels, and requesting that her Majesty will again write to him. Nine days afterwards, there is a letter from Robert Fletcher to Killigrew, urging the necessity of the English Queen's intercession. On the 19th of October, Killigrew writes to Walsingham, begging that Queen Elizabeth may write to the Regent in favour of the Countess of Argyle. At length, on the 5th of March 1574-5, the Earl of Argyle appears before the Regent in Council,

The Countess of Murray and the Great Harry.

Jewels, etc., delivered to King James by Morton in 1578.

Three years afterwards, the Regent was deprived of his office. The Inventory[1] of the jewels, dresses, books, furniture, and hangings which he surrendered to the young King, shows, perhaps, less wreck than might have been looked for after ten years of tumult and civil war.[2] The Great

Fate of the Great Harry.

Harry, it may be added, survived James's accession to the English throne, when its large diamond was taken to adorn a new and still more splendid

Jewel House in the Castle.

jewel, the Mirror of Great Britain.[3] The Jewel House in the Castle was now emptied of all but the Regalia, and some five hundred pieces of plate, weighing about nine thousand ounces.[4] But Holyrood, although stripped of

and in name of the Countess, and of her daughters by the Regent Murray, delivers up ' ane greit H of dyamont, with ane ruby pendand thairat; sex uther jowellis, thairof thre dyamontis, and the uther thre rubyis, intromettit with and kepit be the said Dame Agnes and hir said spous sen the deceis of the said umquhile Erll of Murray.'—(Mr. Thomson's Collection of Inventories, pp. 195-200. Calendar of State Papers relating to Scotland, vol. i. pp. 386-389. Historie of King James the Sext, p. 150. G. Crawfurd's Lives of the Officers of State, p. 101.)

[1] The Inventory of the jewels and other property of the Crown given up by Morton, on the 26th of March 1578, is printed in Mr. Thomson's Collection of Inventories, pp. 203-273, from the original in the Register House. The discharges granted to him are printed in the Acts of the Parliaments of Scotland, vol. iii. pp. 99, 100; and in the Registrum Honoris de Morton, vol. i. pp. 92-100, 102-106, 110-115.

[2] Not a few of the articles which appear in the Inventories of 1561-6, and have no place in the Inventory of 1578, seem to have been in Mary's possession at Chartley and Fotheringhay in 1586-7.—(Prince Labanoff, Lettres de Marie Stuart, t. vii. pp. 231-274.)

The Mirror of Great Britain.

[3] 'A greate and ryche jewell of golde, called the Myrror of Great Brytaigne, contenyninge one verye fayre table dyamonde, one verye fayre table rubye, twoe other lardge dyamondes cutt lozengewise, the one of them called the Stone of the letter 我 of Scotlande, garnished with small dyamondes, twoe rounde perles fixed, and one fayre dyamonde cutt in fawcettis bought of Sauncey.'—(Inventory of Jewels in the Tower of London, 22. March 1605, in Antient Kalendars and Inventories of the Treasury of the Exchequer, vol. ii. p. 305.) We find what remained of the Great Harry—the gold setting, the chain, and the ruby—among the jewels for which the King gave a discharge to the Earl of Dunbar, in July 1606: 'the jewell callit the H, with the chane thairof, and als with the rubie of the samyn.'—(Mr. Thomson's Collection of Inventories, p. 329.)

Crown plate in Scotland in 1617-1621.

[4] Registrum Secreti Concilii: Acta 1621-1625, fol. 30 (10. July 1621). MS. Register House. They were sent to Scotland for the King's use, during his visit in 1617, and after being kept for some time in the Mint, were taken to the Castle. They are thus described: 'Aucht basines and aucht lawers, weyand of Inglishe weyght 771 vnceis, and of Scottis weyght 784 vnceis and tua drop weyght; Fourtie candilstickis, weyand of Inglishe weyght 1004 vnceis, and of Scottis weyght 1021 vnceis and 12 drop weyght; Tuentie beir boullis or coupis, weyand of Englishe weyght 334 vnceis, and of Scottis weyght 340 vnceis; Ten saltis, weyand of Inglishe weyght 203 vnceis, and of Scottis weght 207 vnce; Ten dusane of spoones, weyand of Inglishe weyght 200 vnce, and of Scottis weyght 203 vnce 8 drop weyght; Aucht dusane of trunscheour plaittis, weyand of Inglishe weyght 966 vnceis, and of Scottis weyght 983 vnce 10 drop weyght; Sevintene dusane sevin discheis or plaittis, weyand of Inglishe weyght 5528 vnce, and of Scottis weyght 5630 vnce 12 drop weyght; Sax siluer cop feete, with tua ringis of siluer to tua of the covers of the saidis couppis, weyand altogidder of Scottis weyght threescoir ellevin vnce and ane quarter of ane vnce: Extending in the haill of Scottis weght to threttie-fyue stanes threttene pundis lxxiiij vnce fyve drop weght.'—(Registrum Secreti Concilii: Acta 1615-1617, fol. 108 (13. May 1617). MS. Register House.)

almost everything else,[1] still kept its Wardrobe[2] and its Library.[3] They appear to have outlived the reign of King Charles the First to perish in the fire which consumed all but a corner of the Palace, during its occupancy by the soldiers of the Commonwealth.[4] The tower in which Riccio was murdered withstood the flames; and its chambers are daily crowded by multitudes who, climbing the narrow staircase through which the murderers reached the Queen's Cabinet, yield themselves to the belief that Mary dallied with Darnley and disputed with Knox, under ceilings studded with the cyphers of her son and her grandson. Faith has not everywhere been so unquestioning. It is scarcely remembered now that men once believed that miracles were wrought at the

stately sepulchre at Westminster, into which filial piety or worldly wisdom gathered the ashes of the martyr Queen of Scots.[5]

---

[1] In June 1603, the Chancellor and the Clerk of Register reported to the Privy Council that, on inspecting all the Palace, except the Wardrobe, they 'fand na uthir thingis by the particulers underwritten, except sum buirdes, furmes, and stuillis, nocht worthie to be enrollit : In the first, in the Counsal Hous ane knok : In the Over Chalmer abone the Quenis Cabinet, twa peicis of tapestrie : In the Master of Warkis outwith chalmar, ane fair wrocht pend for a bed, wantand the heid, and bak pend with courtingis for the frontell and the fut ; ane chair coverit with purpill velvott ; ane coverlet of ane buird of reid velvot upoun quhyt saiting ; ane auld covering of ane bed of chainging taffatie : Item, lyand in the transe, be the quhilk thai gang to the wyld bestiall, twa peices of talpestrie.'—(Inventar of the Movables of Halyruidhous, 1603, in the Bannatyne Miscellany, vol. i. p. 185†, note.)

[2] In April 1626, King Charles I. ordered the Master of the Wardrobe in Scotland to take measures for recovering all 'hingings and tapestrie, plate, or other stuffe and plenishing' belonging to the King.—(Secretary Sir William Alexander's Register of Royal Letters, 1626-1631, p. 27. MS. Register House.)

[3] In August 1628, King Charles I. ordered the charge of the King's books in the Palace of Holyrood, which were formerly in the custody of Sir Peter Young, the King's Almoner, to be committed to his son, Patrick Young, keeper of the King's library at Southwick, and commanded the Marquis of Hamilton, as Keeper of the Palace, to put him in possession of the room in Holyrood, where the books were kept, and

of such other rooms as had been occupied by Sir Peter Young.—(Secretary Sir William Alexander's Register of Royal Letters, 1626-1631, pp. 319, 320. MS. Register House.)

There are no means of determining whether Queen Mary's books, preserved in the Castle in 1578, were part of the library at Holyrood in 1628. One volume which, although not in either of the known lists of her books, still bears her arms on the cover, is now in the British Museum, to which it passed from the library of King George III.—'The Actis and Constitutionis of the Realme of Scotland maid in Parliamentis haldin be the rycht excellent hie and mychtie princeis Kingis James the First, Secund, Thrid, Fyft, and in tyme of Marie now Quene of Scottis, viseit, correctit, and extractit furth of the Registers be the Lordis depute be hir Maiesteis speciall commissioun thairto. Anno Do. 1566.' The suggestion of this first attempt at an edition of the Scottish statute-book is due to the Queen's ever faithful follower, John Lesley, Bishop of Ross.

[4] John Nicoll's Diary of Public Transactions, p. 35. Bannatyne Club : 1836.

[5] 'Femina coelo dignissima, ut quae omnes Christi martyres captivitatis supplicio longe superavit ; neque enim ullus martyr XIX. annorum squalorem ac hostilem custodiam sensit. Audio ossa, ad regum Anglorum sepulturam Westmonasterium translata, miraculis clarere.'—(T. Dempsteri Historia Ecclesiastica Gentis Scotorum, t. ii. p. 464. Bannatyne Club: 1829.) Mary's remains were brought from Peterborough to Westminster in 1612. Dempster died at Bologna in 1625.

It remains only to say that nothing has been attempted in the text beyond a faithful representation of originals, in which the hand of a careless or ignorant scribe has but too often darkened the obscurity of the technical or forgotten terms in which they abound. In the interpretation of these terms, a comparison of the two versions, French and English, in which they occa-tech-sionally offer themselves, may be of some service. But more and better help will be found in such works as the admirable glossary which the Comte de Laborde has published as a companion to his Notice des Emaux et Bijoux du Musée du Louvre; the brief but useful vocabulary which M. L. Douët-d'Arcq has added to the Comptes de l'Argenterie des Rois de France, printed by the French Historical Society; the Recherches sur le Commerce, la Fabrication et l'Usage des Etoffes de Soie, d'Or et d'Argent, of M. Francisque-Michel; the Dictionnaire Raisonné du Mobilier Français, of M. Viollet-le-Duc; the Dictionnaire d'Orfévrerie Chrétienne, of the Abbé Texier; Mr. Pugin's Glossary of Ecclesiastical Ornament and Costume; and the Promptorium Parvulorum, edited for the Camden Society by Mr. Albert Way. It will be understood that, wherever in the text words or letters are placed within brackets, they have been supplied by the editor to restore an imperfection, or to correct a mistake, where that seemed advisable.

JOSEPH ROBERTSON.

Register House, Edinburgh,
22d June 1863.

APPENDIX.

No. I.

Inventory of the Vestments of the Chapel Royal of Stirling, delivered by the Sacristan to the Keeper of the Queen's Wardrobe, 11 January 1561-2. (Page xxvii. note 3.)

The Inventor of the Quenis Grace Chapell Royale geir and ornamentis now heir in the Paleiss of Halyruidhous deliverit be Schir James Paterson sacristane at the Quenis command to Serues de Conde Frencheman and varloit of Oure Souverein Ladeis chalmer be Maister Archibald Craufurd her [Gracis] Maister Almoner to be keipit in the Wardrop of Edinburgh ·

Imprimis tua blew damaiss capis stripit with gold ·

Item tua reid welwouss [capis] champit with gold ·

Item ane fyne caipe of claith of gold on blew weluouss feild ·

Item thrie black weluouss caipis for the mort ane of them st[ern]it with gold ·

Item tua tunikillis with ane chesabill of blak weluouss for the mort stand with thrie albis amittis stolis and fannonis and purse ·

Item tua auld alter towallis ·

Item ane frontole and ane pendikill of blak weluouss st[ern]it with gold ·

Item four tunikillis twa chesabillis of fyne clayth of gold with thrie albis stolis fannonis amittis and purse ·

Item ane Mess Buik of parchment with ane nottit Antiphonale of parchment ·

Item ane coffer with lok and key within the quhilk thair is part of this forsaid garniture ·

Item ane pendakill of silk ane frontoll of clayth of gold and purpour velvat ·

All this geyr receivit be me Seruais varlot of chalmer to our Souerane at hyr command the eleuint daye of Janver anno 1561 befor me David Lamerol ·

S DE CONDEZ vallet de chambre de la Royne ·

A Lillebour 11me de Janvier 1561 ·

[A list in English of the Vestments of the Chapel Royal of Stirling, received from the Sacristan by Servais de Conde in 1562, is given in the text, p. 59. The French list, from which it seems to have been translated, is preserved at Preshome among the papers saved from the wreck of the Scots College at Paris; and is here reprinted from the Illustrations of the Reigns of Queen Mary and King James VI., pp. 11, 12.]

Memoyre des Ornement d'Eglise que je resceu du Secretain de la Chapelle de Strellin · 1562 ·

Premierement deux vielle chappe de damas bleu semee de fleur de lis d'or avec les orfres fect d'istoyre ·

Plus ung parrement d'autel avec le soubassement le tout de toylle d'or frisee de bleu et meparty de toylle d'or figurree de rouge frange de soye de mesmes coulleur ·

Plus deux vielle chappe de velours rouge figurree de fleurs d'or garny d'orfre d'or de masse a savoir faux or ·

Plus deux tuniques et une chasuble et une chappe le tout de toylle d'or figurree de velours bleu garny d'orfres fect d'or nues ·

Plus deux tuniques troy chappe et une chasubles avec ung parrement d'ostel et le soubassement le tout de velours noyr semez d'estoilles d'or Et les orfres des dicts ornement sont de velours rouges enriche des armes d'Ecosse et histoyrre ·

Plus une chasuble et deux tuniques de toylle d'or broche de noyr garnye d'orfres d'or fin ·

Plus quatre estolles et six fanons avec sincq saincturre fect de filz blanc ·

Plus six aubes et quatre amycts avec deux vielle nappe d'autel ·

Usee ·

No. II.

Inventory of the Queen's Books in the Castle of Edinburgh delivered by the Earl of Morton to King James VI., 26 March 1578. (Page cii. note 3.)

In the first the saxt and last volume of the Auld Cronicles of England in Frenche · The secound volume · The fyft volume · The fourt volume ·

Lucan Sueton and Salust in Frenche ·

The first volume of the Catologue of Sanctis in Frenche ·

Giron Curtas ·

The thrid volume of Titus Livius ·

The Werkis of Allane Charter ·

Ane Oratioun to the King of Franche of the Quenis awin hand write ·

The ellevint buik of Sanct Augustine · The first buke of Sanct Augustine ·

The first buik of Rolland Amoreuse ·

The Gouernament of Princes writtin in parchement ·

The first buik of Amades de Gaule ·

Ane parte of Plutarche in Frenche ·

Valerius Maximus in Frenche ·

The Legend Aurie ·

La Mere des Historeis ·

The first volume of Vita Christi ·

Foure volumes of La Mere des Historeis couerit with quhite parchement ·

Cronicle Martinan ·

The Play of the Chas ·

The Cronicles of Savoy ·

The Buik of Hunting ·

The Distructioun of Troy ·

The Explanatioun of the Charter of Calice ·

The Lyves of Alexander the Great and vtheris nobles ·

The Decameron of Bocas ·

The Mirrour of Human Redemptioun ·

Boece de Consolation ·

The Gardin of Plesance ·

Tua volumes of Lancilot de Laik ·

Ane greit volume of Cronica Cronicorum ·

Ane Compend of the Cronicles in Spanioll ·

Ane Buk of Devilry ·

Bocas of the Geneologie of the Goddis ·

Cronicle of the Emperiouris and Kingis of Austrice ·

Discours of the Misereis of the Tyme Present ·

The Gardin of Plesance ·

Esaias in Greeik and Hebrew be M[u]nstar ·

Geneologie of the Kingis of France ·

Columell of Historeis [ƒ. l. Treis] ·

The Prothogall of the Chancellarie of France ·

The Regreit of the Duke of Guiss deid ·

Supplement of Devotioun ·

Actis of Parliament of King James the Fyft ·

Historie of the Tyme present be Sanct Fontene ·

The Offices of Cicero ·

The Triumphe of Faith ·

The Triumphe of Pallas ·

The Oratioun [and] the Prayeris of the Auld Cardinall of Lorane ·

The Epistles of Ouid in Frenche Meter ·

The first buik of the [Poemes and the] Novallis of Ronsard ·

Danies Vgieri in Italian ·

The King of Frances Maioritie ·

The nynte buk of the Amades de Gaule ·

Off Penitence ·

Ane Ansuer to the Obiectioun of the Protestantis be Regier Brontanis ·

The Actis of Parliament of Quene Marie of England ·

The Morall Triumphis of Petrark in Italiane ·

Christiane Institutioun in Franche ·

Ane Bischoppis Epistle to the Ministeris ·

Frenche Sonattis in writt ·

Vulgar Lettres of Diuers Noblemen in Italian ·

Salust in Italian ·

The Manuell of the Ingrate Man ·

Errores Amoreuses ·

Elesi vpoun the deid of Joachim de Belly ·

The Armes of the Marques dAlbuif ·

Dictionar in Frenche and Latine ·

Ane vther Dictionar in Frenche and Latine ·

Ane Turk buik of Paintrie ·

The Sege of Troy in Italiane ryme ·

Vigetius de Re Militari ·

The begynning of the Scottis Cronicle in Frenche bie Diennye Savage ·

The levint buik of the Amades de Gaule ·

The Institutionis of Astronomie ·

The first buik of Enguerant ·

Thre buikis of Musik ·

The Margreit of the Quene of Nauarre ·

Ane Epistle to the Quene writtin in Frenche be Diodet Sairell ·

Lyves of Certane of the Illustres be Emelius Probus ·

The Matamorphosis of Ovid in Italion ·

The Institutioun of Lentren ·

The Oliue Augmentit ·

Marcus Aurelius in Italian ·

The Complant of the Vniuersitie of Pareis contra the Jesuittes ·

Orlando Furioso ·

Off the Beginning and Progres of the Realme of France ·

Harang of the Frenche People aganis Rebellioun ·

The Expositioun vpoun the Epistles of Aug[u]s[tine] ·

Supplement of Devotioun ·

The Cardinall of Loyranis Oratioun at the Assembly of Poesy ·

Portuus of Rome ·

Ane Ansuer [of] Ronsard ·

The Misereis of the Tyme Present be Ronsard ·

[R]ecuell de Poesie ·

The Spheir of the Warld ·

The Singular Combat of Dauid and Golias ·

Ane Treatie of the Premiecie of the Peape ·

The Historie of Jasone ·

Pantagruell in Frenche ·

Concionero de Romanses ·

The Sacrifice Evangelick ·

Resolutioun of Certane Christiane Poyntis ·

The Suchingis of Oliuer Magne ·

The Historeis of the Bible in Figures ·

The King of Frances Declaratioun vpon Danvillis Edictis ·

The first buke of Claud Butat in Frenche ·

The Sectis of Hereseis in this tyme ·

The Treateis of Starnislawes bischop of Warne ·

The Manuell of Morall Vertewis ·

Ane Gaddering of Sindry Historeis in Frenche ·

The Buik of Human Policie ·

Clement Marot ·

The Consolationis of Bembo ·

Abrigement of the Art Poetik in Frenche ·

The Defence of the Illustratioun of the Frenche language ·

A Gaddering of Sumpatheis ·

The Epistle[s] of Ignatius ·

The Principallis of Astronomie ·

The Remonstrant of the Emperiour F[r]eid[rich] maid to the Paip ·

The Ordinare of the Money in France ·

The Praiss of Foly in Frenche ·

Four Homoleis anent the Images in France ·

The Intertenyment of Helth ·

The Treatie of the Sacrament be Petir Martir ·

The Ansuer to Johnne Calvynnis Epistle ·

Off the Fals Propheittis ·

Hippocrites in Frenche ·

A Little Buik of the Chas ·

Gadderingis of Rhymes and Peces ·

Remonstrans be the Estaittis in Burgvnye ·

Sangis of the Bible in Frenche be Lancelote de la Carle ·

Ane Exhortatioun to the Kingis Counsall aganis the Trublis ·

Ane Oratioun Buik in write ·

The Maner to tak away the Contrauersie of Religioun be Renatus Benedictus ·

Remonstrance of the Catholik Nobilitie [to] the King ·

The Kingis Apologie aganis the Staittis of Burgunye ·

The Writ of Nicolas Clamanses ·

Bertram vpoun the Sacrament ·

Epithalamium Regis et Regine ·

Ane Grit Dyett Buik of the Duk ·

Tuentie fyve countis and quarternis of the Quene and Quene Regent ·

Certane pacquettis of Frenche lettres and comptis ·

A canues polk with parchment evidentis concerning the auld Erll of Murray Erll of Craufurd and vtheris ·

The Livis of the Paipis be Platine ·

No. III.

Order of the Confederated Lords for coining seventy-four marks of the Queen's plate in the hands of Servais de Conde, 10th July 1567. (Page cxxvii. note 2.)

The Lordis understanding that thar is sum silver wark of the Quenis Majesteis in the handis of her Frensche officiaris quhilkis necessarlie mon be cunyeit alsweill for outredding of sum sowmes of money awand to the saidis Frenschmen als for furthsetting of uther hir Hienes service and in speciall in the handis of Servais de Condy vallet of chambre

    Ane nef of silver ourgilt ·

    Twa coupis wyth thair coveris ourgilt ·

    Ane assay ourgilt ·

    Twa flaskettis ourgilt ·

    Twa gryt coupis ourgilt ·

    Ane chalice and patine ourgilt ·

    Ane bell ourgilt ·

    Twa peces ourgilt ·

    Ane croce ourgilt in the bordis ·

    Twa chopinettis ourgilt in the bordis ·

    Twa greit bassins ourgilt in the bordis ·

    Sex goblettis and ane covering and twa feit of coppis ·

extending to three score fourteine markis · Thairfor ordanis commandis and chargeis the said Servais to deliver the pecis of silver work above specifeit being his handis to Jhone Achesoun hir Majesteis Maister Cunyeour to be cunyeit be him to the effect above mentionat · Subscrivit at Edinburgh the tent day of July the yeir of God ane thousand fyve hvndreth thrie scoir sevin yeiris ·

ATHOLL ·   MORTUN ·   CRAIGMILLER ·
SIR JAS BALFUR ·   JO THESAURARIUS ·

No. IV.

Discharge by the Regent Murray to the Queen's Almoner, of certain pieces of her plate, 13 November 1567. (Pages cxxvii. cxxviii. note 3.)

We James Erl of Murray Lord Abernethy and Regent of Scotland grantis me to haif ressauit be the handis of Maister Robert Richartson treasurer fra the handis of Maister Archibald Craufurd parson of Eglesham this sylver wark under [writtin] quhilk he had in keiping of the Quenis Majestie ·

Imprimis ane sylver chaless with the pate[n] gylt ·

Item twa sylver chandelaris gylt ·

Item ane watter fat with ane watter stik gylt ·

Item ane sylver bell gylt ·

Item ane purse with ane boist gylt ·

Item ane cowip with ane cower and ane sacyer gylt ·

Item ane crowat with ane lyd gylt ·

Item ane flakkon with ane charger gylt ·

Item twa hall crowattis ·

And dischargis the said Maister Archibald hereof be this our acquittance subscrivit with our hand at Edinburgh the thirteenth day of November in the yeir of God 1567 yeris ·

JAMES REGENT ·

No. V.

Inventory of the Queen's Jewels in the hands of Sir William Drury, Marshal of Berwick, General of the English forces at the siege of the Castle of Edinburgh, 1573. (Page cxxxiv. note 5.)

Memor of the Kingis Jowellis now being in the Marschell of Barwickes handes ·

Certane buttonis of gold with rubyes contenand in wecht twa pund sex unces ·

Off garnissingis contenand of wecht twa pund five unces ·

Ane garnissing contening ellevin diamantis quhairof thair is a great dyamant tailzeit and certane perles ·

Nyne great rubyes and fourty greit perlis ·

Thir peces being liand in wed to divers wer brocht to Leith to Grange he then being in the Marschellis handes and be him deliverit to the Marschell ·

Mair ane garnissing of dyamantis esmailled with blak contenand sextene dyamantis and sextene roses of gold betwene ·

Ane les garnissing contenand xviij dyamantis and xix roses of gold betuene ·

Ane carcan contenand xiij diamantis and xiij roses of gold ·

Thir peces wer deliverit to the Marschell of Berwick be Mr Archibald Dowglas ·

Ten diamantis or quhit saphires sett in gold with xj knoppis of gold betuene ·

Ane belt of roses of diamantis and perlis ilkane contenand ten or xx cordelires of gold betwene ·

Thre great rubyes of a jour and a perll of ilkane of thame ·

A hingar of a belt of perll contenand xj knottis with thre perlis in ilkane of thame and xj cordeleris with xiiij perll in ilkane of thame with ane hupe at the end thairof ·

Ane hingand sapheir sett in gold and a great perll at the end of it ·

Ane uther sapheir a jour ·

Thre diamantis with thre rubyes ·

Auchtene knottes of perlis sett in gold with twa perlis in ilkane of thame ·

Ane chayn of perles with twa rankes of perlis with xxiiij merkes of litle dyamantis and small rubyes in gold ten perlis betwene everilk merk ·

Ane garnissing contenand ix roses of rubyes and ten knoppes of perlis with a perll hingand at ilk ruby ·

Ane pair of bracellettis of gold of musk contenand everilk bracelett foure peces and in everilk pece viij dyamantis and vij rubyes and xj perlis in thame baith ·

Twa quaiffis ane collair and ane pair of sleves of perll ·

Fyve great saphires sett in gold ·

Ane carcan of saphers and perlis ·

> Thir peces being in the handes of umquhile James Mosman laid in wod to him be Grange for certane sowmes of money wer agane deliverit be the said Mosman to Grange the day of the randering of the Castell and being thairefter placit be Grange in a coffer within his chalmer quhair he lay in the Castell the same coffer and peces of jowellis become in the Marschell of Barwickes handes ·

No. VI.

Declaration by Sir William Kyrkcaldy of Grange, knight, as to the Queen's Jewels in his keeping in the Castle of Edinburgh, 13 June 1573. (Page cxxxv. note 1.)

The copy of Grange his Declaracione for certen Jewells of the Scottes Quene. 13 Junij 1573.

As for the Juelles whiche I layed in wed to my Lady Hume I redemed them againe after the commynge home of my Lordis Seyton and Fleminnge, as my dischardge therupon will declare.

The Juelles layed in wed to the Secretorie I cannot tell what he hathe done with them.

The Juelles layd in wed to James Mosman which he alledges he delyvered to me againe the day I rendred the Castell in the Generall Sir William Drurys handes, it is of truthe the said James gave me certen geere in an evell favored clowte. What was in yt God is my witnes I sawe not ; but whatsoever it was he gave me, I came therwith to the chamber where then I dyd lye, in the which at that tyme there was bothe Englishmen and Scottishmen, and caste it in an open cofer, and commaunded on of my owne that was stondinge bye to locke the said cofer. But what is become of it sinseen I knowe not, for my coffers were all lefte in my chamber, I thinkinge the same to be sure, because it was geven me to undrestonde that the Generall had gotten graunte of all that was within it to my behoofe, otherwise I might have provided for sundrye thinges that I have loste. And that was because I feared the Generall sholde have inquired me on my honour yf I had either juelles on me or golde ; which truly yf he had I wolde have declared the truthe unto him. And therfore for that respect I brought owt nothinge with me, but the clothe[s] was one me, and fower crownes in my purse, as I will answer to my God. For had I beleved he had not gotten all that was in my chamber, nor yet inquired me on my honour, I sholde have saved a great deale more nor I have done, bothe of juelles and of myne owne proper goodes.   For not only hathe my wiffe and my daughters children loste their own clothinge with some small juelles to the value of a thowsand crownes but aswell an good parte of myne owne stuffe and clothinge, for my coffers were opened and searched thrise or thay came owt at the gates, which I coulde have remedyd yf I had not thought my selfe assured that all that was in my said chamber had not bene promesed unto the Generall by the Regent.   This above wrytten I do by this my hand writt affirm to be true.

Moreover I caused my cossin Pettadro offer to the Regent all that was lefte of the juelles unlayde to wed, with the Crowne, Septure and Swerde, with an accompte of all the juelles I had layde in wed, so that he wolde geve me the sylver that they laye in wed for, provydinge that he sholde not inquire of me to whome they were layde in wed; and required nothinge therfore but the Lard of Pharnyhurste evydentes and myne owne howss and yardes to my wiffe to remayne in.

Item, where it is spoken that there is found in the Invyntorie of the Juelles which I had in kepinge that I have sent certen of the said juelles to my Lady Thame, yt is of truthe that I entended to have geven hir Ladyship some juelles which I did marke on the margent of the said Inventorie.   But bicause she dyd refuse them, yt is blotted awaye in the margent, which here in Godis presence is of truthe.   Further it will appere by some wrytes that had paste betuixt Mr Archibald Duglas and me, that I dyd crave hir Ladyship comminge to the Castell when she was at Lesterick on purpose to have made hir Ladyship some present which also was refused to me.   As also I do testyfie on my honour that I coulde never, by no meanes that I coulde make, gett either the Marshall or his Lady perswaded to receave eny thinge at my handes or at thandes of eny of the Castell, as God is my witnes, but founde him ever deale so uprightlye in the Quene his soveraigne causes, as nowe thend hathe provin, that I and some with me hathe rather cause to complaine nor to thinke we have bene well handled by him ; for truly his perswasions dyd myckell at our handes but toke not so good effect as we looked for, as sondrye of our wrytinges sent to him will testyfie.

Farther bycause it is bruted that I have refte and taken sondry mens goodes and done them great wronges, yt is of truthe, being compelled therto by my enemyes, I have contynued more nor this two yeres in a common cause with some noblemen where there hathe bene some blodshedd and other enormyties donne.   Nottheles I will make this offer nowe when my

u

back is at the wall : Yf eny man can justly accuse me that I have taken eny mans goodes but that which I have paid for, or elles is obliste to paye, I shalbe contente to suffer deathe for the same.

At Leithe, the xiijth of June 1573.

W KYRKCALDY.

I doo afferme this to be a trw copy.

WILL.M DRURY.

I do witnes that the same William Kirkaldye lard of Grange, late Capten of Edin-burgh Castell, dyd not only delyver this his wrytinge in all the effect afforesaid but desiered me to rede the same unto the said Sir William Drury knight, Generall of hir Maiesties forces there, and therupon dyd affirm the same by worde to [be] his dede with further addicion concerninge the same, and therof desiered me to be a witnes. Eodem xiij Junii, 1573.

per me GEORGE BEVERLEY.

This is the true copye of the Declaracione before.

JOHN WILLIAMS.

No. VII.

Examination of Sir Robert Melville in so far as it relates to the Queen's jewels and other moveables, 19 October 1573. (Page cxxxvii. note 3.)

At Halyrudhous the nyntene day of October [the yeir of] God j^m v^c threscoir threttene yeris   In presens [of the] Commendatar of Dunfermling Secretair Principall [till our] Souerane Lord   Mr James M^{c}gill of Rankelour Nether [Clerk] of Registre and Sir John Bellenden of Auchnoule knycht [Justice] Clerk

Robert Mailuile sumtyme of Murdocairny examinat and inquirit   .   .   .   .   .
.   .   .   .

Item declaris that he ressauit ane tikket from the Quene to Servay willing him to deliuer to this deponar the thre gownis and vther thingis that wer in the Cabinett And according thairto this deponar ressauit the samyne according to ane Inuentar subscriuit baith be this deponar and Servay ~~The maist pairt of quhilk grayth wes deliuerit to the Quene attan,rs~~ / And efter my Lord of Murrais hamecumming he desirit to see the grayth in this deponaris hous in Edinburgh specialie ane knok and ane pece of gold weyand vj^{xx} dowcattis / and first contremandit this deponar to deliuer thame Bot thairefter within thre or four dayes be new licence and commandment this deponar send thame to the Quene othir be George Douglas bruther to the Laird of Lochleven or Johne Drysdale and the deponar vnderstandis sensyne that George Douglas gat the knok and the Lady Lochlevin the pece of gold / Item declaris that efter the Quenis cuming furth of Lochlevin quhen sche wes in Hammyltoun she send for this deponar and he deliuerit vnto hir a ring and four or five targattis quhilk ring he hard sensyne that Johnne Betoun conveyit agane fra the Quene to the Quene of England / The targattis he vnderstandis wer not send out of Scotland / bot deliuerit be the Quene to sum in Scotland to be keipit / Thairefter the Quene being in England declaris that be the Regentis licence

this deponar send the thre gownis with his awin bruther Andro to the Quene then being in
Carlile / And all other thing that he ressauit his bruther likuis deliuerit to the Quene at Bow-
toun according to the Inuentar subscriuit be this deponar and Servay quhilk also he gaif the
Quene and ressauit her discharge of the haill / Item declaris that at the Quenis command
being in Lochlevin to ressaue also fra James Moss[man] ane chayn of the Quenis quhairin
wes sum litle dyamantis and wes in Mosmannis handes to haif maid ane garnissing of /
quhilk chayn also this deponaris bruther Andro Mailuile deliuerit to the Quene with the
remanent graith that wes in the Cabinett · Item declaris that he ressauit the Quenis horss to
the nowmer of xxxiiij / quhilkis wer all gevin at hir commandment / Twa the Regent gatt and
twa or thre this deponar kepit quhill efter the Quenis cuming out of Lochlevin and deliuerit
to hir at Hammyltoun / Ane wes slane on a stob in the park All [the] remanent wer disponit
be the Quenis awne commandment and warrand Item as for the graithe of the stabill declaris
that Servie had the keys of the same And as he schew to this deponar send the same to the
Quene partlie to Hammyltoun quhen she wes thair and the rest to hir being in England ·
And denyis to haif had further intromission with ony of the same saulffing in ane coffer left
quhilk this deponar causit cary to the Castell and belevis the same [to] be thair standand as
yet / thair wes ane auld skirt of taffeteis and twa or thre auld harnessingis litle or na gude
worth

Inquirit quha keipit best pairt to thame quhen thai wer in the Castell / quha . . . .
assistit and furnissit thame quhen thay wer in maist strait / Declairis that the cheif furnessing
thai gat wes out of the handes of thame that . . . . jewellis in plege / and that
thair credite vthirways nor be that meane . . . . nor na body wald
mak thame furnessing on obligationis

Inquirit quha wer the principall furnissaris of money to the Castell or of siluer to the cunyehous thair in the tyme of the abstinence or of befoir / Declairis that the principall furneissaris
of money to his knawlege (saulffing it that come out of France Flanderis and England)
wes be the personis to quhom the jewellis were laid in wed and vther moyen or credite
declaris thay had not And as to the personis havaris of the saidis jewellis / belevis that my
Lord Regentis Grace be sic lettres as he hes found knawis thame bettir nor the deponair
And as to his awin knawlege he hes alreddy certifijt his Grace of the same / Affirmyng that
. . wes neuir requirit to counsale in the laying out or putting to plege of ony of thame / And

as to the furnessing of siluer to the cunyehous in the Castell / declaris that himself nowthir maid furnessing nor ressauit ony commoditie of the cunyehous　·　　　　·　　　　·　　　　·

·　　·　　·　　·　　·　　·　　·　　·　　·　　·　　·

Inquir[it]　·　·　·　·　·　·　·　·　[jewel]lis put out of the Castell and quhat wer thay · De[claris] ·　·　·　·　·　·　·　· rememberis the kist quhairin the jewellis were contenit s[end] ·　·　·　·　·　·　·　· putt out of the Castell in the tyme of the troublis afoir the assege of the toun ·　·　·　·　·　· [R]obert Kirkcaldy knew of the putting out of it　Bot quhair the kist wes placeit or quhen it wes brocht thair agane this deponar can not remember nor knawis not quhair it wes placeit during the tyme that it wes out of the Castell / nor in particular quhat wes in it

Inquirit quhat jewellis wer they that the Merschaell gat befoir the assege of the Castell of Edinburgh / ansueris that he gat jowellis fra the Lard at sindrie tymes　Bot quhat thay wer the deponar knawis not

Inquirit quhilk jowell wes it that the Lard of Grange gaif to the Merschaell in Leyth / declaris that he belevis it wes a ring / And as to the jowellis that wer in James Mosmannis handes / declaris that the Lard of Grange schew to the deponair efter thair cuming tō the Abbey quhen thai wer in the chalmer to gidder ·　·　·　·　·　·　·　· ring quhilk he had ressauit fra James Mosman the day of the randering ·　·　·　·　·　·　·　·　·　·　·　· coffer quhilk come in the Mercheallis ·　·　·　·　·

Inquirit quha deliuerit the bracelettis　·　·　·　·　·　·　·　·　·　·　·　·

·　·　·　·　·　·　·　·　·　·　·　·　·　·　·

Inquirit quhat nowmer and quhat kynd of jowellis my Lady Hwme and Alexander ·　·　·　·　· gat and quhairby he knawis the same　Declaris that he knawis thay bayth gat ·　·　·　·　·　· Bot quhat thay wer vnderstandis not nor he saw thame not

Inquirit quhat vther jowellis the Secretar or his wiff gat nor the chayn [Declaris] that he vnderstandis of na vther jowellis that thay gatt / And further ·　·　·　·　·　·　·　·　·　· that at thair being in Leyth with the Merschaell efter thair cuming out of the Castell the Lard of Grange travellit with the Secretaris wyff to haif had the chayn fra hir that wes in hir handes to the effect he mycht haif gevin the same to the Merschaell　Bot sche altogidder refusit to deliuer it /

Inquirit quhat jowellis gat Maister James Kirkcaldy　Off quhat jowellis we[r] thay / and quhen wer thay deliuerit vnto him　And to quhat vse / Declaris that he vnderstandis Maister James Kirkcaldy had sum jowellis / Bot quhat thai wer or quhen thai wer deliuerit to him knawis nott ·

Inquirit quhat jowellis or goldsmyth werk wes it that Helene Achesonis seruand brocht to the Lard of Grange quhen he wes in Leith with the Merschaell / quhat quan[tite] thairof the Merschaell coft quhat thay wer and quhat gaif he for thame [Declaris] that he knawis na thing of this mater saulffing at thair being in Le[ith] Helene Achesone hir self cum to Leyth and speik with the Lard · · · · · · vther thing she did thair or quhat the effect of their sp . . . .
.   .   .   .

Inquirit quhat jowellis Maister James Balfour gat declaris · · · · · · · of ony jowellis that the said Maister James hes quhilk he ressauit · · · · · · · · tyme of the lait troublis Bot now duringe the deponaris remai[ning] · · · · · · · Lethingtoun / ane suldert namyt John Hythe ane of his keparis / quha · · · · · · · wes with the Erll Boithuile quhen he fled away to Orknay shew to this d[eponair] That the Erll Boithuile said thay had gottin of his within the Castell · · · · · · · · · · · · · Quene had gevin him better nor xxᵐ crownis

Inquirit quhat jowellis the Lard of Grangeis wyff hes / ansueris that [he knawis] not / bot quhateuir the Lard had she had as she pleissit / Denyis alsua that he kna[wis the] jowellis that Mergarit Patersoun had ·

Inquirit quhat jowellis had Johnne Simpillis wyff / And gif he knawis that ony of thame wer send to the Quene or not / Declaris that he belevis assuritlie that sindry of the Quenis jowellis and vther thingis wer in the handes of Johnne Simpillis wyff and quhether thay be deliuerit to the Quene or not he can not affirme / Bot this he rememberis That quhen he gaif againe the Quene sic thingis as he had in his handes quhen she wes in Boltoune / and gat hir discharge at the tyme she declarit hir self that she had not gottin the thingis that wer in Johnne Simpillis wyffis handes and said to the deponar that he his self pruvit mair honest [to] hir nor vtheris that she had bene mair beneficiall vnto and that sum folkis wer not thankfull that poyndit hir at thair awne handes ·

Inquirit gif the Lard of Pharnyhirst[is wyff] gat ony of the juellis and quhat thai wer / Declaris he knawis not Bot gif sche gat ony / belevis that the Lard of Grangeis awne wyff vnderstandis of it best of ony ffor of all vtheris thay twa wer maist greit

ADDITIONS AND CORRECTIONS.

Page

xiii., note 4, *add :* State Papers of the Reign of King Henry VIII., vol. viii. p. 674.

xvii., note 4, *add :* In the year 1182, Pope Lucius III. sent the golden rose to King William the Lion. —(Chronica de Mailros, p. 92. Bannatyne Club : 1835. Cf. Lord Hailes, Annals of Scotland, vol. i. p. 149.) 'Une rose d or qui fust done a Edwarde jadiz filz a Roi Henri du donne la Pape' appears in an inventory of the Crown Jewels of England in the year 1356.— (Antient Kalendars and Inventories of the Treasury of the Exchequer, vol. iii. p. 227.) We have a contemporary description of the golden rose presented by Pope Clement VII. to King Henry VIII. of England in 1524 : 'This yere . . . was Doctor Thomas Hanibal . . . received into London . . . as ambassador from Clement bishop of Rome, whiche brought with him a rose of gold, for a token to the Kyng . . . whiche was a tree forged of fine golde, and wrought with branches, leaues and flowers, resemblyng roses : this tree was set in a pot of gold, which pot had thre fete of antike fashion : the pot was of measure halfe a pinte ; in the vpermost rose, was a faire saphier loupe perced, the bignes of an acorne ; the tree was of height halfe an English yard, and in bredth it was a foote. Thesaied Ambassador . . . made an oracion, declaryng the good mind, loue, and fauor, that the Bishop of Rome bare to the Kyng, in token whereof he sent hym that present, which the Kyng thankefully receiued, and deliuered it to him again, and so he bare it open before the Kyng, from the College to the great chamber, and there deliuered it to the Master of the Juell house, and so there ended his legacion.'—(Hall's Chronicle, p. 684. edit. 1809. Cf. State Papers of the Reign of King Henry VIII., vol. vi. p 232.) 'En 1856, la Rose d'Or fut envoyée par le pape Pie IX. à l'Impératrice Eugénie ; la remise s'en fit solennellement dans la chapelle du palais de Saint-Cloud, le 19 Juin, par le Cardinal Patrizzi.'—(Didron Aîné, Manuel des Oeuvres de Bronze et d'Orfévrerie du Moyen Age, pp. 81-83.)

xix., note, col. 1, line 19, *for* ² Inventaire *read* Inventaire

xix., note, col. 2, line 9, *for* Inventarye *read* ² Inventarye

xxix., xxx., note 3, line 16, *add :* Scottish pearls appear among the crown jewels of England in the years 1324, 1338, 1379, and 1605.—(Antient Kalendars and Inventories of the Treasury of

the Exchequer, vol. ii. p. 308, vol. iii. pp. 137, 139, 141, 183, 185, 286.) 'Scotch pearls,' says Mr. Horace Marryat, 'formed an early article of commerce in Sweden. There is scarcely a family of note in Stockholm which does not possess a necklace gathered from the Highland unio. I have sometimes counted as many as twenty or thirty worn by ladies in the same room.—heirlooms inherited by their greatgrandmothers. Though of large size, they are inferior in lustre to those of Norrland.'—(One Year in Sweden, vol. i. p. 465, note.) In 1621, King Charles I. appointed Sir Robert Gordon of Gordonstoun, his Majesty's commissioner for preserving the pearl fisheries in the earldom of Sutherland. The commission sets forth that 'the fischeing and seeking of pearlis in the watteris of this kingdome (a commoditie whilk being rightlie vsed wald proue honnorable to the cuntrey and beneficiall to his Maiestie) hes bene thir diuers yeiris bigane neglectit or vsed at suche inconuenient and vnseasonable tymes as hes doue more harme by the spoill of the broode and qualitie of the pearlis then benefeit by taking thairof ;' that 'the Kingis Maiestie hes als vndoubtit right to all pearlis breiding in watteris as to the mettallis and pretious stones found in the land within his dominionis ;' and that, therefore, His Majesty wishes to provide ' that in tyme comeing no pearles be soght or tane in ony watteris of this kingdome bot at suche tymes and seasonis of the yeir quhen thay ar at thair cheif perfection bothe of cullour and quantitie quhilk wilbe in the monethis of July and August yeirlie.'—(Registrum Secreti Concilii : Acta 1621-1625, fol. 36. 7. Aug. 1621. MS. Register House.) The commissioner, writing a year or two after his appointment, says that ' in the laikes and rivers of Southerland, and cheiflie in Shin, ther are excellent good pearle, some whereof have been sent unto the Kingis Majestie into England, and were accompted of great value.'— (Sir R. Gordon's Genealogical History of the Earldom of Sutherland, p. 6.)

xxxi., note 1, *add :* We have an account of the Queen's will by her accusers : ' This hir ruitit disdayn [for the King] still continewing, a litle before hir deliuerance of hir byrth, in Maij or Junij 1566, in making of hir later will and testament she named and appointed Boithuile amangis vtheris to the tutele of hir birth and yssue and gouernament of the realme incais of hir deceis, and vnnaturaly secludit the father from all kind of cure and regiment ower his

Page

awin childe, avancing Boithuile aboue all
vthers tobe lieutenent generall, gif warres suld
happin in the Princes les aige. Sche disponit
also hir haill movables to vthers beside hir husband. And least reason suld haue owerthrawin
this hir later will amangis the nobilitie eftir hir
deceis, she caused thame gif thar solempnit aith
for observance of the haill contentis thairof
without inspectioun of ony thing contenit thairin.'—(Articles given in by the Earl of Murray
to Queen Elizabeth's Commissioners, at Westminster, on the 6th Dec. 1568. Hopetoun MS.)
The text refutes at least one article of this accusation. That the Queen left none of her
moveables to the King is disproved by the long
list of her bequests to him written by her own
hand.

xxxi., note 2, col. 2, lines 14, 15, *for* April 1566 *read*
March 1567

xxxvii., note 2, *add* : A letter from the Queen to the
Duke of Nemours, written from her prison at
Chatsworth in 1570, shows that she still remembered her old favourite at the French court,
who the year before had lost her husband, the
gallant Viscount of Martigues : 'Je ne finiray
que, premier, je ne vous aye remersciay de la
faveur et courtoysie qu'avés montrée à une
pauvre afflisgée veufe, qui a cest honneur d'estre
vostre asliée, et une que j'ay tousjours aymée
aultant qu'amye peult aymer aultre ; non que
je ne sasche que le parantasge de feu Monsieur
de Martigues vous i a induit, mays pour ce que
je me resants de son bien, je ne puis moygns,
vous escrivant, que de vous prier de continuer à
lui estre favorable et à sa fille, qui est ma filleule.'—(Prince Labanoff, Lettres de Marie
Stuart, t. iii. p. 80.)

xxxviii., line 6, *after* marriage, *add* : She was the
Queen's goddaughter.

xl., note 2, line 1, *for* or *read* of

xlviii., note 2, *add* : William Fowler, secretary to
Queen Anne of Denmark, wife of James VI.,
inscribed his 'Lamentatioun of the desolat
Olympia, furth of the tenth cantt of Ariosto,'
' to the right honourable ladye Marye Betoun,
Ladye Boine.'—(Archaeologia Scotica, vol. iv.
p. 230.)

lxviii., line 6, *on* tartan, *note* : In the autumn of 1562,
during the Queen's progress in the north, there
were payments from the Treasury of £24 'for
ix plaidis to vj allacais in Inuernes,' and of £18
' to Maister Johne Balfour be the Quenis Grace
precept for vj tartane plaidis.'—(Computum
Thesaurarii Reginae Scotorum, Sept. 1562.
MS. Register House.)

lxviii., lxix., note 4, *add* : The edition of the book of
costumes quoted by M. Francisque-Michel is
that of 1567. An edition of 1562 is described
by Mr. Pinkerton in his Scotish Poems Reprinted, vol. i. pp. xxxix.-xli. ; facsimiles of
the figures of 'La Sauvage d'Escosse' (clad in

Page

sheepskins) and 'Le Capitaine Sauvage' (in a
fringed mantle), being given in vol. iii. If this
writer can be trusted, the long loose robe of
the common Highlander, described by Mair
and Lesley in the reigns of King James V. and
Queen Mary, was not wholly disused in the
reign of King George I.: 'Those who came
from the remote Highlands to the rebellion of
1715, were all drest in a long loose coat only,
which was buttoned above and laced below
down to the knees . . . It was of one colour,
and home-made, and was . . . the sole covering that the body had.' This was told to Mr.
Pinkerton by Mr. Dempster of Dunichen, 'on
the information derived from the son of Mr.
Ferguson, a clergyman living at the time.'

xci., xcii., note 9, *add* : Calendar of State Papers relating to Scotland, vol. i. p. 231. Principal
Robertson had not seen the evidence which
proves that Friar Black shared the fate of
Riccio. But the strange feelings which animated
one section of the murderers, did not escape
his notice : ' In the confederacy between the
King and the conspirators, the real intention of
which was assassination, the preserving of the
Reformed Church is, nevertheless, one of the
most considerable articles ; and the same men
who were preparing to violate one of the first
duties of morality, affected the highest regard
for religion.'—(History of Scotland, book iv. ;
Works, vol. i. p. 292.)

xcvii., note 2, *add* : A roll of religious foundations in
Scotland, in the British Museum (Addit. MSS.
24, 277. foll. 14, 15), names ' Magister David
Vocat,' as the founder of the ' Collegium Ec-
clesiae Campi in Laudonia' or Kirk of the
Field. He was master of the Grammar School
of Edinburgh. His foundation of a prebend,
in January 1516-7, is printed in the Registrum
Domus de Soltre, pp. 264, 265.

ciii., note 4, *add* : Servetus obviously borrowed
from Erasmus : ' Scoti, nobilitate, et regiae
affinitatis titulo, neque non dialecticis argutiis sibi blandiuntur.' — (Moriae Encomium,
p. 102, edit. Basil. 1676.) The first dated
edition of this work appeared at Strasburg in
1511, more than twenty years before Servetus'
edition of Ptolemy. The Queen had a copy of
the French translation of Erasmus' satire.

28, line 3, *for* Ma . . . . *read* Ma[ndreis]

30, line 26, *for* [veluot] *read* [viollet]

47, line 21, *for* of the kepair of *read* of the kepair of

62, line 3, *for* Foupertuy *read* Fonpertuy

161, line 6, *for* vnes outanne *read* vne soutanne

161, line 7, *for* pelletier *read* Pelletier

171, line 21, *for* jliures *read* j liures

179, line 6, *for* xv *read* x[x]v

183, line 4, *for* Tragedia *read* Tragedia[e]

TABLE

25. *Nouember* 1561.

IV. Inuentair of the Quenis movables quhilkis ar in the handes of Seruais de Condy vallet of chalmer to hir Grace all ressauit fra Jacques de Ma[ndreis] clerk of the offices of hir Maiesteis house at the Palace of

TABLE. clxv

May ou Juing 1566.

TABLE.

1. *Septembre* 1567.

TABLE. clxvii

20. *May* 1567.

25. *Nouembre* 1569.

APPENDIX.

26. *Feurier* 1560-1.

INUENTAIRES DES MEUBLES

DE LA ROYNE DESCOSSE

DOUAIRIERE DE FRANCE.

MEUBLES DE LA ROYNE DESCOSSE.

[Inuentaire de tous les diamentz rubiz et autres pierreries et tapisseryes et daiz receus par la Royne Descosse de son cousin le Duc de Chastellerault le iij⁰ jour de Juing 1556 .]

Inuentaire des Bagues .

Bagues a mectre aux doitz .

Vne grande table de dyamant .

Vng gros diemant a jour en fir de lance .

Vng diemant taille en fircueil .

Vng diemant a jour taille en triangle poinctu .

Vng autre dyemant a jour taillant en triangle sans fueill .

Vng plus petit dyemant taille en fir de lance .

Vne petite table de diemant .

Vng diemant taille a face .

Vne autre table de diemant moyene .

Vne autre table de diemant moyene .

Vng diemant taille en triangle a fueille ·.

Vne poincte de dyemant fans fueille ·

Vne autre bien petite poincte ·

         Et de diemantz xiii ·

Vng petit rubis a jour ·

Vne poincte de rubis ·

Vne table de rubis ·

· Vng cappochon de rubis a jour ·

Vne table de rubis moyene ·

Vng cappochon de rubis ·

Vng petit rubis plat ·

Trois autres petitz rubis ·

Vng autre moien rubis ·

         Et de rubis xi ·

Quatre emeraudes ·

Trois petitz faffirs ·

        Nombre total xxxi bagues a mectre aux doitz ·

Autres Bagues ·

Vng ecarquant ou il y a fix rubis vne table de diemant et viii coupletz de perles ·

Dix croix de diemant en bouttons ·

Vng refte en daureure ou il y a vij petitz diamentz et fix perles ·

Plus viii coupletz a doubles perles ·

Neuf tables de diemant faictes a bouttons ·

xv boutons rondz a trois perles chacun ·

Onze petites rozes de rubis affauoir cinq emailles de blanc et fix de noir ·

xvii bouttons rauqullarris a trois perlis chacun ·

ii xijes degulhettes de perles trois enfemble a chacune ii perles ·

xv pieces des gullettes a ij perles chacune efmaillees de noir ·

xvj autres pieces defgulhettes emalyees de rouge ·

Vng chiffre emaille de noir ou il y a cinq tables de dyemant ·

Vne enfeigne enlaquelle a vne Sirain et a vne queu Et vng mirour de diemant et vng pigne de rubis ·

Vne enfeigne ou il y a vng Cupido et vng gros cueur de rubis et vng petit rubie en fa main ·

Vne autre enfeigne ou il y a vng mirour de diemant ·

Vne autre enfeigne ou il y a vng rubie et vng oeil de chat ·

Vne autre enfeigne dagatte taillee au bord delaquelle a quatre rubis ·

Vng pognard dor a manche dagatte garny de fix amiraudes de trois gros rubis de trois rubis moiens et de quarant deux petitz rubis de viii petitz diemantz dung gros faphi au brut dune houppe dor et dargent traict ratachee de petitz rubis et quelque brut de perles Ladite houppe garnie dune pointe dargent a vng lazeron dor .

Douze pieces de tappifferie de drap dor et drap dargent frize .

Deux detz de mefmes .

Nous Marie par la grace de Dieu Royne Defcoffe certiffions avoir receu par les mains du Sieur Jaques Hammiltoune gentilhomme de la maifon de noftre coufin le Duc de Chaftellerault tous les diamentz rubiz et autres pierreris et tapifferyes de drap dor et drap dargent frize auec deux daiz de mefme come le tout eft plus aplain en deffus declaire   Dont nous en defchargeons defmaintenant ledit Sieur Hammiltoune parla prefente fignee de noftre main que nous auons auffi faict figner par lun de noftrez fecretaires le iije jour de Juing 1556 .

Marie

Aubelin .

Inuentaire des bacgues de la Royne Defcoffe Douairiere de France ·

Premierement ·

Vng groz collier dor auquel y a fept groz faffiz et neuf chattons de perle et a chacun chatton quatre perles ·

Vne groffe bacgue a pendre facon de · ♄ · enlaquelle y a vng groz diamant taille a faces et deffoubz vng gros rubiz cabochon ·

Vne autre bacgue a pendre enlaquelle y a vng dyamant taille a faces et vne grande efmeraulde ·

Vne autre bacgue a pendre enlaquelle y a vne grande efmeraulde taille a faces et vne groffe perle au bout ·

Vne autre bacgue auffi a pendre enlaquelle y a vne autre efmeraulde ·

Vne autre bacgue a pendre faicte a roulleaux en laquelle y a vne grande table de rubiz ·

Vne autre bacgue auffi a pendre enlaquelle y a vng grand rubiz taille en table carree ·

Vne autre bacgue a pendre enlaquelle y a vng grand rubbiz ballay longuet ·

Vne autre bacgue a pendre en laquelle y a vng autre grand rubiz ballay perce par les deux boutz .

Vne autre bacgue a pendre enlaquelle y a vng grand faffiz taille a huit pampes .

Vne autre bacgue a pendre enlaquelle y a vne roze de dyamant de xij pieces .

Vne autre bague a pendre en laquelle y a vne petite roze de fix diamantz .

Vne grande bordeure en laquelle y a vne grande triangle de dyamantz huit tables que longues que carrees vng dyamant en triangle taille a faces vne autre dyamant taille a faces en facon de pene enrichy de xx perles .

Vne bordeure doreillettes ou il y a vne groffe poincte de dyamans dix tables de dyamans auec xx perles .

Vng carcan ou il y a vne poincte de dyamant taille a faces huit tables de diamant et xvj perles .

Vne cottouere garnye de petitz diamans et de perles .

Vne cinture garnye de dix croix de diamans et de xl petites perles .

Vng dixain de ftraing garny de petites perles .

Vne bordeure de thouret garnye de quatorze tables de diamans et vne triangle de diamant par le meillieu .

Vne bordeure daureillette garnye de xvij moyens diamans .

Vne bordeure de thouret garnye de xvj petitz diamans avec des rozes dor efmaille de noir entre deux .

Vng carcan garny de xiij diamans de mefmes facon .

Vne chefne faicte en facon de petits anneaux ou il en a quatre vingtz vnze anneaux garniz de chacun deux rubbiz et xij tables datente garnye de chacun vne table de rubbiz et vne table de diamant et deux cabochons de rubiz en vne piece attachez a ladicte chefne.

Vng thouret garny de fept cabochons de rubiz et quatre tables de rubiz et quarante groffes perles.

Vne aureillette garnye de huict cabochons de rubiz et xl perles.

Vng carcan de rubiz garny de vne efpinelle et fix cabochons de rubiz et vne table de rubiz auec xxxij perles accompaignez de trois rubiz ballay percez auec vne perle au bout de chacun.

Vne cottouere garnie de petites tables de rubiz et de perles.

Vne cinture garnye de petitz rubiz et de perles auec xxv pieces dicelle cinture.

Vng thouret garny de cinq rubiz les deux font tables fix tables de dyamans et xij perles.

Vne aureillette garnye de cinq rubiz et fept diamans auec xiii perles.

Vne carcan garny de quatre rubiz cabouchons trois tables de diamans dont il y en a vng a faces et huict groffes perles plattes.

Vne autre cinture garnye de dix rubiz cabochons x diamans et xviii perles.

Vne dizain de vaze de criftal efmaille de rouge.

Deux braceletz garniz de petits diamans et de rubbiz enrichy de vnze petites perles.

Vng thouret garny de xv petits rubbiz cabochons et xxviij perles.

Vne aureillette garnye de xvij petits rubiz et xxxii perles.

Vng carcan garny de xj rubiz cabochons de xx perles et de dix petits rubiz ballaiz.

Vng thouret garny de petites fleurs de rubbiz et xvj petites perles · La bordeure daureillettes de mefmes auec le carcan auffi de mefmes ·

Vng carcan garny de xvj tables de rubbiz et xvj petites efmeraduldes · La ou il y a iiii^{xx}iii petites perles ·

Vne petite cottouere de perles efmaillees de verd ·

Vne petite aureillette de petitz rubbiz efmeraduldes et de perles · ou il y a xlix pieces ·

Vng carcan garny de fept efmeraduldes et vj perles ·

Vng collier garny de fept rubbiz cabochons iiii efmeraduldes et iiii neufz de petits diamans et rubbiz ·

Ledit collier donne a Madame de Guife a Calais · ·

Vng thouret garny de xiii faphiz xii pieces de perles ·

Vng carcan garny de ix petites faphiz et vng groz faphiz a jour garny dune perle ·

Six efmeraduldes mifes en chatons ·

Vng thouret de groffes perles ou il y a xxxiii perles et ix pandantes ·

Vne aureillette en laquelle y a lj groffes perles ·

Vng autre thouret de groffes perles auquel y en a xlix perles ·

Vne aureillette en laquelle y a xlvii groffes perles ·

Vng carcan auffi de groffes perles auquel y en a lxiiii perles ·

Vne cottouere auffi de groffes perles de cii perles ·

Vne cincture de groffes perles ou il y en a ij^cvj perles ·

Vng dizain de perles auquel y a cl perles auec vnze marcques a trois perles chacune refte vne marque ou il y a vne perle perduee ·

Quatorze moyennes perles auffi de refte et trois autres jaulnes ·

Vne fuite de velours noir picquee de deux petites perles de compte ·

Vingt trois perles a pendre de plufieurs groffeurs ·

.... efte donne vne a Mernan pour pendre · Depuys vne autre donnee a dit Merna ·

Vng dizain de perles auquel y a xx coupletz et a chacun couplet xxxii perles et lvij perles entre deux ·

Il a efte nue a des coueffes pour Mefdames de Lorraine ·

Cinq cens trente moyennes perles en corde ·

Vng thouret garny de cordelieres de perles ou il y a xii groffes perles ·

Vne aureillette de mefmes ou il y a xiii moyennes perles ·

Vng carcan de mefmes ou il y a huit moyennes perles ·

Vne bordeure garnie de x tables de faphiz blancz ·

Vng petit carcan de cordelieres garny de perles auquel y a xxii perles moyennes ·

Vne aureillette de mefmes garnie de xvj perles vng peu plus groffes ·

Vng petit carcan efmaille de noir ou il y a de petites perles pendentes ·

Vne cinture efmaillee de blanc et rouge a chiffres ou il y a vne pinture du feu Roy Henry ·

Vne cinture de neufz faictz en facon deftaufz efmaillee de blanc · carcan et cottouere de mefmes ·

Vne cinture faicte a chiffre efmaillee de blanc et viollet ·

Vne cottouere de vaze de lappiz ou il y a des perles entre deux .

Deux petits braceletz de table damaſtiſte .

Vne cottouere et vne cinture de griſeliſtes garniz de canons et petites perles a lentour .

     Donnees a Mademoiſelle la Contine .

Vne cinture damatiſte garnie de petites meures de perles .

Vne cinture et cottouere garnie de petites perles et de coural taille a goderons .

Vne autre pareille en laquelle y a dauantaige de turquin .

Le touret laureillette et vne cinture de patenoſtres dor a jour rempliz de ſenteur ou il y a vj^{xx}xv patenoſtres .

Vne cottouere et vng carcan de meſmes .

Vne petite bordeure de ſanteurs garnie de perles laureillette la cinture la cottouere et le gorgeron de meſmes .

Vne paire de patenoſtres de ſanteurs garnies dor .

Vne teſte de martre garnie de deux perles et de pluſieurs petitz rubiiz et ſaphiz . les quatre pattes de meſmes .

Deux hermines . vne auec vne teſte dor eſmaille de blanc et la cheſne de blanc et noir Et lautre de panne de ſoye auec vne teſte de gez couuerte dor et la cheſne eſmaillee de noir .

Vng dizain de cornauille garny dor ou il y a des petits neufz entre deux garniz de perles .

Vne cinture et vne cottouere de cornauille garnye de perles .

Vingt quatre grandes boutonnieres dont il y a xii rozes de diamans et xii rubiz baillayz .

Vne paire de braceletz dor garniz de fanteurs ·

Vne autre paire de braceletz de rubiz et de perles ·

Deux pandans doreille facon de croix de Hierufalen efmaillez de blanc ·

Deux autres facon dencolye garnye de fix petites perles efmaillees de bleu ·

Deux autres garniz de turquoifes et de vermeilles ·

Deux petitz faphis percez auec deux perles auffi pour pendre aux oreilles ·

Vng petit vaze garny de quatre petites perles et trois petits rubbiz ·

Deux cocquilles de verre ou il y a deux petites perles pendantes ·

Deux encollier efmaillez de viollet ·

Deux autre pandans doreille garniz de petis damatifte ·

Deux petis pandans doreille dor empliz de fanteurs ·

Deux autres garniz de quatre petits diamans et de deux petites perles ·

Vng pendant doreille faict en facon de fangs peruiue ·

Vng pandant faict en facon dune tortue ·

Deux autres pendans doreille faict en facon de licorne garniz de deux perles ·

Deux pandans doreille garniz de deux petites efmeraudes ·

Deux petis pandans doreille garniz de deux petites perles en facon de doubles ames ·

Deux moyennes perles a pandre aux oreilles ·

Vng poignart dor du feu Roy Defcoffe garny de rubiz et de diamans · le manche dagatte ·

Ledit poygnar a eftez enuoye a Millor Roven en Engleterre ·

Soixante dix neuf bouttons ronds et entriende garniz de chacun trois perles ·

Soixante douze bouttons dont en y a lxxi garniz de rubiz ballez et lautre ou il ny a rien ·

Vingt fept autres bouttons garniz de faphis dont en y a vng perdu ·

Quatorze chattons auffi garniz de faphis ·

Douze bouttons facon de treffles garniz de chacun trois vermeilies ·

Douze autres boutons pareille facon garniz de chacun trois perles dont en y a deux perdues ·

Vng baffinet efmaille de noir garny dune vieille perle rouffe ·

Quatorze efguillettes et demye de fers de grenaz garniz dor ·

Trente neuf efguillettes et demye de fers garniz de chacun quatre perles dont en y a quatre perdues ·

Quarente fix petis boutons faictz en facon de treffles facon Defpaigne ·

Huict vingtz trois autres bouttons auffi facon Defpaigne ·

Soixante efguillettes de grands fers efmaillez de rouge ·

Vingt cinq pieces pour feruir a vne cottouere garnies de xxv diamans xxv rubiz et de l perles ·

Ce qui eft au Cabinet de ladicte Dame .

Vne pomme platte ou il y a vng mirouer et vng cadren enrichy de deux faffiz et xii rubiz et vne perle .

Vng petit vaze de criftal de roche garny dor et enrichy de deux petites turquoifes et de petis rubiz .

Trois petites noiz de criftal ou il y a trois petites figures dor dedans .

Vne petite cage dor ou il y a vng perroquet dedans .

Vng petit Sainct Francois efmaille de griz .

Deux petitz vazes de jafpe garniz dor .

Vne pomme platte percee a jour efmaille de blanc et de noir .

Vne paire dheures garnies dargent .

Vng petit liure dor efmaille de rouge .

Vng petit boucquet de patenoftres de fanteurs garnies de petites perles et dor .

Vng pigeon dor efmaille de blanc et de noir .

Vne pomme dor percee a jour efmaille de blanc auec deux fonds dargent .

Vne petite pomme faicte dun noyau ou il y a de petites figures taillees .

Vne pomme dor facon Dinde garnye de petits rubiz taincts et de turquoifes .

Vne autre pomme de fanteurs garnie dor .

Vne enfeigne facon de Serine garnie de diamant et dun rubiz qui fert a peigner .

Vne autre enfeigne dun Cupido ou il y a vng petit rubiz au bout dune torche .

Vne autre enseigne dune histoire de laquelle a este oste vng diamant ·

Vne petite enseigne ou il y a vne agatte du camayeux dune femme qui tient vng enfant ·

Vng lyon de nacque de perles garny dor ·

Vng petit vaze dor esmaille de turquin ·

Vne enseigne dor ou il y a vne femme qui chasse Cupido ·

Vng petit mirouer de cristal garny dor ·

Vng petit marc dor ·

Vng plat de cornaline garny dor ·

Vne petite chaufferette dor ·

Vng petit pot dor ·

Vng petit pot dor faict de fil ·

Vng petit mouton dor esmaille de blanc ·

Vng petit liure dor faict en facon de fil ·

Vne petite noiz dagatte ou il y a vne petite Notre Dame que Joseph mene ·

Vng petit lict dor ·

Vng petit flacon dor facon de fil ·

Vne petite pomme dor ou il y a le feu Roy Descosse ·   ·

Vng petit chien dor esmaille de blanc et de noir ·

Vng petit cueur dor perce a jour ou il y a vng petit chiffre ·

Vng petit peigne dor ·

Deux ames dor efmaillees de blanc et de noir ·

Deux faueurs dune torche et dune lance ·

Vne autre lance tournee dun roulleau garnye de flambes de feu ·

Deux langues de ferpentz ·

Quatre petitz panniers dor plains de fruictz ·

Vne roze dor qui fut prefente de la part du Pappe a laquelle y a huit blanches et vng petit faphis au bout ·

Inuentaire of the Queene Regentis movables quhilkis wer deliuerit to me Servay de Conde va[llet] of chamber to the Queene
in prefence of Madamemoifelle de Raulle · The haill wes reffauit
in the moneth of September the yeir of God j^m v^c lxj ·

[*Claithis of Estait* ·]

1 · A claith of eftait of claith of gold / damafkit / fpraingit with reid · [partit]
equalie in breadis of claith of gold and crammofin fatine / furniffit [with]
ruif and taill / thre pandis all frenyeit with threidis of gold and reid filk ·

2 · A claith of eftait of claith of gold / part[it] equalie in breadis / the ane figu-
[rit] with violett filk the vther with grein filk / furniffit with ruif and tai[ll]
with thre pandis / all frenyeit with threidis of gold / grein violett and reid
filk ·

3 · Item ane claith of ftait of blak veluos furnift with ruif and taill [with] thre
pandis / quhairof thair is ane without frenyeis and the taill is [to] the length
of an elne ·

This wes furniffit with ane vther taill fenfyne and frenyeis put to the pand ·

4 · Item ane claith of eftait of broun cramofin veluos / barrit with filuer pafmentis furniffit with ruif / and the taill with thre pandis / all frenyeit with
threid of filuer and crammofin silk ·

5 · Item ane claith of ſtait of blak ſatine / maid of bandis of brodery / furniſit with ruif taill and pandis · The quhilk claith of eſtait is not yet garniſſit ·

Senſyne ſtuffit and garniſſit in the Caſtell ·

All Beddis alſweill ane as other ·

6 · Item ane bed of broderie on blak ſatine / diuidit in bandes / furniſſit with ruif and heade pece / with ſevin pandes and thre vnder pandes / and four coveringis for the ſtowppis · The haill is not ſtuffit nor garniſſit ·

Senſyne ſtuffit and garniſſit in the Caſtell ·

7 · Item ane bed of violett broun veluot / paſmentit with a paſment maid of gold and ſiluer / furniſſit with ruif head pece and pandis / and thre vnder pandis · Off the quhilkis vnder pandis thair is ane bot half paſm[entit] / and thre courtingis of violett dames without frenyeis or paſment vp[on] the same courtingis ·

In Auguſt 1566 · the Queene gaif this bed to the King furniſt with all thingis / and in Februar 1567 · the ſaid bed wes tint in his ludgeing ·

8 · Item ane bed of blak dames garniſit with ruif / heid pece / and pandis and twa vnderpandis / and blak courtenis all freinyeit with blak ſilk ·

[In Str]iueling ·

9 · Item ane bed of blak veluois furniſit with ruif heidpece thre pandis thre ſubpandis and thre curtenis of blak dames freinyeit with blak ſilk ·

. . . this heidpece and the curtenis wes ſtowin ·

10 · Item ane bed of blak veluois garniſit with ruif heidpece and pandis / with twa vnderpandis / and thre curtenis of blak dames / all freinyeit with blak ſilk ·

[This] bed wes brokin to [furn]eis ane vther bed be . . . . . feit and vther thingis . . . . ber 1566 ·

11 · Item ane bed of grene veluot maid of the imperiall like a chapell / garniſit

with ruif heidpece and thre fingle pandis / and thre vnder pandis / foure courtenis all freinyeit with grene filk ·

[15]66 · The tymmer . . . . bed is worne auld . . . . the curtenis wes . . . . . Lochlevin ·

12 · Item ane bed of incarnet veluot garnifit with heidpece and thre fingle pandis ′ and thre curtenis of reid taffety / all freinyeit with reid filk / It is to be vnderftand that the ruif of this bed is bot of quhite taffetie ·

The Coveringis ·

13 · Item ane covering of grene taffetie ftickit and lynit with grene ferge ·

In Lochlevin / and feruis to a bed of grene veluot maid like a chapel · ·

14 · Item ane ftickit covering of blak taffetie ·

[Wo]rn away · in 1565 ·

15 · Item ane auld ftickit covering of reid taffetie ·

16 · Item ane covering of blak plaidis furrit with martick fkynnis ·

17 · Item ane auld ftickit covering of grene taffetie ·

Tapestrie ·

18 · Item ane tapeftrie maid of worfett mixt with threid of gold · of the hiftorie of the Jugement of Salamon the deid barne and the twa wiffis ·

19 · Item ane tapeftrie of the hiftorie of the Creatioun contening nyne peces ·

20 · Item ane tapeftrie of the hiftorie of Roboam contening foure peces ·

In Striueling ·

21 · Item ane tapeftrie of the hiftorie of Salamon contening foure peces ·

22 · Item ane vther tapeftrie of litle Salamon contening thre peces ·

23 · Item ane tapeſtrie of the hiſtories of hunting and halking contening ten
peces ·

A part in Lochlevin and the reſt heir ·

24 · Item ane tapeſtrie of great leavis and flouris contening ſeven peces ·
In the Caſtel ·

25 · Item ane tapeſtrie maid of plantis and flouris contening ſex peces ·
In the Caſtel · ·

26 · Item ane tapeſtrie of the hiſtorie of the hunting of the great vnicorne contening foure peces ·

In Striueling ·

27 · Item a tapeſtrie of ane vther hunting of the litle vnicorne contening ſeven
peces ·

28 · Item a tapeſtrie of the hiſtorie of Mathiolus contening foure peces · (Of
the quhilkis I haue reſſauit bot thrie ·)

29 · Item a tapeſtrie of the hiſtorie of aippis contening ſex peces ·

. . . . foure peces to . . . . in 1563 · The reſt . . . . . and worne ·

30 · Item a great tapeis of Turkie / and ane litle /

The litle ane worne in 1565 · The great remanis ·

Stickes of Silk / great and ſmall peces all meſourit with a Scottis elnwand ·

31 · Item twa peces of blak ſatine contening xlv ellis ·

Deliuerit fra 1561 · to the 1566 ·

32 · Item a reſt of blak ſatine contening xxvij ellis and a half ·

Deliuerit at the foirſaid tyme ·

33 · Item a pece of tannie ſatine contening xx ellis and a half and half a quarter ·

Deliuerit at the foirſaid tyme ·

34 · Item a reſt of quhite dames contening xij ellis and a quarter ·

Deliuerit at the foirſaid tyme ·

35 · Item twa reſtis of gray dames contening xvij ellis and thre quarters ·

Deliuerit at the foirſaid tyme ·

36 · Item a reſt of tannie dames contening ſevin elnis and thre quarters ·

Deliuerit at the ſaid tyme ·

37 · Item a reſt of quhite figurit veluois contening twa ellis and half a quarter ·

Deliuerit at the ſaid tyme ·

38 · Item a pece of blak fuſtiane contening twenty ellis ·

Deliuerit at the ſaid tyme ·

39 · Item a reſt of blak ſatine contening twenty ellis and thre quarters ·

Deliuerit at the ſaid tyme ·

40 · Item a litle pece of quhite ſatine contening ane ell and half quarter ·

Deliuerit in 1564 ·

41 · Item ane litle pece of blak veluois contening thre quarteris and a half ·

Deliuerit at the foirſaid tyme ·

42 · Item ane litle pece of blak ſatine contening ane ell and half quarter ·

Deliuerit at the ſaid tyme ·

43 · Item ane litle pece of blak bowting claith ·

Deliuerit at the ſaid tyme ·

44 · Item ane litle pece of blak reinyeit taffetie contening twa ellis ·

Deliuerit at the ſaid tyme ·

45 · Item ane pece of blak plane chalmillet of filk contening ten ellis and a half ·

> Deliuerit at the foirfaid tyme ·

The Furrenis ·

46 · Item ane pair of wyd flevis of arming flypand bakward with the bordour of the fame ·

> Deliuerit in Januar 1562 ·

47 · Item ane pair of the like flevis of martrikis with the bord of the fame ·

> The bordour deliuerit ·

48 · Item ane pair of the like flevis of jennettis with the bord of the fame ·

49 · Item ane pair of the like flevis / of the fkynnis of neces / with the bord of the fame ·

50 · Item the furring of the foirbreiftis of a fyde cloik of martrickes with the bord of the fame /

> Deliuerit in Nouember 1563 ·

51 · Item half a foirbreift of martrickes / quhilk is fumquhat hoillit and vfit ·

> Deliuerit at findrie tymes in 1563 · 64 · 65 ·

52 · Item fum litle peces of martrickes of the reft of ane foirbreift ·

> [Deliuerit] at the faid tyme ·

53 · Item ane pair of flevis of lufervie flypand bakwart / with the bord of the fame ·

> Deliuerit in December 1563 · and in September 1564 ·

54 · Item ane litle pece of martrickes ·

> Deliuerit in October 1565 ·

55 · Item foure wylie coittis of quhite lambfkynnis ·

> Thre of thame deliuerit in 1564 · The vther in 1565 ·

56 · Item ane pair of flevis of blak pan veluot flypand bakwart / with the bord
of the fame / The ane of thame vncompleit ·

> Ane part deliuerit in 1563 · The reſt in 65 · 66 ·

Of Lyning Claithis ·

57 · Item foure bordclaithis of Scottis lyning ·

> Deliuerit in the pantrie ·

58 · Item fyve burdclaithis of plane lyning ·

> Deliuerit in the pantrie ·

60 · Item aucht ferviottis of vnhemmit great lyning ·

> Deliuerit to Madam moſel de Ralle to rub the Quenis heid ·

61 · Item twa famplar peces of cammes pennit to be fewit ·

62 · Item the reſt of dornick claith to cover the burd contening twenty ellis
and a half ·

> Deliuerit in the pantrie ·

63 · Item ane pece of holland claith contening ane ell and a half ·

> Deliuerit in 1562 to Madam moſel de Rale for the Queene ·

64 · Item twa reſtis of holand claith reſſauit be Madam moſel de Ralle to mak
nicht quaiffis for the Queene · And fwa I am chargit with nathing of
that ·

> Madam moſel de Ralle tuke the fame for the Queene ·

65 · Item ane reſt of great lyning contening ten ellis thre quarteris ·

> Deliuerit in 1562 ·

66 · Item ten peces of lyning great and fmall the haill contening j^c and foure
ellis .

> Deliuerit in 1562 ·

67 · Item fyve peces of quhite lyning contening lxvj ellis ·

Deliuerit in 1562 ·

Off rownd Gloibbis / and Paintrie ·

68 · Item twa gloibbis / the ane of the heavin / and the vther of the earth ·

69 · Item sex cartis of findrie cuntreis ·

70 · Item twa paintit broddis / the ane of the Mufes / and the vther of crotefcque or conceptis ·

71 · Item aucht paintit broddis of the Doctouris of Almaine ·

Off Gownis ·

72 · Item ane gowne of blak dames with lang flevis borderit with veluiot ·

Deliuerit in Maij 1563 ·

73 · Item ane gowne of blak dames with great flevis borderit with veluot ·

Deliuerit in the faid moneth ·

74 · Item ane gowne of blak dames without flevis ·

Deliuerit in Julij 1565 ·

75 · Item ane gowne of blak fatine with lang flevis borderit with veluot ·

Deliuerit in Maij 1563 ·

76 · Item ane gowne of blak taffeteis / with great flevis borderit with veluot ·

Deliuerit in Maij 1563 ·

77 · Item ane dule gowne of furring / and the body of fteming ·

The body takin away ·

78 · Item ane hude of arming ·

Deliuerit in December 1561 ·

D

Off Cloickes mekle and litle .

79 · Item ane cloik of blak veluot richt on baith the fydes .

[Deliu]erit in Junij 1563 ·

80 · Item ane cloik of blak fatine lynit with pan veluot ·

Deliuerit in Julij 1565 ·

81 · Item ane cloik of blak fteming garnifit on the foirbreift with jennettis /
and the bord of the fame / and nathing in the reft ·

The fteming deliuerit in September 1563 · and the furring in Maij 1567 ·

82 · Item ane cloik of fteming / the foirbreiftis lynit with arming / and borderit
with the fame ·

The fteming deliuerit in Januar 1562 ·

83 · Item ane cloik of ferge droppit fingle /

Deliuerit in Merche 1562 ·

84 · Item ane auld cloik of blak taffetie furrit with quhite lambfkynnis / and
the foirbreiftis of arming / and the bord of the same ·

Deliuerit in Januar 1562 ·

85 · Item ane cloik of blak fatine borderit with veluot / and furrit with gray
furring ·

The fatine deliuerit in Februar 1562 ·

86 · Item ane auld litle blak cloik of fatene furrit with martrickes ·

Deliuerit in Auguft 1565 ·

87 · Item ane royall cloik of violett veluot without furring or vther thing ·

Deliuerit in September 1563 ·

88 · Item ane ftomach of armenis ·

Deliuerit in Januar 1562 ·

89 · Item ane cloik of blak dames borderit with veluot ·

　　Deliuerit in Julij 1565 ·

Off Doublettis Vaskenis and Skirtis ·

90 · Item ane doublett of blak veluot / and the vaſkene of the ſame ·

　　Deliuerit in December 1563 ·

91 · Item ane vther doublett of veluot and the ſkirt of the ſame ·

　　Deliuerit in December 1564 ·

92 · Item ane doublet of ſatine with the vaſkene of the ſame ·

　　Deliuerit in Februar 1562 ·

93 · Item ane vther doublett of ſatine / with the ſkirt of the ſame ·

　　Deliuerit the ſaid tyme ·

94 · Item ane doublett of chammillot of ſilk with the vaſkene of the ſame ·

　　Deliuerit in October 1561 ·

95 · Mair twa tymmer beddis ·

　　Ane worne in 1566 ·

96 · Mair twa ſchrynis and ane coffer ·

　　Ane deliuerit in October 1564 · the vther in December the ſame yeir ·

Mr Johnne Wod ·

Inuentair of the Quenis movables quhilkis ar in the handes of
Seruais de Condy vallett of chalmer to hir Grace / All reſſauit fra
Jacques de Ma . . . . clerk of the offices of hir Maieſteis houſe
in the moneth of Nouember 1561 . at the Palace of Halyrude-
hous the xxv of the ſaid moneth and yeir .

In the first the Claithis of Estate .

1 . Item ane claith of eſtate of freſit claith of gold and ſiluir / partit equalie /
a breid of claith of gold and ane vther of ſiluir . And vpoun the ſiluir / cordeleris knottis of gold quhairof thair wantis ſum faſſis / furniſit with thre
pandis and the taill / and all freinyeit with threid of gold .

In Julij 1566 . it wes brokin to put crammoſie veluot in place of the claith of ſiluir . It
is in Striueling .

2 . Item ane claith of eſtate of grene veluot in the quhilk thair is ane great
trie / and perſonageis / and ſcheildis / all maid embroderie / furniſit with
thre pandis and the taill / all freinyeit with grene ſilk and threid of gold .

3 . Item ane claith of eſtate of freſit claith of gold / and traitis of violet ſilk /
partit equalie / with violet veluot / furniſit with thre pandis and the taill /
the nukis only freinyeit .

4 . Item ane claith of eſtate of claith of gold / and drauchtis of violett

filk / partit equalie / with violett veluot / quhair thair is the armes of Scotland and Lorayn with crownit cyphers / all in broderie furnefit with thre pandis and the taill / all freinyeit with threid of gold and violet filk ·

5 · Item ane claith of eftait of veluot / yallow incarnet and blew furnifit with thre pandis and the taill / all freinyeit with filk of that fame cullouris ·

6 · Item ane claith of eftate of blak veluot / furnifit with thre pandis / and the taill / all freinyeit with blak filk ·

In Februar 1567 · it wes tint in the Kingis ludging ·

7 · Item ane claith of eftate of crammofie veluot of heich cullour / furnifit with thre pandis and the taill / all freinyeit with threid of gold and crammofie filk / and pafmentit with pafmentis of gold ·

In Striueling ·

Off Claithis of Estate / without taillis ·

8 · Item ane fals ruif without tale of grene veluot maid in broderie with great treis perfonages and fcheildis and branches of holine / furnifit with thre double pandis and ane fingle / all frenyeit with grene filk and threid of gold except the fingle pand ·

9 · Item ane clayth of eftate without the tale of clayth of gold / with drauchtis of blak / diuidit equalie / with gray veluot / and furnifit / with foure fingle pandis without ony freinyeis or lyning ·

Efterwart it wes furnifit at the babtifme of the Prince ·

10 · Item ane claith of eftate without the taill of crammofie dames furnifit with foure fingle pandis and freinyeit with reid filk ·

Of Beddis maid in Broderie ·

11 · Item ane bed of crammofie broun veluot / maid in broderie work and leiffis

of claith of gold / with fum hiftories maid in the figure ovaill / furnifit
with ruif heidpece and fex pandis and thre vnderpandis / all frenyeit with
threid of gold and crammofie filk · with thre curtenis of crammofie dames /
pafmentit with gold / and frenyeit with the fame / and alfo foure coveringis
for the bed ftowppis ·

12 · Item ane bed of broderie work of foure cullouris of fatine / reid blew yallow and quhite / pourfeilliet with fals gold and filuir / furnifit with ruif
and heidpece / and thre fingle pandis / and twa vnderpandis / all freinyeit
with counterfait gold and filuir / with thre courtenis of taffetie of the fame
cullouris / without ony thing vpoun thame ·

13 · Item ane bed of frefit claith of gold / with drauchtes of reid filk / in figure
of jennettis and perfonageis and brancheis of holine / furnifit with ruif
heidpece / thre fingle pandis / twa vnderpandis / and all freinyeit with threid
of gold and crammofy filk ·

14 · Item ane bed maid of crammofie veluot / enriched with phenixes of gold
and teares with a litle cantaillie of gold / furnifit with ruif heidpece thre
fingle pandis and thre vnderpandis / all freinyeit with gold and crammofie
filk ·

15 · Item ane bed of blak veluot enrichit with armes and fpheris / with bordis
of brodere work of claith of gold furnifit with thre fingle pandis / with ruif
and heidpece / without ony vther garnifing ·

16 · Item ane bed diuidit equalie in claith of gold and filuir with drauchtes of
violet and gray filk / maid in chiffers of · 𝔄 · and enrichit with leiffis and
branches of holine / furnifit with ruif heidpece and thre fingle pandis twa
vnderpandis freinyeit with gold and violett filk with thre plane courtenis ·

17 · Item ane bed of fcarlett [veluot] bordit with broderie of blak veluot /
furnifit with ruif heidpece thre pandis twa vnderpandis thre curtenis of

taffetie of the fame cullour without freinyeis / The bed is furnifit with freinyeis of the fame cullour .

Deliuerit in Merche 1564 . to Johnne Semples wiff .

18 . Item ane bed all maid in broderie work of gold / of the hiftorie of the Workis of Hercules furnifit with fix pandis / ruif / heidpece / and thrie vnderpandis / quhilk is nother ftuffit nor garnifit .

Efterwart furnifit in the 1566 .

19 . Item ane bed of crammofie veluot enrichit with knottis of luif and . ⚹⚹ . furnifit with ruif heidpece / thre fingle pandis and thre vnderpandis / all haill togiddir without ony enrichement / and thre fingle curtenis of crammofie dames .

In Linlythgow in the handis of Ferriar .

20 . Item ane bed of violet broun veluot / enrichit with claith of gold and filuir / with chiffres and flouris fewit with gold and filk / furnifit with ruif heidpece / fevin pandis and thre vnderpandis . It is not yit furnifit nor ftuffit .

Wes efterward furnifit in 1566 . yeir .

21 . Item thre pandis of quhite and blew fatine / maid with broderie work of claith of gold droppit with reid filk interlacit / All pourfeillit with counterfait gold .

In Merche 1567 . the Quene gaif the faid pandis to Schir James Balfour .

22 . Item ane bed equallie diuidit in claith of gold and filuir maid in figure of pottis full of flouris with broderie work of lang roundis callit ovaill / quhairin the hiftories ar contenit / furnifit with ruif heidpece / fex pandis / thre vnderpandis ~~It is not yit ftuffit nor garnifit.~~

In Striueling . Efterward furnifit in anno 1566 .

Off pafmentit Beddis ·

23 · Item ane bed of incarnet dames maid like a chapel furnifit with ruif heidpece and pandis / and vnderpandis / with ane freinyeit heid abone / of reid
veluot / and curtenis of dames / all freinyeit with filuir and crammofie filk
and pafmentit with filuir ·

> This bed wes brokin in 1566 · and the pafment put vpoun curtenis and coveringis of
> grene chalmillet reinyeit with gold · The curtenis to ferve to the litle bed of crammofie
> veluot pafmentit and freinyeit with gold / with fingle pandis / And the covering feruis to
> the bed of phenix / And the reft to mak burd claithis and coveris to ftuillis of eafes / And
> the freinyeis of filuir feruis to the bed of grene veluot in broderie ·

24 · Item ane vther bed of quhite veluot pafmentit with ane pafment of gold
and violett filk / furnifit with ruif heidpece / thre fingle pandis / and thre
fingle curtenis of quhite taffete / and twa plane vnderpandis ·

25 · Item ane bed of crammofie veluot of heich cullour pafmentit with gold
furnifit with ruif heidpece and pandis / thre vnderpandis / and thre curtenis
of crammofie dames / all pafmentit and freinyeit with gold and crammofie
filk ·

In Striueling ·

Off plane Beddis not enrichit with ony thing ·

26 · Item ane bed of quhite dames furnifit with heidpece of taffeteis / and the
ruif / The thre pandis and twa vnderpandis of dames / and thre courtenis
of taffetie not freinyeit ·

27 · Item ane vther bed of quhite dames furnifit with ruif / heidpece / thre
pandis / twa curtenis of quhite taffetie not freinyeit ·

28 · Item ane bed of grene dames / furnifit with ruif / heidpece / and thre fingle pandis and thre curtenis of the fame ftuff vnfreinyeit ·

> The Quene gaif this bed to the Lord Huntlie in 1565 ·

29 · Item ane bed of veluot reid yallow and blew furnifit with ruif heidpece and thre fingle pandis and thrie vnderpandis haill togidder / all freinyeit with filk of the fame cullour / with thre curtenis of dames of the fame cullouris unfreinyeit ·

30 · Item ane bed of violett dames furnifit with ruif / without a heidpece / only foure pandis / and thre curtenis of violett dames vnfreinyeit / all the reft freinyeit ·

Off Cannabeis ·

31 · Item ane cannabie of grene taffetie freinyeit with grene / quhilk may ferue for any dry ftuill or a bed /

32 · Item ane cannabbie of orange taffeteis crifpit with gold and violet filk with the vnderpand haill togidder · all freinyeit with gold and violett filk / with the knop of trie ·

33 · Item ane litle cannabie of crammofie fatine of thre quarter lang furnifit with freinyeis and faffis maid of gold and crammofie filk / mony litle paintit buttonis all feruing to bear to mak fchaddow afoir the Quene ·

34 · Item ane auld cannabie of grene ferge worne away and brokin ·

> Worn away ·

35 · Item ane cannabie of yallow varian taffetie freinyeit with reid and yallow filk quhilk may ferue for ane ftuill of eafe ·

> Loiffit in the Kingis ludging quhen he deit in Februar 1567 ·

E

Of Chyris Falding Stuillis and Laich Stuillis ·

36 · Item ane heich cheir of crammosie veluot enrichit with branches of claith of gold in broderie / freinyeit with gold and crammosie silk ·

37 · Item twa auld faulding stuillis of crammosie veluot ·
> Worne away ·

38 · Item thre auld laich stuillis of crammosie veluot ·
> Worne away ·

39 · Item ane stuill of ease coverit with crammosie broun veluot .

40 · Item ane vther stuill of ease coverit with leddir / and bandit about with irne ·

Of Coveringis / and Claithis ganging about the Bed / for warmnes .

41 · Item ane covering of incarnet taffeteis stickit and strypit with siluir pasmentis and freinyeit with siluir and incarnet silk ·
> At the baptisme of the Prince the pasment wes tane away and seruis to the bed of phenix ·

42 · Item ane claith of reid scarlett gaing about the bed freinyeit beneth with crammosie silk ·

43 · Item twa coveringis of holane claith steickit ·
> The ane worn away ·

44 · Item ane covering of quhite mantill ·

45 · Item ane covering of blew taffetie stickit ·
> In 1567 . wes tynt in the Kingis ludging ·

46 · Item ane covering of reid taffetie ftickit ·

In Auguſt 1566 · this covering gevin to the King ·

47 · Item ane covering of varian taffetie ftickit borderit with a cordoun of gold vpoun the ſticking / maid in broderie ·

Preſentlie it feruis the bed of cyphers of · 𝕸 · callit the Bed of Amitie ·

48 · Item ane great covering of eſtate of crammoſie veluot heich culloure / paſmentit with gold / and buttonit with gold buttonis on the nukis / freinyeit round about with gold and crammoſie filk ·

In Striueling / and feruis to the bed of crammoſie veluot with double pandis ·

49 Item ane covering of crammoſie ſatine / lynit with taffeties only / ~~quhilk is imperfyte~~ ·

Efterwart wes perfytit to furnis the bed of crammoſie broun veluot maid in broderie ·

50 · Item ten ſingle blankettis / quhilkis feruit the beddis of the brodinſters / quha wrocht vpoun the great pece of broderie ·

Deliuerit fen the yeirs of 1561 · to 1566 ·

Off Burd Claithis ·

51 · Item ane burd claith of violett broun veluot droppit with flouris de lice maid in broderie work of threid of gold / to the nowmer of fifty / wanting freinyeis and lyning ·

In September 1563 · The violet veluot wes emploit for to mak ſtuillis of eafe and heich chearis and falding ſtuillis ·

52 · Item ane burdclaith of grene veluot lynit with grene taffetie without freinyeis ·

In Lochlevin ·

53 · Item ane burdclaith of crammoſie veluot of heich cullour / lynit with taffetie and freinyeit with gold and crammoſie filk ·

It wes worne away in the Quenis chalmer 1566 ·

54 · Item ane evill litle burdclaith of grene ·

     Worne away ·

Off Cusscheonis of all sortis ·

55 · Item foure cufscheonis of crammofie veluot ftuffit with fethirs /

     Twa of thame deliuerit in Julij 1565 · to ferue in the Chapel ·

56 · Item foure cufscheonis of reid veluot ·

     Worne away in the Quenis chalmer · and part tynt in the Kingis ludging ·

57 · Item thre cufscheonis of grene veluot ·

58 · Item thre cufscheonis of claith of gold figurit with reid ·

     Employit in October 1566 ·

59 · Item twa cufscheonis of claith of gold figurit with reid / quhairof the vnder fyde is of crammofie veluot ·

     Employit in October 1566 ·

60 · Item ane cufscheoun of grene fatine maid in broderie work in figure of litle fcheildis and branches of holine

61 · Item fex cufscheonis of work of filk fewit / lynit with reid leddir ·

62 · Item thre fewit worfet cufscheonis lynit with reid leddir ·

Of auld Beddis of all sortis ·

63 · Item ane bed maid of ane auld pece of tapeftrie of the figure of branches of holine / garnifit with ruif and pandis / thre vnderpandis / The ruif is different fra the ftuff of the reft ·

64 · Item ane bed maid of the hiftorie of the Huntar of Coninghis / garnifit with ruif and foure pandis ·

65 · Item ane bed maid of ane vther pece of auld tapeſtrie of the Huntar of Coninghis · The ruif is of bukrem / and the reſt of the furniſing lyke this laſt bed ·

66 · Item ane vther bed maid of ane auld pece of tapeſtrie of the hiſtorie of SOUUIENNE VOUS EN / furniſit with ruif and foure pandis / and freinyeit with threid reid quhite and blew ·

67 · Item ane vther bed maid of ane auld pece of tapeſtrie in the figure of branches of holine mixt a litle with threid of gold · furniſit with ruif and thre pandis only / Of the quhilk thair is bot twa freinyeit with red quhite and blew ſilk ·

68 · Item ane bed maid of ſewit worſett with the figure of Satires and levis of treis / furniſit with ruif and heidpece and thre pandis / all freinyeit with reid and grene worſett / with thre auld curtenis of blew ſerge of diuers cullouris ·

69 · Item ane bed maid of ſewit ſilk / quhairin thair is perſonages · furniſit with heid pece and thre pandis / freinyeit with euill ſilk counterfait / reid blew and yallow / with the ruif of tapeſtrie / and thre auld courtenis of reid taffetie without freinyeis ·

70 · Item thre beddis of reid ſerge furniſit with ruif and pandis / all freinyeit with worſett / with nyne curtenis of ſerge ·

Ane deliuerit in December 1565 · Ane vther to Pochonmer 1568 ·

71 · Item ane bed of reid chalmillett furniſit with ruif and heid pece and thre pandis / all freinyeit with reid worſett / with thre curtenis of reid ſerge ·

72 · Item ane bed of auld reid ſerge / garniſit with ruif and pandis / all freinyeit with reid worſett ·

73 · Item ane vther auld bed of reid ferge diuidit equalie with grene ferge furnifit with ruif and pandis / all freinyeit with reid worfett ·

Off Tapestreis of all sortis ·

74 · Item ane tapeftrie of heich cullourit crammofie veluot · maid in broderie / quhilk is not yit compleit ·

    Brokin to mak a claith of eftait in *anno* 1566 ·

75 · Item ane tapeftrie maid of frefit claith of gold equalie diuidit in bredis of claith of filuir contenand xij peces fmall and great / and the haill alfweill gold as filuir contenand lxj bredis / In quhilk vpoun the claith of filuir thair is cordeleir knottis of claith of gold maid in broderie / quhilkis knottis hes faffis of threid of gold quhairof thair is fum loiffit /

    This tapeftrie wes brokin and crammofie veluot equallie diuidit with the claith of gold puttin in place of the claith of filuir ·

76 · Item aucht peces of tapeftrie of grene veluot / quhairin is the figures of great treis / and the reft droppit with fcheildis / and brancheis of holine / all maid in broderie ·

77 · Item ane tapeftrie of the hiftorie of the Triumphe of Veritie contening aucht peces ·

    Ane part in Striueling ·

78 · Item ane tapeftrie of the hiftorie of the Battell of Ravene contening fevin peces ·

79 · Item ane tapeftrie of the hiftorie of the Jugement of Paris contening aucht peces ·

80 · Item ane tapeftrie of the hiftorie of the Huntis of the Sangleir contening fex peces ·

81 · Item ane tapeſtrie of the triumphe of ane aſſault of ane toun contening fyve peces ·

82 · Item ane tapeſtrie of the hiſtorie of ſcheiphirdis contening ſevin peces ·

83 · Item ane tapeſtrie maid be litle branches wrocht with ſum gold / the ground of this tapeſtrie is of the cullouris reid quhite and blew / and contenis thre peces ·

84 · Item ane tapeſtrie maid with the figure of perſonages / quha cuttis the holine / continand fouretene peces ·

    Part in Linlythgow ·

85 · Item ane tapeſtrie of the brancheis of holine wrocht a litle with threid of gold contening ſex peccs ·

86 · Item ane tapeſtrie of the Armes of the hous [of Longovaill] of aucht peces ·

    In Striueling ·

87 · Item ane tapeſtrie of the hiſtorie of the Saling of Eneas contenand aucht peces ·

88 · Item ane tapeſtrie of the hiſtorie of the Workes of Hercules contening aucht peces ·

89 · Item ane tapeſtrie of litle grene flouris vpoun yallow ground / contening ſevin peces ·

90 · Item ane litle pece of tapeſtrie like a burdclaith cuttit in twa ·

91 · Item ane tapeſtrie of the Huntar of Coninghis contening ſevin peces ·

    In Februar 1567 · ſex of thir peces wes tint in the Kingis gardrop at his death ·

92 · Item ane tapeſtrie maid of reid quhite and blew / in the quhilk thair is ane

trie with ane reafoun Souuienne vous en / and the reft droppit with litle·branches / contening twelf peces ·

93 · Item ane tapeftrie of litle grene flouris contening twa peces ·

94 · Item ane tapeftrie in the quhilk thair is ane tre / and the reft droppit with litle branches of fmall flouris contening fex peces ·

95 · Item ane tapeftrie of the hiftorie of Calueris and Moris contening foure peces ·

96 · Item ane auld tapeftrie in the quhilk thair is ane trie / and the reft droppit with fmall grene flouris ·

Off Turquie Tapeis for the flure ·

97 · Item twa auld tapeis of Turquie worne away ·

  Thair remanis a part ·

98 · Item xxiiij Turkie tapeis fum great fum litle ·

  Part worne and part tint in 1565 and 66 ·

Off Messe Claithis ·

99 · Item ane chafiable of crammofie veluot furnifit with a ftole and a fannoun only ·

  Deliuerit for the Chapel in Julij 1565 ·

100 · Item ane claith of crammofie veluot to hing abone the alter / and ane vther to hing beneth · quhairin thair is a crucifix and the Quenis armes / and the reft droppit with fternis of gold / all maid in broderie ·

  Deliuerit at the faid tyme ·

101 · Item ane tapeis vnder fute of the said veluois lynit with bukrem :
    Deliuerit at the said tyme ·

102 · Item ane corporall cais of crammofie veluot maid in broderie ·
    Deliuerit at the said tyme ·

Sum Harnessingis ·

103 · Item half a littar of crammofie veluot freinyeit with gold and filk ·

104 · Item twa litle fut mantillis of the same veluot / freinyeit with gold and crammofie filk ·

Of Tymmer Beddis ·

105 · Item ane tymmer bed that feruit for the incarnet dames / pafmentit with filuir ·

106 · Item ane tymmer bed that feruit for the bed of crammofie veluot of heich cullour pafmentit with gold ·

107 · Item ane tymmer bed that feruit for the bed of reid ferge ·
    Takin for the King in 1566 ·

108 · Item ane tymmer bed that feruit for the bed of veluois incarnet yallow and blew ·

109 · Item ane tymmer bed that feruit for the quhite veluois bed pafmentit with gold and violett filk ·

110 · Item ane tymmer bed that feruit for the broun crammofie veluot bed / enrichit with the phenix in broderie ·

111 · Item ane tymmer bed that feruit for the bed of claith of gold and claith of filuir and chiffers ·

F

112 · Item ane tymmer bed that feruit for the bed of reid ferge ·

113 · Item twa vther tymmer beddis ·

114 · Item ane tymmer bed that feruit for the bed of crammofie veluot em-
broderit with claith of gold and hiftorie ·

115 · Item ane tymmer table paintit and gilt with the treflis of the fame ·

Of sum restis and peces of Claith of Gold and Silk and vther small geir ·

116 · Item aucht reftis and litle peces of crammofie veluot contening xviij ellis
and thre quarters in the haill ·
Deliuerit at findrie tymes in 1565 · and 66 ·

117 · Item foure quarters of a coitt of claith of gold frefit with cantailyeis of
gold and filuir ·
Deliuerit in Julij 1565 ·

118 · Item the reft of blak veluot brochit with gold contening ten ellis and a
quarter ·
Deliuerit at the faid tyme ·

119 · Item twa litle peces of claith of gold maid in broderie of bordis and
leiffis / ilk pece contening an ell ·
Emploit to work in Merche *anno* 1564 ·

120 · Item ane litle pece of claith of gold traiffit with yallow contening ane ell
and thre quarters ·
[Deliuerit in September] 1563 ·

121 · Item ellevin peces of frefit claith of gold and filuir fum great fum fmall /
quhilk feruit for a caparifon to a hors ·
Deliuerit in September *anno* 1566 ·

122 · Item ane collet of aürange hew / quharin is bandis of claith of claith of
gold twa fingar braid ·

> Employit in Aprile 1566 ·

123 · Item half a fcheild and the half of the Order of France all maid in
broderie ·

124 · Item fevin quaiffis of claith of filuir cordonit with blak filk / and the
railyettis of the fame ·

125 · Item ane man of armes coitt without flevis of claith of gold frefit with
filuir ·

> Deliuerit in Julij 1565 ·

126 · Item fyftene cuffcheonis of auld claith of filuir ·

> Employit in Aprile 1566 ·

127 · Item ane reft of auld claith of filuir contening twa ellis and thre
quarteris ·

> Employit at the faid tyme ·

128 · Item threttene litle cuffcheonis of plane claith of gold / fewit togidder ·

> Deliuerit and employit in *annis* · 1565 · and 66 ·

129 · Item the hude of a cannabie of claith of gold brochit with blak / without
freinyeis / maid of ellevin peces ·

130 · Item fourty litle fcheildis in a litle pacquet ·

131 · Item ane litle pacquet of lyvelie leiffis of holine ·

132 · Item ane hatt of blak veluois enrichit with the bord and cordoun of
threid of filuir ·

133 · Item ane pacquet of blew freinyeis and threid of gold contening fex [ellis] ·

The freinyeis wes put to the claith of eftate that it wes takin fra in Nouember. 1567 ·

134 · Item ane band of claith of gold brocheit with blak / contening a quarter in breid /

135 · Item ane reft of auld plane claith of gold / contening twa ellis thre quarters / in thre litle peces ·

The haill deliuerit and employit in *anno* 1564 · to the 66 ·

136 · Item ane vther litle pece of plane claith of gold contening a fute alfweill in lenth as in breid ·

Employit in *anno* 1565 ·

137 · Item ane pacquet of freinyeis of violet filk and threid of gold / quhilk freinyeis hes feruit to the pandis of ane claith of eftate of violett veluois and fatine brocheit with gold ·

The freinyeis hes bene put to the claith of eftate quhairfra they wer takin · Reffauit 1 eln thre quarters 1 half ·

138 · Item ane band of quhite veluois quhilk is of twa fingair braid cordonit with a cordoun of filuir in broderie / and it is in xxij peces ·

139 · Item twa egles maid in broderie of threid of gold ·

140 · Item ane quarter of freinyeis of crammofie filk ·

It wes put to the bed of broun crammofie veluot in broderie in Auguft 1566 ·

142 · Item thre bredis of claith of gold frefit with gold reinyeit with quhite / everie breid contening twa ellis and a half and half quarter /

Employit in Aprile 1566 ·

143 · Item fyvetene cuſſcheonis of freſit claith of gold and reinyeit with quhite / ilk cuſſcheoun contenand ane quarter and a half or thairby ·

> Employit in the ſaid tyme ·

144 · Item ane vther pece of the ſaid claith / contenand a quarter ·

> Deliuerit in October 1564 ·

145 · Item thre quarters of freſit claith of gold reinyeit with violett / with ane vther litle pece contening half ane ell and half a quarter ·

> Employit in Januar 1566 ·

146 · Item fyve ellis and thre quarters of freſit claith of gold reinyeit with blak / contening in the haill to fyve litle peces / a half of the laich of a coit thairin contenit / figurit with ſcaillis ·

> The claith of gold wes employit in Februar 1566 · and the laich of the coit de-
> liuerit in Januar 1566 ·

147 · Item ane mekle auld curtene of quhite taffetie without freinyeis ·

148 · Item thre curtenis of grene dames without freinyeis ·

> Thay wer brokin to be maid a pavillon to a bed in *anno* 1566 ·

149 · Item twelf lang taillit buttonis of threid of gold to be ſett vpoun the cover of honoure of crammoſie ſatine ·

> Employit vpoun the cover in *anno* 1566 ·

150 · Item ane ſeck of leddir quhairin thair is findrie litle peces of grene veluot ·

151 · Item twelf litle cuſſcheonis of blak ſatine brochit with gold / quhilkis ſeruit the claith of eſtate of violet veluois and of blak ſatine brocheit with gold ·

Of Scheittis and Lyning Claithis great and small ·

152 · Item fourty round fcheittis quhilkis feruit to the þrowdinftaris that
wrocht vpoun the tapeftrie of the crammofie veluois ·

> A part deliuerit in *anno* 1561 · to 67 · Ane reft ·

153 · Item thre feruiettis of dornick ·

> Deliuerit to the pantrie ·

154 · Item fex great feruiettis of dornik quhilkis wer not cuttit ·

> Deliuerit to the pantrie ·

155 · Item twa feruiettis of dornik ftickand togidder ·

> Deliuerit to the pantrie ·

156 · Item fevin feruiettis damafkit ·

> Deliuerit to the pantrie ·

157 · Item twa burdclaithis and ane claith for the copburd damafkit ·

158 · Item ane great claith of lyning without feme ·

159 · Item fex feruiettis for banquettis ·

> Deliuerit to the pantrie ·

160 · Item ane bed of layn fewit with filk of diuers cullouris / garnifit with
thre curtenis and with thre vther litle peces / and the heidpece of the
fame ·

161 · Item ane tyke of a bed reinyeit with blew ·

162 · Item twa great mekle bordclaithis of dornik contenand fouretene ellis the
twa ·

> Deliuerit to the pantrie ·

163 · Item twa litle peces of claith of caddes / with twa vther litle peces / the haill contening foure ellis ·

164 · Item thre litle peces of freinyeis of counterfait gray filk quhite and violet / with fum vther litle peces / the haill weand a pund ·

165 · · Item ane pece of round lyning contening liiij ellis thre quarters ·
> Deliuerit in Februar 1562 ·

166 · Item ane vther pece of round lyning contening liiij ellis ·
> Deliuerit in Aprile 1562 ·

167 · Item auchtene fcheittis of hollane and lyning alfweill great as fmall auld and new ·
> Part vfit and deliuerit in Februar 1567 · Twa tint in the Kingis ludging ·

168 · Item ane fcheit of lyning maid of thre bredis ·

169 · Item twa dufand of codwaris of holane claith ·
> Part worne and partt tynt ·

170 · Item xxviij curcheis of holane claith ·

171 · Item auchtene burdclaithis of dornik great and fmall ·
> Deliuerit in the pantrie ·

172 · Item thretty aucht commoun fcheittis great and litle auld and new · (A part of thame reffauit ·)
> Quhairof thair wes put in the chalmer coffer at hir departing furth of France as it appearis be the memoir of the kepair of the hous of Fecan / quhilkis I haue not reffavit ·

173 · Item ten vther fcheittis of round lyning ·
> Foure of thame deliuerit in Julij 1565 ·

174 · Item twa auld burdclaithis half worne ·

175 · Item ane pece of dornik to mak burdclaithis / contening xxxv ellis of lenth and twa ellis of breid ·

176 · Item twelf fcheittis of lyning / quhairof thair is twa of thre breidis / and the reft twa breidis and a half ·

Of Schrynis and Cofferis ·

177 · Item ane fchrene garnifit with quhite irne ·

178 · Item ane vther fchryne quharin wes the tapeftrie of claith of gold and claith of filuir ·

179 · Item ane vther fchryne quhairin wes the tapeftrie of grene veluot ·

180 · Item ane auld worne coffer ·
     Brokin ·

181 · Item ane ward of a mat of round lyning for the mekle bed of eftate ·

182 · Item ane coffer of filk vpoun cammes maid of nedill work / quhairin is the bed of layn wrocht with filk ·

183 · Item ane vther coffer maid in broderie vpoun reid fatine / quhilk is without ony garnifing ·

Of Mattis / Palleissis / and Bousters ·

184 · Item ten pallies ane and vther ·

185 · Item ten mattis mekle and little ·

186 · Item ten bowfters / the haill to ferue to the faidis beddis ·

Mr John Wod ·

The Inuentar of the movables of vmquhile the Erll of Huntlie quhilkis wes deliuerit to me [Servay de Conde vallet of chamber to the Quene] be James Stewart gentleman to the Erll of Murray / all reffauit in December · 1562 ·

1 · In the firft a bed of violett veluois garnifit with ruif heidpece / thre fingle pandis and twa vnderpandis freinyeit with violett filk / thre curtenis of violett dames and a covering of gray taffeteis ftickit ·

2 · Item ane bed of grene dames garnifit with ruif heidpece thre fingle pandis twa vnderpandis and thre curtenis / all pafmentit with filuir paf[m]entis / and freinyeit with filuir and grene filk · Togiddir with a covering of grene taffeteis ftickit and ane litle burdclaith of grene veluot ·

Changeit fenfyne in a foure nukit bed / The burdclaith loiffit in the Kingis ludging in Februar 1567 ·

3 · Item ane bed of blak figurit veluot garnifit with the ruif heidpece and thre fingle pandis / thre vnderpandis / and thre courtenis of taffeties · all enrichit with pafmentis of gold and filuir / and freinyeit with gold and filuir / and a burdclaith of blak veluot garnifit in like maner / and lynit with bukrem ·

Deliuerit quhen the Quene wes at Hammyltoun ·

4 · Item ane bed of tannie dames garnifit with ruif heidpece / thre fingle pandis

G

and twa vnderpandis / all freinyeit with tannie filk / with thre fingle courtenis / and twa coveringis of tannie taffeteis ftickit ·

Ane of thir coveringis deliuerit in Februar 1564 ·

5 · Item ane bed of crammofie veluot of heich cullour / garnifit with ruif heidpece / thre fingle pandis and twa vnderpandis / and thre curtenis of crammofie dames / all freinyeit with threid of gold and crammofie filk / and
enrichet vpoun the feames with a litle biffet of gold / Ane burdclaith of
that fame freinyeit with gold and crammofie filk · and ane covering of
reid taffetie ftickit ·

In Auguft 1566 this covering gevin to the King and changeit the courtenis ·

6 · Item ane claith of eftate of crammofie fatine figurit pirnit with gold / furn-
fit with ruif and taill / thre fingle pandis / the haill freinyeit with gold and
crammofie filk ·

In Lochleavin ·

7 · Item ane auld bed of yallow and blew taffetie furnifit with ruif heidpece
and thre fingle pandis all freinyeit with filk of that fame cullour with thre
curtenis of taffeteis of that fame cullour ·

8 · Item ane bed of yallow dames maid like a chapel / furnifit with ruif and
heidpece and thre pandis / twa vnderpandis / thre curtenis and foure coueringis for the ftowppis / all freinyeit with yallow filk ·

This bed wes maid foure nukit in December · 1566 · The curtenis wes brokin / and
vtheris putt in thair place ·   In Linlythgow ·

9 · Item ane bed of frefit claith of gold / diuidit equalie in breidis of claith of
filuir champit / furnifit with ruif heidpece / thre fingle pandis / and thre
vnderpandis / and foure coveringis to the ftowppis / thre curtenis of yallow
damas / ane covering of ftickit taffeteis / and ane burdclaith of veluot / the
haill freinyeit and pafmentit with filuir and yallow filk ·

. . . . . this bed wes brokin to mak the claith of gold ferue to a claith of eftate / and

alſua to mak coveringis to the ſtouppis of beddis of the claith of ſiluir to another bed ·
The reſt employit in that ſame yeir ·

10 · Item ane covering of quhite fuſtian to put on a bed ·

Worne away · Condempnit ·

11 · Item ellevin tapeſtrie of gilt leddir ·

12 · Item twa cuſſcheonis of figurit crammoſie veluot droppit with gold ·

13 · Item foure cuſſcheonis of blak veluot ·

A part employit in work · Reſſauit j ·

14 · Item twa cuſſcheonis of yallow veluot ·

15 · Item twa cannabeis of blak dames ·

In Julij · 1565 · ane deliuerit · Reſſauit j ·

16 · Item fyve pece of auld tapeſtrie maid in the figure of burdis and great
leiffis of treis ·

17 · Item mair ane bed of blak veluot furniſit with ruif heidpece / thre ſingle
pandis and twa vnderpandis / the haill freinyeit with blak ſilk / thre curtenis of dames and ane covering of blak ſtekit taffeties ·

Vther mouables quhilkis I reſſauit fra Maiſter Johnne Balfoure ·
vallet of the Quenis chalmer · in December · 1562 ·

18 · In the firſt fourty peces of tapeſtrie of all ſortis mekle and litle auld and
new ·

In Februar 1567 · ſex peces wes tynt in the Kingis chalmer and fyve peces in the hall /
and ane tynt in the great hall of Striueling / Reſſauit xxxiij peces ·

∞ · Item twa burdclaithis of blak tryp veluot figurit with twa cuſſcheonis of the ſame ·

Ane brokin in *anno* 1566 · Reſſauit j ·

19 · Item foure litle burdclaithis of grene claith part gude part euill ·

Part of thir worne away in 1565 · Reſſauit twa ·

20 · Item ane litle cuſſcheoun of blak veluot quhilk ſeruis to put vnder a buke ·

21 · Item ane pece of quhite plaidis ſingle / contening ten ellis ·

Deliuerit at ſindrie tymes · in *anno* 1563 · and 64 ·

22 · Item ten duſand of playne ſerviettis ·

Deliuerit in the pantrie ·

23 · Item foure duſand of dornik ſeruiettis ·

Deliuerit in the pantrie ·

24 · Item xxij copburd claithis part mekle part litle ·

25 · Item fourty drying claithis of all ſortes ·

Deliuerit xij in the chalmer on Skir Furiſday at the weſching of the pure folkis fete ·

26 · Item nyne burd claithis mekle and litle ·

Deliuerit in pantrie ·

27 · Item ten duſand of damaſkit ſerviettis ·

Deliuerit in pantrie ·

28 · Item foure dornik burdclaithis ·

Deliuerit in pantrie /

29 · Item ſextene burdclaithis damaſkit of ſindre ſortis ·

Deliuerit in pantrie ·

30 · Item twelf pair of fcheittis meklę and litle ·

> Part worne away ·

31 · Item twelf burdclaithis mekle and litle ·

> Deliuerit in pantrie ·   ·

32 · Item ten pece of caippis / chafubles / and tvnicles / all of claith of gold /
and thre of thame figurit with reid / and the reſt with quhite and yallow /
The thre quhite is auld ·

> In Merche 1567 · I deliuerit thre of the fareſt / quhilk the Quene gaif to the Lord Boithuil /
> And mair tuke for hir felf ane caip / a chafable / foure tvnicles to mak a bed for the
> King / all brokin and cuttit in hir awin prefence · Reſſauit ane ·

33 · Item nyne peces of caippis / chafubles and tvnicles / all of claith of gold ·
thre figurit with reid ·

> Part brokin employit · Reſſauit part ·

34 · Item ane claith of eſtate to be borne on foure ſtouppis of violett crammofie veluot / quhilk hes na thing bot foure pandis / enrichit with broderie
and freinyeis without ony vther thing ·

35 · Item ane covering of the alter maid of claith of gold figurit with grene /
without ane vnderpand ·

36 · Item ane auld caip of claith of gold figurit with quhite ·

37 · Item ane caip of claith of gold figurit with blew ·

38 · Item twa caippis / ane chafuble / and twa tvnicles / all of reid veluot ·

> Deliuerit ·

39 · Item foure caippis / ane chafuble and twa tvnicles / all of blew veluot ·

40 · Item ane chafuble / twa tvnicles / foure caippis / all of grene veluot /
quhairof thair is twa figurit ·

> In the end of the yeir 1564 · all this wes employit be the Quenis command ·

41 · Item ane pece of grene veluot of ane quarter breid and ane ell lang ⁄ quhairupoun thair is fum broderie ·

    Employit at the fame tyme ·

42 · Item ane auld caip ane chafuble and twa tvnicles ⁄ all begareit with diuers cullouris ·

42 · Item ane auld caip of quhite dames ·

43 · Item thre vther auld caippis of quhite dames ·

44 · Item ane chafuble and twa tvnicles of blak dames ·

45 · Item twa auld foirbreiftis of caippis ·

46 · Item ane vther auld caip begareit ·

47 · Item ane chafuble and twa twnicles of reid fkarlet ·

    Gevin be the Quene ·

48 · Item ane auld claith afoir the alter ⁄ and ane vther auld caip ·

49 · Item diuers ftoyllis and fannonis of findrie fortis ·

50 · Item mair Maister Johnne Balfoure deliuerit ane mytir to Madam mofel de Ralle ⁄ quhilk mytir wes inrychit with findrie ftanes not verie fyne ⁄ all the reft coverit with fmall perlis ·

A ne vther Inuentar of the Vefshellis of Glaffe ⁄ quhilk I reffauit fra Alexander Bog porter · in December · 1562 ·

51 · In the first ane gilt bafine with the cais ·

    Reffauit the bafin ⁄ wantis the cais ·

52 · Item twa blew flaccownis garnifit with tin ·

> Reffauit ·

53 · Item ane vther blew flaccoune ·

> Reffauit ·

54 · Item ane figure of a manis heid maid of maber ·

55 · Item foure gilt chandillers .

> Reffauit ·

56 · Item the figure of ane doig maid in quhite laym ·

> [To the] King ·

57 · Item ane litle ymage of Sainct George maid of tyn ·

> [To the] King ·

58 · Item ane munk and a nun / in twa litle buiftis ·

> To the King ·

59 · Item ane Samaritan woman and hir well / maid of trie ·

> Reffauit ·

60 · Item ellevin plaittis of findrie fortis maid of quhite anameling ·

> Reffauit v · mair viij quheit / j of wandfaffon / iij of diuers collouris / vther thre colourit plane / ij of quheit and gold / [t]ua quheit fawfars ane lefs and a mair · Reffauit viij blew gilt / j brokin / j quheit bafing gilt / i bafing and lair with aipis wormes and ferpentis / tua litle blew glaffis / ane litle blew difch / twa brokin coveris in form of laweris / five platis / ane lawer gilt / ane lawer with a cowp and a cover of copper enamallit ·

61 · Item twa gilt facers ·

62 · Item twa litle barrellis and a litle thre futit pott ·

> Reffauit ·

63 · Item twa pottis with thair coveris / and vther twa to drink beir without coveris ·

64 · Item ane pilgreimmes difche ·

 Reffauit ·

65 · Item ane aip ·

66 · Item twa blew laveris with ane gilt coup ·

 Reffauit / wantis j ·

67 · Item ane litle laver blew gilt ·

 Reffauit ·

68 · Item ane quhite vais ·

 Reffauit ·

69 · Item ane cowp of jafp with the cover ·

 Reffauit ·

70 · Item twa gilt fpvnis ·

71 · Item thre heich goblettis / twa coverit and ane without a cover ·

 Reffauit · ij in the Registry ·

72 · Item twa cowppis coverit / and fex vther cowppis ·

 Reffauit viij ·

73 · Item ane glas and fex litle culing fannis of litle wandis ·

 Wantis glas ·

M'' Johnne Wod ·

Memorandum of fum graith / within a cais reſſauit fra Lethingtoun / the tyme that he brocht the pictour of the Quene Regent
out of France · 1563 ·

1 · Firſt · The brod of the pictour of the Quene Regent ·

2 · Thre vaſkenis of reid ſatine pirnit with gold ·
  Deliuerit ·

3 · Thre vther vaſkenis of quhite ſatine pirnit with ſiluir ·
  Deliuerit ·

4 · Nyne ellis of claith of gold figurit with blew ·
  Deliuerit ·

5 · Thre ellis and a quarter of gray ſatine pirnit with gold ·
  Deliuerit ·

6 · Ane reſt of columbe taffeties contening nyne ellis ·
  Deliuerit ·

7 · Mair ſevintene cuſſcheonis ſewit with ſilk and gold ·

8 · Mair ten mekle round peces of ſewit work of ſilk and threid of gold ·

9 · Mair ane litle pece of gais of ſiluir and quhite ſilk ·

10 · Mair twa coittis of grene veluot bandit with claith of gold ·
  Deliuerit ·

11 · Mair twa coittis of violet veluois bandit with claith of ſiluir ·
  Deliuerit ·

12 · Mair ane vther coitt of blew veluot weill auld and worne ·
  Preſentlie wes deliuerit to Merna ·

H

Memorandum of that quhilk I haue reſſauit of ane preſent quhilk
my Lady Ruthven maid to the Quene in the Juſtice Clerkis ludging · 1564 · in June ·

1 · Firſt ane litle claith of eſtate of claith of gold reinyeit with reid / quhilk
hes bot thre bredis in braidnes / furniſit with thre ſingle pandis / the haill
freinyeit with gold and reid ſilk ·

This wes brokin to cover the flure about the Quenis bed · Reſſauit · Reſſauit the freinyeis
wantand findry partes of the gold contenand iij eln iij quarteris double freinyeit ·

2 · Mair ane vther claith of eſtate of the fame ſtuff / quhilk hes bot twa
bredis in braidnes / furniſit with ruif taill and thre ſingle pandis / all freinyeit with gold and reid ſilk ·

3 · Mair ane vther litle claith of eſtate of claith of gold reinyeit and figurit
with tanne / furniſit with thre ſingle pandis / ruif and taill / all freinyeit
with reid ſilk and tanny ·

4 · Ane burdclaith of claith of gold reingyeit with reid without freinyeis or
lyning ·

Memorandum of the ornamentis of the Kirk quhilk I reſſauit fra the Kepair of the Chapel of Striueling · 1562 ·

Firſt twa auld caippis of blew dames droppit with floure delice of gold / with the foirbreſtis maid in hiſtories ·

Alſua ane cover of the alter with the vnderpand / all of frefit claith of gold with blew / and diuidit equalie in bredis of claith of gold figurit with reid / freinyeit with ſilk of the ſame cullour ·

Mair twa auld caippis of reid veluot figurit with flouris of gold / furnifit the foirbreiſtis with counterfait gold ·

Mair twa tvnicles ane chaſuble and a caip / all of claith of gold figurit with blew veluot / the foirbreiſtis of broderie work of gold and ſilk ·

Mair twa tvnicles / thre caippis / ane chaſuble with the cover of ane alter ·and the vnderpand / all of blak veluot droppit with ſtarnis of gold · The foirbreiſtis of thame of reid veluot enrichit with the armes of Scotland and hiſtories ·

Mair ane chaſuable and twa tvnicles of claith of gold / pyrnit with blak / furnifit with the foirbreiſtis of fyne gold ·

Mair foure ſtoillis and ſex fannonis with fyve beltis maid of quhite threid ·

Mair ſex abbis and foure amytis with twa auld alter claithis ·
    Worne ·

Inuentaire de tous les ahabillemens de la Royne tant vngs que aultres faict a Liflebourg · et premier jour de Feburier mil cinq cens foixante vng · Lefquelz meubles font de prefant auecq les aultres meubles de la Royne dans Labbaye de Liflebourg ·

Et premierement ·

Vne robbe de toylle dor damaffee bandee de troys bifets dargent faict entre deux de petitz cordons dargent faict en plume ·

Vne robbe de toille dargent frifee dor et dargent et traffee de vert bordee de paffement dor · Ladite robbe faicte a bourletz ·

Vne robbe de toille dargent frifee dor et dargent et traffee de foye cramoyfye et bordee dung paffement dor faict a bourletz ·

Vne robbe faicte a bourletz de toylle dor toute couuerte de broderye de cordon dargent faict en feullaiges le font rambly de foye viollete et bordee dung paffement ·

Vne robbe de veloux noyer faict a grand manches toutes couuertes de broderye bandee et chamaree de cannetille dor et cordon · Le refte de la dicte robbe eft faict par ondes dudict cordon ·

Vne robbe de veloux vert faicte en bourletz toute couuerte de broderye ginpeure et cordon dor et dargent et bordee dung paffement de mefmes ·

Item vne robbe de damas cramoyfy viollet faicte a bourletz toute couuerte de
broderye la bande de cannetille dor et brodee dune treffe dor ·

Donne a Madame dArgille en ce moys de Decembre 1566 ·

Vne [robbe] de fatin gris faict en bourletz toute couuerte de broderye de gumpeure dor cordon dor et bordee de paffement dor ·

Vne robbe de fatin bleu faicte a borletz toute couuerte de broderye en faffon de
palmes faicte dargent · le refte cordonne dor et bordee dung paffement dor
et dargent ·

Vne robbe de fatin cramoyfy fect a bourelles toute couuerte de broderye en
faffon de roffe et feullages faictz dargent · et le refte cordonne dor et bordee
dung paffement dor ·

Vne robbe de fatin incarnat faicte a bourletz et bandee dune bande de brodere
de gumpeure dargent · Ladicte robbe eft femee de petitz fleuron dargent
et bordee dune treffe dargent ·

Vne robbe de fatin blanc faicte a manches longues toutes chamarees de bandes
de broderye faicte de gumpeure dor cordonne dor et bordee dune treffe dor ·

Vne robbe de fatin geaulne faicte a manches longues toute couuerte de broderye
gumpeure cordon dargent et bordee de paffement dargent frife ·

Les Robbes de Toille Dor et Dargent pleine ou brochee dor et dargent ·

Vne robbe de toille dargent faicte a bourles toute goffree et bordee dune treffe
dargent ·

Vne robbe de camellot cramoyfy brochee dor faicte a bourletz et bordee dune treffe dor .

> Au moys Daouſt la Royne a donne ladicte robbe a Foupertuy .

Vne robbe de camellot blanc brochee dargent faicte a manches longues bandee de deux paſſement dor faicte a jour et a troys nattes dor et bordee dune treffe dor .

Vne robbe de ſatin cramoyfy brochee dargent faicte a borletz et bordee dune frange dargent .

Vne robbe de taffetas cramoyfy viollet broche dor faicte a bourletz et bordee dune treffe dor .

Item vne robbe de toylle blew a grande manche rayee dor et dargent et paſſement dor et dargent alentour .

Item vne robbe de ſattyn orengee rayee dargent et paſſement dargent alentour .

Item vne robbe de weloux noyr figuree lowttye femee de geyn pewyrs dor et bordee de martriques .

Item vne manteau royale de veloux wiolett .

Les Robbes de Couleur lesquelles sont Enrechies tant dune sorte que aultre .

Vne robbe de reſeu blanc faicte a borletz toute femee de roſes et boullon dargent et bordee dune franges dargent .

Vne robbe de ſatin cramoyfy faicte a manches longues toute chamaree de biſette dargent . la bande femee de perles par petitz fleuron de troy perles .

> La Royne en a faict prendre les perles et a donnez ladite robbe a Madamoiſelle de Leui-
> ſton laynee ce jourdhuy xje jour de Januier mil vᶜ lxiiij .

Vne robbe de fatin jeaulne dore toute goffree faicte a manches longues toute
chamaree de bifette dargent bordee dung paſſement geaulne goffre dargent .

Donne a Madamoiſelle de Beton ce moys de Decembre 1566 .

Vne robbe de fatin bleu faicte a manches longues toute chamaree dung bifette
dor et dargent toute faicte par bandes bandee de deux paſſement dargent
faicte a jour a troys bifette de meſme aſſauoir le tout dor et dargent .

Vne robbe de fatin blanc faicte a borlette toute chamaree dung petit paſſement
dor faicte a jour et bande de petitte natte dor faicte a fleuron .

Vne robbe de camellot de foye blanche faicte a manches longues bandee dung
paſſement dor et dargent faictz a double eſcaille .

Vne robbe de veloux cramoyſy par petis carreaux figure faicte a bourletz
bande de troys paſſement dargent faict a jour et bordee dung paſſement
dargent .

Donne a Madame de Marre ce moys de Decembre 1566 .

Vne robbe de damas cramoyſy de hault coulleur faicte a manches longues
bandee dung paſſement dor et dargent bien larges faictz a jour et bordee
dung paſſement dor et dargent .

Vne robbe de damas orenge faicte a borletz bande dung grand paſſement
dargent faictz a jour et bordee dung paſſement de foye orenge goffre de
filles dargent .

Vne robbe de damas bleux faicte a borletz bandee dung grand paſſement dargent faicte a jour .

Vne robbe de damas collombez faicte a borletz bande dung grand paſſement
dor et dargent faictz a jour .

Vne robbe de veloux cramoyſy faiɛte a grandz manches les poignes de loup
feruier et gie de meſme ·

> Au mois de Januier 1564 la Royne a faiɛt prendre les poignetz de loups ceruiers et le
> bord pour mettre en vng manteau de velours noir · La Royne a donnez ladite robbe a
> Margueritte Habron a moy de May vᵒ lxvij ·

Vne robbe de taffetas jeaulne changeant bien paille faiɛte a borletz bordee de
troys petitz bors de meſme auecq troys petites nattes dor ·

> La Royne a donnez ladite robbe a la petite fille Madame Datel au moy de Nouembre ·

Vne robbe de taffetas changeant rayee de rouge et jeaulne faiɛte a manches
longues bordee de veloux cramoyſy cordonnee dargent ·

Vne robbe de creſpe blanc raye de ſoye blanche faiɛte a bourletz bordee de
frange dargent ·

Vne robbe de reſeu blanc faiɛt a borletz dont le corps de ladite robbe eſt double
de toille dor cramoyſye bordee dune bizette blanche ·

Vne robbe de ſtamine blanche faiɛte a bourlettes bordee de ſatin blanc deſ-
couppee ·

> Ladite robbe au moys de May la Royne a donne a Nicolle la Folle ·

Vne robbe de ſtamine blanche faiɛte a manches longues bordee dung paſſement
de ſoye noire et blanche et les manches chamaree de meſme paſſement ·

Vne robbe ronde de toille blanche raye de ſoye cramoyſye faiɛte a manches
longues bordee dung paſſement de ſoye cramoyſye et ſoye blanche ·

Les Robbes de Soye Noire tant vnes que aultres · Et premierement ·

Vne robbe de veloux noyer faiɛte a bourletz tout le bor couppe par eſcaille
bordee dune frange dargent et le tout de ladite robbe eſt de reſeu dargent faiɛt
a mode de paſſement et roſe par deſſus ladite robbe dont elle eſt toute
couuerte ·

Vne robbe de veloux noyer faicte a borletz bande de deux bors de broderye faicte de perles cordonnes dargent et cannetille .

Vne robbe de fatin noyer faicte a borletz toute chamaree dung paffement dargent faicte a jour et dung bifet dargent faict par ondes .

Vne robbe de veloux noyer faicte a manches longues bandee dung grand paffement dor et dargent faicte av jour et bordee dune treffe dargent cordonnee dor .

Vne robbe de veloux noyer faicte a manches longues / lefdites manches defcouppes par petittes lofenges enrechies de treffe et jazerant dargent auecq la bande de mefme et couppee alentour par efcaille bordee dune treffe dargent .

    Nota · Nocht found ·

Vng bas de robbe de veloux noyer figure par petis carre / la bande defcouppee a jour doublee de fatin incarnat enrechye dung bifet dargent et bordee dung paffement dargent .

    Madame de Marticgues a prins le corps de ladite robbe ·

Vne robbe de veloux noyer faicte a manches longues defcouppee garnye de boutonnier et chenetz dor et sur le deuant de ladite robbe cent mil aultres chofes ·

Vne robbe de veloux noyer ronde faicte alEfpagnolle le corps defcouppe et double de fatin incarnat bordee et bandee de bifette dor en faffon de cheuron ·

    Le xvij jour de Januier mil v° lxiiij la Royne a donnez ladicte robbe a Madamoifelle de Leuifton laynee ·

Vne robbe de taffetas noyer faicte a manches longues / lefdites manches chamarrees et le refte bandee dune bande faicte par cheureon dune petitte natte et frange dor ·

    La Royne a donnez ladite robbe a Madamoifelle de Leuifton laynee le xviij jour de Januier mil v° lxiiij .

I

Item vne robbe de weloux noyr faicte alAfpaignolle toute femee de grayns de geis en faffhon de buttymens ·

Vne robbe de camellot de foye noyer faicte alEfpagnolle / le corps et les manches chamarees dung bifette de foye noire femee de petitte murez noire auecq la bande de mefme ·

La Royne a donnee ladite robbe a Margueritte Carotte ·

Vne robbe ronde de camellot de foye noire faicte a manches longues garnye de boutonnier fur lefdites manches et fur le deuant de ladicte robbe faicte de fil dor et foye noire bordee dune treffe dor et foye noire ·

Le xme de Defembre 1562 la Royne a donnee ladite robbe a Madamoyfel de Seton ·

Vne robbe de crefpe de foye noire raye dor faicte a borletz bordee dune petitte frange dor ·

Vne robbe de crefpe faicte a bourletz · la bande defcouppee par lofenges et cordon dargent femee de rofe et petis fers de getz noyer ·

Vne robbe de crefpe noyer brodee de mefme faicte a longues manches ·

La Royne la prinfe pour luy feruir · Depuys a efte donnee a Monfieur de Ledinton ·

Vne robbe ronde de farge de Fleurance faicte a longues manches bordee dung petit paffement noyer auecq deux tortis de veloux noyer ·

La Royne la faict prendre pour luy feruir ·

Vne robbe de crefpe noyer ronde faicte a longues manches bordee de fatin noyer par pistaunc garnye sur les manches et deuant de ladite robbe de petitz fertz de getz noyer ·

La Royne la prinfe pour luy feruir · Depuys a efte donne a Monsieur Ledinton ·

Vne robbe de ftammen noyer faicte a longues manches bordee de frange de foye noyre et les manches defcouppees et garnye de petis fers de getz ·

La Royne la faict prendre pour luy feruir ·

Vne robbe ronde de ſarge daſquot faiɕte alEſpagnolle et a longues manches
chamarree et bandees de ſatin bordee de frange noyre garnye de petitz ferts
de getz noyer ·

Tous les Manteux · tant vng que aultres ·

Vng manteau a coullet carre faiɕt de toille dargent damaſſe et borde dung
paſſement dargent garny de parement de loupt ſeruier ·

> La Royne a commende donner ledit mantheau a Seruais de Condez pour faire vng liɕtz
> pour ſon ſeruice et leſdits paremens onſt eſtez pris pour mettre en vng mantheau de ſatin
> raye dargent ·

Vng manteau ront de taffetas gris faiɕt alEſpagnolle tout couuert de broderye
de petitz jazerant dargent et tout double de panne de ſoye blanche et
borde dung grand paſſement dargent ·

Vng manteau de ſatin blanc gomfre faiɕt a coullet carre tout chamarre de troys
petitz cordons dor et garny de boutonnieres dor ·

Vng manteau de camellot de ſoye blanche faiɕt alEſpagnolle bande de deux
paſſement dor faiɕt a jour et borde dune treſſe dor ·

Vng manteau a cuer de taffetas cramoyſy faiɕt a coullet carre bande de deux
paſſement faiɕtz a jour et troys biſettes de fil dargent faiɕt a double parement ·

Vng manteau de taffetas blanc raye et mouſchettes de meſme faiɕt alEſpagnolle bande de deux treſſes dor et garny ſur le deuant et ſur les manches de
grandes boutonnieres de fil dor ·

> Donne a Flamin ·

Vng manteau de taffetas noyer raye et mouchettes de meſme faiɕt a coulet carre bande dung petit paſſement et deux franges dargent et borde dune treſſe dargent .

Au moy de May mil v° lxvij la Royne a donnez ledit mantheau a Maiſtreſſe Catenay .

Vng manteau de taffetas noyer raye et mouchettes faiĉt a coullet carre le parement de panne de ſoye noire et borde de veloux noyer .

La Royne la donnez a Madamoiſelle de Flamy lan v° lxv .

Vng manteau de taffetas noyer faiĉt a coullet carre borde dung paſſement dor les manches chamarres .

Vng mantheau de taffetas noyer faiĉt alEſpagnolle borde dune treſſe dargent garny de boutonniers ſeullement ſur le deuant .

Le xvij jour de Januier mil v° lxiiij la Royne a donnez lediĉt mantheau a Madamoiſelle de Leuiſton laynee garny de lij placque dargent et de dixhuiĉt bouton dargent a longue queux .

Vng manteau de taffetas noyer faiĉt alEſpagnolle et borde de veloux noyer .

Vng petit manteau de chambre faiĉt de veloux noyer enrechie dune bande de petite natte dargent faiĉt en faſſon de treffles .

Les Vasquines de Toille Dor et Toille Dargent .

Vne vaſquine de toille dargent friſee bordee de paſſement dargent .

Deliurez ladite vaſquine a Ceruays de Condez pour paracheuer vng liĉt au moy de Mars mil v° ſoixante ſix .

Vne vaſquine de toille dargent friſee auecq le corps et bourletz figuree et friſee de rouge .

Vne vaſquine de toille dargent figure et toute cordonnee alentour de la figure de cordon dor feĉtz en broderie .

Vne vafquine de toille dor traffe de foye vyollette damaffe de mefme bordee dune paffement dor ·

Vne vafquine de toille dor cramoyfye bordee dune petitte frange dor ·

> La Royne la donne a Madamoifelle de Leuifton la jeufne le landemain de ces nopces et les manchon de mefmes qui fut le viij° jour de Januier ·

Vne vafquyne de toille dor crammoyfe bordee dune petitte frange dor ·

Vne vafquyne de toille dor frifee et bordee dung paffement dor ·

Vne vafquyne de toille dor plaine auecq le corps de mefme faict a bourletz bordees dung paffement dor ·

> Donne a Monfieur de Ledinton en ce moys de Decembre 1566 ·

Vne vafquyne de toille dargent pleyne auecq le corps faict a bourletz borde dung paffement dargent ·

> La Royne la donnee a Madamoifelle de Leuifton laynee le Samedy iij° jour de moy de Mars mil v° lxv auant Pafques ·

Vne vafquyne de toille dor frifee dor et dargent et traffee de vert bordee dune traffe dor dont le derriere de ladite vafquyne eft de taffetas geaulne ·

Vne vafquyne de fatin viollet chamarree par bandes de broderye faicte par cheuron de cannetille dargent bordee dung paffement dargent ·

Vne vafquyne de camellot blanc broche dargent et bordee dune traffe dargent ·

> La Royne la donne a Madamoifelle de Beton en ce moys de Decembre 1566 ·

Vne vafquyne de refeul dargent auecq de petites hoppes de foye noire doublee de tocques dargent et le derriere de ladite vafquyne eft de taffetas blanc ·

Les Vasquines de Broderye et Passementees ·

Vne vafquyne de fatin bleux · auecq la piece faicte alEfpagnolle enrechye de bandes de broderye faicte dor et dargent ~~laquelle neft encore parfaicte~~ ·

Vne vafquyne de fatin noyer enrechye dune bande de broderye dargent bordee dune treffe dargent ·

Vne vafquyne de fatin incarnat enrechye dung large paffement dargent feullement fur le deuant et lentour de petittes nattes dargent faicte par entrelatz et bordee dune treffe dargent ·

Vne vafquyne de fatin collombe enrechye dung grand paffement dor faict a jour feullement sur le deuant et alentour eft bordee dune treffe dor ·

Vne vafquyne de fatin orenge enrechye dune bande faicte dune bifette dargent ·

Vne vafquyne de fatin incarnat bandee dung paffement dor et dargent faict a jour bordee dung paffement dor ·

Vne vafquinne de fatin geaulne daure enrechye dune bande de broderye faicte de ginpeure dargent bordee de treffe dargent ·

Vne vafquyne de fatin cramoyfy enrechye dune bande dung paffement dargent faict a jour et borde dung paffement dargent ·

Au moy de Feuurier la Royne donne laditz vafquine a Mademoyfel de Beton ·

Vne vafquyne de fatin incarnat bandee dung paffement dor faict a jour ·

Le Samedy iij^e jour de moys de Mars la Royne la donnee a ladite Leuifton laynee ·

Vne vafquyne de fatin gris bordee de paffement dor ·

La Royne la donnee a Mademoifelle de Leuifton laynee le xvij^e jour de Januier 15[6]4 ·

Vne vafquyne de fatin blanc bandee dung paffement dor faict a jour ·

Vne vafquyne de fatin blanc enrechye dune bande de paffement faict dor et dargent ·

Vne vafquyne de fatin noyer enrechye dune bande faicte de troys bifettes dor auecq la piece et manches longues ·

Vne vasquyne de toille raye de foye viollette et fil dargent bordee dung petit paffement faict de foye viollette et dargent ·

Vne vafquyne de fatin cramoify auec le cors faicte a hault collet auecq des petites efcailles et vng bor de veloux cramoify cordonnez dargent ·

La Royne la donnee a Maiftreffe Cadenay au moy de May vᵉ lxvij ·

Les Vasquynes ausquelles ou il n y a nul Enrechissement ·

Vne vafquyne de fatin blanc defcouppee par lofenge ·

Vne vafquyne de fatin blanc defcouppee et mouchetee ·

Vne vafquyne de fatin blanc auecq le corps ·

Au moys de May 1562 · la Royne la prin pour luy feruir · La Royne a vfee ·

Vne vafquyne de fatin noyer auecq le corps et les bourletz ·

La Royne la vfee ·

Vne vafquyne de fatin noyer defcouppee et chamarree de tortis de veloux noyer · ·

La Royne la prinfe pour luy feruir / La Royne la [vfee] ·

Vne vafquyne de taffetas noyer mouchete ·

La Royne la prinfe pour luy feruir · La Royne la [vfee] ·

Plus vne verdugall ~~souerte~~ de taffetas noyer ·

Tous les Deuant de Cottes tant vngs que aultres ·

Vng deuant de cotte de toille dor frifee et traffee de rouge ·

Au moys de May 1562 · la Royne a donne leditz deuan a Madame de Flamy ·

Vne deuant de cotte de toille dor damaffee et traffee de noyer .

> La Royne la donnez a Madame dArguille le xiiije jour de Januier 15[6]4 . et les manchons et la pieffe de mesme .

Vng deuant de cotte de toille dor incarnat frife dor .

Vng deuant de cotte de toille dargent frifee dargent .

> La Royne la donnee a Madamoifelle de Leuifton laynee le Dimenche iiije jour de Mars ve lxv auant Pafques .

Vng deuant de cotte de fatin cramoyfy tout couuert de broderye de petis cordons dor faict par feuillages .

Vng deuant de fatin blanc chamarre en trauert de bande de broderye faict de cordon dor .

Vng deuant de cotte de veloux bleux tout couuert de broderye defcouppe a jour et double de tocque dargent .

Vng deuant de cotte de fatin incarnat tout couuert de broderye faict par grand feullages auecq du veloux bleux et petit cordon dor et dargent .

Vng deuant de cotte de toille dargent goffree tout couuert de broderye de ginpeure de plufieurs couleurs en faffon de quannetille et cordon dor .

Vng deuant de cotte de toille dor tout goffre .

Vng deuant de toille raye de veloux viollet et dargent .

Vng deuant de cotte de fatin blanc mouchette ..

> La Royne la donnez a la petite fille la Lauendiere .

Vng deuant de cotte de fatin cramoyfy defcouppe et mouchette .

Vng deuant de cotte de refeul dargent et foye incarnat double de fatin cramoyfye .

Vng deuant de cotte de crefpe crefpeu blanc raye dor ·

Vng deuant de toille de foye blanche raye dor ·

Les Abillemens de Deul assauoir ceulx qui sont auecq les meubles ·

Vng grand manteau royal garny de parement darmyne lentour de mefmes et le refte double de taffetas blanc ·

Vne robbe deftamer noyer faicte a grande peliffon de menu vert ·

La Royne la donnee a Madame de Cotiquant au mois de Nouembre 1563 ·

Plus vne aultre robbe de mefmes ·

Les Masques assauoir ceulx qui sont sur les tables auecq les meubles ·

Vne robbe de camellot rouge onde faicte a la Picarde auecq vng deuanteau de fatin geaulne ·

Vne robbe ronde faicte alEfpagnolle faicte par petitz boullons dargent faulx ·

Vne robbe de fatin blanc faicte alEfpagnolle par boullon et femee de peties boutons de verre ·

Vne robbe de fatin incarnat blanc et bleux boullonnee de tocque dargent et frange dargent ·

Plus troys tappis vertz qui couurent lefdits habillemens contenant chacun deux aulnes et demye ou enuiron ·

Condamnee ·

K

Je confeſſe avoir veu moy Seruez de Condee vallet de chambre de la Royne tous les abillemens de la Royne cy deſſuz comprins en ſe preſent Inuentoyre leſquelz ſont de preſent avecques les aultrez meublez de ladite Dame dont je fine la preſente ·

S De Condez ·

Inuentaire des bagues de la Royne ·

Premierement · Bacgues a pandre ·

Vng gros collier auquel y a fept gros faffis et neuf pieces garnies de quattre perles chacune qui font lentredeux dun collier ·

Vne groffe bague a pendre facon de · ♄ · en laquelle y a vng gros diamant en lorenge taille en face et deffoubz vng gros rubiz chabochon garniz dune petitte chefne ·

Vne autre bague a pendre en laquelle y a vng diamant a lorenge taille a faces et au deffoubz vne grande efmeraude et vne perle platte ·

Vne autre bague a pendre en laquelle y a vne grande efmeraude a faces mifes hors doeuure ·

Vne autre bague a pendre en laquelle y a vne autre efmeraude ·

Vne autre bague a pendre faicte en rouleaux en laquelle y a vne grande table de rubiz ·

Vne autre bague a pendre en laquelle y a vng grand rubiz ballay taille en table carre garny dune groffe perle ·

Vne autre bague a pendre en laquelle y a vng grand rubiz ballay longue .

Vne autre bague a pendre en laquelle y a vng grand rubiz ballay perce par les deux boutz .

Vne autre bague a pendre en laquelle y a vng grand faffiz taille a huiƈt pampes efmaille de blanc et rouge garny dune grofs perle .

Vne autre bague a pendre en laquelle y a vne rofe de diamant de dix pieces efmaillee de rouge .

Vne autre bague a pendre en laquelle y a vne petitte rofe de diamans garnie de fix pieces .

Vne croix garnie de fept diamans dont y a deux tables deux triangles deux diamans taillez a face et vne poynte de diamans et deux rubiz cabochons .

Vne croix garnie de cinq tables de diamens et troys moiennes perles pendantes laquelle a efte baillee a la Royne a Sainƈt Jeanfton .

Acoustrement de Groz Diamens .

Vne grande brodure en laquelle y a vne grande triangle de diamens / huiƈt tables de diamens que longues que carrees / vng diament taille a faces / vng autre diament taille a faces de pene garnye de dix entredeux / et a chacun entredeux y a deux perles .

Vne brodure doreillettes ou il y a vne groffe poynte de diamens / dix tables de diamens garnye de dix entredeux / et a chacun entredeux y a deux perles .

Vng carcan ou il y a vne groffe poinƈte de diament taille a faces / huiƈt grandes tables de diamens garnies de huict entredeux / et a chacun entredeux y a deux grosses perles ·

Vng cottouere garnie de dixhuict pieces / et a chacune piece y a deux diamens reste vne piece quoil y a faulte dun diament et dixhuict entredeux garniz de six perles chacun entredeux et xxxvj · s · esmaillees de rouge et vng entredeux qui est de reste ·

Vne saincture faicte de fil garnye de dix croyx de diamens taillez a faces enchassee en bassinetz esmaillez de rouge et de dix entredeux / et a chacun entredeux y a quattre perles et dixneuf cordelieres esmaillees de rouge ·

Vng dizain destrin garny de quinze pieces / et a chacune piece y a six poinctes destrin et quatorze entredeux garny chacun entredeux de quattre perles ·

Vng dizain de cristal ou il y a xiiii vases de cristal garniz dor en facon de vase / et au bout du dizain y a vng gros vase garny dor et quatorze patenostres dor esmaillees de blanc ·

Autre Acoustrement de Diamens esmaille de blanc ·

Vne brodure de thouret garnie de xiiii tables de diament et vne triangle de diament au meilleu faicte a jour facon destaux esmaillee de blanc et seize petitz entredeux faictz en maniere de feuille esmaillez de blanc ·

Vne brodure doreillettes pareille facon garnie de xvii moiene diamens et xviii entredeux ·

Autre Acoustrement [de] Diamens esmaille de noir ·

Vne brodure de thouret garnie de seize diamens et dixsept roses dor entredeux esmaille de noir ·

Vne brodure doreillettes pareille facon garnye de dixhuiᴄ̇t diamens et xix rofes entredeux pareille facon ·

Vng carcan garny de treize diamens et treize entredeux de pareille facon ·

Aultre Acoustrement de Rubis et Diamens ·

Vne chefne faiᴄ̇te en facon de petis anneaux ou il y a iiii^{xx} xi anneaux garniz de chacun deux rubiz et douze tables datente / chacune table garnie dune table de diamens et dun rubiz / et deux cab[o]chons de rubiz en vne piece attachez a ladite chefne ·

Groz Rubis garniz de Perles enfillees ·

Vng tour[e] garny de fept gros rubiz cabochons et quattre tables de rubiz et quarante groffes perles qui font les entredeux ·

Vne aureillette garnie de vnze rubiz cabochons et quarante perles qui font lentredeux ·

Vng carcan de rubiz garny de vne efpinelle et fix rubiz cabochons vne table de rubiz auec xxxij perles accompaignees de troys rubiz ballays percez / auec vne perle au bout de chacun ·

Vne cottouere garnie de feize pieces / et a chacune piece y a deux rubiz tant cabochons que tablit / feize entredeux de perles / et a chacun entredeux y a deux perles et trentedeux · ʂ · efmaillees de rouge et blanc ·

Vne fainᴄ̇ture garnie d'vnze pillers / et a chacun piller y a neuf petis rubiz / xxi pillers / et a chacun piller y a neuf perles / et xxij entredeux garniz de deux perles chacun et au bout de ladite fainature y a vng vafe dor garny de trente perles alentour dudit vafe et vne perle au bout dudit vafe .

Aultre Acoustrement [de] Rubis Diamens et Perles .

Vne brodure de toure garnie de cinq rubiz les deux font tables fix tables de diament et douze entredeux garniz de chacun vne perle .

Vne aureillette de fix rubiz et fix diamens et treize entredeux et a chacun entredeux y a vne perle .

Vng carcan garny de troys diamens / lun taille a faces et deux en tables / et quattre rubiz cabochons / huiat entredeux garniz de chacun vne groffe perle platte / et xiiii autres petittes pieces qui feruent dentredeux efmaillees de blanc et rouge .

Vne fainature garnie de neuf diamens dont y a fix tables et troys taillez a faces / huiat rubiz cabochons / et xvij entredeux garniz de chacun vne [perle] .

Refte de lacouftrement cy deffus de fept pieces dont y a troys tables de diamens / defquelles deux font grandes et vne petitte / troys rubiz deux en table et vng cabochon / et vne piece garnye dune perle .

Deux braffeletz garniz de chacun quattre pieces / et a chacune piece y a huiat diamens / et fept tables de rubiz / et a chacun braffelet y a quattre entredeux garniz dune perle les huiat entredeux .

Aultre Acoustrement [de] Rubis esmaille de blanc .

Vng toure efmaille de blanc garny de quinze rubiz cabochons et quatorze entredeux garniz de chacun deux perles .

Vne aureillette de mefme facon garnie de xvij petis rubiz cabochons et xvj entredeux garniz de chacun deux perles ·

Vng carcan de mefme facon garny d'vnze rubiz cabochons dix entredeux garniz de chacun deux perles et dix rubiz balays qui font pendant au dit carcan ·

Aultre Acoustrement [de] Rubis en roses ·

Vne brodure de toure garnie de dix rofes de rubiz / dix entredeux garnis de chacun quattre perles / xix pieces faictes a fleurs efmaille de blanc et de verd ·

Vne brodure doreillette garnie de neuf rofes de rubiz / dix pieces garnies de quattre perles chacune / et dixhuict entredeux efmaillez de blanc et verd ·

Demeure de refte de loreillette vne piece garnie de quattre perles et deux entredeux efmaillez de blanc et verd ·

Vng carcan garny de fept rofes de rubiz huict pieces garnies de chacun quattre perles quinze petitz entredeux et vingthuict perles pendantes ·

Vng carcan garny de neuf pieces et a chacune piece y a deux tables de rubiz et deux petittes efmerauldes et quattre vingtz neuf perles ·

Vne cotouere garnie de xxvij pillers garnies de petittes perles et xxvij entredeux garniz de deux perles chacun efmaille de verd ·

[Rubis Esmerauldes et Saffiz ·]

Vne petitte aureillette garnye de douze rubiz cabochons douze efmeraudes et xxv entredeux garniz de chacun vne perle ·

Vng carcan efmaille de noir garny de fept efmeraudes fix pieces garnies de chacun vne groffe perle et quatorze entredeux ·

Vng toure efmaille de blanc et rouge garny de treize faffiz et treize entredeux garnis de chacun quattre perles ·

Vng carcan de mefme facon garny de neuf petitz faffiz vng gros faffiz a jour ou pend vne groffe perle et dix entredeux garnis de chacun quattre perles ·

Six efmeauldes en chattons garnies de leurs baffinetz ·

Vng petit faffiz a jour pandant pour frotter les yeux ·

Vne bordure garnie de dix tables de faffiz blancs et vnze entredeux facon deftaux ·

Vingt cinq pieces qui feruent a faire vne chefne garnie chacune piece dun diament dun rubiz et deux perles ·

Les vingt cinq pieces cy deffus efcriptes ont efte prinfes pour faire vne cottouere auec des perles ·

Acoustrement de Perles enfillees ·

Vng tour[e] de groffes perles ou il y en a xxxiij et neuf pendantes en poire et trentetroys petittes perles qui font lentredeux ·

Vne oreillette en laquelle y a li groffes perles ·

Vng toure auquel y a xlix groffes perles ·

Vne aureillette en laquelle y a xlvij groffes perles ·

Vng carcan auquel y a lxiiij groffes perles ·

L

Vne cottouere en laquelle y a cij groffes perles · et y a dauantaige a la cotouere pour lalonger xlviij perles qui eft en tout cl perles ·

Vne faincture de groffes perles ou il y a deux cens fix perles ·

Vng dizain de groffes perles ou il y a cliiij perles et vnze marques garnies de troys groffes perles chacune refte dune marque quoil y a vne perle perdue · vne houppe au bout dudite difain ou il y a xxij groffes perles ·

Quatorze moyennes perles de refte et troys perles jaulnes ·

Vne fauiéte de velours noir ou il y a deffus cij perles ·

> Ladite fauiéte balle a Seruais pour mectre a vng collet ·

Vingt troys perles a pendre de plufieurs groffeurs ·

> La Royne en a deux pour pendre a fes oreilles · Vne pendue a vng rubiz balay / vne a vng faffiz taille a viij pampes / et deux donnees a Marnac ·
>
> Il a efte prins des perles cy deffus a pandre pour mectre a vne croix de diamens et rubiz vne groffe perle ·

Cinq cens trente moyennes perles en corde ·

> Il y a efte prins defdites cinq cens trente perles a vne coueffe qui a efte faicte pour la Royne ou il y a des rubiz cinq cens dix / et vingt qui reftoient ont efte mifes a allonger la cottouere de rubiz et diamens ·

Aultre Acoustrement de Perles ·

Vng toure garny de treize groffe perles en chattons et douze cordelieres qui feruent dentredeux garnies de perles efmaille de noir ·

Vne aureillette garnie de treize chattons a perles et douze cordelieres qu feruent dentredeux garnis de perles ·

Vng carcan garny de huiét perles en chattons et neuf cordelieres de perles qui feruent dentredeux ·

Vne bordure de toure garnie de xvij baffinetz / et a chacun y a vne groffe perle et de petittes perles alentour / et feize entredeux garniz de petittes perles efmaillez de noir ·

Vne aureillette garnie de xxij baffinetz et a chacun y a vne moyenne perle et xxj entredeux garniz de petittes perles ·

Vng petit carcan efmaille tout de noir ou il y a de petittes perles pendantes et de petitz grains noirs entredeux ·

      Contenant dixhuict pieces ·

Vng autre petit carcan efmaille de noir garny de douze pieces garnies de chacune vne perle et vnze entredeux facon de baftons rompuz entrelacez garniz de chacun vne perle pendante ·

      Hotman a baille cedit carcan · lequel n'eft au vieil Inuentaire ·

Vne cottouere garnie de trente quattre lappis en vaze et xxvj perles qui font lentredeux auffi en maniere de vafe ·

Vne faincture garnie de xxxij pieces damatifte / fept pillers dor xxxix meures de perles entredeux / et au bout vne pomme damatifte de deux pieces ·

Vne faincture et cotouere garnie de petittes perles et de coural taille a godrons ·

Vne faincture de grifolicques garnies en maniere de vafes et de petittes oliues entredeux efmaillees de rouge ·

Vne faincture et cotouere garnie de perles de coural taille a godrons et de turquin ·

Vne petitte brodure de faincture de toure ou il y a xxxvj grains a jour pleins de parfum garniz de petitz grains dor a jour ·

Vne aureillette de mefme ou il y a xxx grains de mefme et troys qui font de refte ·

Vne faincture de mefme ou il y a liij grains de mefme facon ·

Vng petit carcan de grains a jour pleins de parfum et de petitz grains dor entredeux ·

Vng gorgerin garny de petitz grains dor a jour pleins de parfum et de petittes perles entredeux ·

Vne faincture ou il y a dixfept pillers et a chacun piller y a xxviij petitz grains dor a jour emplis de fenteurs et xviij entredeux / a chacun entredeux y a fix defdits grains et de petittes perles vne pomme au bout de ladite faincture ou il y a fept pendant garniz de fix petitz grains chacun et vng au bout ·

Vne cottouere ou il y a xvij pillers de pareilz grains / et a chacun piller y en a xviij · refte deux qui ny en a que quinze et feize entredeux garniz de cinq grains chacun et de petittes perles ·

Vne paire de patenoftres de fenteurs contenant lj paftenoftres et fix pilliers garniz de petis grenatz ·

Vne bordure dor de fenteurs ou il y a xxiiij pieces et xlviij perles qui font entredeux ·

Vne bordure doreillette de mefme ou il y a xxix pieces et lvi perles ·

Vne paire de braceletz garniz de quattre tables de rubiz et huict perles chacun bracelet ·

     La Royne les a donnez ·

Deux petitz braceletz de tables dematifte ·

Deux braceletz dor percez a jour pleins de parfum ·

Vne tefte de marte garnie de rubiz diamens et faffiz auec deux perles / les quattre pattes de mefme · Il y a faute dun rubiz a la tefte ·

Vne teſte de marte de criſtal garnie de turquoyſe alentour les quattres pattes de meſme ·

Vng bracelet fait a facon de ſerpent ·

Vne ſainẽ ture dor garnie de cornalins auec les entredeux de perles ·

Vng dizain garny de cornalins de meſme ·

Vne cotouere garnie de cornalins de meſme ·

Vne cotouere de grains de griſolicques ronds de meſme ·

Vne ſainẽ ture et vne cotouere dor eſmaille tout de noir faiẽ te en facon de pillers et vne houppe dor au bout en facon de cloche contenant cent treize pieces attachees auec des petitz cheſnons ·

Vne cheſne dor faiẽ te a chiffres eſmaillee de blanc et rouge faiẽ te a jour ou il y a xliiij pieces auec vne painẽ ture du feu Roy Henry ·

Vne cheſne dor eſmaillee de blanc et violet faiẽ te a chiffres contenant lix pieces ·

Vne cheſne a ſaindre faiẽ te en facon deſtaux eſmaille de blanc contenant xlv pieces ·

Vne cotouere de meſme facon contenant lxv pieces ·

Vng carcan de meſme facon contenant douze pieces auec de petis pendans ·

Vingtquattre grandes boutonnieres dont y a douze grandes roſes de diamens et douze autres grans rubiz ballays tant en tables qu'en cabochons ·

Soixante dixneuf boutons ronds et en triangle garniz de chacun troys perles ·

Vingtſept autres boutons garniz de chacun vng ſaffiz reſte vne pierre perdue ·

Quatorze autres petis chattons garniz de petitz ſaffiz ·

Douze boutons garniz de chacun troys vermeilles ·

Douze boutons de mefme facon garniz de chacun troys perles / dont y en a deux perdues ·

Vng baffinet efmaille de noir garnie dune vieille perle rouffe ·

Quinze efguillettes et demye [de] fers de grenatz garnies dor ·

Trenteneuf efguillettes et demye de fers garnies de chacun quattre perles / dont en y a quattre perdues ·

Soixante vnze boutons garniz de chacun vng rubiz balays ·

Quarante fix boutons faictz en facon de treffles facon dHyfpaigne ·

Huict vingtz troys autres boutons auffi facon dHyfpaigne ·

Soixante efguillettes de grande fers efmaillez de rouge garnies de petittes perles alentour ·

Cinquante boutons dor a jour efmaillez de noir ·

Quattre vingtz treize boutons et demye de fenteurs ou pend vne petitte perle chacun ·

Vingt troys boutons faictz a rofes garniz de chacun troys perles ·

Quattre vingtz vng boutons de meures de perles ·

Vne paire de braceletz dor garniz de criftal blanc rouge et verd ·

Vng carcan efmaille tout de verd auec des perles entredeux et de petis grains efmaillez de rouge ·

Vne faincture de gros grains de criftal / ou il y a li gros grain treize .oliues efmaillees de rouge et verd garnies de petittes perles et xl gros grains dor entre-deux efmaillez de rouge et verd ·

Vne cotouere garnie de petis grains de criftal et de grains de verre verd et entredeux de petittes oliues efmaillees de rouge ·

Vne autre faincture garnie de porceline de verre verd accouftree dor ·

Vne cotouere de mefme garnie de xlvij grains dor efmaillez de blanc ·

Brodeures dor ·

Vng corps de faincture dor garnie de xix pieces taillees de baffe taille efmail-lees de blanc auec vng entredeux faictz de fil fans efmail ·

Vne brodure de thoure garnie de xvj pieces et xvii entredeux ·

Vne aureillette de pareille facon garnie de   pieces et de xv entredeux efmaillez de rouge ·

Vne brodeure de toure faicte en coeurs efmaillez de blanc et verd garnie de xxxix pieces ·

Vne aureille de femblable facon garnie de xlv pieces ·

Vne brodeure de toure de femblable facon efmaille de blanc et verd et rouge garnie de xlviii pieces auec de petis pendans de fleurs ·

Vng collet de perles et grenatz ·

Pendans doreille ·

Deux pendans doreille faictz en facon de croix de Hierufalem efmaillez de blanc ·
        · La Royne les a donnez ·

Deux autres pendans doreille facon dencolie garniz de fix petittes perles ·

Deux autres pendans doreilles garniz de turquoyfes et de vermeilles ·
La Royne les a donnees par eftraines a Madame de Leuifton ·

Deux petis faffiz garniz dune perle chacun ·

Vne petitte bague garnie de quattre petittes perles et troys rubiz ·

Deux autres pendans doreille de deux coquilles de verre vert et vne perle chacun ·

Deux emolies efmaillez de violet ·

Deux autres pendans doreille garniz de petittes amatiftes ·

Deux autres garniz de quattre petis diamens et deux petittes perles ·

Deux petis pendans doreille dor emplis de fenteure ·

Deux pendans ·

Vng autre pendant faict en facon de tortue ·

Deux autres pendans doreille faictz en facon de licorne garniz de deux perles ·

Deux perles garnies de quattre petittes efmerauldes ·

Deux petis pendans doreille garniz de deux petittes perles en facon de doubles ames ·

Deux autres femblables ·

Deux moiennes perles a pendre aux oreilles ·

Deux autres perles faictes en poire a pendre a loreille lefquelles font cottees en marge cy deuant ·

Vne hermine auec vne tefte dor efmaillee de blanc et la chefne de blanc et noir
garnie de rubiz diamens et perles auec les pattes de mefme .

Vne autre hermine auec vne tefte de gez noir couuerte dor et la chefne efmaillees de noir .

Vne autre hermine la tefte dor efmaillee de blanc .

Vne marte garnie dune tefte dor auec rubiz diamens et perles .

Vne autre hermine fans garniture .

Treize vingtz quattre groffes perles achaptees de Jean Guilbert orfevure
dEdinbourg comprins quattre que lorfevure de la Royne a rendu qui eftoient
deffus vne paire dheures dor .

> Il a efte ofte xxvij perles pour enuoyer a Paris pour faire boutons / Et le refte a efte prins
> pour faire vne cottouere qui eft de diamens et de rubiz en chattons .

Vne chefne a vne marte blanche garnie de quarente fept patenoftres dor et
quarente fept entredeux a jour .

M

Memoire de ce qui eſt sus la Couronne ·

Premierement du grant touret de diamans xi diamans et vng du carcan Sont xii en tout ·

Item du gros touret de rubis huict rubis ·

Item du carcan de rubis diamans et perles trois diamans vng rubi et huict perles ·

Item au hault trois rubis a iour et trois perles en poire ·

Item de la cotoire de perles enfillee cent et quatre ·

Item le Henri et les deus emeraudes et la table de rubi ·

Item quatre chatons de braceles des rubis et diamans et au quatre chatons y a vi perles ·

Fin ·

M̃emoire de ce qui eſt sus le Surcot ·

Premierement a ce qui eſt autour de la carrure yll i a vi diamans ſinq rubis et x chatons de perles ·

Item a ce qui borde tout lentour du ſurcot ill y a xix diamans xvii rubis et xxxvii perles et · · · · · chatons ·

Item les trois grandes pieſces que la Roine a achetes et a chaicune vn perle au bout ·

La crois de rubis et diamans et vne perle au bout ·

Le grous rubi ballet et vne perle au bout ·

Les deus autre grans rubis a pandre ·

Item deus pieſces du collier ·

Item quatre diamans et deus rubis femes par le corſet ·

Fin ·

Memoire de ce qui eſt ſus la Coiſe ·

Premierement vne brodure ou ill y a finq diamans quatre rubis et dis chatons de perles ·

Item vne aultre brodure ou ill y a quatre diamans finq rubis et quarante perles enfillees ·

Item toute la cotoire de rubis diamans et perles ·

Item ill y a ſeme ſus la coiffe vi rubis finq diamans et vii chatons de perles que petis que grans ·

Inuentaire de la Royne ·

Premierement · Bacgues a pandre ·

*Ie veulx quelle soyt
iointe a la Couronne
de ce pays par vn acte
pour memoyre de moy et
du lieu dou ie layeue ·*

Vne groffe bacgue a pandre facon de / ♄ / en laquelle
y a vng groz diamant taille a faces et au deffus vng
groz rubiz cabochin garny dune petitte chefne ·

*Ie laysse cestissi aus-
si de mesme ·*

Vne aultre bacgue a pandre en laquelle y a vng ~~grize~~
gros diament taille a faces et au deffus vne grande efmeraulde et vne perle platte au bout ·

*Ie la laysse a Ma-
dame de Martigues ·*

Vne aultre bacgue a pandre en laquelle y a vne grande
efmiraulde myse hors ~~dheure~~ deuure ·

Elle neft pas renue de France ·

*Ie la laysse a ma tante
Madame de Guise ·*

Vne aultre bacgue a pandre en laquelle y a vne grande
efmiraulde ou pend vne groffe perle au bout ·

*Ie la laysse a ma
cousine Daumalle les-
nee ·*

Vne aultre bague a pandre faicte en roulleaux garnye
dune grande table de rubiz ou pend vne groffe perle ·

*Ie le laysse a ma fille-
ule fille du Marquis ·*

Vne aultre bague a pandre en laquelle y a vng grand
rubiz baillaiz en table efmaille de blanc ·

Ie le laysse a mon cousin de Guise .

Vne aultre bacgue a pandre en laquelle y a vng grand rubiz ballez long .

Ie le laysse a ma cousine de Guise .

Vne aultre bacgue a pandre en laquelle y a vng grand rubiz ballez perce par les deux boutz .

A la fille du Marquis ma filleule .

Vne aultre bacgue a pandre en laquelle y a vng grand faffize taille a huict pampes efmaille de blanc et rouge .

A la Couronne comme les deus autres en memoyre de laliance de Lorrayne .

Vne grande croix garnye de fept diamans deux en table deux en triangle deux taille en face et vne pointe et deux rubiz cabochons ou pend vne groffe perle au bout .

A ma filleule .

Vng groz collier garny de fept groz faffiz et neuf entredeux garnis de iiij perles chacun .

Groz Diamens .

Pour ornemant de toutes les Roynes qui ne les pourront iamays changer dœuure ni donner seullemant les reseuoir par la mayn de celui qui guardera les subdites bagues auuesques la Couronne et mourant les remetra la pour demeurer a la Couronne de toutes les Roynes .

Vne brodeure de tours en laquelle y a vne grande triangle de diament huict tables de diamens que longues que carrues vng aultre en triangle taille a faces / vng aultre diamant en table taille a faces garnye de dix entredeux chacun entredeux garny de deux perles .

Vne brodeure illettes doreillettes ou il y a vne groffe poincte de diament et dix tables de diamens garniz de dix entredeux / chacun entredeux de deux perles .

Vng carcan ou il y a vne groffe poincte de diamant taille a faces huict tables de diamens et huict entredeux garny chacun entredeux de deux perles .

Vne cottouere garny de dixhuiƈt pieces [et a] chacune piece y a deux diamens reƒte [vne] piece qui a faulte dun diament et dixhuiƈt entredeux garniz de ƒix perles chacun entredeux / et xxxvj / s / eƒmaille de rouge et vng entredeux qui eƒt de reƒte .

Vne ƒainƈture de fil garnye de dix crois de diamens taillez a faces enchaƒƒez en baƒƒinetz eƒmaillez de rouge dix entredeux / et a chacun entredeux y a quatre perles xx cordelieres eƒmaillees de rouge .

Vng dozain deƒtain deƒtrin garny de quinze pieces et a chacune piece y a vi poinƈtes deƒtain et quatorze entredeux chacun entredeux garny de quatre perles .

Vng dizain de criƒtal ou il y a quatorze bazes vaƒes de criƒtal garniz dor et autour du dizain y a vng grize baze groƒƒe vaze auƒƒy garny dor et xiiij patenoƒtres dor eƒmaillez de blanc .

Aultre acoustrement de Diamens esmaillez de blanc .

A ma cousine de Guise . Vne brodeure de thuioir thouret garny de xiiij tables de diamens et vne triangle de diamens au meilleir faiƈte a jour facon deƒtaux eƒmaillez de blanc et ƒeize petis entredeux faiƈtz en maniere de feulles eƒmaillez de blanc .

A celle A ma cousine de Guise aussi . Vne brodeure doreillettes pareille facon garnye de xvij moyens diamans en table et xviij entredeux .

Aultre acoustrement de Diàmans esmailles de noir ·

A ma cousine Dau-
malle ·

Vne brodeure de ~~touoir~~ touret garnye de feize diamens dixfept rofes dix entredeux efmaillez de noir ·

Vne brodeure ~~doreilleir~~ doreillettes pareille fachon garny de dixhuiƈt diamens et dixneuf rofes dor qui font vn entredeux pareille facon ·

Vng carcan garny de treize diamens et treize entredeux de pareille facon ·

·

Acoustrement de groz Rubiz et grosses Perles ·

A la mayson de Guise
pour demeurer tous-
iours a lesne ·

Vng tours garny de vi groz rubiz cabochons et cincq tables de rubiz garny de quarante perles groffes qui font vng entredeux et trois rubiz baillaiz pandant percez ou pend vne perle au bout ·

Vne aureillette garnye de onze rubiz cabochons quarante perles qui font lentredeux ·

Vng carcan garny de vne ef[pine]lle et fix rubiz cabochons et xxxij perles qui font lentredeux ·

Vne cottouere garnye de xvij pieces garnye chacune piece de deux rubiz tant cabochons que tables et xvj entredeux de perles et a chacun entredeux y a deux perles et xxxij · s · efmaillez de blanc et rouge ·

Vne fainƈture garnye de vnze pilliers et a chacun pillier

y a neuf petiz rubiz xxj pillier et a chacun pillier y a
neuf perles / et xxij entredeux garny de deux perles
chacun / et au bout de ladite faincture y a vng vaze dor
garny de xxx perles alentour ·

Le perle perdue que pandoyt au bout ·

A la Couronne de ce pays ·

Vne chefne faicte en facon de petis anneaulx ou il y a
iiij^xx xi anneaux garniz de chacun deux rubiz douze
tables datente chacune table garnye d'une table de diament d'un rubiz et deux cabochons de rubiz et vne
piece attache a ladite chefne · Il y a faulte de deux
rubiz au petis anneaux ·

Acoustrement de Rubiz esmaillez de blanc ·

~~Au fils ayne du Marquis~~ ·
A ma cousine la fille du Marquis ma fille-ule ·

Vng brodeure de toure garny de xv rubiz cabochons et
xiiij entredeux garny de chacun deux perles ·

Vne aureillette garnye de xvii petis rubiz cabochons et
xvj entredeux garny de chacun deux perles ·

Vng carcan de mefme facon garny de vnze rubiz cabochons dix entredeux garny de chacun deux perles et
dix rubiz baillaiz qui font pendant au dit carcan ·

Vne faincture de coural contenante xl merques de coural
acouftre dor et quarante pilliers de perles ·

32 feulement receus · tant dun que de lautre ·

Vne cottouere de mefme contenante xlvij marques de
coural aufi acouftre dor et xlvij pilliers de perles ·

44 feulement · Receus iij de coural et 3 de perles ·

N

Acoustrement de Rubiz Diamans et Perles ·

Le reste de cest acous-
tresmant aux esnez
Daumalle ·

Vne brodeure de thou[r]et garniz de cincq rubiz trois
font tables fix tables de diamans douze entredeux garniz
de chacun vne perle · ·

Vne aureillette garnye de vj rubiz et fept diamens do[nt]
y a vne grande table au meilleu douze entredeux chacun
entredeux y a vne perle ·

Le carquant a la
Couronne de ce pays ·

Vng carcan garny de trois diamens lun taille a faces et
deux en ta[b]le[s] quatre robiz cabachons huiét entredeux garniz de chacun vne perle platte / et quatorze
petittes pieces qui feruent entredeux / efmaillez de blanc
et rouge ·

A luy mesmes ·

Vne cottouere garnye de xxv pieces chacune piece
garnye dun rubiz d'un diament / et ij° lvij perles qui font
lentredeux ·

Vne fainéture garnye de neuf diamens do[nt] y a cincq
tables quatre ta[il]les a faces huiét rubiz cabochons et
xvij entredeux garniz de chacune vne perle ·

Refte dudit acouftrement fept pieces do[nt] y a deux
tables de diamens deux rubiz cabochons vne table de
rubiz et deux chattons garnye chacun vne perle ·

Rece us vij diamant et vne perle · Faut vne table diament ·

Acoustrement de Rubiz et Turquoyses ·

A Madame de
Martigues ·

Vng brodure de touret facon de foleil garnye de douze

rubiz cabochons garniz de perles alentour / et treize turquoyfes qui font lentredeux .

Vne aureillette garnye de douze rubiz cabochons auffy
garny de perles alentour et xiij turquoyfes qui font lentredeux .

Vne faincture de coural garnye de xxiiij grains de tur-
que et lvne xxij grains de coural taille a godrons et
xlvij pilliers de perles et vne houppe autour le tout
acouftre dor .

    Sen fault vne houppe .

Vng carcan de mefme facon garniz de neuf rubiz
cabochons garniz de perles a lentour et de neuf turquoyfes qui font les entredeux .

Vne cottouere garnie de xxvj grains de turquin xxvj
grains du coural taille a [g]odrons et lj pilliers de perles .

Acoustrement de Rubiz en rose .

*A Madame Dar-
guilles .*

Vne brodeure de touoir garnie de dix rofes de rubiz
dix entredeux garny de chacun iiij perles et dixneuf
pieces faictes a fleurs efmaillez de blanc et vert .

Vne brodeure [dore]ille[tte] garnye de neuf rofes de
rubiz dix pieces garnies de iiij perles chacune et xviij
entredeux efmaille de blanc et vert .

Vng carcan garny de fept rofes de rubiz huict pieces

garnyes de chacun quatre perles quinze petiz entredeux et xxviij perles pandantes .

Demeure de refte de laureille vne piece garnye de
quatre perles et deux entredeux efmaillez de blanc et
vert .

A la fille de Mons-
sieur de Martigues .　　Vng carcan garny de neuf pieces et a chacune piece y
a deux tables de rubiz et deux petites efmeraulde et
iiij^{xx} ix perles .

A elle la cotoire aussi .　　Vne cottouere garnye de xxvij pilliers de petites perles
et xxvij entredeux garny de deux perles chacun .
　　Sen fault .

Rubiz et Esmeraulde .

A la fille de mon frere
de Mora .　　Vne aureillette garnye de douze rubiz cabochons douze
efmeraulde et xxv entredeux garny de chacun vne
perle .
　　Sen fault .

Vng carcan efmaille de noir garny de fept efmer-
aldes vj pieces garnyes de chacun vne groffe perle
et xiiij entredeux .

Six efmeraulde en chattons garnyes de leur baffinetz .

Acoustrement de Saffiz .

A laisne fils de la
mayson du Marquis .　　Vne brodure de tours efmaille de blanc et rouge garnye

de xiij faffiz et xiij entredeux garniz de chacun iiij perles ·

Vng carcan de mefme facon garny de neuf petiz faffiz et vng gros faffiz a jour ou pand vne groffe perle et dix entredeux garniz de chacun iiij perles ·

Vne brodeure doreillette garnye de dix tables de faffize blancs et vnze entredeux facon deftaux ·

Vne cottouere garnye de xxxiiij ~~lappins~~ lapis en vaze et xxxvj pieces qui font lentredeux garniz en vaze ·

Vng faffiz perce a pandre garny de deux feulle dor ~~faint~~ fans efmail qui fert a frotter au yeux ·

Refte de brodeure quelle a eu aultre fois deux cabochons garny chacune pieche dun rubiz cabochon vng entredeux garny dune perle vne aultre piece fans rubiz / vne petite pieche garnye trois petis diamans en triangle et trois qui ont efte ·

Acoustrement de Perles enfillees ·

A la mayson de Guise ·

Vng toure garny de xxxiij groffes perles neuf perles pendantes en poire et xxxiiij perles qui font lentredeux ·

Vne aureillette garnye de xlvj groffes perles ·

Vng carcan garny de lxiiij groffes perles ·

Vne cottouere garnye de cent foixante quatre groffes perles ·

Vne faincture garnye de deux cens fix perles ·

Vng dizain garny de vnze marques dor garnye chacune marque de trois perles et vnze pilliers chacun pillier y a xiiij perles et vne houppe au bout garny de perles ·

A celle Daumalle · Vng autre touret garny de cincquante groffes perles
Sen fault vne perle ·

Vne aureillette garnye de cincquante vne groffes perles/ Demeure de refte cincq perles du moyen touoir touret et de laureillette quatre groffes perles auffy de refte du · · · rez touoir ·
Sen fault vne [perle] ·

Vng cordon de bonnet garny de douze chattons dor a chacune chatton garny dune perle et vij^{xx} viij perles enfillee qui font de entredeux ·
Sen fault ·

Seize perles garnyes en pandant doreille tant rondes que en poire ·
Sen fault vne perle ·

Acoustrement dor garnyes de Perles ·

A celle du Marquis · Vne brodure de thoure garnye de treize chattons garniz de chacun vne perle xij entredeux faictes a cordelieres garnyes de xviij perles chacune cordeliere ·

Vne brodeure doreillette garnye de treize piece chacun

piece garnye d'une perle et douze entredeux a cordeliere garnies de xv perles chacune piece ·

Vng carcan de mesme facon garny de huict chattons chacune chatton garny dune perle et neuf entredeux garny de quinze perles chacun en facon de cordelieres ·

A la fille de Madame de Martigues ·

Vng aultre ~~theuoir~~ touret faict en baffinetz garny de xv baffinetz chacun baffinet garny d'une perle dor et alentour defdits baffinetz de petittes perles et xvj entredeux garniz de petittes perles ·

Vne aureille de mesme facon garnye de xx baffinetz garny de chacun vne perle et xix entredeux garniz de petittes perles ·

Refte du toure deux pieces garniz de chacune vne perle ·

Refte de laureillette quatre pieces deux a perles et deux entredeux ·

Vng carcan faict en facon de battons rompuz garny de douze pieces a perles et vnze entredeux ou pend chacun vne petitte perle ·

A ma sœur ·

Vng aultre petit carcan faict a canons efmaille tout de noir garny de xviij pieces ou pend de petittes perles et petittes grains noires ·

Acoustrement de Senteurs ·

A ma sœur Darguilles ·

Vng touoir garny de xxv pieces faictes a jour plains de

parfum tant longues que pouroint et xlvj perles qui
font les entredeux .

Vne aureille de mefme facon garnye de xxix pieces tant
longues que rondes et cent huict perles qui font les entredeux .

Vng gorgerin garniz de petis grains dor a jour plains de
parfum et de petittes perles entredeux .

Vne cottouere garnye de petis grains dor faictz a jour
plains de parfum / et y a xvij pilliers garnies de xv grains
de petites perles / et xvj aultres petis pilliers cincq grains
garniz de perles / et de petis grains de parfum qui font
lentredeux .

Vne faincture de mefme facon garnie [de] xvij pilliers
chacun pillier garny de xxiiij grains / et xviij aultres petis
pilliers garniz de perles et vj grains / et vne pomme au
bout ou pend vj pendant de mefme grains .

Aultre acoustrement de Senteurs .

A Madame de Mora .   Vng tours garny de xxxvj patenoftre dor a jour plaines
de parfum garnies de petis grains dor a jour entredeux .

Vne aureillette de mefmes garnye de xxxiij patenoftres
de mefme .

Vne cottouere de mefme facon contenante iiij^{xx} ix patenoftres dore plaines de parfum et de petis grains a jour
et de grains dor qui font lentredeux .

Vng petit carcan de petit grains a jour plains de parfum
et de petis grains dor qui font entredeux ·

Vne ſainƈure garnie de liij patenoſtres en a jour plaines
de parfum ·

Vne paire de patenoſtres de ſenteurs garnye de lj patenoſtres et vj pilliers garniz de petit grenatz a jour entredeux ·

Sen fault 32 ·

Sainctures Damaſſiſte Jaspe et Cornaline ·

A Madame de Mar ·　Vne ſainƈure garnye de xxxij pieces damaſtiſte vij
pilliers dor xxxix meures de perle entredeux / et au bout
vne pomme damaſtiſte de deux pieces ·

~~Sen fault~~ ·

A sa fille ·　Vne ſainƈure de ~~grozolieques~~ chryſolithes contenante
lvij pieces grains rondes garniz en vaze et de petittes
olliues entredeux eſmaille de rouge et vng vaze au bout ·

~~Sen fault~~ ·

Vne cottouere de meſme contenante xlix pieces garnye de
chacun deux grains et de petittes olliue[s] entredeux
eſmaille de rouge ·

~~Sen fault~~ ·

A Iene Stuart ·　Vng dizain de cornaline garnye de xiiij cornalines en
vaze et xiiij entredeux garniz de chacun iiij perles / et au
font pend vng grand [v]aze garny de vj cornalines ·

Sen fault ·

o

Vne cottouere garnye de xl pieces garnye de chacun vne coraline et xxxix entredeux garnies dune perle chacun · ~~Son fault~~ ·

Vne faincture garnie de xxviij pieces chacun piece garnye dune coraline et xxvij entredeux garniz de chacun deux perles ·

Brasseletz ·

A Madame de Mar · Vne paire de brasseletz garniz de chacun iiij pieces et a chacune piece y a huict diamans et vij tables de rubiz ' et huict entredeux garniz dvne perle [chacun] ·

A Madame de Briante · Vne aultre paire de brasseletz damatiste ·

A Madame de Cric · Vne aultre paire de brasseletz garniz de cornaline lappines et agate et lentredeux de doubles ·

A Madame de Leuinston · Vne aultre paire de brasseletz dor a jour empliz de parfum ·

Pandans doreille ·

Aus dames dArguilles de Mar et de Leuinston · Deux perles en poires ·
Sen fault ·

Deux aultres perles garnies de trois esmeraulde chacune ·

Deux aultres perles rondes ·
Sen fault ·

Aus dames d'Ar-
guilles de Mar et de
Leuinston ·

Deux faffiz garny dune perle chacune ·

Deux aultres pendans doreille damaftrifte ·

Deux aultres petis pendans faiⅽt en peu creu garniz de
petis rubiz ·

Sen fault vne ·

Deux aultres perles en poire petites acouftre dor ·

Sen fault vne ·

Deux aultres pandans garny de diamans ·

~~Sen fault~~ Vne auecques deux groffes perles ·

Vne piere que Gendrot a achaiⅽte ·

Vne perle platte qui neft point percee ·

Deux pendans doreille facon dencolye efmaillez dazur ·

Deux aultres pandans de mefme facon efmaillez de bleu
garniz ~~et inperle~~ de iij perles chacun ·

Deux pendans en fempirviue ·

Deux pendans efmaillez tout rouge ·

Deux pendans vers en coquille ·

Deux pannier dor ·

Vng pendant en tortue ·

Deux pandans de fenteurs ·

Huiᛃ pendans de chiffres de plufieurs fortes .

Deux pandans en [v]aze .

Martes .

A Madame de Martigues .　　Vng loup feruier garny d'une tefte de marte de criftal acouftree dor efmaillee de rouge garnye de xxj tourquoifes quatre ~~pafte~~ pattes auffy de criftal garnyes chacune patte de trois turquoyfes / et vne chefne contenante quatre vingtz xiiij paftenoftres .

La chefne eft donne au Roy .

A Madame d'Arguilles .　　Vne marte garnye dune tefte dor et au col cincq chattons garniz de iij rubiz et deux diamans et deux rubiz au deux yeux deux perles pendantes aux aureilles et quatre pattes dor .

A Madame de Mar .　　Vne marte blanche garnye dune tefte dor garnye de feize rubiz cincq diamans et deux faffis / deux perles pendantes aux aureilles / quatre patte chacune garnye cincq rubiz et vng diamant .

A Madame de Mora .　　Vne marte jaulne garnie dune tefte dor garnie de huiᛃ rubiz cincq diamans deux pendans doreille efmaillez de rouge vne chefne dor garnye de viij pieces a chiffres et huiᛃ effeu entredeux / et quatre pattes dor efmaillez de blanc .

A Madame dHatel .　　Vne hermine garnie [dune] tefte [de getz] garnie de trois rubiz et deux diamans deux rubiz aux yeulx deux perles aux oreilles / les quatre pattes dor efmaillez de blanc .

A Madame de Leuin-
ston ·

Vne aultre hermyne garnie d'une tefte efmaillee de blanc
et mouchettee de noir / vne chefne efmaillee de blancq et
noir / et les quatre paftes de mefmes ·

Vne hermine fans ~~grantnor~~ garniture ·

A Ien Stuart ·

Vne penne de foye garnye dune tefte de getz garnye dor
auec fa chefne efmaille dor et de noir / le quatre pattes de
mefmes ·

~~Bordons~~ Boutons de Perriees ·

Au Roy ·

Douze grans boutonmens garnis de douze rofes de diamens ·

Douze aultres pieres grans de rubiz ballaiz ·

Au Roy ·

Quatre cens quatre bottons en facon de panache efmaille
de blancq garniz de chacun vng rubiz ·
    Sen fault 14 ·

Au Roy ·

Lxxj boutons tant grans moyens que petis garnis de
chacun vng rubiz ballay ·

Vingt fept bottons garniz de chacun vng faffiz / refte vng
qui na point de piere a vng ·

Treize petis chattons garniz de chacun vng faffiz ·
    Sen fault vne ·

Douze bottons garniz de trois vermeilles chacun ·
    Donne au Roy ·

~~Boudous~~ *Boutons de Perles* ·

Au Roy ·

Quatre vingtz bouttons dor efmaillez de blanc et noir garniz de chacune vne perle ·

Douze boutons garniz de chacun trois perles / Il y a fault de deux perles ·

Vingt trois bottons a [r]ofe garniz de chacun trois perles ·

Trente fept defguillettes garnye de chacun iiij perles ·

Quinze efguillettes et demye de grenatz garnye dor ·

Quatre vingtz boutons de ~~meueres~~ meurs de perles ·

Soixante vne efguillettes dor et de perles efmaillez de rouge ·

A Madame de Boduel ·

Vne couiffe garnye de rubiz perles et grenatz .

Vng collit auffy garny de rubiz perles et grenatz ·

Vne paire de manches garnies de rubiz perles et grenatz ·

A Francoys mon nepueu ·

Quatre vingtz treize boutons de fenteurs garniz de cha-cune vne petitte perle ·

Vne piece de licorne garnye dune ~~chaine~~ chayne dargent · Sen fault ·

Cincquante huict en triangle garniz de chacun trois perles efmaillez de rouge blancq et vert ·

Cent cincq ~~poitiers~~ petis bottons dor ron[d]es efmaillez de rouge garny de chacune vne perle ·

Sen fault de vne pour vne bonnett ·

Cincquante boutons dor percez a jour efmaillez de noir xxxiij faict en treffle facon dEfpaigne ·

Sen fault xxxiij · Mergrett hes the xxxiij ·

Huict vingt trois aultres boutons facon dEfpaigne efmaille de griz blanc et noir ·

Sen fault vij ·

Cent quatorze efguillettes a pompons dor fans efmail a font bruny ·

Cincquante quatre et demy de fers defguillete faictz en facon de trianger efmaillez de blancq ·

Sen fault 31 et vj ·

A Lesuiston lesnee · Quatre vingtz deux efguillettes xliiij petittes de mefme facon efmaillez de blancq ·

A la ieusne · Soixante cincq efguillettes dor facon de cheuilles fans efmail ·

Sen fault vne ·

A mon nepueu · Quatre vingtz trois petites boutons efmaillez de blanc et noir en croiffant ·

Quatre vingtz dix neuf boutons a jour qui vallent deux ~~a fouze~~ efcus et demy ·

Soixante vnze boutons efmaillez de blanc griz et noir garniz de perles a lentour ·

Ces botons ont efte enuoye en Engleterre ·

Quatre vingtz dixhuiĉt efguillette dor efmaillez de blanc et noir ·

Sen fault · On dict a Loychtlewin ·

A ma tante de St Pierre ·

Vng grand mirouer efmaille de blanc et de noir au dedens chiffres ou eſt la figure de la Royne dAngleterre auec vne efguillette ferree dor / et la pareille eſt a vne montre ·

Sen fault ·

Souuenances pour me ramanteuoir a mes bons amys ·

Bagues a mettre au doy · Premiere[m]ent ·

A la Courone ·

Vne grand table de diamant efmaille de rouge ·

Cest celui de quoy ie fus espousee · Au Roy qui la me donne ·

Vne autre bague de diamant efmaille de rouge ·

A mon beau pere ·

Vne pointe de diamant en groſſe heuure efmaille de noir ·

Sen fault ·

A ma belle mere ·

Vng diamant taille en face ·

Vng autre diamant en pointe efmaille de noir ·

A la Contine pour souuenance ·

Vng diamant en pointe taille en face efmaille de blanc et rouge ·

A mon frere de Mora ·

Vng diamant en pointe fans feuille ·

Au Conte de Mar ·

Vne table de moyfe auec deux diamans ·

Au Conte Boduel ·	Vne table de diamant emaille de noir ·
Aux quatre Maries ·	Quatre autres petis diamant de diuerse façon ·
Au Conte d'Arguilles ·	Vng ruby sans feuille esmaille de blanc ·
Au Conte Hontelay ·	Vng ruby cabochon esmaille de blanc ·
Au Conte d'Atel ·	Vne table de ruby esmaille de blanc et noir ·
A ma sœur	Vng ruby caboche esmaille de bleu et rouge ·
Aus dames de Cric de Ceston et de Leuinston	Troys bagues garnye de petis rubys ·
A Iemes Balfour ·	Vne grande emeraude emaille de blanc et rouge ·
~~*A Madame Donuille*~~ *A Iosef pour porter a celui que ie luy ay dit ·*	Vne emeraude emaille de blanc ·
A l'Esuesque de Lendors ·	Vng grand safi esmaille de blanc ·
Aus filles ·	Vne dousaine de petites bague dor sans piere ·

Il sen fault vne chesne que vous naues pas ecrite esmaylle de blanc et rousge que ie laysse a Madamoyselle de la Souschee ·

Marie R

P

Inuentoyre dernier des pierreryes que la Rayne a achefte dernierement .

Au filleul du feu Roy .	Vne grande bage a pendre ou il y a vne emeraude vng ruby vng fafi et fept petis diamans · Sen fault ·
Les deus autres a Charles et a Loys ·	Deux autres bages a pendre ou il y a chafcune vne emeraude et vng ruby et vne perle au bout · Sen fault vne · Receau lautre ycy ·
Au Roy ·	Vne chefne de diament et de perle dont il y a 24 pieces garnye chafcune de deux diamans et 24 cordeliere de perles ·
Au Roy ·	Vng refte de pareille facon ou il y a 8 pieces garnye chafcune de deux perles et 9 cordeliere de perles · · Sen fault 3 pieces de deux diamants et 4 cordeliers de perles ·
A mon oncle le Cardinal ·	Vne bage a mettre au doy garnye de vne emeraude · Sen fault ·
Lune au Roy et lautre a mon nepuueu ·	Deux chefnes de ruby et de diamans et de perle ayant 12 pieces chafcune garnye dun ruby et dun diamant et 24 perles chafcune · Sen fault · Le Roy a perdu vng diamant ·

Au Roy .   Vne chefne dor efmaille de blanc contenante deux centz
pieces et chafcune piece deux diamans ou il y a dix
diamans de perdu ·

Sen fault ·

Marie R

Marie Semiston

Jentends que cestuissi soyt execute
au cas que lenfant ne mesururue
mays sil vit ie lefoys he rit ier
de fout MARIE

Inuentaire des Brodures .

A Flamy ·

Vne brodure dor efmaille de blancq et rouge contenante xxxvij pieces ·

~~Sen fault~~

Vne brodure dorellette de mefme facon garnye de lj piece efmaille de blancq et rouge ·

Vne cottouere de mefme facon contenante foixante piece efmaille de blanc et rouge ·

Vng quarquan efmaille auffy de blancq et rouge garny de vingt vne piece ·

Vne chefne a faindre en femblable facon contenante lij pieces efmaillez de blanc et rouge et vng vaze pandant au bout ·

Tout sen fault ·

Aultre acoustrement ·

A Leuinston laysnee ·

Vne brodure du toure contenante xxv pieces efmaille de blanc et noir facon de godrons ·

Vne brodeure doreillette de pareille facon contenante xxvij pieces efmaillees de blanc et noir ·

Vne cottouere de femblable facon contenante lx pieces de pareille facon efmaillee de blanc et noir ·

Vng carcan efmaille de blanc et noir contenant dixfept pieces et a chacune piece y a vng petit pandant .

Vne chefne a faindre de femblable facon contenante liiij pieces efmaillees de blanc et noir et vng vaze au bout .

Aultre acoustrement dor ·

A Leuiston la ieusne　Vne brodure de thouret a fons bruny garny de vingt neuf pieces .

Vne brodeure doreillettes de mefme facon contenante xxxiiij pieces .

Vne cottouere contenante lxvj pieces de mefme facon .
Sen fault ·

Vng carcan contenant xxvij pieces ·
Sen fault ·

Vne chaifne a faindre contenante lxvj pieces et vng vaze au bout ·
Sen fault .

A Marguerite ·　Vne aultre paires de brodeures dor et cordelieres contenante xxix pieces ·

Vne brodeure doreillettes contenante xxxvij pieces de femblable facon ·

A Beton ·　Vne aultre paires de brodeures a fons brung deffoubz efmaillez de blanc contenante xxxvj pieces ·

A Beton .   Vne brodeure doreillette garny de xlix pieces de mefme facon .

Aultre acoustrement dor et de blanc .

A Ceston .   Vne brodeure de toure contenante xxxiij pieces efmaillez dor et de blanc partye en cordelieres .

Vne brodeure doreillette de mefme facon contenante xxxj pieces .

Vne fainƌure de mefme facon contenante xl pieces .

Aultre acoustrement .

A Marie Ersquin .   Vne brodeure garnye de quarante fept pieces efmaillez de blanc vert et rouge et xx femper viuantes pendent .

Vne aultre toure efmaille de blanc et vert contenant xl pieces .

A Maystre Ien Stuart .   Vne aureillette de mefme facon contenante xlv pieces .

Sainctures .

A Tore .   Vne chefne dor a ~~fainƌure~~ cendre efmaille de noir contenante lvj pieces tant vazes pillieres que entredeux et vng vaze pendant au bout .

Vne cottouere de mefme facon contenante lvj pieces tant vazes pilliers que entredeux .

[A] *Madame* [de]
Mar ·

Vne aultre faincture efmaille de blanc et rouge contenante xlvj pieces faicte en facon de rofes et chiffres ou
pend au bout vne grande ro[f]e ou eft le pourtretz du
feu Roy Henry ·

A Lucresse ·

Vne aultre chaifne a faindre faicte en facon de chiffres
efmaillee de blanc et dazur contenante lviij pieces ou
pend au bout vng grand chiffre ·

A Beton ·

Vne aultre chefne a faindre efmaille de blanc facon def-
taulx contenante xlv pieces ·

Vne cottouere de mefme facon contenante lxv pieces ·

Vng carcan de mefme facon contenant douze pieces auec
de petites pandans ·

A Madame de
Hontelay ·

Vne paire de patenoftres dagatte faicte en vaze contenante xxiiij garniz dor auec de petis grenatz entredeux
garniz dolliues vng pillier dagatte garny dune perle auec
vng petit dieu et deux merques toutes dor garniz de
cinq rubiz chacun et vne hourre au bout ·

Vng dizain ~~garny~~ de fept pillieres dagatte acouftrez
de cinq aultres pilliers dor garniz de vermeilles et du
turquin et vnze entredeux a jour fans efmail ·

Sen fault dvnce · Donne a Marguerite pour bouter au Cabinet ·

A la ieusne Contesse
de Hontelay ·

Vng dizain de criftal garny de dix vazes et vng pillier
de criftal au bout et dix grans efmaillez dazour percez
a jour ·

A Madame de Leuin-ſton .

Vne paire de patenoſtres contenante lxv grains rondes de grenaz et ſept pilliers de verre garny dor / et vng pillier de grenat et dor eſmaille dazur ·

A Flamy .

Soixante dix de groz grains dor a jour plains de parfum faiɗz de deux pieces ·

     Sen fault ·

A Marie Arſquin ·

Vne ſainɗure de criſtal contenante lj groz grain de criſtal rond xiiij olliues en ~~fais dEſcoſſe~~ facon deſt-aux de poix eſmaillez de vert et rouge garnies de perles / Et xl petis beſains eſmaillez de rouge et vert et vng groz vaze de criſtal qui pend au bout ·

Vne cottouere garnye de ſoixante quatorze grains tant verre que criſtal garniz dolliues et petis grains entredeux ·

Vne paire de braſſeletz de meſmes ·

Vng carcan du meſme ·

A Iame Stuart ·

Vne ſainɗure de verre vert garnie dor et grains de por-celine ·

Vne cottouere de meſme garnye de bezand dor eſmaillez de blancq ·

A Lesuiston lesnee ·

Vne corde de coural contenante lxiij pieces faiɗes en vaze ·

     Il a eſte faiɗ vne cottouere et vne ſainɗure garnye de gerbes dor et de perles ·

Vne aultre corde de coural contenante treize groſſes pieces auſſy en vaze ·

A Lesuiston lesnee . Vng aultre corde de coural contenante xxxviij pieches plus petites auffy en vaze ·

> Receu ycy xxxviij ·

Vne refte de patenoftres ou il a neuf meures de perles et des grains dargent entredeux ·

Vne faincture ~~nottouere~~ et cottouere de perles garnie bleu et grains noir faict a roifteau ·

> Item haill acouftrement of gold of couter carcan and chefne of 66 pyecis ·

[signature: Marier]

[signature: Marie Semston]

Inuentaire des Pierreries qui font en Cabinet de la Royne ·   ·

Premierement ·

Au Roy ·	Vne / ♭ / dor garnye dun rubiz cabochon et vne perle pandante au bout ·
Au Roy ·	Vng Sainct Mychel faict de quatorze diamens ·
A mon frere ·	Vne rose garnye de quatorze diamens vng rubiz et vne perle pandante au bout ·
Au Roy ·	Vne aultre rofe garnye de xvij diamens et cinq perlcs pandantes ·
A mon frere de Sᵗ Croys Au Roy ·	Vne aultre rofe garnye de dix diamens efmaillee de rouge et vert ·
	Vne aultre petitte rofe garnye de vj diamens ·
A mon frere de Sᵗ Croyx ·	Vne croix garnie de cinq tables de diamens et trois perles pandantes ·
A Josef pour bailler a que ie lui ay dit dont il ranuoir aquitance ·	Vne bacgue garnye de vingt vng diamens tant grands que petis ·
Au Conte Boduel ·	Vne enfeigne ou il y a vne ceruine garnye de vnze diamens et vng rubiz ·

A mon nepueu ·   Vng tableau garny de cinq rubiz · / vne esmeraulde ·

A Monssieur de Hontelay ·   Vne fleur de lis guarnye de cinq diamens et vne perle pandante et vne chesne esmaillee de rouge blanc et noir et neuf pilliers de perles qui font les entredeux ·

A Marguerite ·   Vne painɗure de la Royne garnye dune croix de ~~diame~~ cinq diamens ·

Au Roy ·   Vne montre garnye de dix diamens deux rubiz et vne corde d'or ·

Au Roy ·   Vng petit cadren garny de huiɗ diamens deux rubiz vne perle pandante vne petitte chesne dor ou il y a atache au bout vne poire dor pleine de parfum garnye de petittes turquoyses et grenatz ·

A la ieusne Leuiston ·   Vne aultre montre garny de douze rubiz et deux grands saffiz auec vne ~~qu~~ perle pandante au bout ·

A Alexandre Ersquin ·   Vng cueur dor garny de trois diamens vng rubiz et vne perle pandante ·

A Artus Asquin ·   Vne enseigne garnye dun ~~rubi~~ saffize et vne perle pandante au bout ·

A Iosef que son frere mauoyt donne ·   Vne aultre enseigne garnye de dix rubiz en tortue auec vne perle pandante au bout ·

Il y a vne petite boyte dargent entre ses mayns que ie lui donne et il y a deus cueurs dor de mes entrees auuesques vne comme vne rose et vn hault goubellet couuert et vn bouclier et quelque Notre Dames que ie veus etre enuoyees a ma tante de St Piere et toutes les petites besoignes de cabinoit   Ie laysse mes liuures qui y sont ceulx en Grec ou Latin a luniuersite de Sintandre pour y commancer vne bible Les aultres ie les laysse a Beton Ie laysse mon linge entre mes troys fammes et ma chambre et la vayselle de mes cofres entre les vallets de fourieres tapissiers et huissiers pour etre vandu a leur profit et des troys filles qui la guardent   Tous mes ouurasges maches et collets aus quatre Maries a Iene Stuart a Marie Arsquin Sonderland et a toutes les filles ·

Marie R

Iantands que cestuissi sorte aeffect ·

Marie R

Memoire de tout ce qui a efte diftribue des draps de foye et aultres chozes depuis le larriuee de la Royne en Ecoffe commençant au premier jour de Septembre 1561 jufque au premier jour de Januier 1564 auant Pafques   Le tout deliure par moy Seruais de Condez vallet de chambre de ladicte Dame et le tout deliure a laune de France ·

Premierement au mois de Septembre 1561 ·

Jay deliure au cordonnier de la Royne deux tiers de velours noir pour faire des fouliers pour ladicte dame et demie aulne de taffetas pour doubler lefdictz foulliers ·

Plus jay deliure aux femmes de chambre trois quartiers de toille pour allonger vng vieil drap ·

Plus jay deliure au tapiffier xxvij aulnes de gros caneuas pour faire deux paillaffes et vne enueloppe afcauoir lune pour Courfelles et laultre pour la Folle auec lenueloppe ·

Plus deliure fept aulnes de toille pour faire vne paire de draps pour ladicte Courfelles ·

Plus deliure au cordonnier demie aulne de velours noir pour faire vne paire de foulliers et vne paire de pantoufles pour la Royne ·

Plus deliure a Francoyfe femme de chambre de la Royne deux aulnes dEfcoffe deftamet viollet pour faire des chauffes pour la Royne auec vne aulne de taffetas viollet et vne once de foye viollet ·

Plus il a efte defrobbe dedans la falle de la Royne vng doffier de lict de velours noir lequel eftoit tendu dedans ladicte falle ·

Plus deliure a ladicte Francoyfe deux aulnes dEfcoffe deftamet blanc pour faire des chauffes pour la Royne auec vne aune de taffetas blanc vne once de foye blanche et vne once de foye noire le tout pour lefdictes chauffes ·

Plus jay deliure a Dauid tapiffier xxxvij aulnes et demie tant deftamet verd que carife pour faire vne tapifferie pour le cabinet de la Royne ·

Plus jay deliure a Francoyfe vng quartier de taffetas bleu et vne once de foye bleue ·

Plus je deliure deux petitz tappis de drap verd lun pour mettre en la garde-robbe de la Royne et laultre en fa librarie ·

Memoire de ce que jay diftribue durant le mois de Octobre audicte an 1561 ·

Premierement jay deliure a la gouuernante de la Jardiniere cinq aulnes de toille blanche pour faire trois paires de callefons pour ladicte Jardiniere auec quelques mouchoirs ·

Plus deliure a Francoife vne aulne de taffetas noir pour faire vng taffetas pour la Royne ·

Plus jay deliure cent douze aulnes de toille pour garnir quatre litz des filles et

a chafcun lict quatre draps et eftoict pour Flami Fonpertuis Beton Ceton et
Leuifton .

Plus je deliure xxiiij aulnes de toille pour garnir deux litz pour leurs femmes .

Plus je deliure a Madamoifelle de Raalle xiiij aulnes de toille pour lui faire
deux draps pour fon lict .

Plus jay deliure vne vafquine de camelot noir de la feu Royne pour feruir a la
Royne .   (94 .)

Plus jay deliure xxx aulnes de toille aux femmes de chambre pour leur faire
quatre draps pour leurs litz .

Plus je deliure a Courfelles vij aulnes de toille pour lui faire vne aultre paire
de linceuz .

Plus pour la femme de Madamoifelle de la Souche xij aulnes de toille pour lui
faire des linceux .

Plus jay deliure a la gouuernante de la Jardiniere x aulnes de toille pour lui
faire vne paire de linceux .

Plus je deliure a Mernard dix aulnes de toille pour lui faire quatre linceux et
neuf aulnes et demie de toille pour lui faire des chemifes .

Plus je deliure a Jacques le tailleur deux tiers de camelot noir pour relargir vne
vielle vafquine de la feu Royne .

Plus je deliure a Michelet et a Mernard vj aulnes de toille pour doubler leur
habillement de mafque .

Plus je deliure a Michelet et Eftiene xx aulnes de toille pour leur faire deux paire de draps ·

Plus je deliure a Madamoifelle de Raalle vng refte de toille de Hollande qui a efte employe pour faire des chauffes pour la Royne contenant xviij aulnes ·

Plus je deliure a Madamoyfelle de Raalle vne aultre demie piece de toille de Hollande qui a efte employee a faire des coeuurechefz pour la Royne et auffi a racoutrer le lict de la Royne lequel eftoict en partie brufle ·

  Ces deux articles font vng piece entier ·

Plus je deliure au tailleur de Monfieur Danuille xvj aulnes de toille pour doubler des habillementz de mafque ·

Plus je deliure vng refte de toille blanche en prefence de Madamoifelle de Raalle pour faire vne fouille pour le matelatz qui fert au lict de la Royne ·

Plus je deliure a Madamoifelle de la Souche demie aulne de toille pour paffer de lhuille pour la Royne ·

Plus je deliure a Jacques le tailleur vne refte de camelot noir fans ondes contenant xj aulnes et demie pour ayder a faire vne robbe pour la Royne ·

Plus je deliure a Jacques le tailleur vng quartier de fatin noir pour faire vng manchon pour la Royne ·

Plus je deliure au dict tailleur vng tiers de fatin noir pour faire vng aultre manchon a caufe que le premier eftoict trop petit ·

Plus je deliure de la fourrure de martre pour doubler lefdictz manchons ·

Plus je deliure a Henry clerc de chapelle xij aulnes de toille pour faire des linfeulx pour Hannibal ·

Memoire de ce que jay deliure durant le mois de Nouembre audicte an 1561 .

Premierement je deliure demie aulne de velours noir pour faire vng bonnet pour Hannibal et vne ceinture .

Plus je deliure a Pierre Martin tapiffier lx aulnes de mechante toille de quoy eftoient emballes les meubles de la Royne dont il en a efte faict cinq paillaffes pour ceux qui font la garde .

Plus je deliure a Jacques le tailleur xx aulnes de fatin noir pour les deliurer aux filles de la Royne quand ilz ont prins le fecond deuil .

Plus je deliure au dict tailleur vne aultre aulne de fatin noir pour vne fille qui vient a la Royne nommee Ros .

Memoire de ce que jay distribue durant le mois de Decembre audicte an 1561 .

Premierement je deliure au Pelletier le chapperon de deuil de la feue Royne auec deux aultres petitz morceaux dhermine dont le tout a efte employe pour border des robbes aux filles quand elles prindrent le fecond deuil . (78 .)

Plus je deliure a Henry clerc de chapelle demi quartier de velours noir pour mettre au cierge de la Royne le jour du bout de lan du feu Roy .

Plus je deliure a Eftiene le chantre vij aulnes de velours noir pour lui faire vng foye chauffes et lui bender vne cappe .

Plus je deliure au dict Eftiene vj aulnes de fatin noir pour lui faire vng pourpoinct et bender fa cappe par dedans et emplir fes chauffes .

R

Plus par le commandement de la Royne je deliure a Madamoiſelle de Raalle vne martre et vne hermine a mettre a lentour du col garnies de teſtes et piedz dor emailles et les colletz deſdictes martre et hermine garnies de pierres et perles reſerue que a la bride de la martre il fault vne perle laquelle martre et hermine jauois receus auec les meubles de la feu Royne ·

Plus je deliure vne aulne de toille pour acouſtrer les perruques de la Royne ·

Plus jay deliure au tailleur trois quartiers et demi de ſatin noir pour doubler le cofps d'une robbe faicte a lEſpagnolle pour la Royne ·

Plus je deliure a la gouuernante de la Jardiniere vng drap des brodeurs pour faire des mouchouers pour ladicte Jardiniere ·

Plus je deliure a Dauid le chantre viij draps des brodeurs pour la garniture de ſon lict auec vne couuerte deſdicts brodeurs ·

Plus il a eſte deliure ſix couuertes deſdicts brodeurs a ceux qui font la garde la nuict en la ſalle de la Royne ·   (50 ·)

Plus il a eſte entame vngs poignetz dhermine pour border et chamarrer vne robbe a lEſpagnolle pour la Royne ·

Fin de la ſuſdicte annee ·

Marie R

Memoire de tout ce que jay deliure durant lannee 1562 commencant le premier jour de Januier ·

Premierement ·

Je deliure a Madamoifelle de Raalle trois quartiers de frize rouge pour enuelopper vne martre et hermine pour mettre a lentour du col · Ladicte frize eft de la tapifferie des brodeurs ·

Plus je deliure a Jacques le tailleur vne aulne de Hollande pour faire des braffieres de nuict pour la Royne ·

Plus je deliure au cordonnier trois quartiers de velours noir pour faire vne paire de mulles et deux paire de foulliers pour la Royne ·

Plus jay deliure au dict cordonnier vng quartier de taffetas pour doubler lefdicts foulliers ·

Plus je deliure au clerc de chapelle demi quartier de velours noir pour mettre au cierge de la Royne ·

Il a efte prins vng farcot dhermines pour border les robbes des filles · (88 ·)

Il a efte employe des poignetz dhermine pour faire des parementz a vng manteau de nuict et border des robbes des filles · (46 ·)

La Royne a prins pour lui feruir vng manteau de eftamet noire garni de parementz dhermines .   (82 ·)

Il a efte pris pour la Royne vng manteau de taffetas mouchette pour faire vne
cotte et lhermine dudiƈt manteau a efte pris pour border les robbes des filles .
(84 ·)

Memoire de ce que je distribue au mois de Feburier 1562 ·

Je deliure a Francoife trois aulnes de fatin noir pour mettre dedans fes coffres
au partement de la Royne pour aller a Sainƈt Andre ·

La Royne a donne a Marnard vng manteau de fatin noir pour lui faire vne
robbe de nuiƈt ·   (85 ·)

La Royne a donne a Seruais vne vafquine et vne paire de vielles braffieres de
fatin noir ·   (92 ·)

La Royne a donne a Baltazar vne paire de braffieres et vng deuant de fatin
noir ·   (93 ·)

Plus la Royne a prins vng poignet de panne de foye noire ·

Memoire de ce que jay deliure au mois de Mars 1562 ·

Je deliure demie aulne demi quart de fatin noir pour faire vng collet pour la
Royne ·

La Royne a donne a Seruais vng manteau de farge drappe tout fimple ·   (83 ·)

Memoire de ce que jay distribue durant le mois d'Apuril 1562 et May audicte an .

Je deliure vng quartier dEcoffe de velours noir pour faire des mules pour la Royne .

Memoire de ce que jay distribue durant le mois de Juing .

Je deliure a Jacques le tailleur vng quartier de fatin noir pour faire deux touretz de nez pour la Royne et vng quartier de taffetas pour les doubler .

Memoire de ce que jay distribue durant le mois de Juillet 1562 .

Memoire de ce que jay distribue durant le mois d'Aoust 1562 .

Je deliure a Jacques le tailleur fept aulnes de fatin noir pour faire vne cotte pour la Royne auffi deux touretz de nez deux cornettes et deux mafques .

Plus je deliure au dict Jacques trois quartiers de taffetas pour doubler lefdictes befougnes .

Plus je deliure a Francoife demi quartier de taffetas noir pour mettre a vne paire de chauffes pour la Royne .

Memoire de ce qui a este distribue durant le mois de Septembre 1562 ·

Je deliure a Pierre Odri brodeur iiij draps et vne couuerte des celles qui feruoient aux brodeurs en France ·

Memoire de ce que jay distribue durant le mois de Octobre 1562 ·

Je deliure a Baltazar vallet de chambre vne piece de fatin noir contenant quarante trois aulnes trois quartz quand la Royne eftoict au nord ·

Memoire de ce que jay distribue durant le mois de Nouembre 1562 ·

Je deliure a Jacques tailleur vne aulne et trois quartz de fatin noir pour faire vne piece d'ung corps a lEfpagnolle pour la Royne et demie aulne de taffetas pour doubler ledict corps ·

Plus je deliure au cordonnier vng tiers de taffetas noir pour doubler deux paire de foulliers pour la Royne ·

Plus jay deliure a Mathieu menufier vne aulne et demie de fatin noir pour doubler vng coffre de nuict pour la Royne ·

Plus je deliure au dict Mathieu vne aulne et trois quartz de fatin noir pour couurir les atibois du lict de fatin noir faict de broderie ·

Plus je deliure au tapiffier Pierre Martin xix aulnes de fatin noir pour faire vne couuerte au lict de fatin noir faict de broderie ·

Memoire de ce que jay distribue durant le mois de Decembre 1562 ·

Je deliure a Marnard cinq aulnes et demie de satin noir pour lui acomplir vng habillement ·

Plus je deliure a Madamoiselle de Ceton deux aulnes de satin noir ·

Plus je deliure a Madamoiselle de Raalle huict aulnes de plette pour seruir a mettre les bagues et seintures de la Royne ·

Plus je deliure a Estiene vallet de chambre trois aulnes et vng quart de satin noir pour lui faire vng pourpoinct et vne paire de manches a vng vieil pourpoinct de satin ·

Plus je deliure a Jacques tailleur demie aulne de satin noir pour faire vng deuant d'ung corps a lEspagnolle dune robbe de sarge dascot ·

Plus je deliure a Jacques le tailleur demie aulne de satin noir pour faire vng collet a lEspagnolle pour porter aux champs pour la Royne ·

Plus je deliure a tapissier cinq aulnes et demie de plette blanche pour picquer et mettre au seintures et dorures de la Royne ·

Fin de la susdicte annee 1562 ·

Marie R

Memoire de ce que jay distribue en lan 1563 a commencer au mois de Januier.

Premierement.

Je deliure a Monfieur du Vaux alors quil fut hors de page trois aulnes et demie de fatin noir.

Plus je deliure a Adrian vallet de chambre trois aulnes de fatin noir pour lui faire vng pourpoint.

Plus vne aulne et demie de damas blanc pour faire fix gibefieres de bergers pour des mafques au nopces de Monfieur de Sainct Cofme.

~~Plus jay deliure a Jacques le tailleur deux manteaux de mafque faictz de taffetas blanc pour faire daultre forte dhabillements a ceux qui jouoient du lut pour lefdicts mafques.~~

Efface pour ce quil eft efcript en vng aultre endroict.

Plus jay deliure a Jacques le tailleur deux aulnes de fatin noir pour faire vne paire de braffieres pour la Royne.

Plus je deliure au dict tailleur vne aulne et demie de tafetas noir ray pour border vng manteau pour la Royne lequel eft de vellours a deux endroictz.

Plus je deliure a Eftiene vallet de chambre deux aulnes de fatin noir pour mettre dedans des chauffes.

Plus a Francoife femme de chambre je deliure trois aulnes de Hollande pour faire des chauffes pour la Royne .

Plus la Royne a donne a Marnard trois pieces de tapifferie des finges . (29 .)

Memoire de ce que jay deliure durant le mois de Feburier 1563 .

Jay deliure vng drap pour faire des frotouers pour la Royne .

Plus deliure a Jacques le tailleur fept aulnes et vng quart de fatin noir pour faire vne bafquine et vne paire de braffieres pour la Royne .

Plus je deliure a Francoife trois aulnes de Holande pour faire des chauffes pour la Royne .

Durant le mois de Mars 1563 .

Durant le mois de Apuril 1563 .

Memoire de ce que jay deliure durant le mois de May 1563 .

Je deliure a Jacqueline quatre draps pour coucher la Jardiniere auec vne couuerte blanche . (50 .)

Plus je deliure a Jacques tailleur trois quartiers de fatin noir pour faire vng corps de cotte pour la Royne .

s

Plus la Royne a donne vne robbe de damas noir a Leuifton laifnee · (72 ·)

Plus la Royne a donne vne robbe de damas noir faicte a grandes manches a Madamoifelle de Raalle · (73 ·)

Plus la Royne a donne a Madamoifelle de la Souche vne robbe de fatin noir a manches longues · (75 ·)

Plus la Royne a donne a Madamoifelle Leuifton la jeune vne robbe de taffetas noir a grandes manches · (76 ·)

Memoire de ce que jay distribue durant le mois de Juing 1563 ·

Je deliure fept aulnes de Hollande pour faire fix paire de callefons pour la Royne ·

Plus jay deliure a Madamoifelle de Raalle vne aulne de plette pour enuelopper des coiffes et colletz pour la Royne ·

Plus quand la Royne alla en Argueil je deliuray a Baltazar vne plette bigarree pour la Royne ·

Plus trois quartiers de plette pour enuelopper vng collet de perles et grains noirs lequel jay faict ·

Plus la Royne a prins pour lui feruir vng manteau de velours a deux endroicts · (79 ·)

Memoire de ce que jay deliure durant le mois de Juillet 1563 ·

Il a efte rompu trois habillementz de taffetas blanc borde de rouge lefquelz feruirent a abiller des joueurs aux nopces de Monfieur de Sainct Cofme ·

Memoire de ce que je deliure durant le mois d'Aoust 1563.

Il a efte prins vng morfeau de toille dor enuiron vng tiers et vne demie aulne en vng aultre morceau le tout pour feruir a la broderie de velours vert.

Memoire de ce que je deliure durant le mois de Septembre 1563.

Je deliure a Madamoifelle de Leuifton laifnee onze aulnes de damas gris pour lui faire vne robbe.

Plus je deliure a Jacques le tailleur deux chanteaux de damas gris broche dor pour faire vne robbe a vne poupine.

Plus je deliure a Jacques le tailleur trois quartz et demi de toille dargent et de foye blanche pour faire vne cotte et aultre chofe a des poupines.

Plus jay deliure a Madamoyfelle de Seton et Leuifton vne aulne trois quartz de toille dor figuree.   (120.)

Plus je deliure a Jacques le tailleur onze aulnes et demie de fatin tanne pour faire vng manteau rond pour la Royne.

Plus la Royne a faict rompre vng vieil manteau royal pour faire vng tapis et garnir des pilliers de lict de velours viollet faict a fleurs.   (87.)

~~Plus la Royne a donne a Madamoifelle de Seton et Leuifton vng morfeau de toille dor frize contenant vne aulne trois quartz.~~

Efface pour ce quil eft efcript cy deuant.

Plus a efte pris la queue dung dees de velours noir laquelle queue neftoict que dune aulne de France de long pour remettre au lict duquel on auoict desrobbe le dossier ·

Plus pour paracheuer de rabiller ledict lict il a este prins le soubassement et les rideaux dung aultre vieil lict de velours noir ·

Plus a este pris vng tapis de velours viollet seme de fleurs de lis pour faire couurir deux chaires et deux placetz ·   (51 ·)

Plus la Royne a donne a Seruais vng manteau destamet lequel auoict les parementz de jennette ·   (81 ·)

Memoire de ce que jay deliure durant le mois dOctobre 1563 ·

Je deliure a Jacques le tailleur six aulnes de satin tanne pour faire vne juppe pour la Royne ·

Plus il a este prins vne aulne et vng quart de toille dargent pour faire vne pierre faicte en broderie au grand dees de velours cramoysi la ou font assis deux poetes pour le fondz dudict dees ·

Plus a este prins vne aulne et vng quart de toille pour doubler ladicte toille dargent ·

Plus je deliure viij paires de draps pour les lictz des femmes de chambre ·

Memoire de ce que je deliure durant le mois de Nouembre 1563 ·

Je deliure a Jacques le tailleur neuf aulnes de damas blanc pour faire vne soutanne pour la Royne ·

Plus je deliure a Jacques le tailleur huict aulnes de damas tanne pour faire vne soutane pour la Royne .

Plus je deliure a Jacques le tailleur six aulnes et demie de damas gris pour faire vng petit manteau pour la Royne .

Plus je deliure a Madamoiselle de Raalle vne aulne de toille pour faire des sacs pour mettre des pappiers .

Plus je deliure a Jacques le tailleur deux tiers de satin tanne pour faire vng corps de cotte pour la Royne .

Plus je deliure deux aulnes et demie de satin noir pour faire deux colletz quatre cornettes et deux touretz de nees .

Memoire de ce que jay deliure durant le mois de Decembre 1563 .

Je rompu vng soye de velours bleu pour faire trois grands bonnetz a la Souisse pour faire des masques .

Plus je deliure a Madamoiselle de Ralle demie aulne de toille pour faire des ataches pour des perruques pour la Royne .

Plus je deliure a Estiene vallet de chambre de la Royne vng quartier dung vieulx soye de velours bleu pour faire des colletz pour les petitz chiens de la Royne / et vng aultre quartier a Ferriere .

Plus je deliure au Pelletier du bord de martre de la garniture dune robbe et vng manteau pour border vng manteau de damas tanne .

Plus je deliure audict Pelletier de la martre neuue pour doubler et paracheuer de chamarrer ledict manteau .

Plus a efte prins pour enrichir les pilliers dun lict de broderie faict par fleurs les bordz dung foye de velours bleu ·

Plus je deliure a Nicollas tapiffier fix aulnes de Holande pour doubler deux paires de braffieres pour la Royne lefquelles font piquees ·

Plus je deliure a Jacqueline vng bonnet de velours bleu pour Nicolle ·

Plus je deliure quatre aulnes de groffe toille pour enuelopper la planche que on chauffe au lict de la Royne et pour feruir denueloppe pour les foulliers et vaiffelle ·

Plus je deliure a Jacques tailleur vne vafquine de cotte de velours noir des habillementz de la feu Royne pour feruir a la Royne · (90 ·)

Plus je deliure vng parement de manteau de martre lequel eft des fourrures de la feu Royne auec le bord de mefme et auffi de la martre pour eflargir ledict parement · (50 · 51 · 52 ·)

Plus de deliure vng poignet de loup ceruier des fourreures de la feu Royne pour paracheuer de fourrer les parementz dung manteau de velours noir pour la Royne auec les bords de mefme · (53 · 54 ·)

Fin des trois fufdictes annees [1561 · 1562 . et] 1563 ·

Memoyre de tout ce que je distribue en lannee 1564 · commanſant au premier jour de Januyer .

Premierement en Januier ·

Je delliure a Nicollas tapiſſier ſept aulnes de canneua pour fairre vng mattellas
pour les famme de chanbre de la Royne ·

Plus a Jacquelinne vng vieux dras pour fairre des vieux linge pour la Folle ·

Plus je delliure vng vieux dras pour vne poure famme Franſoiſe laquelz eſtoiƈt
en couche au petit lieƬz ·

Plus je delliure au famme de chanbre trente aulnes de toylle pour fairre deux
pairre de dras pour eux ·

Plus je delliure a Jacquelinne xij aulnes de toylle pour fairre ſix chemiſe et des
coyſe a Nicolle ·

Plus a Courcelle ix aulnes de toylle pour luy ferre vj chemiſe ·

Plus a Jacque tailleur demy aulnes de ſatin noyr pour fairre des tourre de ne
pour la Royne ·

Plus a Jacque tailleur ij aulnes j quart et demy de taffetas chengent pour fairre
vne robbe a la fille batarde de Monſieur de Sanƈt Croy ·

Plus demye aulnes de vieux velous cramoysi pour bander ladicte robbe .

Plus a Pierre Martin tapissier iiij aulnes de canneua pour fairre deux gran sac lung pour metre le linge salle et lautre pour metre les soullier et autre chose pour la Royne .

Plus a Jehan de Conpiengne vj aulnes de gro canneua pour enpaqueter ce qui fut enuoye en France a Madame de Monmoransy .

Plus a Jehan de Conpiengne xiiij aulnes de satin tanne pour les fincq robbe de drapt tanne .

Plus a Mademoyselle Beton et Leuiston vne piece de passement fet dor et dargent pesant xxij onse [con]tenant xxxij aulnes .

Plus a Madame de Briande demye aulnes de Hollandes pour fairre doubler xiij pairre de manchettes pour la Royne .

Plus a Jehan de Conpiengne vng tier de satin noir pour faire des bandeaux pour la Royne .

Durant le moys de Feuuerier .

Je delliure a Jehan de Conpiengne troy rest de taffetas orangie chengent contenant xxviij aulnes demy cart qui furt enploye pour les masque qui fit la Royne le jour de son bonque .

Plus a Mademoyselle de Rallez xxiiij aulnes de toylle pour luy ferre ij pairre de dras pour garnir vng lict que la Royne luy ast donne .

Plus a Jehan de Conpiengne iij aulnes de taffetas chengent pour fairre vne robbe a la petitz fille que garde Jacquelinne et fut pour le jour du banquet de la Royne .

Plus je enploye deux vieux dras del lin pour couurir deux licornne et deux pan qui feruir le jour de banquet de la Royne ·

Plus au tapiffier ij aulnes de groffe toylle pour netoyer les armoyrie de la falle du balle ·

Plus vne aulne de toylle pour frifer de perruque pour la Royne lequel je delliuree a deux foys ·

Plus a Mademoyfelle de Rallez iiij aulnes de toylle pour fairre des frotoy pour la Royne ·

Plus a Mademoyfelle de Ralle vne aulnes de pletz pour eneuloper des feinturre de la Royne ·

Plus a Michel famme des fille vne aulnes de toylle pour luy doubler le corps dunne robbe que la Royne luy aft donnee ·

Plus je delliure a Jacquelinne viij aulnes de toylle pour fairre huict chemife au petis enfans quelle gard ·

~~Plus je delliure au Pelletier vng pongne de louferuie et vng morfeaux de lautre pour metre a vng [parrem]ent de manteaux pour la Royne ·~~

Plus a Jehan de Conpiengne troy piece drapt ou eftamet noyr pour fairre des abillement aux paiges ·

Plus xvj aulnes de veloux noyr pour fairre vng manteaux a queu pour la Royne lequelz aft des parrement de louferuie ·

Plus xxiiij aulnes de veloux noyr pour fairre vne robbe a Mademoyfelle Leuifton lenee et vne autre robbe a Mademoyfelle de Beton ·

Plus a Jacques tailleur iij aulnes ij tier de veloux pour border vng mantaux de fatin pour la Royne lequel eft foure de martre ·

T

Plus a Jacque tailleur vne piece de futainne blanche frifee qui aft efte enploye a vng manteaux vne vafquine et des braffier pour la Royne laquel piece contenoict xx aulnes .

~~Plus je delliure a Jehan de Conpiengne troy piece deftamet rouge pour fairre des manteaux et dauantier au fille .~~

    Efface pource quil eft efcript plus anplement fi apres .

Plus je delliure audict Conpiengne du treilly jaune et viollet et du paffement . le tout pour fairre vne robbe a Nicolle .

Plus au tapiffier iij coffre a mullet pour les garnyr de plet lefque feruent a la chanbre de la Royne ordinnairement .

Plus a Baltafar vng autre coffre pour metre les abillement de la Royne pour porter par pays .

Plus a Jehan de Copiengne vng moyen coffre carre lequel ferme a deux ferrure auec vng caddena .

Plus a Jehan de Conpiengne iij pannache affauoir deux de jes noyr pour metre fur des chappeaux pour la Royne .

Plus au brodeur vne aulnes vng cart de veloux noyr pour fairre des boutons pour les fincq robbe tannee .

Deurant le moy de Mars .

Je delliure a Jehan de Conpiengne fincq piece deftaminne noyr pour fairre des robbes aux fille .

Plus a Monfieurs dAfquin vng harnoy de chaffe pour feruir a la Royne auec la houfe de mefme .

Plus vne autre piece deftaminne noir pour parracheuer lefdictes robbe ·

Plus a Jehan de Conpiengne iij aulnes iij quars de toylle de Hollande pour fairre fix pairre de chofe pour la Royne ·

Plus a Jehan de Conpiengne xviij aulnes et demye veloux noyr qui ont eftez enployee a bander et chamarer fincq robbe tannee et a vng manteaux et vne deuantier de drapt dAngleterre tanne et bande de quatre doicbt auec les parrement du manteau double de veloux et pour fairre vng fac a metre les mouchoye ou leftre pour la Royne et vne coyffe doublee de taffetas Plus pour vne robbe de taffetas frangie fect a bourrelle et manche decoupee et bordee Et aufit en aft eftez fect dudict veloux pour bander labillement du petit garfon que gard Jacquelinne affauoir manteau faye et choffe ·

Au moy dApuril rien et

·

Deurant le moys de May ·

Je delliure a Etienne vallet de chanbre iij aulnes de fcarllatin rouge pour luy ferre vng faie et des chofes ·

Plus je delliure audict Eftienne iiij aulnes et demye de veloux noyr pour bander le faye et lefdictes chofe auec xxxvij aulnes de bifet dargent et foye cramoyfie ·

Plus audict Eftienne iij aulnes de veloux blanc figurre pour doubler lefdictes chofe ·

Plus a Marguerit famme de chanbre deux paire de dras qui font chacun dras de troys toylle lefquelz feruent au lictz de la Royne ·

Plus je delliure a Jehan de Conpiengne fincq aulnes de veloux noyr qui ont eftez enploye a ferre ce qui fenfuyt affauoir Deux aulnes demy cart pour parracheuer les manteaux deftamet rouge Plus vng cartier pour vng fac a metre des mouchoye Plus demy aulnes demy cart pour fairre vng corps de robbe pour la Royne .

Plus je delliure au clere de chapelle iij aubes et iij any et feintur .

Plus vne aulnes demy cart pour fairre troy bors fur vne robbe de taffetas pour la Royne .

Plus je delliure au parfumeur vng cartier de veloux noyr pour fairre des collie au petit chien que la Royne aft enuoye a France .

Deurant le moys de Jung .

Je delliure au brodeur vne aulne de veloux pour fairre vng coffre pour la Royne pour metre papier et autre chofes .

Plus vne aulne troy cart de fatin noyr baillee au menufier pour doubler ledict coffre .

Plus a Jehan de Conpiengne ij aulnes demy cart de damas blanc pour ferre des braffier pour la Royne .

Plus a Jehan de Conpiengne viij aulnes troy cart et demy deftamet rouge pour commancer les manteaux et deuantier des filles .

Plus vne autre piece contenant xj aulnes demy cart .

Plus vne autre piece contenant xiij aulnes vng cart . Le tout pour ferre lefdictes manteaux et deuantier .

Plus a Jehan de Conpiengne xiij aulnes de taffetas mouchetez pour fairre vne robbe pour la Royne ·

Plus a Jehan de Conpiengne vne piece deſtaminne blanche pour fairre vne ſoutainne pour la Royne ·

Durant le moys de Jullet ·

Je delliure a Jehan de Conpiengne xiiij aulnes de veloux noyr pour bander les manteaux et deuantier deſtamet rouge pour les dammes et damoyſelle ·

Plus je delliure a Jehan de Conpiengne vne piece deſtaminne blanche pour fairre vne robbe pour la Royne auec vng autre reſt ·

Plus a Eſtienne vallet de chanbre iiij aulnes et demye de veloux noyr pour luy bander vne cappe et des choſe ·

Plus audit Eſtienne v aulnes de ſatin noyr pour doubler des choſes et fairre vng pourpoin ·

Plus a Baltaſar ij piece deſtaminne blanche pour metre a ſon coffre pour porter au voyage que la Royne fit en Arguylle ·

Plus demy cartier de veloux pour fairre vne gan pour la Royne lequel ſert pour tirrer de larc ·

Plus a Jehan de Conpiengne xv aulnes i quart de ſatin noyr pour fairre deux juppe et manche de meſme et pour larder des bandes ſur la robbe de taffetas noyr auec vng pourpoin qui ſert auec la robbe tanne ·

Plus a Jehan de Conpiengne i quartier de veloux noyr pour fairre vne grand bource pour la Royne lequelz ſert a metre les mouchoy ·

Au moys d'Aoust rien ·

Deurant le moys de Septembre ·

Je delliure a Monſieurs de Leuiſton eſcuyer vng harnoy de chaſſe feᵭ a la riſtre lequelz ſert pour la Royne auec la houſe de meſme ·

Plus xij chappeaux de veloux noyr borde dor et cordon dor ·

Plus a Jehan de Conpiengne lvij aulnes quart et demy de veloux noyr pour fairre des robbes au filles ·

Plus a Jehan de Conpiengne xxij aulnes vng quinſiemme de veloux noyr pour fairre vne robbe pour la Royne fet en treuffle de perlles ·

Plus a Pierre Martin tapiſſier ij aulnes et demye de veloux cramoyſy vieux aſſauoir de celuy que je reſceu de France pour garnir quatre pillier de liᵭ · et fut a la venue du Conte de Leno ·

Plus au menuſier vne aulne de meſme veloux pour couurir deux ſiege pliant ·

Plus au Pelletier du louſeruie qui eſtoiᵭ de reſt des pongnes pour en ferre vng louſeruie pour la Royne lequel aſt eſtez garny et aproprie pour mettre au col de la Royne ·

Plus je delliure au mulletier de litier vng ſac de veloux noir ·

Deurant le moys dOcttobre ·

Je delliure a Jehan de Conpiengne ix aulnes de taffetas noyr a grograin pour fairre vne robbe pour la Royne ·

Plus a Jehan de Conpiengne v aulnes de damas viollet pour fairre vne robbe a la petitte fille de Madamme dAtelz ·

Plus a Jehan de Conpiengne vng cartier et demy de toille dor frifee et traffee de blan pour ferre des manche a ladiéte fille · (144 ·)

Plus vne bandez de toylle dor plenne auec vng autre morceau · le tout pour metre en bande fur ladiéte robbe ·

Plus a Jehan de Compiengne vj aulnes ij tier et demy de taffetas tanne turquin pour fairre vne juppe auec le corps et manche · le tout pour la Royne ·

Plus je delliure vne garderobes au fille de Galletas · (96 ·)

Durant le moys de Nouembre ·

Je delliure a Mademoyfelle de Flamy et Beton ij pellifon dAllemaingne lefquelz font blan · (55 ·)

Plus au Pelletier vng pellifon de mefme pour en ferre vng cottillon pour la Royne · (55 ·)

Plus au brodeur demye aulnes de toylle dor pour ferre les pallemier du hocqueton de Goguelu fourrier des logis ·

~~Plus a Jehan de Conpiengne ix aulnes de taffetas noyr a grograin pour fairre vne robbe pour la Royne ·~~

Efface parce quil eft efcript cy deffus ·

Deurant le moys de Desembre ·

Je delliure a Jehan de Conpiengne xiiij aulnes de cammellot de foye noyr pour fairre vne robbe pour la Royne ·

Plus je delliure vne garderobe au tapiffier de la Royne · (96 ·)

Plus je delliure a Jehan de Conpiengne xiij aulnes de veloux pour fairre vne robbe de perlle laquel eft fect en fafon de boutonier et de roffe ·

Plus audict Conpiengne vij aulnes troy quars de veloux qui me reftoict de tous les veloux et eftoict pour commanfer la robbe de perlle laquel eft touttes couuert de les damours et conpartiment ·

Plus je delliure a Mademoyfelle de Leuifton vng deuan et des braffier de veloux noyr de la feux Royne · (91 ·)

Fin de la fufdicte anne · 1564 · et jufques au premier jours de Mars · 1565 · auan Pafque ·

Marie R

La fudictz anne a eftez contez jufque a Mars a raifon que je men alloye en France ainfin ne reft a conter pour lannee prefent · 1565 · que ix moys ·

Mars ·

Plus il aft eftez oublie a efcriptre en ceft prefente annee afauoir deux piece de toylle dor fect de broderie par bors contentant chafcunne bande vne aulnes lefquelz ont eftez enploye a fairre le bort de la queu de gran detz de veloux cramoify en broderie · (119 ·)

Plus vng li&tz de fcarllatte viollet fe&t par bande de broderie fe&t de veloux noy
~~garny~~ a Mademoyfelle de Sanple garny de fon dofiel pante foubaffement et
rideau auec vne couuet taffetas piquee ·   (1 7 ·)

Plus il aft eftez prin trois chappe deux tunique et vne chaffuble le tout de
velours verd · lequelz ornemet ont eftez ronpu pour garnir tout le li&t
douuraiges en broderie et fleurs meparty de vert et defdi&ts flurs ranply par
carreau dargent · et auffit pour fairre vne hault chefez deux fieges et vne chefe
perfee a eftez prin vne morfeau contenant j aulne ·

Plus je delliure a Mademoyfelle de Rallez xij gros feruiet [pour] fairre des
frotoy [pour] la Royne ·

Plus il aft eftez perdu a Lifcot vne piece de tapifferie des chaffeur de congne
entre les mayns de Monfieur de Sain&t Jehan durant le temps quil eftoi&t capitainne dudi&t chateaux ·

Memoyre de tout ce qui aſt eſtez delliure des meubles et dras de ſoye par moy Seruais de Condez vallet de chanbre de la Royne · le tout feĉt en lan · 1565 · commanſant au moys de Mars ·

Premierement durant le moys de Januier au moys de Feuuerier ·

Je ne conte rien durant Januier Feuuerier ~~ne Mars~~ parce quil eſt contez ſur lannee preſidente ·

Durant le moys de Mars ·

Je delliure a Jehan de Conpiengne vij aulnes iij quars de taffetas noy pour fairre vng manteaux pour la Royne ·

Plus je delliure a Jehan de Conpiengne ij aulnes et demye de taffetas noy a grograin pour fairre deux corps de robbe et vng deuan · le tout pour la Royne ·

Plus je delliure a Jacques tailleur v aulnes demy cart de taffetas changent pour fairre vng cottillon pour la Royne ·

Durant le moys dApuril ·

Durant le moys de May et Jung ·

Durant le moys de Jullet ·

Je delliure a la Royne ij chapeaux de taffetas noir auec vng chapeaux de veloux noyr garny de pannache ·

Plus je delliure a lecuyrie les chapeaux de veloux noyr garny de cordon dor lefquelz feruent au dammes et fille ·

Plus a Madamme de Sainct Croy vng cotte de fatin cramoyfy broche dor fect par carre ·

Plus je delliure a Mademoyfelle de Ralle vne martre joune et vne aultre blanche ·

Plus au Secretairre Dauit vne piece de veloux noy broche dor contenant x aulnes i quart · (118 ·)

Plus a Baltafar vallet de chanbre vne piece de toylle dor figurre de bleu contenant ix aulnes i quart ·

Plus audict Baltafar vne cotte de toylle dargent pleynne auec la moytie dunne aultre de mefmes toylle ·

Plus a Jacques tailleur fix aulnes fatin noyr pour fairre vne vafquinne pour la Royne ·

Plus a la Royne vng petit pauillon qui fert donbre deuan fa Maieftez lequel eft a fon cabinet ·

     Depuys remys au meubles ·

Plus vng vieux faie de veloux ~~viollet~~ vert auec ij bonnet bleu et leur pan-nache · le tout donne au foulz du Roy ·

Plus a la famme dudiĉt Seruais la Royne luy aft donne vng manteaux noir doubles de panne de foye auec vne robbe de damas fans manche · lefquel abillement reftoyent de la feux Royne · (80 · 74 ·)

Plus au Seigneur Franfifque vng manteaux de damas de reft defdiĉt abillement · (89 ·)

Plus iij aulnes i quart de fatin tanne broche dor pour meftre dedans des chaufes pour le Roy ·

Plus vng reft de martre pour fourrer vng chappeaux pour le Roy ·

Plus vng caparanfon de drap dor auec le corps de mefmes · (125 ·)

Plus vng aultre caparanfon fans corps delliure a Baltafar · (117 ·)

Plus la Royne a prin vng chapeaux a famme feĉt de veloux noyr garny dar-gent lequelz eft au cabinet ·

     Depuys remys au meubles ·

Plus il aft eftez vfez iiij pairre de linfeuil a la chanbre de Monfieur de Lufurie afauoir vne de lin et les autres commun ·

Plus je delliure du vieux veloux vert de reft des vieux faye pour regarnyr les pillier du liĉt de veloux vert feĉt a grue ·

Plus je delliure a la chanbre de la Royne ij sieges pliant et iij tabourrez le tout de velour cramoysi auec ij carreau · (37 · 38 ·)

Plus je baille a la Chapelle vng parrement dostel auec le soubassement la chassuble le tolle et fanon vng tapie de pie auec ij carreaux · le tout de veloux cramoysy · auec le corporalle · (55 · 99 · 102 · 100 ·)

Plus a lecuyie vng harnoy de cheual fet a la ristre lequel sert pour la Royne ·

Plus pour metre au lictz du Roy assauoir a celluy qui se port au chan je delliure ij orillier et iiij taye pour lesdicts orrillier ·

Plus vne chese persee couuert de veloux viollet auec vng bassin qui sert a porter au chan pour le Roy ·

Plus au parfumeur vne garderobbe platte pour metre des besongne pour le Roy ·

Plus vne petitte table laquel se port au chan pour le Roy ·

Plus ij tapie de Turquie se port au chan pour le Roy · dont lung a estez perdu et lautre vsez ·

Plus a la chanbre de la Royne il ast estez mys par son conmandement vng aultre tapie de pie a la ruel de son lictz a rayson de quoy lautre estoict vsez ·

Plus a Standy escuyer de lecuyie du Roy donne par le conmandement de la Royne vne paillasse mattellas trauersin ij pairre de dras ij couuert dont lunne nest que de blanche des brodeur auec ij orrillier et iiij taye · (50 ·)

Plus vne couuert de taffetas noir qui ast estez vsee au lictz de la Royne auec vng pauillon de damas noyr pour sa garderobe .

Durant le moys d'Aoust ·

Je delliure vng petit manteaux de fatin noyr fourre de martre lequel fert a la Royne · (86 ·)

Durant le moys [de] Septembre ·

Je delliure a Marguerit famme de chanbre iiij martre entier ·

Plus a Mefire Pierre preftre ij nappes dautes ij aubes et ij amy ·

Durant le moys d'Octtobre ·

Durant le moys de Nouembre ·

Je delliure a Monfieurs de Sainct Croy iiij aulnes de toylle dargent damaffee pour luy mettre dedans des chaufes ·

Plus a Jehan de Conpiengne x aulnes de veloux violle pour fairre vng manteaux de nuyct pour le Roy ·

Plus v cartier de veloux noyr baillie a Jehan de Conpiengne pour doubler les parrement dung riftre viollet pour la Royne ·

Durant le moys de Desembre ·

Je delliure a Jehan de Conpiengne j aulnes et demye de taffetas blan pour doubler vne pairre de braffier de fatin blan pour la Royne ·

Plus vne piece de futainne noyr contenant xx aulnes .

Plus je delliure a Pierre Matin tapiffier vne aulnes de taffetas viollet pour piquer vng ecuyffon pour metre fur leftomac de la Royne auec vng bonnet .

Plus a Jehan de Conpiengne vj aulnes de taffetas noyr pour doubler vne vafquinne de fatin noyr pour la Royne .

~~Plus a Jehan de Conpiengne xj aulnes de taffetas blan pour doubler vng manteaux de fatin cramoyfy raye dor auec vne pairre de braffier et vne vafquinne de toylle dargent pleinne pour la Royne .~~

~~Plus je delliure a Merguerite famme de chanbre quatre martre .~~

Le tout efface parce quil eft efcript en aultre lieux .

Plus a Jehan de Conpiengne xj aulnes demy cart de taffetas blan pour doubler vne pairre de braffier de fatin blan auec le deuan vne autre pairre de braffier de toylle dor et le deuan de mefme et vng manteaux de fatin blan raye dor .

Plus au Secretairre Dauit iiij aulnes de veloux noyr .

Plus a Jehan de Conpiengne vne aulnes demy quart de fatin blan pour fairre vng deuan de cottes pour la Royne .

Plus vne aulnes et demy de taffetas blan pour le doubler .

Plus vne aulnes de veloux noyr delliure audict Jehan de Conpiengne pour fairre des tourre le ne et cornet pour la Royne .

Plus au fellier du Roy iij aulnes et demye de vieux veloux cramoyfy pour recouurir vne felle darmines pour lecuyrie du Roy auec les eftriuier couuert de mefme .

Plus a Jehan de Conpiengne iiij aulnes de toylle dargent plainne pour fairre vng deuan et des braffier pour la Royne .

Plus a Jehan de Conpiengne x aulnes de taffetas blan pour doubler lefdicts braffier auec vng manteaux de fatin cramoyfy ray dor ·

Plus vng pongne de panne de foye noyre lequel eftoict entamme ·

Plus a Jehan de Conpiengne iij cartier dung bas de cottez rouge ray dor pour fairre vne pairre de braffier pour la Royne auec le petit chanteaux de lautre cartier ·

Plus iij aulnes et demye de plect blanche pour doubler vng manteaux de fatin cramoyfy ray dargent dont ladicte plect eft en doubles ·

Plus vne aulnes et demye de taffetas rouge pour doubler · · · · · es braffier de mefmes ledict manteaux ·

Plus je delliure vng ciel de lictz de farge rouges garny de pantes et rideau au filz de Monfieurs de Codinguan ·

Plus je delliure a Jehan de Conpiengne demye aulnes de taffetas noyr pour doubler troys orrilletz et iij tourre le nez pour la Royne ·

Le tout aulnes de France ·

Fin de lannee · 1565 · jusques au premier jour de Januier enfuyuant ·

Memoyere de tout ce que je delliure durant lannee · 1566 · conmanſant des le premier jours de Januier ·

Premierement je delliure au Secretairre Dauid quatre aulnes de toylle dor figurree par eſcaille · le tout en ſincq morſeaux ·   (146 ·)

Plus je delliure a Jehan de Conpiengne ſincq aulnes et demye de pleςt blanche pour doubler vneſ outanne de ſatin joune pour la Royne ·

Plus je delliure au pelletier viij aulnes de vieux bor de martre pour ayder a border ladiςte ſoutanne ·

Plus je delliure a Pierre Martin tapiſſier vij aulnes de vieux veloux cramoyſi pour ferre vng tapis de table ·

Plus je delliure vj aulnes de taffetas rouge armoyſi pour doubler lediςt tappis ·

Plus vij aulnes iij quars et demy de toylle dor friſee dor et traſſee de noyr delliuree au tapiſſier pour ferre des pillier de liςtz · dont le tout eſtoiςt en ſincq morſeaux ·   (146 ·)

Plus je delliure a Jouachin vng tier de toylle dor pleinne pour racoutrer ſon hoqueton ·

Plus je delliure au tapiſſier vj aulnes iij quars de vieux velous cramoyſi pour

x

ferre vng petis tapis et iiij pillier au lictz de veloux cramoyfi venu de Monfieur de Hontelles ·

Plus je delliure a vng coutellier iij quartier de veloux noyr pour fairre viij fourreaux a des dacques dEcoffe ·

Plus je delliure a Jehan de Conpiengne iij aulnes et demye de toylle dor plainne
pour fairre des flanbe fur vj abillement de mafque pour des famme · le tout en
viij morfeaux ·　(128 ·)

Feuuerier ·

Premierement je prin ij aulnes de toylle dor pleinne pour ferre la broderie de
la crepinne du lictz fect de toylle dor et toylle dargent et houppes ·

Plus je delliure a Jehan de Conpiengne xij aulnes de fatin blan pour ferre vng
manteaux a queu pour la Royne ·

Plus vij aulnes de taffetas blan pour doubler ledict manteaux ·

Plus iij aulnes de toylle dargent damaffee pour ferre les parrement dudict manteaux ·

Plus xij aulnes de toylle dargent plainne pour fairre vne robbe a la fille de
Madamme de Hontelles pour le jour quel fut marriee a Monfieur de Bodouel ·

Plus vj aulnes de taffetas blan pour doubler les manche et la queu de ladicte
robbes ·

Plus au clercq de chappelle ij aubes ij amy et vne nappe · le tout pour feruir
a la chappelle de la Royne ·

Plus je delliure a Jehan de Conpiengne xij aulnes de fatin cramoyfi pour fairre
vng manteaux a queux pour la Royne ·

Plus vij aulnes de taffetas armoyfi pour doubler ledict manteaux ·

Plus delliure audict Conpiengne iiij aulnes i quart de toylle dor frifee dor et traffee de noyr pour ferre vng parrement de manteaux pour la Royne ·

Mars ·

Je delliure a Jehan de Conpiengne ij tier de toylle dargent plainne pour ferre ij coyffe pour la Royne vng jour de Parllement ·

Plus je enploye vng bas de cotte de toylle dargent plainne pour parracheuer la broderie du gran faux cielz fect en broderie par cordellier ·

Apuril ·

Je enploye vj carre de toylle dor plainne pour parracheuer la broderie dudict faux cielz · (128 ·)

Plus je enploye fur ledict cielz xv carreaux de toylle dor frifee et traffee de blan pour referre les pantes dudict cielz · (143 ·)

Plus je enploye xv carreaux de toylle dargent plainne fur lefquelz on a fect des cordellier · (126 ·)

Plus je enploye audict cielz iij les de toylle dor frifee et traffee de blan contenant ij aulnes iij quars chafcun lez · (142 ·)

Plus je enploye vng les de toylle dargent plainne au fon dudict faux cielz contenant ij aulnes iij quars · (127 ·)

Plus je enploy plufieurs bande de toylle dor frifee dor lefquelles eftoient dedans vne toyllet joune pour ferre la broderie de deſſus les carreaux de toylle dargent dudiɛt cielz · (122 ·)

Plus je delliure a Baltaſar xx aulnes de veloux noir pour metre au coffre de la Royne ·

May ·

Je delliure a Jehan de Conpiengne vj aulnes de ſatin blan pour ferre vng petis manteaux pour la Royne ·

Plus je delliure audiɛt Conpiengne vj aulnes iiij quars de ſatin cramoyſi pour fairre troy pairre de braſſier pour la Royne ·

Plus audiɛt Conpiengne vj aulnes iij quars de ſatin blan pour ferre iij pairre de braſſier pour la Royne ·

Plus je delliure au tailleur du Roy v aulnes de ſatin blan pour ferre vng petis manteaux pour le Roy alors quil eſtoiɛt mallade pour porter au liɛtz ·

Jung ·

Je delliure a Jehan de Conpiengne iiij aulnes vng cart de taffetas rouge armoyſi pour doubler ij pairre de braſſier de ſatin cramoyſi pour la Royne ·

Jullet ·

Je delliure au tapiſſier xlv aulnes de veloux cramoyſi pour fairre vng dees et

le cielz meparty dudict veloux et toylle dor frifee dor · et xx aulnes de bougran pour le doubler ·

Plus je delliure au tapiffier lxxx aulnes de paffement de filz dor et dargent
dung doicbt de largeur pour mettre fur des rideaux et vne couuert · le tout de
cammellot rouge raye dor ·

Plus je delliure audict tapiffier ij aulnes et demye de toylle dor traffee de rou-
gue pour ralongir vng lees de la tapifferie de toylle dor frifee mepartie de
veloux cramoyfi et aufit pour en ferre vne fimple pantes pour le cielz de
mefme parce que au parrauan ledict cielz nauoict que quatre fimple pantes ·
(58 ·)

Plus par le conmandement de la Royne je ronpu vng lictz de toylle dor et
toylle dargent fect a fimple pantes · dont la toylle dor dudict lictz a eftez
enploye a ferre vng dees meparty de veloux cramoyfi · Et la toylle dargent
dudict lictz a eftez enployee pour ferre viij pillier de lictz · lung pour le lictz
de toylle dor et toylle dargent et lautre du lictz damitie · (9 н ·)

Plus je enploye j aulnes de fatin cramoyfi pour ferre les houppes en broderie
de deffus les pilliers du lictz de toylle dor et toylle dargent et crepinne de
houppes ·

Aoust ·

Je delliure a Jehan de Conpiengne vj aulnes de fatin cramoyfi pour fairre vne
cotte pour la Royne ·

Plus je enploye vng vieux faye de veloux viollet pour ferre des pillier a vng
lict de veloux viollet paffemente dor et dargent fect a jour ·

Plus je delliure a Jehan de Conpiengne x aulnes de toylle dargent damaſſee pour ferre vne couuert a Monſieur le Prinſe pour le jour de ſon bapteſme .

Plus alors que la Royne a donne le liċtz de velours viollet au Roy il y auoiċt vng pairre de linſeul de toylle de Hollande leſquelz ne me furrent poinċt randu a raiſon que les vallet de chanbre du Roy me dirrent que la auoiċt donne tout ce qui eſtoiċt audiċt liċtz .

Plus je enploye iiij aulnes de toylle dor plainne qui reſtoient du liċtz de feux Monſieur de Hontelles leſquelz je enploye a ferre de la broderie pour le grand dees de veloux cramoyſi en broderie · . (9 н ·)

Septembre ·

Je delliure vne cotte et le cartier dunne aultre le tout de cammellot de ſoye rouge raye dor pour doubler des choſes a Monſieur de Morra · le tout delliure a ſon tailleur ·

Plus je delliure audiċt tailleur iij aulnes de toylle dargent plainne pour doubler des choſes audiċt Sieur ·

Plus je delliure iij aulnes de meſmes toylle dargent pour doubler des choſes a Monſieur dArguylle ·

Plus je delliure a Monſieur de Hontellez iij quartier de bas de cotte de cammellot de ſoye rouge ray dor pour doubler des choſes ·

Plus je delliure a Monſieur de Bodouelz iij cartier de bas de cotte de cammellot blanc raye dargent pour luy doubler des choſes ·

Plus au tapiſſier quatre viengt aulnes de paſſement feċt dor et dargent pour mettre fur vne grand couuert de parrade de cammellot de foye verd auec les rideaux de mefmes · le tout chamarre dudiƌ paffement ·

Plus delliure audiƌ tapiffier lvj aulnes de vieux paffement dargent qui eftoiƌ fur les conturre du liƌz de damas incarnal lequel aft eftez ronpu et enploye a daultre chofes · lediƌ paffement a eftez mis fur les rideaux de damas viollet qui feruent au liƌt damitie ·   (23 ·)

Plus audiƌ tapiffier je delliure lv aulnes de petitte frange dor qui fut deffet de deffus des abillement de mafque · laquelz frange a eftez mife fur des vieux rideaux de damas rouge qui feruent au liƌtz de veloux cramoyfi a fimple pantes ·

Plus audiƌ tapiffier lxx aulnes de canneua pour fairre des paillaffe et des enuelope ·

Plus audiƌ tapiffier quatre viengt aulnes de pleƌt blanche pour fairre teindre pour doubler des couuert piquee ·

Plus je delliure audiƌ tapiffier iiij livres vij onfe de foye de plufieurs coulleur tant pour piquer des couuert que pour fairre conture ·

Plus xj piece de toylle dor frifee dargent delliuree au Roy pour fairre vng caparanfon ·   (121 ·)

Plus au fellier de la Royne iij aulnes. de veloux noyr pour ferre des cuyfines pour aller a cheualle a la riftre et pour ferre des chapperon a des felles ·

Plus je delliure a Baltafar xxi aulnes de fatin cramoyfi pour metre dedans les coffre de la Royne ·

Plus au tapiffier ix aulnes de taffetas blan acord pour ferre vne couuert de taffetas blan pour le liƌtz de veloux blan ·

Octobre ·

Je delliure au tapiffier xij aulnes de taffetas viollet pour fairre vne couuert au lict damytie ·

Plus audict tapiffier xxiiij aulnes de taffetas noyr pour ferre deux couuert lunne pour le lictz de veloux noyr paffemente et lautre pour le lictz de veloux noyr ·

Plus audict tapiffier xiij aulnes et demye de taffetas rouge pour ferre vne couuert au lictz de veloux cramoyfi paffement dor fet a fimple pantes ·

Plus audict tapiffier vne aulnes et vng cart de veloux cramoyfi pour ralongir le doffier du lictz des fenix ·

Plus audict tapiffier quatre carreaux de vielle toylle dor doubles de mefmes pour ferre vng foubaffement au lict de jennet et vng au lictz damytie · et pour ralongir vng des foubaffement du lictz des fenix ·   (58 · 59 ·)

Plus audict tapiffier deux aultre vieux carreaux pour ferre vng foubaffement au lictz de veloux cramoyfi paffemente dor fect a fimple pantes · et pour ralongir le foubaffement du lictz des las damours ·

Plus audict tapiffier trois pantes de veloux noyr dung vieu lictz pour ferre des pillier au lictz de veloux noyr figurre et paffemente dor et dargent · et pour ralongir le doffier dudict lict ·   (10 ·)

Plus je enploye le doffier dudict vieux lictz qui me reftoict encor pour en ferre vng petis tapis ·   (10 ·)

Plus audict tapiffier iiij aulnes de petit paffement fect dor et dargent pour enrichir les pillier dudict lictz ·

Plus je enploye ix aulnes de veloux cramoyſi pour parferre tout ce qui reſtoiꝶ a ferre au grand dees de veloux cramoyſi en broderie ·

Plus audiꝶ tapiſſier je luy ay feꝶ mettre le frange du liꝶz de damas incarnal au dees de veloux cramoyſi et toylle dor ·   (23 ·)

Plus je feꝶ mettre la frange dargent dudiꝶ vieux liꝶz ſur les pantes du liꝶz de veloux verd et douuraiges ·   (23 ·)

Plus les troys rideaux dudiꝶ vieux liꝶz je les feꝶ ſeruir au liꝶz des las damours ·   (23 ·)

Plus je fes ſeruir la couuert pique dudiꝶ vieux liꝶz au liꝶz des fenix · (23 ·)

Plus le reſt du damas dudiꝶ vieux liꝶz jen eſt feꝶ ferre vng tapis et couuri des cheſez perſee ·   (23 ·)

Plus je enploye les rideaux dung petit liꝶz de damas joune a rayſon quilz eſtoient trop petis a ferre vng ſoubaſſement vng doffier vng tapis et vne cheſe perſee que je fes couuri du reſt dudiꝶ damas ·

Plus je mys troys aultre rideaux de damas joune audiꝶ liꝶz leſquelz reſtoient du liꝶz de toylle dor et toylle dargent feꝶ a ſimple pante ·

Plus au tapiſſier ij cens aulnes de futainne blanche pour faire des mattellas et trauerſin et orrillier ·

Plus je delliure audiꝶ tapiſſier ix aulnes de taffetas viollet pour doubler les pantes dung ciel meparty de toylle dor traſee de noyr et veloux gris au quelz cielz je fes remetre ſes frange et le remonter ·

Plus au menuſier x aulnes de veloux cramoyſi pour couurir deux hault cheſe troys ſiege plian et vne cheſe perſee ·

Y

Plus audiɛt menuſier viij aulnes de doublurre rouge pour mettre ſoubz le veloux deſdiɛt cheſe ·

Plus vne aulnes et vng cart de bougran pour doubler ladiɛte cheſe perſee ·

Plus au tapiſſier xv aulnes de toylle dargent damaſſee pour ferre vne couuert de parrade pour le liɛtz de toylle dor et toylle dargent crepine de houpes ·

Plus xiiij aulnes de taffetas blan pour doubler ladiɛte couuert ·

Plus au tapiſſier iiij^{xx} v aulnes de petitz paſſement feɛt dor et dargent pour meſtre ſur les conturre de ladiɛte couuert et ſur la couuert de ſatin cramoyſi ·

Plus au menuſier iiij aulnes iij quars de veloux cramoyſi pour couurir vne aultre cheſe et deux ſiege plian ·

Plus au menuſier iij aulnes et demye de veloux noyr pour couurir vne hault cheſe et vng ſiege plian ·

Plus iiij aulnes et demye de veloux viollet pour couurir vne hault cheſe et vne ſiege plian ·

Plus vij aulnes de veloux verd pour couurir vne hault cheſe vne cheſe perſee et vne ſiege plian ·

Plus vne aulnes et vng cart de bougran pour doubler ladiɛte cheſe perſee ·

Plus iiij aulnes de doublurre pour doubler la hault cheſe ·

Plus au tapiſſier xxx aulnes de toylle de Lion pour doubler vj mattellas ·

Plus je ronpu vng tapis de trippe de veloux noir figurree de quoy jen eſt prin iiij aulnes pour couurir vne cheſe perſee et vng ſiege plian ·

Plus au tapiſſier ſincq aulnes et demye de veloux viollet pour ferre vng tapis ·

Plus je delliure au paffementier lv paque tant filz dor que filz dargent tant a
.vne foys que aultre pour toutes les befongne quil a fe& par mon conmandement · xij efcheueaux pour paque ·

Plus audi& paffementier xxvij liures xj onfe de foye cramoyfie ·

Plus en foye de coulleur tant vne que aultre vij liures v onfe et demye ·

Plus je delliure a Pierre Odry brodeur pour ce quil aft fe& tant en filz dor que
filz dargent tant pour la crepinne des houpes que pour le bor du grand dees de
veloux cramoyfi en broderie la cantite de ij paque qui font viengt et quatre
efcheueau ·

Plus je delliure audi& brodeur tant a vne foys que a vne aultre vne liures ij
onfe de foye afauoir de plufieurs coulleur ·

Plus je delliure au menufier vij onfe et demye de foye tant cramoyfie que
daultre coulleur · le tout pour coudre touttes les frange et veloux de toutte
chefe fiege et aultres chofes quil aft fe& ·

Plus je delliure a Madamme de Mars vj gro efcheueaux de filz dargent pour
Monfieur le Prince ·

Plus pour touttes la broderie du gran faulx cielz fe& a doubles pantes meparty
de toylle dor et toylle dargent fur laquelz toille dargent on a fe& des cordellier
en broderie ou il aft entre iiij paque iij efcheueaux tant or quarient ·

Plus pour tout la foye quil aft faillu pour fairre touttes la broderie dudi& cielz
jliures vj onfe de foye joune ·

Plus pour touttes la foye quil aft entre a ferre la crepinne du li&z fe& de toylle
dor et toylle dargent tant dunne coulleur que daultre iiij liures xiiij onfe
afauoir tant cramoyefie que aultre coulleur ·

Plus troys liurs et demye tant filz dor que filz dargent qui font vj paque vij efcheueaux .

Plus je delliure pour le grand dees et aufit de ce que je enploye tant pour rabatre que pour pourfiller tout ce qui eft feét audiét dees v liures tant dunne coulleur que dautre .

Plus pour fix aulnes de bor pour le grand dees auec deux aulnes que je fet ou il aft entre iij paque et demy tant filz dor que filz dargent .

Plus au tapiffier xlix aulnes de bougran tant pour doubler tapis que cielz de liétz et aultre chofes .

Plus au menufier xij peaux de marroquy de quoy il en aft eftez couuert iiij chefe et iiij fiege pliant .

Plus audiét tapiffier viij aulnes de taffetas verd pour doubler les pantes du liétz de veloux verd et douuraige .

Plus je delliure au tapiffier xlvj aulnes de petit paffement feét dor et dargent pour chamarer la couuert de liétz de jennet et celle du liétz de fenix et pour enrichir les pillier dudiét liétz et pour vng tapis de table et aufit les pillier du liétz damytie .

Plus je delliure au tapiffier xxij aulnes et demye de veloux cramoyfi pour ferre trois tapis et des pillier au liétz de fenix .

Plus xviij aulnes de bougran rouges pour doubler lefdiét tapis et les pilliers cy deffus diétz .

Plus vne pairre de linfeulz et vne payllaffe qui ont eftez perdu vne durrant le temps que Monfieur du Croc eftoiét depar defa . .

Nouembre ·

Je delliure au menufier iij aulnes et demye de veloux noyr pour couurir vne hault chefe ·

Plus au menufier viij aulnes et demye de veloux cramoyfi pour couurir ij hault chefe et iiij fiege plian ·

Plus au tapiffier xij aulnes de taffetas rouge pour ferre vne aultre couuert pique pour le lictz de veloux incarnal ·

Plus au tapiffier vij aulnes de veloux cramoyfi pour ferre vng aultre tapis de tables ·

Le tout delliure a launes de France ·

Desembre neant ·

Faict a Edinbour le xxxj^e de May · 1567 ·

Marie R

Delliurance de lannee · 1567 · conmanfant au premier jours de Januier jufques au premier jours de Jung audict an ·

Premierement Januier Feubuerier et Mars ·

Je delliure troys aulnes et demye de toylle dargent damaffee pour paracheuer vng lictz a double pantes auquel lictz je enploye la couuert de toylle dargent qui auoict feruy au baptefme de Monfieur le Prinfe que jauoye refceu de Baltafar · laquel eftoict de mefme toylle dargent ·

Plus pour mepartir ledict lictz je delliure quatre chappe de toylle dor frifee dor trafee de plufieurs coulleurs ·

Plus je delliure pour fairre les rideau audict lictz viengt aulnes de taffetas raye dor que jauoye refceu de Baltafar ·

Plus je delliure foyfant et quinze aulnes de paffement fect dor et dargent dung doicbt de largeu[r] · le tout pour metre fur les conturre dudict lictz ·

Plus je delliure vng paque de petitte dantelle qui aft eftez coufue enfemble pour metre fur les conturre des rideaux dudict lictz contenant quatre vingt aulnes ·

Plus je delliure a Jemmes Baffour capitainne du Chafteau de Lillebour troys pantes de broderie fect dor faux meparty de fatin blanc et bleu fans nulz aultre chofes · (21 ·)

Plus il aſt eſtez enploye deux chappe vne chaſuble et quatre tunique fe∂ de toylle dor friſee dor et traſee de pluſieurs coulleurs pour fairre vng li∂z meparty de toylle dargent damaſſee et veloux cramoyſi enrichy de grand fleurs de gro poin et aultre choſes ·

Et pour fornir la toylle dargent pour ledi∂ li∂z je reſceu de Baltaſar vng manteaux a manche longues auec vng bas de cot de meſmes ·

Plus je reſceu dudi∂ Baltaſar dix aulnes de veloux cramoyſi pour meparty ledi∂ li∂z ·

An moys d'Apuril ·

Je delliure a Janne famme de Tierry deux vieux linceulz pour luy ayder a ferre ces couches ·

Plus je delliure a Pierre Odry brodeur troys aulnes de toylle dor en pluſieurs morſeaux pour fairre la broderie du li∂z meparty de toylle dargent toylle dor et veloux cramoyſy ·

Plus je delliure audi∂ Pierre Odry pour le meſmes li∂z demye aulnes de toylle dargent pour fairre la broderie · le tout en pluſieurs morſeaux ·

Plus je deliure deux paire de dras de lin pour ſeruir au li∂z de la Royne ·

Au moys de May ·

Je delliure a Baltaſar troys mars troys onſe et demye de paſſement dor fe∂ a jour lequelz auoi∂ deux doicbt de largeur ·

Plus je delliure a Monfieur le Duc dOrquenez vng parrement dung gran manteaux de fourrurre de jennet pour luy feruir a vng manteaux de nuyct · (81 ·)

Decherge des meubles que jauoye feƈ porter au logis du feu Roy · laquelle doibt eſtre atachee auec lannee · 1567 · au mois de Feburie · Leſquelz meubles ont eſtez perdu ſans en rien recouurer · Et y auoiƈ vne chanbre ſalle et garderobe garnye ainſy quil ſenſuyƈ ·

Premierement vng lictz de veloux viollet a double pante paſſemente dor et argent garny de boys paillaſſe mattellas trauerſin et vne couuert de taffetas bleu piquee et deux aultre couuert et vng orrillier et enuelope · (7 · 45 ·)

Plus vne petitte table auec le tapis de veloux verd · (2 H ·)

Plus vne hault cheſe couuert de veloux viollet auec le ſiege ·

Plus xvj piece de tapiſſerie tant a ſa chanbre que ſalle et garderobe tant grand que petitte · (91 · vj piece · 18 H ·)

Plus a ſa ſalle vng dees de veloux noyr a double pantes · (6 ·)

Plus vne cheſe hault couuert de cuyere ·

Plus vne cheſe perſee couuert de veloux garnye de deux baſſin ·

Plus vng petis tapis de Turquie et vng pot de nuyƈ pour ſa chanbre ·

Plus vng petitz lictz de damas joune et verd feƈ a grue garny de boys pail-

z

laiffe mattellas trauerfin et fa couuert piquee de taffetas vert auec deux aultre couuert et vne enuelope ·

Et vng pauillon de taffetas changent a fa garderobe ·   (35 ·)

Fe& a Edinbour le xxme de May · 1567 ·

Plus il aftez perdu vng piece de tapifferie a Lifcot de liftoyre des chaffeur de cogny durant le baptefme de Monfieur le Prinfe ·   (84 ·)

Plus aufit perdu a Eftrellin au baptefme de Monfieur le Prinfe vne piece de tapifferie de gro feuillage et vng petis tapis de Turquie ·   (18 H ·)

Et deux dras de lin au logis de feu Roy ·   (167 ·)

Plus il aft eftez ~~perdu~~ vfe a Faclan deux gro dras des li&z qui eftoient audi& Faclan ·

Marie R

Decherge des Abillemant de Mafque et dOrnemant dEglife et de quelque Liures auec tous les Painture et quelque Tableau delliure a Maiftre Jehan Houde · fignee de Monfieur de Mora et Maiftre Jehan Houd ·

The Inventareis off the Buikis / Ornamentis / and Mafkyn Cleifs reffauit be Maifter Jhone Wod and James Murray vpoun the xv day of November the yeir of God j^m v^o lxix yeiris frome Serues Franchmane ·

BUIKIS ·

1 · Herodian ·

2 · The firft buik of Frofart ·

3 · The Hiftorie of Palmarine ·

4 · The Aftrologie off Baffentyne ·

5 · The Hiftorie of Herodote ·

7 · The Hiftorie of Paradyn · in tua volumes ·

8 · The Horologe of Princis ·

9 · The firft volume of Horos ·

10 · The Corniclis of Sawoy ·

11 · Zenophone Ceropedia ·

12 · The buik of Afriĉt and the Negotiatiounis ·

13 · The Cofmographie of Appiane ·

14 · The Art of Fyir ·

15 · The Myrrour of Polecie ·

16 · The Ethicis of Ariſtotill ·

17 · The firſt buik of Noveau Chriſtian ·

18 · The tua buikis of Paulus Amelius ·

19 · The Deſcriptioun of the Province of the Yndianis ·

20 · The Inſtitutioun of Patience ·

21 · Tymee of Plato ·

22 · The Illuſtratioune of the Gaulis ·

23 · The Sympoſie of Plato ·

24 · The Hiſtorie of the Varis againis the Turkis ·

25 · Ane Arreſt Memorable of the Seneit of Tulloſe ·

26 · The buik of Statutis concerning the Ordour of Sanct Michaell ·

27 · Diſcourſs of the Hiſtoreis of Loraine and Flanderis ·

28 · The firſt part of the Promptuarie of Medallyeis ·

In quarto ·

1 · The Succeſſioun of the Armes of Longove[lle] ·

In octauo ·

1 · Diuerſs Leſſounis of Peter Meſſee ·

2 · The Hiſtorie of Ethiopia be Diodore ·

3 · The Hiſtorie of Chelidon of the [Instit]utioun of Princis ·

4 · The Lyf of Charles the Maine ·

5 · The Inſtitutioun of ane Chriſtiane Prince be the Beſhope Seneſorie ·

6 · The Princeps of Aftronomie ·

7 · Leon the Hebrew of Luif ·

In decimo sexto ·

1 · The Paragon of Vertew ·

LATYN BUIKIS ·

1 · Commentarij Romane Reipublice per Volfangum Lazium ·

2 · Tabule Ptolemei · in pergameno ·

3 · Lutherus in Genefim ·

4 · Variarum Lectionum Joannis Oldendorpij ·

5 · Henrici Loriti Annotationes in Titum Liuium ·

6 · Seueri Boetij Commentarij in Topica Ciceronis ·

7 · Blondi Roma Reftaurata ·

8 · Harmonia Ofiandri ·

9 · Officiorum Ciceronis libri tres ·

10 · De bello Rhodio libri tres ·

11 · Cornucopia Lingue Latine ·

12 · Virgilius ·

13 · De Natura et Gratia ·

14 · Petri Angeli Carmina ·

15 · Harmanni Reformatio · in duo volumina ·

16 · Quinti Horatij Flacci opera ·

17 · Ludouici Regii Confolatio ·

18 · Antonij Maffe contra Vfum Duelli ·

In octauo ·

1 · Diogenes de Vita et Moribus Philofophorum ·

2 · Caluinus contra Seruetum ·

3 · Commentarij in Georgica Virgilij ·

4 · Pfalmi Buchquhannani ·

5 · Fabrica Strabuli ·

6 · Hodepori Bizantini Opera Quatuor ·

7 · Diui Michaelis Regij de Principibus Chriftianis ·

10 · Tria volumina Ciceronis · in velin ·

10 · Ciceronis Opera · in 9 voluminibus deauratis ·

11 · Diodorus Siculus · deauratus ·

12 · Publij Virgilij Opera ·

In decimo sexto ·

1 · Compendium Patricij Senenfis ·

Greca Volumina ·

1 · Atheneus Grece ·

2 · Luciani Opera ·

3 · Chrifoftomus in Epiftolas Pauli · in 3 voluminibus ·

4 · Platonis Omnia Opera ·

5 · Eufebij Pamphili de Evangelica Preparatione ·

6 · Herodotus ·

7 · Commentarij in Aphthonij Progymnasmata ·

8 · Commentarij Lingue Grece ·

9 · Isocratis Orationes ·

10 · Sophoclis Tragedia cum commentariis ·

11 · Geographia Ptolemei ·

12 · Demosthenis Orationes ·

13 · Dictionarium Hysichij ·

14 · Commentarij in Platonem ·

15 · Homeri Elias et Vlissea ·

16 · Institutiones Lingue Grece ·

In quarto ·

1 · Mercurij Trismegisti Poemander ·

In octauo ·

1 · Euripides cum scoliis ·

3 · Luciani pars prima et secunda · in duobus voluminibus ·

Resauit fra Serwais · 25 · Novembris · 1569 ·

Mr Johnne Wod ·

The Inventarie of the Ornamentis deliuerit to James Murray .

Inprimis of ftoillis and fannounis **xxxij** .

Item ane covertour of ane altar of cleith of gold champit with grene veluat . (35 H ·)

Item ane foir frontell of ane altar of blew dames .

Item four caipis of quheit dames .

Item ane chefabill and tua twnykis of blak dames .

Item ane chefable and tua twnykis of crammafie veluat .

Item tua caipis of cleith of gold figurit with blew veluat .

Item ane caipe ane chefible and tua twnykis of blew weluat .

Item ane chefible and tua tunikis of cleith of gold figurit with reid .

Item ane chefible three caipis and tua twnykis of cleith of gold figurit with reid veluat .

Item ane felle of blew purpour weluat to be careit on Corpus Chrifteis day with four pandatis and with brouderie of cleith of gold about the borderis of the fame .   (34 H ·)

Item ane chefible and tua twnykis and tua caipis brouderit wark with King Edwart his armes .

Item ane chefible tua twnykis and ane caip of quheit veluat figurit with gold .

Item tua twnykis of quheit dames with flouris one the fame .

Item ane auld caip of filk .

Item ane auld caipe of greine figurit weluat ·

Item ane chefible tua twnykis of cleith of gold figurit with blew veluat

Item tua caipis of blew dames figurit with flouris of gold ·

Item ane frontell of blak weluat with ftarnis of gold with ane subueftment of the fame ·

Item ane chefible and tua twnykis of blak weluat ·

Item ane caipe of blak weluat ftarnit wyth gold ·

Item mair tua caipis of blak weluat ·

Item ane chefible and tua twnykis of pyrnit cleith of gold ·

Item tua caipis of champit crammafie veluat and flouris of gold in the fame ·

Item ane parrament of ane aultar with fubueftment thairof the ane half thairof of crammafie veluat fteikit with gold and the vther half interlefit with cleith of gold fteikit with blak veluous ·

The Inventarie of the Mafkyne Cleife ·

Item ane coit of blew fatyn with ftarnis of toig ·

Item thre leauche coitis of crammafie fatyn pyrnit with quheit ·

Item tua of the fame dowblit with variand tauffateis ·

Item thre coitis of greine veluat raynit with yellow · with bodeis and flewis of yallow fatyn ·

Item tua coitis of yallow fatyne champit with greine with bodeis and flewis of the fame ·

2 A

Item tua coitis of the fame champit with blew · the ane thairof the bodeis and flewis of yallow fatyne ·

Item tua coitis of quheit tauffateis figurit with blew with bodeis and flewis of quheit ·

Item tua coitis the ane of reid and the vther of blak ~~fatyne~~ champlet ·

Item vj leauche coittis of yellow fatyne lynit with fum toige of filuer ·

Item ane coit of reid fatyne with bodeis and flewis of quheit begareit in the bodeis with toige ·

Item ane vthir coit of quheit fatyn with bodie and flewes of the fame ·

Item ane coit of quheit reid and blew tauffateis hingand full of fchakaris ·

Item ane coit of quheit armefing tauffateis hingand full of fchakaris ·

Item vj coitis begareit with quheit and reid fatyne and dropit with cleith of gold ·

Item ane howd of blew reid and quheit tauffateis with fchakaris ·

Item four bodeis tua aprounis the ane of yallow fatyne and the vthir of greine tauffateis ·

Item tua pair of flewes of yellow fatyne ·

Seruees of Condy / ye fall deliuer to our feruitouris James Murray and Mr Jhone Wod · the haill ftuiffe and buikis heir aboue expremit · togidder wyth aucht bredis of the new Doctouris · item xxviij payntit clethis of Flanderis wark of the gretaft volume and fywe payntit clethis of the fmall volume · quhilk falbe, weill allowit to yow keiping this prefent for your varrand fubfcriuit wyth our hand · At Edinburght the xxiiij day of Nouember the yeir of God ane thoufand fywe hundrith thre fchoir and nyn yeiris ·

[signature]

Item mair reffauit the Commentareis vpoun the Pfalmes ·

Item the Cathefifme in Englis ·

Item ane buik of Prayeris in Latine ·

Item the Pfalmes of Dauid and Prayeris on the fame in Latine etc ·

Item mair tayne be my Lordis Grace hym felf vj fyndrie buikis ·

Item tayne be my Lordis Grace and brint vj Mefs Buikis ·

XXV Nouembris and in the fame moneth dywerfs tymis befoir all this geyr abuif expremit refaued be James Murray and me Mr Jhone Wod at my Lord Regent his Gracis command · and layd in his keipping ·

Ita eft ·

Mr Jhonne Wod ·

Inventaire et estimacion des pierres précieuses tant en œuvre, brodures, carquans, colliers, chattons que autres joyaulx affectez à la Couronne de France, que la Royne Marie a, après le trefpas du feu Roy Françoys Deuxième de ce nom, que Dieu abfolve, remis ès mains du Roy, et qui ont efté baillez en garde à la Royne Mere de fa Majefté, ayant efté lefdictes prifées et eftimacions faictes par François du Jardin orfèure du dict Seigneur Roy, Pierre Redon orfèure et vallet de chambre du Roy de Navarre, et par Henry du Boux auffi orfèure du dict Seigneur Roy de Navarre, en la préfence de nous Jehan Babou fieur de la Bourdaiziere, Triftan de Roftain fieur de Brou, gentilzhommes ordinaires de la chambre d'icelluy Seigneur Roy, Maitres Florimond Robertet fieur D'Alluye confeiller fecrétaire d'eftat et des commandemens et finances, Nicolas Legendre fieur de Villeroy auffi fecrétaire des finances, Charles de Pierremue fieur de Lezigny confeiller et maiftre d'hoftel ordinaire, et Charles le Prévoft fieur de Grantville, auffy confeiller et intendant des finances d'icelluy Seigneur, commis et depputez par le dict Seigneur pour ceft effect, fuivant la commiffion qui pour ce nous en a efté expediée, de laquelle la teneure eft tranfcripte à la fin du dernier de ces deux Inventaires; ayant lefdictes pierreries et tout le contenu en ceftuy cy efté remys dans le coffre duquel elles avaient efté tirées, et le tout baillé en garde et mis entre les mains de Mademoifelle du Gauguier l'une des Dames de la Royne, par le commandement dicelle Dame.

Et premierement

[1.] Embrodure de touret faicte à canettes efmaillée de rouge, et à tous les bijoulx y a des F. couronnées, garnie de neuf tables de diamans de plufiers grandeurs, et huict coupplets de perles entre deux en chafcun defquelz y a des perles.

Le premier defquelz dyamans de la dicte brodure, eftant ung peu longuet et efcorné des quatre coings, a efté eftimé II. mil écus.

Le fecond eftant diamant à plain fond, efcorné d'un coing, a efté eftimé III. mil v. cens écus.

Le troifiefme eftant diamant foible, efcorné d'ung coing, a efté eftimé IIII. mil écus.

Le quatriefme eftant diamant efcorné de deux coings, à demy fond, a efté eftimé XVI. mil écus.

Le cinquiefme eftant diamant taillé de lozanges par deffus, faible et ung poinct au millieu, a efté eftimé VI. mil écus.

Le fixiefme eftant diamant longuet et efcorné d'ung coing, à demy fond, a efté eftimé VIII. mil écus.

Le feptiefme eftant diamant à plain fond, efcorné d'ung coing, a efté eftimé IIII. mil écus.

Le huitiefme eftant diamant longuet, à plain fond, a efté eftimé III. mil écus.

Le neufiefme eftant diamant longuet, efcorné de troys coings, a efté eftimé II. mil v. cens écus.

Les quarente perles eftans de huiĉt couppletz ont efté eftimées l'une portant l'autre v. cens écus.

De la valleure de la diĉte brodure, fans l'or, XLIX. mil v. cens écus.

[2.] UNG CARQUANT de pareille façon auquel y a cinq dyamans, deux en groffe poinĉte, une grande table taillée à face et deux petites tables, dont y en a une rompue par la moiĉtié, et fix coupplets de perles entre deux, où y a à chacune cinq perles.

Le premier diamant defquels, eftant efcorné d'ung coing, a efté eftimé VIII. cens écus.

Le fecond, eftant à fix poinĉtes, a efté eftimé x. mil écus.

Le troifiefme eftant en table longuette efcorne d'ung coing, où y a une lozange deffus, a efté eftimé VIII. mil écus.

Le quatriefme eftant en une grande poinĉte, ung peu longue, a efté eftimé xx. mil écus.

Le cinquiefme eftant diamant foible, caffé en deux, a efté eftimé II. cens écus.

Et les perles de la diĉte brodure, en nombre de trente, ont été eftimées II. cens L. écus.

De la valleur dudiĉt carquant, fans l'or, XXXIX. mil II. cens L. écus.

[3.] UNG GRANT COLLIER d'or, garny de unze grans dyamans, avec dix cordelieres garnies chacunes de cinq groſſes perles rondes.

Le premier deſquels diamans, eſtant taillé en triangle, a eſté eſtimé III. mil v. cens écus.

Le ſecond eſtant un peu longuet, à demy fond, a eſté eſtimé II. mil écus.

Le troiſieſme, eſtant en poinĉte, taillé à facettes, a eſté eſtimé III. mil écus.

Le quatrieſme, eſtant diamant en façon de coeur, plat deſſus et taillé à facettes par dedans, a eſté eſtimé III. mil écus.

Le cinquieſme, eſtant en poinĉte longue et taillé a faces, a eſté eſtimé IIII. mil v. cens écus.

Le ſixieſme, eſtant taillé en façon de fuzée, a eſté eſtimé III. mil écus.

Le ſeptieſme, eſtant taillé en poinĉte, long et taillé à faces, a eſté eſtimé VIII. mil écus.

Le huitieſme, eſtant diamant en poinĉte, eſcorné par le bout, a eſté eſtimé II. mil écus.

Le neufieſme, eſtant foible et en table, a eſté eſtimé II. mil v. cens écus.

Le dixieſme, eſtant une belle table, eſcorné d'ung coing, ayant le teinĉt taſche, a eſté eſtimé III. mil v. cens écus.

Le unzieſme, eſtant carré, eſcorné de deux coings, a eſté eſtimé xv. cens écus.

Et les perles, eſtant en nombre de ſept vingtz, ont eſté eſtimées XIIII. cens ecus.

De la valeur du diĉt collier, sans l'or, xxxvII. mil ix. cens écus.

[4.] Quatre autres tables de diamans fervans pour allonger le dict collier.

Le premier defquelz eftant longuet et efcorné d'ung coing, taillé à faces, a efté eftimé vi. mil écus.

Le fecond, eftant carré, eftimé ii. mil écus.

Le troifiefme eftant carré, efcorné de deux coings, a efté eftimé xv. cens écus.

Le quatriefme, eftant longuet, a efté eftimé ii. mil v. cens écus.

De la valleur des dicts quatre diamans xii. mil écus.

[5.] Ung autre collier en groffe oeuvre, émaillée de plufieurs coulleures, garny de cinq groffes émerauldes, dont y en a deux frellées de caffures, trois cabochons de rubby, ung beaucoup plus gros que les autres, et ung grenat et dix cordelierès en chacunes defquelles y a six perles.

La première defquelles emerauldes, eftant rompue, a efté eftimée vi. cens écus.

La feconde, eftant en cabochon, rompue en troys pieces, a efté eftimée viii. mil écus.

La troifiefme eftant grande émeraulde, d'affez mauvaife façon, et une petite vene au milieu, a efté eftimée xii. mil écus.

La quatriefme, eftant en triangle, a efté eftimée iiii. mil écus.

La cinquiefme, eftant longue et efcornée d'ung bout, a efté eftimée iiii. mil v. cens écus.

Elle a efté rompue à l'entrevue de Bayonne, quant elle fut preftée à Madame.

Et le premier cabochon de rubby, glaffeux, a efté eftimé IIII. mil écus.

Le fecond, eftant longuet, a efté eftimé II. mil v. cens écus.

Le troifiefme, en forme de triangle, cabochon, a efté eftimé xv. cens écus.

Le quatriefme, qui eft ung grenat, a efté eftimé c. écus.

Et les perles eftant au nombre de foixante ont ete eftimées xII. cens écus.

De la valeur dudi& collier, fans l'or, xxxvI. mil IIII. cens ècus.

[6.] DOUZE ÉMERAULDES en chattons de canettes, les bijoulx efmaillés de rouge et blanc, avec des F. pour faire une bordure.

La premiere, carrée, a été eftimée vI. cens ecus.

La deuxiefme, cabochon a triangle, eftimée III. cens écus.

La troifiefme, auffi en cabochon, platte deffus, eftimée v. cens écus.

La quatriefme, en cabochon plus petite que l'autre, a efté eftimée c. L. écus.

La cinquiefme, eftant plus petite, en triangle, a efté eftimée c. écus.

La fixiefme, en façon de triangle, ung peu plus petite, a efté eftimée c. écus.

La feptiéfme, eftant du Perou, haute eflevée, a efté eftimé II. cens écus.

La huitiefme, eftant en façon de table, fourde, a efté eftimé c. écus.

La neufiefme, en table et longuette, eftimée II. cens L. écus.

La dixiefme eftant longuette, poinctue par ung bout, a efté eftimée v. cens écus.

La unziefme, en façon de triangle, platte, eftimée c. L. écus.

La douziefme, auffi en façon de triangle, a efté eftimée II. cens écus.

De la valleur des dictes douzes émerauldes III. mil c. L. écus.

[7.] UNE GRANDE CROIX compofée de neuf diamans : affavoir : cinq grans tables, faifans la croix, au plus hault au deffoubz ung diamant quafi rond et trois autres diamans en larmes, en fers de lance, taillez en faces, faifans le pied de la dicte croix ; auquel pied pend une perle en poire. Laquelle croix ainfi garnie a efté eftimée tout enfemble L. mil écus.

[8.] UNE FORT GRANT TABLE de diamans à plain fond, ung peu longue, efcornée de deux coings, accompagnée d'une groffe perle en oeuf, qui eft celuy que achepta le Roy François Premier, et luy coufta foixante cinq mille efcuz fans le perle, laquelle a efté eftimee XII. cens écus, et par ainfi ladicte bague revient à LXVI. mil II. cens écus.

[9.] UNE AUTRE GRANT TABLE de diaman foible, plus fpacieufe que la précédente, efcornée de troys coings, à laquelle pend une autre groffe perle quafi ronde, eftimée le tout XXV. mil écus.

[10.] UNG GROS RUBY ballay à jour, percé d'une broche de fer, appelé l'oeuf de Naples, auquel pend une perle en forme de poire eftimé LXX. mil écus.

[11.] UNE BAGUE d'ung A. Romain, garnie d'ung gros rubby ballay mis en griffe, eftimée XXV. mil écus.

[12.] Ung autre rubby ballay, en façon de demy oeuf, avecque une perle en poire eftimé ii. mil v. cens écus.

[13.] Ung ruby fans feuille, qui a efté ofté de la poincte de Milan, enchaffé d'or pour pendre, eftimé x. mil écus.

[14.] Ung grant ruby ballay, faict en cofte, percé en trois endroicts, pendu à quinze perles au lieu de chefne, eftimé l. mil écus.

[15.] Deux perles en poire eftimées ii. mil écus.

Summe total de la valleur des fufdictes bagues perpectuellement affectez à la Couronne iiii. cens lxxviii. mil ix. cens écus.

Faict a Fontainebleau le xxvi.e jour de Feurier l'an mil cinq cens foixante.

JEHAN BABOU.   DE PIERREMUE.
LEGENDRE.   LE PREVOST
ROBERTET.

AUTRE INVENTAIRE ET ESTIMACION des anneaulx ou bagues trouvez en ung baguier, pareillement affe&ez a la Couronne, et qui ont efté auffi remis es mains du Roy comme les autres bagues du précédent Inventaire, et dont la prifée et eftimacion en a efté faicte par les orfèures et en la préfence de nous foubz fignéz et cydevant nomméz, fuivant la commiffion à nous expé-diée, ainfi que dict eft cy devant; ayant les dictes bagues ou anneaulx après lefdictes Inventaire et prifée parfaictz efté remis dans le dict baguier et au coffre duquel ils avoient efté tiréz, et le tout mis entre les mains de la dicte Damoifelle du Gauguier, par le commandement de la Royne.

Et premierement

[1.] UNE GROSSE POINCTE de diaman garnie en ung anneau émaillé de noir eftimée VI. mil écus.

[2.] Ung diamant à doz dafne et en lozange eftimé VIII. cens écus.

Il a efté prins pour envoyer en Efpagne à la femme du Prince d'Evoly le IIIme Mars mil v. cens LX.

[3.] Ung autre diamant en table, foible et efcorné de deux coings, eftimé III. cens écus.

L'un des dicts dyamans a efté auffi ènvoye le dict jour à ung Docteur Efpagnol.

[4.] Ung autre diamant en table, efcorné de deux petits coings, efmaillé de rouge à feuillaige, eftimé II. cens LX. écus.

[5.] Ung autre diamant auffi en table, efmaillé de rouge, à feuillaige, eftimé II. cens L. écus.

> Les deux tables de diamanz efmaillées de rouge ont efté prinfes pour meftre à deux bagues à pendre dont le Roy à fon facre à faict don à Mefdames de Lorrayne le 15ᵉ Mars 1561.

[6.] Ung grant table de rubby longuette, efmaillée de noir, eftimée II. mil V. cens écus.

> La dite table de rubby prinfe par le Roy le xIIIᵉ Fevrier 1562 pour donner à la Royne d'Efpagne.

[7.] Ung rubiz longuet en cabochon, efcorné, où il y a de petitz trophées, eftimé II. cens écus.

[8.] Une petite table de rubiz émaillée de blanc alentour, eftimée XL. écus.

[9.] Une chaufferette de ruby émaillée de verd eftimée XXX. écus.

[10.] Ung petit coeur de rubiz émaillé de verd eftimé XV. écus.

[11.] Une petite table de rubiz émaillée de noir eftimeé XV. écus.

[12.] Une fpinelle émaillée de blanc eftimée II. cens écus.

[13.] Ung grenat émaillée de noir eftimé XV. écus.

[14.] Une amatifte orientalle émaillée de blanc et noir eftimé XL. écus.

[15.] Une autre amatifte auffi émaillée de noir à huict pens eftimée LXXII. écus.

[16.] Une autre amatifte en griffe émaillée de blanc eftimée XL. écus.

[17.] Une autre amatifte émaillée de viollet eftimée L. écus et demy.

[18.] Une efmeraulde en table efmaillée de blanc et pourpre eftimée VIII. cens écus.

Ladite efmeraude a efté prinfe pour envoyer á la Ducheffe d'Alve le XIme jour d'Avril 1562.

[19.] Une aultre émeraulde longuette auffi émaillée de blanc et de rouge eftimée L. écus.

[20.] Une autre émeraulde fans émail eftimée C. écus.

[21.] Une petite poincte de diamant efmaillé de noir eftimée XX. écus.

[22.] Une petite table de diamant, ayant alentour quatre petitz rubys émaillés de noir, eftimée VIII. cens écus.

[23.] Une grant table de faphyr à une bague émaillée de noir eftimée CL. écus.

[24.] Ung autre faphyr émaillé de blanc eftimé LXX. écus.

[25.] Deux turquoifes en deux bagues fans émail eftimées XV. écus.

[26.] Une bague, ou il y a ung criftal et une nunciation dedans, eftimée XX. ecus.

[27.] Une pierre bleue à une bague émaillée de blanc eftimée III. écus.

Somme totale des fufdictes bagues XII. mil XIIII. écus et demy.

2 c

Ensuict la teneur de la commission.

CHARLES par la grâce de Dieu Roy de France a nos amiz et féaulx les Sieurs de la Bourdaizière et de Roftaing gentilfhommes ordinaires de notre chambre, Maitres Florimond Robertet fieur D'Alluye noftre confeiller fecrétaire d'eftat et de noz finances, et Nicolas Legendre fieur de Villeroy auffi fecrétaire de nos finances, Salut. D'aultant que aultre Inventaire, appréciation et eftimation, que nous avons ordonnè faire par noz lettres cy atachées, foubz le contre feel de noftre chancellier, des bagues, joyaulx, pierreries et chofes précieufes de noftre cabinet de ce lieu de Fontainebleau, Nous voullons auffi Inventaire et eftimation et appréciation eftre faicte des autres bagues et pierreries affectées à noftre Couronne que noftre très-chere et très-amée bonne feur la Royne d'Efcoffe Douairière de France a remys en noz mains. A ces caufes, nous vous mandons, commectons et ordonnons par ces préfentes que en la préfence de noz améz et féaulx les Sieurs de Lezigny noftre dict confeiller et maiftre-d'hoftel ordinaire, et de Grantville Maiftre Charles le Prévoft l'ung des intendans de noz finances, vous faictes faire inventaire defdictes bagues affectées à noftre dicte Couronne et icelles avalluer et eftimer par noz chers et bien améz Françoys du Jardin, Pierre Redon et Henry de Boux orfèvres par nous commis à faire l'eftimation des bagues de noftre dict cabinet, laquelle eftimation vous ferez adjoufter fur le dict Inventaire, ainfi qu'il vous eft mandé faire pour le regard defdictes autres bagues, et le dict Inventaire faict et parfaict figné de vous ou de troys de vous, et femblablement des dicts Sieurs de Lezigny et de Grantville, vous rapporterez par devers nous pour le regard ou en faire ce que adviferons. De ce faire vous avons donné et donnons plain pouvoir, puiffance, auctorité, commiffion et mandement fpécial. Donné à Fontainebleau, le xviii° jour de Février, l'an de grâce mil cinq cens foixante, et de noftre règne le premier. *Signé* CHARLES, *et au-deffoubz,* Par le Roy, De L'Aubespine. *Et fcellees a fimple que de cire jaulne.*

Faict à Fontainebleau le xxvi° jour de Février l'an mil cinq cens foixante.

Jehan Babou. De Pierremue.
Legendre. Le Prevost.
Robertet.

Nous CHARLES par la grâce de Dieu Roy de France certiffions à tous qu'il appartiendra que toutes les pierres précieufes tant en œuvre, brodures, carquans, chattons, anneaulx ou bagues que autres joyaulx affectéz à noftre Couronne, que noftre très-chère et très-amée bonne feur la Royne d'Efcoffe Douairière de France a, après le trefpas de feu noftre tres-cher Seigneur et frère le Roy François dernier décedé, que Dieu abfolve, remis en noz mains et de noftre très-honnorée Dame et Mère la Royne, cy-devant fpéciffiéz et déclairéz par les deux Inventaires et appréciation qui en ont par noftre commandement et ordonnance efté faictz, par noz améz et féaulx Jehan Babou feigneur de la Bourdaizière, Triftan de Roftain feigneur de Brou, gentilz hommes ordinaires de noftre chambre, Maiftres Florimond Robertet feigneur de Dalluye noftre confeiller fecrétaire d'eftat et de noz finances, et Nicolas Legendre feigneur de Villeroy auffi noftre confeiller et fecrétaire de noz finances, en la préfence de noz améz et féaulx les Seigneurs de Lezigny noftre confeiller et maiftre d'hoftel ordinaire et De Grantville l'ung des intendans de noz finances, et appelléz pour faire la dicte appréciation François du Jardin, Pierre Redon

et Henry de Boux orfèvres, fuivant noz lettres de commiffion cy-deffus
tranfcriptes, ont par les deffufdictes efté remifes ès mains de noftre très-
honnorée Dame et Mère et de nous qui les avons bailléz en la charge èt garde
de noftre chère et bien amée Damoifelle Claude de Beaune veufve du feu
Seigneur Dugauguier, l'une des Dames de noftre Dame et Mère, de toutes lefquelles pierres précieufes, brodures, carquans, colliers, bagues, anneaulx que
autres chofes deffufdictes et cy-devant fpéciffiées, Nous avons iceulx Seigneur
de la Bourdaizière, de Roftain, Dalluye et Villeroy, de Lezigny et de Grantville, et femblablement iceulx Du Jardin, Redon et De Boux, en tant que
befoing feroit, defchargéz et defchargeons par ces préfentes fignées de noftre
main.   Faict audict Fontainebleau le dernier jour de Avril l'an mil cinq cens
foixante et ung.

CHARLES.

DE LAUBESPINE.

NOUS CHARLES par la grâce de Dieu Roy de France certiffions à tous
qu'il appartiendra que, lors de l'entreveue par nous faict dernièrement à Bayonne
avecques noftre très-chère et très-amée feur la Royne d'Efpaigne, une
efmeraulde longue et efcornée d'un bout contenue au premier des deux Inventaires cy-devant tranfcriptz, feuillet quatreiefme, article troifiefme, a efté
rompue, ayant efté preftée à noftre très-chère et très-amée feur Marguerite de
France, ainfi qu'il eft cotté à la marge du dict article.

Auffi que le IIII.e jour de Mars mil cinq cens foixante, nous avons prins ung
diamant à doz-d'afne et en lozanges, eftimé VIII. cens écus, contenu au fecond
Inventaire, article II.e, et icellui envoyé à la femme du Prince Devoli.

Plus avons prins ung autre diamant en table, foible efcorné de deux coings, eftimé III. cens écus, contenu au III.ᵉ article du fecond Inventaire, et icelluy envoyé à ung Docteur Efpagnol.

Plus avons prins deux autres diamants, contenuz ès IIII. ou vᵉ articles dudict fecond Inventaire, le premier à table efcorné de deux petitz coings, efmaillé de rouge à feuillage, eftimé II. cens LX. écus, l'autre auffi en table efmaillé de rouge à feuillage, eftimée II. cens L. écus, et d'iceulx faict préfens, lors de noftre facre, à noz coufines de Lorraine.

Plus avons prins une grande table de rubbis, longuette, efmaillée de noir, contenu au VI.ᵉ article du dict fecond Inventaire, eftimée II. mil v. cens écus, et icelle envoyée à noftre dicte feur la Royne d'Efpaigne.

Plus avons prins une émeraulde en table, efmaillée de blanc et rouge, contenu au dict fecond Inventaire, article XVIII.ᵉ, eftimée VIII. cens écus, et icelle envoyée à la Ducheffe D'Alve, le XI.ᵉ d'Avril mil cinq cens foixante-deux.

CHARLES.

De Laubespine.

INDEX OF PERSONS.

2 D

Martigues (Martiques), Sebastian of Luxembourg, Viscount of Martigues, (afterwards Duke of Penthievre) ; the Queen's bequest of a jewel to his daughter, 100.

Mary, the Blessed Virgin, and St. Joseph, figures of, 16.

—— of Lorraine (or Guise), Queen Dowager and Regent of Scotland (daughter of Claude, first Duke of Guise, wife of King James V. of Scotland) ; inventory of her moveables delivered to a valet of the Queen's chamber, 18-27 ; her portrait brought from France by Secretary Maitland of Lethington (in 1563), 57 ; robes, furs, etc., which belonged to her, 127, 129, 130, 142, 152.

—— Stewart, Queen of Scots, Dowager of France, 7, 15, 24, 33, 35, 36, 39, 49, 51, 53, 54, 64, 66, 71, 74, 75, 84, 87, 91, 93-124, 125-167, 173, 175, 176, 191, 202, 203 ; jewels, tapestry, etc., delivered to her by the Duke of Chatellerault (3. June 1556), 3-6 ; priced list of the crown jewels of France, delivered by her to King Charles IX., after the death of her husband, King Francis II. (5. December 1560), 191-205 ; inventory of her jewels (in 1561), 7-17 ; jewels, etc., in her cabinet (in 1561), 15-17 ; inventory of her mother's moveables delivered to a valet of her chamber (September 1561), 18-27 ; inventory of her moveables delivered to a valet of her chamber by the clerk of offices of her household (November 1561), 28-48 ; inventory of the late Earl of Huntly's moveables, etc. delivered to a valet of her chamber (December 1562), 49-54 ; inventory of glass, porcelain, etc., delivered to a valet of her chamber (December 1562), 54-56 ; articles delivered to a valet of her chamber by Secretary Maitland of Lethington (in 1563), 57 ; list of things gifted to her by Janet Stewart, Lady Ruthven (June 1564), 58 ; vestments of her chapel royal of Stirling delivered to a valet of her chamber (in 1562), 59 ; inventory of her robes in the Palace of Holyrood (1. February 1561-2), 60-74 ; inventory of her jewels (in 1561-2), 75-92 ; inventory of her jewels, etc., with marginal notes in her own hand bequeathing them to persons so named by her in the event of the death of herself and her infant (in 1566), 93-124 ; jewels in her cabinet (in 1566), 122-123 ; list of silks, etc., delivered by a valet of her chamber after her arrival in Scotland, in each month (from 1. September 1561 to 1. June 1567), 125-176 ; inventory of her furniture lost in the King's lodging at the Kirk of the Field (in February 1567), 177-8 ; inventory of her books, church vestments, masquing clothes, pictures, etc., delivered to the Regent Murray (November 1569), 179-187.

Mary Stewart, Queen of Scots, Dowager of France ; necklace given by her to the Duchess of Guise at Calais (August 1561), 10 ; sheets put in her chamber coffer, on leaving France (August 1561), 47 ; her second mourning (November and December 1561), 129 ; her observance of the first anniversary of the death of King Francis II. (5. December 1561), 129 ; her journey to St. Andrews (February 1562), 132 ; her journey to Aberdeen and Inverness (October 1562), 134, 135 ; her masquerade (December 1563), 141 ; her masque and banquet (in February 1564), 144, 145) ; little dog sent by her to France (May 1564), 148 ; her marriage ring (July 1565), 112 ; her gift of cloth of silver for the wedding dress of Lady Jane Gordon, Countess of Bothwell (22. February 1566), 162 ; her coiffes of cloth of silver for the Parliament (March 1566), 163 ; her bequests of her jewels, etc., made before the birth of her son (19. June 1566), 93-124 ; her bequest of her marriage ring to the King, who gave it to her (1566),

2 E

INDEX OF PLACES.

THE END.

LaVergne, TN USA
14 July 2010
189529LV00004B/19/P